Communicating

Many accounts of human communication suggest that we are limited to communicating through words, visual images, the mass media and by digital means. This perspective underestimates the multisensory qualities of much of our human interconnecting and the multiple sounds, touches, sights and material objects that humans use so creatively to interconnect both nearby and across space and time.

Ruth Finnegan brings together research from linguistic and sensory anthropology, alternative approaches to 'material culture' and 'the body', non-verbal communication, cultural studies, computer-mediated communication and illuminating work on animal communication. Examples from both western and non-western cultures, together with plentiful illustrations, enrich and deepen the analysis.

The book uncovers the amazing array of sounds, sights, smells, gestures, looks, movements, touches and material objects that humans use so creatively to communicate – resources consistently underestimated in those western ideologies that prioritise 'rationality' and referential language.

Focusing on embodied and material processes, and on practice rather than text, this comparative analysis challenges the underlying cognitive and word-centred model common to many approaches to communication.

The second edition of *Communicating* includes a new preface, updates to take account of recent work, an additional chapter covering ethereal non-verbal non-bodily communicating such as telepathy and dreams, fresh illustrations, a new conclusion and an updated bibliography.

This authoritative but accessible book is an essential transdisciplinary overview for researchers and advanced students in language and communication, anthropology and cultural studies.

Ruth Finnegan is Emeritus and Visiting Research Professor in Sociology at the Open University, UK. Her previous publications include *Oral Literature in Africa* (1970/2012), *Oral Poetry* (1977/1992), *Information Technology* (1987), *Literacy and Orality* (1988), *The Hidden Musicians* (1989/2007), *Oral Traditions and the Verbal Arts* (1992), *South Pacific Oral Traditions* (1995) and *Tales of the City* (1998).

Figure 0.1 Palimpsest, 2010
Sonata mulattica; our beautiful multisensory world. From a series of Jack Leibowitz's photographs of South Africa's environmental objects, this one inspired by Rita Dove's life of the nineteenth-century virtuoso violist George Bridgetower: the son of a white woman and an 'African prince', he travelled to Vienna to meet Beethoven whose subsequent sonata was dedicated to him. As well as the obvious auditory and visual associations we can almost feel the grainy texture, scent the fragrance (Credit: Jack Leibowitz).

Communicating

The multiple modes of human communication

Second edition

Ruth Finnegan

Routledge
Taylor & Francis Group

LONDON AND NEW YORK

Second edition published 2014
by Routledge
2 Park Square, Milton Park, Abingdon, Oxon OX14 4RN

and by Routledge
711 Third Avenue, New York, NY 10017

Routledge is an imprint of the Taylor & Francis Group, an informa business

First edition published by Routledge 2002

British Library Cataloguing in Publication Data
A catalogue record for this book is available from the British Library

Library of Congress Cataloging in Publication Data
Finnegan, Ruth H.
Communicating : the multiple modes of human communication / Ruth Finnegan. -- Second Edition.
pages cm
Includes bibliographical references and index.
1. Interpersonal communication. I. Title.
HM1166.F56 2014
302.2--dc23
2013019544

ISBN: 978-0-415-83778-1 (hbk)
ISBN: 978-0-415-83780-4 (pbk)
ISBN: 978-1-315-86987-2 (ebk)

Typeset in Perpetua
by M Rules

Printed and bound in Great Britain by
TJ International Ltd, Padstow, Cornwall

For my grandparents and my grandchildren,
now and to come, and all the intervening
and extending links in between

Contents

Figures

Boxes

Preface to the first edition

As I sit here tapping into my computer I have memories of story-telling in West Africa with its songs, movements and actively performing audiences, of the calls, colours and scents from sparkling displays of produce laid out to entice buyers in a Fijian market, and of the shared experiences, somatic and visual not just acoustic, of musical performances in England. I think of the gestures and unspoken signals of everyday living and of contacts across distance through telephones, letters, presents; also of those variegated family heirlooms, material contacts with earlier generations. I cannot forget either the experiences of reading authors from the long past, Homer's rhythms and cadences as well his words, and the body-stirring excitements of Greek dramatic metres, with their dances and choruses.

All these, it seems to me, are ways that human beings interconnect with each other – modes of communicating. And yet so many accounts seem not to take on this full multisensory range, presenting instead a thinner more parochial view of communicating, as if it is limited to words or, at best, to recent expansions in visual images and the ramifications of currently expanding information technologies. Words are indeed wonderful, and my personal and scholarly life has been imbued with them – but there is so much else too.

This book developed out of such reflections. Looking back at my own experiences, I felt the need for a wider view of communication. There seemed a place for a book which could draw together something of the many current insights into the importance of *all* the senses in our human interconnecting, of material objects, contacts across space and time, and the significance of experiential dimensions of human life, not just the cognitive. Too many of our assumptions and analyses have been logocentric or unidimensional, cutting out the dynamic processes of gesture, movement, dance, often even sound itself.

The book also grows out of my earlier research. In studying first story-telling in Sierra Leone, then oral poetries and performances in Africa and elsewhere, processes of literacy and orality, Fijian and English music-making, and urban tales, I have for long, I now realise, been involved not just with the anthropology of expressive art and performance but also, in the broad sense, with communication. Going in the same direction too, perhaps, was my initial training in the beautiful works of Greek and Roman literature. Back in 1973 Robin Horton and I edited a collection on *Modes of Thought*. Now, a quarter of a century or so later, I wish to keep the comparative perspective of that work but to suggest a more multifaceted conspectus than we altogether envisaged then, and to direct attention not to thinking but to the multiply overlapping processes, intricate and thickly interwoven, through which people actively interconnect.

This book is about communication, then, but communication in a wider sense than adopted in many studies. It is narrow too in focusing on different dimensions from those pursued in many other specialist works. It looks to embodied performances and human artefacts rather than to 'texts', to multidimensional shared and active processes rather than the transfer of messages. It has little to say about evolutionary origins in prehistoric times, or about the brain, mental representations, technical transfers of data, the arguably capitalist tendencies of the modern mass media, or new globalising trends. Nor does it address detailed questions about the effects of human communicating and how far these should be judged 'good' or 'bad'. Rather it focuses on charting the modes by which people interconnect in the world – the multiple bodily resources we can draw on and the multifarious arts and artefacts which we humans create. In one way this is an unambitious undertaking: merely a kind of catalogue of the various modes and resources used in human communicating with some accompanying commentary. But that in itself is actually a staggering task – an attempt to capture something of the amazing creativity of human beings as they deploy an equally amazing range of resources.

Such an endeavour, even narrowed down, is necessarily interdisciplinary, with all the costs and benefits that that implies. It draws most directly on the insights and findings from anthropology, the discipline in which I am most rooted; I much value both its fertile combination of comparative perspective with meticulously detailed ethnography, and a series of illuminating recent studies, not as widely known outside the discipline as they should be. The comparative contexting and the examples from many areas of the world, not just the modern west, are important dimensions of my approach. Also relevant have been certain converging strands across a range of disciplines in both the social sciences and the humanities to do with emotions, 'the body', the anthropology of the senses, and a concern with process, not least the micro-processes and non-verbal dimensions of face-to-face interaction. I have also inevitably drawn on work in, for example, social history, social psychology, sociolinguistics and linguistic anthropology (a specially rich and developing field), art history, material culture and, not least, animal communication.

Any attempted synthesis must fail to do full justice to the subtlety of much of this work and inevitably omits many of the finer debates. Because I hope this book will be accessible to readers with a variety of backgrounds I have tried not to overload the text with detailed argument, references and up-to-the-minute reports (specialists, please forgive me for not citing all the important works); I have tried to add further references in brackets or notes to enable others to follow up – or dispute –

the interpretations here. Overall I would like to think that the book might open up new channels for those not aware of the riches of this transdisciplinary work, as it certainly has for me, even if the cost is a curtailed coverage of any one area.

Some short remarks on the book's format and presentation might be useful to the reader. First, it is in one way linear with an unfolding argument and series of descriptions. But in another way there is no right order: by the end the separate points have become inextricably mixed. We are now more conscious of non-linear communication, and of the possibilities of organising communication in multiple orders. It is the same here. Some will wish to start with the relatively abstract discussion of communication and theoretical perspectives in Chapter 1, others with Chapter 2's treatment of the basic resources that humans have for communicating. Others again may prefer the concluding chapters, or turn at once to the more detailed examples of modalities of communication in Part II, in a way the heart of the volume.

Second, the figures are integral to the book. They are not meant just to decorate it but to be part of the account. In practical terms, and as the social world now is, it would be hard to provide a properly multisensory volume. But the pictures can at least serve as some token that our communicating does not lie in words alone, nor just in visible written marks on a piece of paper, but is also realised in wider multidimensional processes – all part of the remarkable multiplex world of human communicating.

Finally, the book refers to examples from throughout the world. Scattered cases cannot of course prove a particular thesis; rather they are intended to illustrate the overall position taken up here and to open up our imaginative grasp of what can be involved. They are presented as examples of resources, processes or artefacts that *can* be used for communicating and in some cases have been so used; but it should not be assumed that they are always used in this way. Different people, groups, cultures or historical periods have differing conventions and occasions, and part of the multiplicity referred to in the title of this volume lies in the versatility of our manifold communicative processes.

Preface to the second edition

Ten years later . . . From one perspective I have in no way changed my views since writing the first (2002) edition. I still believe communicating is best treated in a pragmatic way as human interacting – a process – rather than either the *products* of human minds or the verbal, rational and cognitive dimension of human life. I would still urge that in the study of communication we must be prepared to go further than technological mechanisms and think beyond the speculative boxes of evolutionary or psychological theorising. Neither do I think it sufficient to focus on just one kind of culture (by default, no doubt, that of twentieth-century Europe).

There has been a spate of new writing since the first edition of this book, referred to at appropriate places in the text rather than gathered up here. There is still much – too much in my view – based on assumptions queried throughout this volume. But much has also, encouragingly to me, been on somewhat similar lines to mine, a route to the opening of minds to the many-sided aspects of human cultures through the ages, guided but not limited by the insights of comparative anthropology: the burgeoning (and welcome) pragmatist approach to speaking, the sociology and anthropology of the body, dialogic approaches, new cultural studies, and fresh insights into memory, imagination and consciousness. In particular there has been a flurry of mind-blowing research into multisensory topics. Even more justifiably than in 2002 we can truly speak of a 'sensory turn' in the humanities, taking it even further than the perspectives fore-shadowed in the first edition of this work and bringing new insights into the nature not just of communicating but of human nature itself.

As I reflected in the original Preface, an intractable problem in the first edition, to my eyes at least, was that though it – rightly – devoted much attention to communicating across distance, across space, contact across *time* remained a puzzle. How could it be possible? Must not death and oblivion render us blind, incommunicado? There seemed no appropriate tool to get a purchase on the question of how, given the mortality of earthly life and the succession of new generations, this could ever be practicable. For of course just the sheer survival of the products of human culture – in books, libraries, museums, schoolrooms – could surely not be enough. Writing, it is true, and other long-lasting and seemingly imperishable artefacts do indeed provide some element of continuity – is this truly contact between human *minds*? And if not, is this really to 'communicate' in the truly human senses implied here? And if not contact between human beings, human *persons*, is it indeed *communication*?

And yet – do not all religions of the past and present in their different ways assume a link beyond the present, an understanding across the generations, some bridge between life and death? Studies of memory and – increasingly fashionable nowadays – of brain and consciousness shadow out a continuity. Does not quotation – the carrying on and re-enactment of others' words, above all of those loved and revered – offer us a way to enter and re-enact the minds and thoughts – and wisdoms – of others from past times, near or far? As I found in my study of the nature and history of quotation (Finnegan 2011), quoting has been experienced as a mode of personal contact, conceptualised by those involved as an experiential means of direct communicating. Here indeed is a mode of contact – communication, not just with family members, dead as well as alive (though they may be the most mentioned and present in our thoughts and on out lips) but with earlier generations – with other congenial souls across centuries as across the continents. Now as in the past we do indeed find means of contact across time. And let us not forget the mode of connection that somehow takes us beyond the here and now of our mortal world – surely we have all experienced some touch of that? The new chapter 8 describes such access and communion.

And then in the end I return perforce to the multisensory. It is true that at times the senses are not simultaneously exploited. In the settings of day-to-day bodily presence the skills of contact across space and time, so wonderfully and miraculously developed in the appropriate contexts, are not needed. But for the most part, and counter-intuitively to us children of the linguistic turn whose eyes are too readily closed to all but the verbal, they work in concert – still the key theme of this book. In hidden and continuingly subtle ways they link humanity to humanity through their multiple modes. And not just in our everyday earthly lives but, equally earthly, in that contact with (however we term it) the somehow *beyond-the-here-and-now* – or, if you will, in our experience of dreams, of trance, telepathic communion and heaven-return journeys – *all* the senses are, least expected, still in play.

And finally: we know from other studies that muscles well exercised enlarge and vivify the corresponding portions of the brain: violinists mastering the unnatural movements of their play, chess prodigies who have come just to 'know' the right moves, even – as I noticed an hour ago – ourselves able to cut the nails of our dominant hands (strange indeed!). The skills of our movements and senses, above all vision and audition, we have learned and exercised in like manner. We both inherit and transmit them – together with the linked brain skills that result from and enable them – to and from our co-members of the great race of humankind.

Now, perhaps, are we on the brink of revivifying those skills of mutual knowing –

communicating through a multitude of modes, not least those skills of communicating through and by the ether so sadly atrophied in the controversially scientistic age of the twentieth century? Do they still lurk unseen in our brains from previous ages, to increase and bequeath to our grandchildren?

Acknowledgements

A book on human interconnection should certainly have some acknowledgement to make to those others who have been embroiled in one way or another in the process of creating it. Not surprisingly I have many thanks that I wish to express here.

In a relatively formal sense – but no less sincere – let me thank first the Faculty of Social Sciences of the Open University for help with research expenses and for other support over many years and also, within it, the Pavis Centre for a generous grant towards the heavy cost of the illustrations. Among my favourite places are libraries, and I have happy memories of many. I have benefited especially from the marvellous collection in the library of the School of Oriental and African Studies, University of London, and also, extensively, from the resources of the British Library both in central London and its great Inter-Library Loan service; though like others I still mourn the beauties of the old Round Reading Room I cannot fault the great service and wonderfully helpful smiling staff now in the 'Humanities 2' Reading Room at St Pancras. The Open University library has been an unfailing support for years and I am more grateful than I can properly express to my many colleagues and friends there, old and new. For the more recent stages, let me also acknowledge with real gratitude the friendliness and professionalism of those at Routledge, especially Christabel Kirkpatrick and Louisa Semlyen, and of Mike Hauser at M Rules, who between them so constructively smoothed the book's final completion and production.

In a way everyone with whom I have interacted over the years, both academically and in other ways, has helped my understanding. My thanks to all of them. Certain individuals have given particular help, often without knowing they were doing so, by encouraging me to pursue bits and pieces of this book, reinforcing or challenging my approach, providing references and ideas, or just generally taking an interest. The list is actually endless but let me mention in particular (and in alphabetical order) Dick Bauman, John Clarke, Drew Gerstle, Peter Hamilton, John Hunt, Tim Ingold, Ray Ison, Helga Kotthoff, Gunther Kress, Thomas Luckmann, Rachel Murray, David Parkin, Rees Pryce (and others from that hugely stimulating 'DA301' Open University course), Jurgen Streeck, Brian Street, Greg Urban, Elizabeth Whitcombe and Stephen Yeo; also Di-An McCormick for her much appreciated help on the Chinese calligraphy and its background in Figure 5.10 and David Lowenthal for his enormous kindness in saving me from so many mistakes at the eleventh hour. I also most gratefully acknowledge the stimulating comments of members of seminars or conferences to which I have, in various forms, presented some of the ideas behind this book, especially those at the conference on 'Aesthetic forms of communication' at Konstanz in 1997 and the ever-bracing group of anthropologists and others in the University of Edinburgh. Other scholars have greatly influenced my thinking over the years, often at a distance and mostly unknowingly on their part; they would not necessarily agree with my approach here and some alas are now dead, but I must still mention Howard Becker and John Blacking (both in their different ways constant sources of inspiration), Dick Bauman, Peter Burke, Steve Feld, Ulf Hannerz, Roy Harris, Dell Hymes and Joel Sherzer.

I have very special thanks to Paul Smith and to John Hunt for their invaluable help with the illustrations: Paul for his support and expertise in searching out and advising on the illustrations both generally and severally, something I could never have managed on my own; and John for not only scanning them all in, advising on the detail, taking photographs, and producing the artwork but also, like Paul, for his creative suggestions, enthusiasm and staying serene when I was panicking. Let me thank them too not just for this recent help but also for the warmth and wonderful intellectual stimulation of their colleagueship over many years – I have learnt so much from each of them.

My friends, family and co-singers in local choirs all helped too, not least my grandchildren; they were all part of my learning about communication. And my husband David Murray: as ever there are too many debts and interactions to list, but let me at least cite his help in taking, finding and allowing me to reproduce some of his photographs – not just that but the shared experiences in many lands and many phases of our family life which was their setting.

Illustrations

The sources of the illustrations are given in their captions. Many are by now out of copyright but I wish to acknowledge permission to reproduce the figures listed below.

First, special thanks are due to the following not only for permission to publish personal photographs or artwork or to reproduce personal items, but often for suggesting and locating them as well:

Kenneth Cragg (for assistance with 5.12), Andrew Crowley (10.4), Andrew Gerstle (10.3 caption and figure), John Hunt (photographs 1.2, 5.4 (OS map, centre right), 5.10, artwork 4.6, 5.5, 5.9 caption, 5.1 box), David Murray (photographs 1.1, 3.1, 3.3, 5.1, personal permissions 1.2, 3.4, 5.10), Bill Rolston (6.1 – photographs from his book *Drawing Support. Murals in the North of Ireland,* Belfast: Beyond the Pale Publications, 1992).

I also gratefully acknowledge the following: 'Communicating is not just words', 'The principal varieties of mankind', 'West African drums', 'Mosque in Sierra Leone', 'The Hallelujah chorus', 'The Laughing Buddha', 'Calligraphy and picture: a Chinese fan', reproduced by permission of David Murray; 'Teaching of heaven and hell: the Doom painting, Chaldon', © Crown Copyright, NMR; 'The disappointed ones', reprinted by permission of Kunstmuseum Bern; 'Communication in movement and posture: Indian dance' and 'The painted rickshaw', reprinted by permission of Julia Hollander, Liba Taylor and Hutchison Picture Library; 'An ancient system of finger notation', reprinted by permission of the British Library, shelfmark HS 74/76; 'From an Assyrian tale of a lion hunt', 'Ashanti goldweights' and 'Marshall Island stick chart', © The British Museum; 'The Bayeux Tapestry – 11th century', by special permission of the City of Bayeux; 'Mappa Mundi', © The Dean and Chapter of Hereford Cathedral and the Hereford Mappa Mundi Trust; 'True and False Preaching', © Kupferstichkabinett, Staatliche Museen zu Berlin – Preussischer Kulturbesitz. Photograph: Jorg P. Anders; 'Dr Saunderson's Palpable Arithmetic, 1740', reproduced by permission of the Bodleian Library, University of Oxford, shelfmark GG53 Jur; 'Noli me tangere' and 'The Virgin of Louvain', reproduced by permission of Bridgeman Art Library; 'Murals from the north of Ireland', reprinted by permission of Bill Rolston from his book *Drawing Support. Murals in the North of Ireland*; 'Performance script for the Japanese Noh play *Izutsu*', courtesy Hinoki Publishing Company, Tokyo, and C. Andrew Gerstle; 'Indian carpet', courtesy of the Atlantic Bay Gallery, London; 'The wise men of Gotham and their goose', reprinted by permission of the Library of Congress, LC-US262-1514; photograph of the St William window, York Minster, © Andrew Crowley; '*Ramayana* illustration', © The V & A Picture Library; 'Notating movement: the Benesh movement notation system', © Rudolf Benesh, London 1955, courtesy of the Benesh Institute, London; Patrick Baldwin photograph © Patrick Baldwin; photographs or artwork in Figures 1.2, 4.6, 5.4, 5.5, 5.9 (caption), 5.10 and box 5.1, courtesy of John Hunt; 'Story of the magical breadfruit tree', reprinted by permission of Bishop Museum, Honolulu, photograph by Christine Takata; 'The Shahadah: a calligraphic declaration of faith', courtesy Kenneth Cragg and the Institute of Islamic Studies, Rawalpindi; 'Knots that declare the measure', reprinted by permission of Vandenhoeck and Ruprecht Publishing Company; 'Monkey tails', reprinted from M. Moynihan, 'Communication in the titi monkey', in *Journal of Zoology*, 150, 1966, Fig.1, p. 83, courtesy of Cambridge University Press; 'Poems as pictures' (Apollinaire), courtesy of Éditions Gallimard.

In a few cases copyright holders could not be traced or did not respond despite our efforts; the publishers would be glad to hear from any that have been omitted.

Part I

Foundations

1 Communicating humans . . . but what does that mean?

Like other living creatures human beings interconnect with each other. When you come to think about it, this is actually something remarkable – that individual organisms are not isolated but have active and organised ways of connecting with others outside themselves; that we can reach out to others beyond the covering envelopes of our own skins.

How do we do it? And what resources do humans have at their disposal for achieving this? The answer is in a way simple: we work through the resources of our bodies and of our environment. Unpacking that short statement is less easy, however. It leads into a vast and wonderful field of the complex resources that human beings draw on to interconnect with each other. It is these manifold resources and the many ways we use them that are explored in this book.

Rather than plunging at once into definitional issues let us start with four short examples to preview the general approach to communication in this volume. A more extended discussion of contending perspectives can then bring it into sharper focus, before we return to a more direct consideration of human communicative resources in Chapter 2 and later.

Communication and human interconnectedness

Three people are standing around discussing a recent event they all feel strongly about. They are interchanging spoken comments, partly taking turns, partly interrupting, capping and overlapping each other, and formulating their annoyance and surprise through gesture and body positions as well as words. One shows round a memo, pointing to specific bits of it, additionally inflaming their anger. They gasp, tut-tut or 'hm' from time to time in acknowledgement or agreement (partial at least) with each other's comments and actions, or as a way of expressing ironic or mock-incredulous reactions. One is more lukewarm, but all three show their active involvement through mutually recognised actions like eye contact, direction of their gaze, body movements, facial expressions, postures and occasional touches. They move in to stand closer, and increasingly formulate and build up a shared sense of indignation about what had happened.

Face-to-face interaction among a small number of people is one obvious instance but not of course the only context for communicating. Take another example. Among the highlights of the year among the Limba rice farmers of northern Sierra Leone in the 1960s were the rites surrounding boys' initiation into manhood. The night before the boys were taken off to be secluded in the bush there was a grand and public ritual thronged with hundreds of people from throughout the chiefdom. The boys wore the special garb traditional for these rituals, an obligatory mark of the occasion. All through the night they displayed their prowess in special dances, incredibly vigorous and demanding with powerful gymnastic gyrations and hand-springs. Expert drummers sounded out the emotive patterned beats appropriate for the occasion, engaging both dancers and spectators over the long hours with their body-stirring rhythms. Whistles were blown, songs sung, and the crowds, above all the principals in the rite, contributed their shouts and movements. Every now and then friends or relatives rushed up to touch one of the dancers or give a gift in token of their support and admiration. Speeches of welcome and admonition were made by local dignitaries. Fires and lamps lightened the gloom, itself part of the atmos-phere. So too was the olfactory ambience from the aromas of food, palm wine, closely touching crowds and perspiring dancers. Through these colourful perfor-mances people marked the public validation of the boys' approaching status-change, a major occasion for the community, enacted through these highly specific and recognised multisensory processes. Individuals signalled their personal allegiances and involvement, the boys demonstrated their fitness for elevation to manhood, and through their speeches the elders conveyed both their own leading positions and what they presented as the age-old values of *malimba ma*, 'the Limba way'. All these multiple communicative processes were mediated not through publication in writing but through publicly shared and multifaceted enactment.[1]

Humans also interconnect at greater distances – not so easy perhaps but made possible through our ingenious uses of material objects and technologies. So as a third example consider a personal letter and photograph sent through the post. Simple at first sight, this again has multiple dimensions, though in different ways from the other two cases. The visual marks on the material page – written words, format, punctuation, handwriting – are one obvious dimension. But others matter too. Even before the letter is opened up, the envelope and its handwritten address visibly declare its specific character not only to the named addressee but also to others in the household where it is delivered. The appearance and feel of the paper and the layout on the page are relevant too, accepted conventions which in this case clearly indicate personal intimacy not officialese. So are the handwriting, the non-verbal visual signs (a squiggle of a diagram, 'x's at the end (for kisses), exclamation marks), the crackle of paper and envelope, and, not least, the enclosed photo-graph, a human-made artefact which also plays its part. The communicating is experienced in the context of (more, or less) shared understandings and associations between the various participants – participants who include not only letter writer and addressee but in this case a number of other people involved in different ways and at various removes, including others in the recipient's household among whom the letter is mentioned or read aloud, the photograph circulated, or the interpretations formulated – some more interested or more directly involved than others. And if time passes and the letter and photograph are looked at again, other forms of interconnecting may come into play for those later users. The specific ways in which people engage in 'mediated' communicating of this kind vary with different individuals, contexts and conventions. But the communicative process is always likely to be more complex than just a chunk of information transmitted once-and-for-all by fixed marks on a sheet of paper.

The final short example is one where the enactors were involved in yet further temporal and spatial dimensions beyond the momentary occasion: the memorial service for the British Poet Laureate Ted Hughes in May 1999, a large-scale ritual in Westminster Abbey drawing on the multiple resources conventionally deployed on such occasions. There were jointly sung hymns; choir anthems; a visually colourful procession; organ, piano and guitar playing; the olfactory and spatial ambience of the building; the closely pressed throng; spoken and read words; and a ringingly declaimed oration. And then came the dead poet's unseen voice reciting 'Fear no more the heat of the sun', with all its resonating associations for an English-speaking gathering.

> One by one, line by line, the looking stopped and the listening went on: 'The sceptre, learning, physic must, all follow this and come to dust'. . . . And now for a few moments, he was back with us. It was as though he was moving from the pews of the living into the poets' corner of the dead. . . . The crowd that flowed away out of the Abbey was both different from and the same as the one which arrived.
>
> (Stothard 1999: 24)

The occasion drew not only on written and remembered words, first formulated centuries ago and long handed-down through people's creative chains of experience, but also on recent auditory technology for storing and transmitting recorded sounds, all set within a multidimensional process with its plurality of participants.

These four short cases foreshadow the approach in this volume. They assume a view of 'communicating' that is not confined to linguistic or cognitive messages but also includes experience, emotion and the *unspoken*. Communicating is envisaged as creative human process rather than transport of data or meeting of 'minds', and goes beyond the preoccupation with 'information' and 'the information revolution' typical of much current discussion. It encompasses the many modes of human interacting and living, both near and distant – through smells, sounds, touches, sights, movements, embodied engagements and material objects.

These interconnecting processes are necessary ones for collective human life. We humans are notably social animals. We live in interacting groups, larger or smaller depending on the context and purpose. Through these we bring up our children, order our affairs, make decisions (the disputed and disastrous as well as the happy ones), express ourselves, share out our complementary tasks, our space and our material resources, avoid (more or less) treading on each other's toes, conduct our lives, and collaborate in the joint enterprises of collective living. Humans are dependent on webs of interconnectedness for their basic modes of growth and livelihood as well as the rich arts and practices of human cultures. In a whole series of organised ways we formulate and share information, ideas, activities, experiences, resources and emotions, and in so doing – for good or ill – engage interactively with each other.

Human creatures call on a vast array of resources for this interconnecting: the examples above represent only the minutest sample of the amazingly diverse ways in which they do so. We use gestures, sounds, writing, images, material objects, bodily contacts, supported by the more or less agreed conventions through which we variously recognise such usages as purposive forms of interaction and mutual influence. Through activating our voices, touches and movements we can share wishes or emotions with others; make visible movements of our bodies to encounter or avoid each other in public places; utilise pictorial displays, visually codified graphics, and three-dimensional artefacts to interconnect over space or time. Deploying these communicative resources is fundamental to our human existence. As the anthropologist Ray Birdwhistell put it in 1968 (dated in language perhaps but an eloquent summary nonetheless):

> Because of a complex division of labor, man's performances are seldom isolated actions in themselves. The social performance of a given member of society is by definition incomplete; task accomplishment is dependent upon continuative, coordinate, parallel, or complementary individual or subgroup behaviors. . . . Flexibility and adaptability demand continuous and reliable feedback, contribution, and correction between the performing membership. . . . All [the] directly or indirectly influenceable somatic systems within the living body provide potentials for human interconnectedness.
>
> (Birdwhistell 1968: 25, 26)

Birdwhistell's conception of communication as the active dimension of human interconnectedness underlies the approach in this volume.

The approach here builds both on this and on the related tradition of pragmatist writers like Dewey, Cooley and Mead, of Simmel, and the symbolic interactionist school. Certain more recent developments – extensions to this general tradition – are also particularly pertinent for this analysis of communication and can usefully be discussed together here.

First, a number of analysts have been progressively turning away from decontextualised and passive models of human life towards emphasising instead the complex creative processes through which human beings actively interact. Changing interpretations of language have paralleled this, especially a move away from a model of language as *product* – thus best studied as formal text – to that of language as *action*. The dramatistic approaches of Erving Goffman and Kenneth Burke and the pragmatic analysis of 'speech acts' by the philosopher Austin and others have been matched by a similarly active approach to other forms of linguistic interchange like the ethnomethodological micro-analyses of conversations and small-group encounters. Comparable perspectives are found in the ethnography of speaking, performance and experience by anthropologists and sociolinguists (such as Vic Turner, Dell Hymes, Dick Bauman or Joel Sherzer) and in the expanding interdisciplinary work on language and social interaction which emphasises the processual dimensions of language – exchange rather than thought. Some of these streams date back some time but they are now flowing together in a fresh view of speech and communication: not independent systems of signs for conveying decontextualised pieces of information but modes of social action, created by interacting human agents in specific situations.[2]

These perspectives highlight the active and processual nature of human life and the role of creative human action in forming the human world, linking into the increasing emphasis on process and interaction within social theory more generally. In Dick Bauman's phrase, 'Society is communicatively constituted, produced and reproduced by communicative acts' (1992: xiv): not a predetermined entity over and above individuals but emergent in and through their actions and experiences. Communication is to be found in the creative mutual interacting of individuals or groups in specific contexts rather than in abstract systems of codes or the transmission of bounded 'messages'. Communicating is not a once-and-for-all transfer of some referential content, but develops as the interactors jointly and severally co-construct the process.

Second, there is now increasing awareness of *all* the channels of human interaction, non-verbal and material as well as linguistic. As will emerge in later chapters, a sensitivity to the multisensory aspects of communicating is in some ways nothing new. But recent years have seen a revival of interest, implicitly challenging the focus on 'meanings', 'symbols' and verbalised articulations found even in some of the interactionist work mentioned above. New approaches to material culture, museology and cultural history draw attention to the role of human-made artefacts and their multisensory dimensions; comparable trends are found in the comparative anthropology of the human senses, aesthetic anthropology, and some of the burgeoning writing on 'the body'. Cultural historians, anthropologists and others are querying the assumption that communication has to be conceived as centred on the written word or intellectual meanings, while studies of language point to the co-ordination of verbal and gestural activities in the actual processes of speaking and include affective as well as referential aspects. The result is a greater sensitivity to the variegated channels of human interaction – through smells, sounds, touches, sights, movements, material artefacts – and the significance of shared experiences, dynamic interactions, and bodily engagements beyond the purely cognitive.[3]

These transdisciplinary developments both reinforce and extend the earlier pragmatist and interactionist traditions, and underlie the approach in this volume. The focus is on active interconnectedness through a range of modes. This is to take a broad view of communication which includes all the channels open to human interaction, whether auditory, visual, kinesic, proxemic, tactile or olfactory. Humans are not solely intellectual or rational creatures, and their communication through human-made artefacts and through their facial expressions, dress or bodily positionings form as relevant a part of their dynamic interacting as verbally articulated sentences. Human beings, in short, draw on a multitude of resources to interconnect with each other and in so doing interactively create their human world.

Figure 1.1 Communicating is not just words
In ways both unique to themselves and typical of how human beings often interact, these two children are communicating through eyes, heads, faces and bodies, as well as through their close spatial positioning (Photograph: David Murray).

Perspectives on communication

This view of communication runs counter to some currently influential approaches. Accounts in the standard social science literature commonly assume an essentially cognitive model, with its 'information', 'messages', 'codes' and 'meanings'; after (perhaps) a nod to non-verbal processes, they tend to concentrate either on verbal language or, more topically, on the 'mass media' and 'new information technologies'. Alternatively the focus is on face-to-face communication, omitting any substantive consideration of the equally human processes of communicating at a distance.[4] Even in anthropology, reference works often do not fully capitalise on the discipline's long interests in communication or the extensive and highly pertinent recent work by anthropologists, and frequently say little about 'communication' as such whilst waxing eloquent on linguistic matters.[5] Overall, current accounts provide a narrow viewpoint on communication and, with it, on human life.[6]

Contending approaches have long been a feature of analyses of communication. Indeed our everyday metaphors for communication are themselves multiple (see the perceptive account of these metaphors in Krippendorff 1993). We variously envisage communication as container, conduit or transmission; as control; as war; as dance-ritual. The more explicit academic statements overlap and intertwine with these images, often carrying with them powerful if unspoken connotations about what it is to be human. Something of the spread of current approaches is illustrated in Box 1.1.

Box 1.1 A sampler of statements about 'communication'

Note: not all were proposed as formal definitions but they are nevertheless succinct statements encapsulating key points in distinctive perspectives on communication.

1

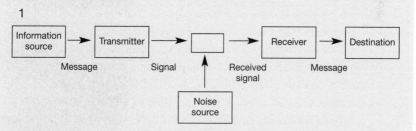

(This figure is after Shannon and Weaver 1964 [1949]: 7, 34, a classic and still influential formulation of the 'communication theory' approach, typically cited in this diagrammatic form.)

2   'Communication occurs when one organism (the transmitter) encodes information into a signal which passes to another organism (the receiver) which decodes the signal and is capable of responding appropriately' (Ellis and Beattie 1986: 3, psychology).

3   'A process that involves the transmission of messages from senders to receivers' (Berger 2000: 271, media research).

4   'Social interaction through messages' (Fiske 1990: 2, textbook in communication studies).

5   'A negotiation and exchange of meaning in which messages, people-in-cultures and "reality" interact so as to enable meaning to be produced or understanding to occur' (O'Sullivan *et al.* 1994: 50, the 'structuralist approach' as summarised in a standard reference work).

6   '[We make] meaning by forging links between three different orders of things: what we might broadly call the world of things, people, events and experiences; the conceptual world – the mental concepts we carry around in our heads; and the signs, arranged into languages, which 'stand for' or communicate these concepts. . . . We can translate [our thoughts about the world] into language, make them 'speak', through the use of signs which stand for them – and thus talk, write, communicate about them to others' (Stuart Hall 1997: 61–2, cultural studies).

7   'Communication Studies is about how human meanings are made through the production and reception of various types of sign. It is about visual and verbal sign systems and the technologies used to articulate, record and convey them' (Corner and Hawthorn 1993: 2, communication studies).

8   'Communication is behavior resulting in the transfer of information among organisms, with the purpose of modifying the behavior of all participants involved in the process' (Beeman 1997: 73, dictionary of anthropology).

9   'Communication is action on the part of one organism (or cell) that alters the probability pattern of behavior in another organism (or cell) in a fashion adaptive to either one or both of the participants' (Wilson 1975: 176, 581, sociobiology).

10   'A speaker perceives a state of affairs, that is, constructs a mental model representing it. The speaker intends to communicate certain aspects of this situation to a listener, and so, taking into account common knowledge, utters some appropriate words. The listener perceives these words and, again taking into account common knowledge, is able to grasp the content of the speaker's immediate communicative intention. The listener constructs a mental model representing the relevant features of the original situation. A message may then

pass in the opposite direction, and, as a result, the two participants may share a mutual knowledge that the act of
communication has been successfully consummated' (Johnson-
Laird 1990: 9, cognitive psychology).

11 'Communication is a process involving two information-processing
devices. One device modifies the physical environment of the
other. As a result, the second device constructs representations
similar to representations already stored in the first device. . . .
[An individual's] mental representations . . . get communicated:
that is, first transformed by the communicator into public representations, and then re-transformed by the audience into mental
representations' (Sperber and Wilson 1995: 1; Sperber 1996:
25 – interdisciplinary cognitivist approach).

12 '"Language" refers to the most frequent form of communication
among human beings. It is unique to the human species' (Comrie
1997: 274, dictionary of anthropology).

13 'The human faculty of language seems to be a true "species
property", varying little among humans and without significant
analogue elsewhere. . . . There is no serious reason today to
challenge the Cartesian view that the ability to use linguistic signs
to express freely-formed thoughts marks "the true distinction
between man and animal" or machine. . . . The faculty of language is largely responsible for the fact that alone in the
biological world, humans have a history, cultural evolution and
diversity of any complexity and richness' (Chomsky 2000: 3,
linguistics/cognitive science).

14 'Communication is not something additional to or separable from
the rest of human life and the constantly changing circumstances
that it presents, but an integrated part of it. . . . There is no message that is independent of the activities involved in its
formulation and interpretation, and no such process which is
independent of the particular communication situation in which it
operates' (Harris 1996: 13, 20, on integrational linguistics).

15 'Communication is a social activity. . . . Most of communication's
key features make sense only when understood as somehow
forged in the linking of different individuals' (W. J. Smith 1997: 7,
31, ethology/animal communication)

16 'Communication is the dynamic aspect of interconnection'
(Birdwhistell 1968: 27, pioneer in anthropological research on
bodily communication).

Box 1.1 is a selective sampler, far from any attempt to cover myriad definitions of 'communication'.[7] But it can serve as some illustration of both contrasts and recurrent themes, themselves bound into widespread assumptions about the nature of communication and of humanity. The following sections give some commentary on certain of these threads.

Communication as information

The strongest single theme is the idea of communication as a matter of the intellect. We constantly encounter terms like 'information', 'message', 'meaning', 'coding', 'mental representations', 'thoughts'. Even in otherwise contrasting theoretical perspectives, there seems to be an underlying model of communication as ultimately something cognitive, prototypically formulated in spoken or written words. Contextual and 'intertextual' dimensions, if mentioned at all, seem to be secondary, perhaps even counter-productive. The emotive overtones of touch, the subtle cadences of the heard voice, or the visual apperception of bodily gesture or material art – since the informative content is presupposed as central, all these come in as, at best, an afterthought.

This often goes along with the assumed equation of 'communication' with language. Despite the wider claims of their titles Saville-Troike's *The Ethnography of Communication* (1989) and Habermas's *On the Pragmatics of Communication* (1998), for example, are all about language (its practice and theory respectively), whilst anthropological textbooks regularly take it for granted that learning about 'communication' means exploring aspects of verbal language.[8] A standard reader on 'communication theory' explains its coverage as 'understanding the "flow" of information': its 'uniting focus' is the idea of 'linguistic processes. . . . Linguistics provides the foundations and touchstone for communication theory. . . . Language is the central institution of any society' (Cobley 1996: 1).

That this model of communication looks credible is partly due to the widely held view of language as *the* unique characteristic of human beings and thus naturally central to truly human communicating. The non-linguistic processes of touch, olfaction, kinesics, vision or non-vocal audition seem of little moment compared to the wonderfully developed human power of speech. This impression is strengthened by influential ideologies about language and the human destiny. In Locke's 'scientific' approach language and knowledge should be stripped of contextual and emotive associations, for what matters is abstraction and decontextualisation. Human beings communicate through propositional and rational verbal formulations – or should do so to be fully human – rather than through the 'lower' forms of non-verbal or emotional activities. This referential view of language, an unstated and unquestioned premise in many approaches to communication, is further reinforced in images of communication as container or conduit in which objectively existing messages and statements reside and are transmitted (Krippendorff 1993: esp. 5–9).

But this model is starting to seem less convincing. The reasons partly lie in the widening interests in contextual, pragmatic and *non*-referential dimensions of communication and of language mentioned in the last section. Nor is the Lockean position the only ideology of language, for the contending philosophies of Herder and similar thinkers stressed not reference but feeling and imagination, championing intertextuality, context, emotion and sensory celebration.[9] The perspective in this volume, as in some recent work in (among other areas) linguistic anthropology, performance studies and ethnomusicology, inclines towards Herder's tradition in not focusing solely on decontextualised meaning but also embracing emotion, context and multisensory enactment. Verbal language furthermore seems less and less like a self-standing autonomous system, the site for truly human representation, but as in practice inextricably intertwined with 'gesture, pantomime, graphic depiction' and other modes of human interaction (Kendon 1991: 216).

It is of course true that the exchange of factual information plays some part in human communicating. It is true too that human interaction does indeed draw extensively on verbal resources. But so much else in our processes of communicating goes beyond the 'factual' or – not necessarily the same thing – the purely verbal. Think of the claims conveyed through a person's dress or demeanour; the subtle interaction between the two children in Figure 1.1; the aesthetic or spiritual experiences communicated through musical, danced, theatrical or religious performances; the effectiveness of pictures of the 'varieties of mankind' or of doom (Figures 1.2, 1.4); the shared emotions generated in a group gathering (recall the initiation and memorial ceremonies above, but more everyday occasions too); the unspoken sympathies expressed through visual and tactile means, unambiguous even if not fully conscious. Such processes are all fully part of our communicating. But they get squeezed out in a model of communication where information or referential language set the framework.

This same basic theme is prominent in three currently influential approaches to communication: those that see it principally as transporting messages; as sharing meanings; and as transferring mental representations between minds. Though it involves some well-trodden ground, some commentary on these contrasting yet overlapping perspectives (among some others) will help to elucidate the view of communication in this volume.

Transporting messages

The 'Sender–Message–Receiver' model with which many accounts of communication commonly open deserves the first attention, set out in classic form in the first example in Box 1.1 above. Communication is initiated by a sender 'encoding' an idea, observation, or other piece of information as a 'message'. This is transmitted and, having survived more or less accurately depending on the distortions ('noise') on the way, reaches the 'receiver' who 'decodes' it at the other end. The straight-line

PRINCIPAL VARIETIES OF MANKIND

process is concluded by the successful receipt of the message. This basic idea has a long history, but the version commonly cited as starting off mid-twentieth-century 'communication theory' was formulated in an engineering context. Shannon and Weaver, working for the Bell Telephone Company, were interested in having messages transmitted fully and accurately over the wires. For them, the 'fundamental problem of communication' was that of 'reproducing at one point either exactly or approximately a message selected at another point' (Shannon and Weaver 1964: 31). More subtle and complicated versions have since been extensively developed, especially in mass media studies, focusing on obstacles to accurate transmission (introduced for example by the status, personality or social conditions of sender or receiver) and/or on influences of feedback. Though much criticised and qualified, in essentials this basic sender–message–receiver image remains enormously influential, by implication if not overtly. It is still often referred to as 'communication theory' par excellence (O'Sullivan *et al.* 1994: 51, Cobley 1996: 1).

The model has its attractions. It fits certain aspects of human communicating, especially the transmission of messages at a distance through electrical/electronic media, and melds satisfyingly with the familiar 'conduit' metaphor. The problem lies in its implications and its focus, both now criticised as implying a narrow, mechanistic and ultimately unrealistic view of what is involved in communication.

Its prime emphasis is on transporting 'the message'. But in the active practices of interacting human life, does a 'message' possess some objective independent existence even in its initial formulation, let alone over the 'transmission process'? As Sless neatly puts it, the message is not 'a distinct entity which can be analysed separately from author or audience' (Sless 1981: 25). One might wonder too whether the 'exact transmission of a message' is always either people's prime aim in communicating or in practice feasible in most of the interactive processes of human living. Just as the cognitive-referential model of language is now being challenged by more active models concerned as much with experience and context as decontextualised meaning, so too surely with communication more generally. The 'message' dissolves into a fluid, situational and multiplex process. It is a process through time, furthermore, where mutual understanding and influence may eventuate *during* the interaction, not just in a concrete message enunciated

---

Figure 1.2 Visual representation of the human world: 'the principal varieties of mankind' A picture by the lexicographer Sir James Murray, possibly copied from another similar illustration, powerfully conveying a late nineteenth-century vision of the nature and ranking of mankind: the Chinese honourably placed, others at the edges and below, and the 'Briton' at the centre. It communicates as effectively as words – in some ways more so, for the spatial juxtapositions work more economically and immediately than a single-line written presentation. The original, in ink drawing and colour, is of a size to hang on a wall and pass on its vision to the viewers (in private possession, reproduced by permission of David Murray. Photograph: John Hunt).

beforehand, and continue even after the apparent 'conclusion' of the message-transfer at its 'destination'. Such emergent interaction is not well served by describing all this as 'noise' – rather, it is a positive dimension of much human communicating.

A parallel point is made by Mikhail Bahktin. Although focusing primarily just on speech his account of people's interactive creativity is well worth quoting: this aspect is often simply omitted in message-transfer approaches to communication. He queries the 'graphic-schematic depictions' of speech communication that present the listener as passively receiving the spoken message:

> When the listener perceives and understands the meaning (the language meaning) of speech, he simultaneously takes an active, responsive attitude toward it. He either agrees or disagrees with it (completely or partially), augments it, applies it, prepares for its execution, and so on. . . . Of course, an utterance is not always followed immediately by an articulated response. An actively responsive understanding of what is heard (a command, for example) can be directly realized in action (the execution of an order or command that has been understood and accepted for execution), or it can remain, for the time being, a silent responsive understanding (certain speech genres are intended exclusively for this kind of responsive understanding, for example, lyrical genres), but this is, so to speak, responsive understanding with a delayed reaction. Sooner or later what is heard and actively understood will find its response in the subsequent speech or behavior of the listener. . . .
>
> The scheme distorts the actual picture of speech communication, removing precisely its most essential aspects . . . the active role of the *other* in the process of speech communication.
>
> (Bakhtin 1986: 68–70)

Many comparable critiques have been made of the sender-focus in these transmission models, with their implication that the 'receiver' has only a receptive rather than active part. As Streeck well points out (1994) in the context of communicating through gestures, the 'audience' is simultaneously a co-author in the communicative process. Though more complex versions of the basic model now suggest something of a two-way process with feedback loops, the concept of a specific (albeit modifiable) *message* still remains.

A further strand also often survives even in the qualified versions: the assumption that there are essentially two main parties in the process, sender and receiver. This has several problems. There is the obvious point that in any process of communicating there are commonly more than two participants. Of course the *categories* might still be twofold: sender (or author) and receiver (audience) – but in practice is it often as simple as this? Even in two-way conversations, with their well-studied conventions for 'turn-taking', there is multiplex overlapping interchange not just because people are speaking at once but also because they may be simultaneously communicating through body movement, posture, facial expression and paralinguistic sounds. Many communicative situations involve multiple participants, perhaps playing different roles or taking a mediating position but all contributing in their own ways to the process. It can be multiply complex. There can be eavesdroppers, interrupters, people who are present but do not at first regard themselves as participants and yet gradually become involved, or the ongoing bodily movements or sequential postures of someone from one viewpoint the 'audience' but from another the 'sender'. Ignoring these complicated interactions by focusing on a message being transmitted *from* one party *to* another misses so much of what is going on. Even in the ostensibly one-way transmission systems of broadcasting to which this model has been extensively applied the concept of 'audience' is now recognised to be more complex and creative than pictured in the simple sender–receiver model, paralleling the active rather than purely 'receptive' processes through which readers engage with texts.[10] Some of these complexities might be built into the dyadic model – but it would then become so complicated as to exceed its usefulness. Equally important it would still divert attention from the multiply interconnecting and creative interactions by people participating in plural roles typical of much communicating.

In the elusive context of communication over time as well as space the two-sided model sometimes proves illuminating. The interchanges of handwritten letters or of electronic email messages are obvious examples. But even there, while the distinction between 'sender' and 'recipient' may seem easy to draw in technical terms, it may in social terms be multiplex indeed. Think of the differential responses and actions among different recipients of 'copied-in' email messages; or the potentially diverse ways that, say, paper, handwriting or address may be interpreted not just by a letter's overt addressee but those others involved in the process. There are even more complexities with examples like reading a book – whether recent novel or ancient Greek epic – or attending the performance of, say, a nineteenth-century symphony. Difficult to get a grip on in any approach to communication, these are little illuminated by the dyadic model: for even if we can pinpoint the 'recipient(s)', who exactly is the 'sender' and whose the 'message'? Or is this not 'communicating' at all? It is more illuminating to think of communication not as a two-sided relationship between two protagonists but as multidimensional processes involving a number of enactors participating to different degrees and in different ways.

The sender–message–recipient model can sometimes be appropriate, and I will not totally avoid the vocabulary of 'message', 'transmission' or 'reception'. But when taken as *the* model, with its connotations of message as distinct entity, of straight-line transportation to a final specified destination, and of dyadic transfer, it implies a narrow view of the processes by which human beings actively interconnect with each other.

Finding meaning

A second major set of perspectives is partly linked to reactions against the 'message-transmission' model. Rather than 'message' or 'data', the key terms are now 'meanings', 'signs', 'signifying systems', 'texts', 'symbols' and 'codes'. Communication is about how 'human meanings are made through the production and reception of various types of sign' (Corner and Hawthorn 1993: 2) and, in theory at least, participants play some part in negotiating or exchanging shared meanings rather than receiving predefined transmitted messages.

These approaches have been enunciated with particular force by writers in the semiotic and structuralist traditions and, most recently, in cultural studies. They cast a fresh perspective on communication by their rejection (usually) of the sim-plified 'sender–message–receiver' model, their emphasis on 'meanings', and their notable readiness to include visual images, material artefacts and the works of the body in their studies of communication. Structural linguistics provides the ultimate inspiration in many cases, with semiology as the science studying 'the life of signs within society' (de Saussure 1960: 16). That these 'signs' are not just those of verbal language is made clear both in detailed analyses and in general comments such as Roland Barthes's seminal assertion that 'images, gestures, melodic sounds, objects, and the compounds of these substances that can be found in rites, protocols or spectacles' can all be taken to constitute 'if not "languages", at least systems of meaning' (Barthes 1964: 1, as translated in Mattelart and Mattelart 1998: 69). Language is the paradigm. Stuart Hall summarises 'the semiotic approach':

> Since all cultural objects convey meaning, and all cultural practices depend on meaning, they must make use of signs; and in so far as they do, they must work like language works, and be amenable to an analysis which basically makes use of Saussure's linguistic concepts.
>
> (Hall 1997: 36)

Such analyses focus on the rules and codes by which meanings are constructed and ideologies expressed in systems of signs. They have been applied to fields as diverse as soap powder, fashion magazines, newspaper photographs, clothes, architecture, film, television programmes, literary texts, or museum exhibitions – among many others (Barthes 1972, 1983; Hall 1997). Mary Douglas (1975) 'deciphers a meal' by elucidating the coding that structures the menu and decodes the symbolic rules in Christmas dinners; indeed 'all material possessions carry social meanings and [are used] as communicators' (Douglas and Isherwood 1980: 59). Structuralist approaches in archaeology assign meaning to the objects they discover. Funeral goods, pot decorations, rock art, or settlement layouts form a 'communicative medium . . . [which] can be regarded as a kind of text, a silent form of writing and discourse; quite literally, a channel of reified and objectified expression' (Tilley

1989: 189). Communication is emphatically not confined to the verbal channel for we also communicate through clothing, houses, images, representations in film or literature, and our material goods generally.

This breadth is illuminating indeed. However, this set of perspectives, useful though they are, also diverge in certain respects from the viewpoint of this volume. First, the 'meanings' are usually sought in abiding or widely applicable codes with less interest in the specificities of varying experiences, interpretations or performances. All analysts of communication, of course, to some extent draw attention to patterning of which the actors themselves may be relatively unaware (expressive bodily movements for example). But structuralist analyses, often moving at a high level of abstraction, tend to combine authoritative pronouncement with quite speculative interpretation. Sometimes, it seems, the meanings are 'found' as much through the analyst's ideology, self-reflection or verbal wizardry as from ethnographic investigation of the processes among actual participants.

A second divergence revolves around the emphasis on terms like 'sign' and 'code'. Relevant in certain cases, these yet imply a closer one-to-one correspondence with some 'correct' set of meanings, to be solved by the analyst, than is really appropriate for the subtle and multiplex interactions – emotional, emergent and value-laden as much as cognitive – commonly involved in human communicating. Some systems of communication do indeed stand out as consisting of more or less standardised and codified signs, and these must be treated in due course (see Part II). But using 'code' and 'sign' of *all* forms of communicating loses the distinction between the more explicit systems and the less standardised (if nonetheless effective) conventions, giving the misleading impression that all human communicating belongs to the former type.

The problem is compounded by the primacy given to systems of 'signs' and 'codes' in their own right. But just as the concept of self-existing languages 'out there' is giving way to an appreciation of the fluid processes of actual speaking, so too there must be doubts about picturing systems of codes as independent of their activation by human communicators in specific settings. Roy Harris (1996) characterises as 'segregationist' the structural-linguistics view which presupposes the autonomy of the sign *vis-à-vis* its users and uses. Instead, he argues, signs are created in and by the act of communication:

> For the segregationist, communication presupposes signs: signs and sign systems exist apart from and prior to the communicational purposes to which they may or may not be put. For the integrationist, on the contrary, signs presuppose communication: they are its products, not its prerequisites.
>
> (Harris 1996: 7)

In their communicating humans often draw, indeed, on a rich store of (relatively) shared resources in particular cultures or situations. But seeing these as systems of independently existing signs is to miss the creative processes in which they are actualised by specific human beings in particular contexts: these are open-ended resources rather than 'a pre-determined set of options' (Harris 1996: xi).

There is also, third, the paradox that despite their welcome inclusion of other than just verbal forms of communicating, *linguistic* images feature so strongly in these approaches. Much is made of the 'linguistic turn' and of terms like 'text', 'reading', 'discourse', 'mode of address', 'say', 'speak' or 'poetics', all carrying connotations of linguistic representation and, ultimately, verbalisable meaning. Objects are 'texts' whose 'meaning' it is for the analyst to find. Sometimes 'text' is indeed an appropriate term, and one dimension of certain genres may well be some degree of verbal entextualisation. But to use it as blanket metaphor obscures differences. This set of images fits poorly with many forms of communicating – music and other performance arts for example or experiences formulated through touch, smell or gesture. A predominantly linguistic paradigm inevitably limits our view of the multiple modalities of human communicating, affective as well as referential.[11]

For all its insights this perspective de-emphasises the active processes of interconnecting between human actors in favour of the transcending power of the 'sign' and of largely linguistic imageries. So although I will certainly from time to time draw on this rich body of work, the view of communication in this volume diverges from its somewhat abstract and cognitive emphasis with its tendency to play down the contextual and creative dimensions of communicating.

Mind, brain and mental representations

Communication is sometimes presented as essentially something of the mind. This is to take a particular position on the long western debates about the mind–body relation, 'Cartesian dualism' being just one version among many. Plato and his followers envisaged the intellectual part as the highest in the tripartite human soul; similarly the 'mind' is the seat of reason, the leader, the charioteer who drives the horses. Enlightenment perspectives set mind above body, intellectual capacities above the 'lower' and more 'animal' emotions. At least partly in the same tradition is the view that it is in the mind that our acts of communication originate and are formulated, with action following on from the mind's command.

The view that the mind is *the* site, origin and even definition of purposive human action shapes cognitivist approaches to communication. Recent analyses in evolutionary psychology often take this line (see below pp. 24–5), but it is widely influential, often dated to the 'cognitive revolution' from the 1950s. Noam Chomsky recently summarised its basic presuppositions:

> The cognitive perspective regards behavior and its products not as the objects of inquiry, but as data that may provide evidence about the inner mechanisms of the mind and the ways these mechanisms operate in executing actions and interpreting experience. . . . The approach is 'mentalistic' . . . concerned with

'mental aspects of the world' . . . It undertakes to study a real object in the natural world – the brain, its states, and its functions.

(Chomsky 2000: 5–6)

Communication is here a matter of 'mental representations', 'internal states' or 'mental concepts' in the mind. Thus Johnson-Laird describes communicating as starting when one speaker constructs a 'mental model', then utters words to convey this to a listener. 'A prerequisite for genuine communication', he writes, 'is the ability to construct internal representations . . . [and] communicate them to others' (Johnson-Laird 1990: 10; see also Johnson-Laird in Box 1.1, pp. 10–11).

The mind itself, and with it human communication, is sometimes further conceived in terms of information processing, a computational metaphor long associated with cognitivist perspectives. Human minds – indeed human beings generally – are pictured as computer systems. To recall the statement quoted earlier (Box 1.1, p. 11):

> Communication is a process involving two information-processing devices. One device modifies the physical environment of the other. As a result, the second device constructs representations similar to representations already stored in the first device. . . . [An individual's] mental representations . . . get communicated: that is, first transformed by the communicator into public representations, and then re-transformed by the audience into mental representations.
>
> (Sperber and Wilson 1995: 1; Sperber 1996: 25)

In some versions of this perspective mind is identified with 'the brain'. This is reinforced by research into links between physical locations in the brain and specific types of behaviour. Such approaches can only have tangential relevance for our understanding of communication as an embodied process, however. A model that equates speaking (for example) with physical events in the brain is not only liable to the charge of reductionism but closes down other routes to analysing the many-dimensional processes of communicating.

These mentalist and information-based approaches are far from the perspective assumed in this book. To see human communicating – and humanity – essentially in terms of mental representations and information-processing not only accords ill with a view of communication as an interactive process but also directs attention away from the communicative potential of the body as a whole and of the modes other than verbal language through which in practice we interconnect – through dancing, for example (see Figure 1.3). As Brenda Farnell neatly expresses it in her study of dance, the logocentric and intellectual focus of such studies exclude a large part of the subject by 'stopping at the neck' (1995b: 9).

This is not to say that no issues remain, for the question of how far communication has to be 'intentional' is always difficult. One line is to presuppose verbally articulatable ideas or propositions as prerequisites for communication, and/or

Figure 1.3 Communication in movement and posture: Indian dance
The specialised tradition of Indian classical dance uses highly formalised postures and movements, especially facial expressions, eyes, hand formations and head movements, to depict
specific objects, states and abstract concepts. Conventional attire, stage, ornaments and
audience all play a part in this danced and dramatic form of communication. Left: Manipur
State Dance, Nanglar Kooth Trissur Keraba. Right: Stylised hand formation (lion)
(Photographs: Julia Hollander/Liba Taylor/Hutchison Picture Library).

self-conscious intentions or internal representations in the mind. This is explicit in
cognitivist approaches but a challenge for other approaches too. But is this again to
over-emphasise verbalisation? Communicating *is* sometimes highly verbal, self-
conscious and reflective, linked to articulated words or ideas. But it does not *have*
to be in words to influence our actions nor always take the form of mentally
formulated ideas. The point was put well by Tim Ingold:

> Conduct that is spontaneous – carried out without previous thought or reflec-
> tion – may still be informed by *intention in action* although not preceded by a
> *prior intention* (Searle 1984: 65). Much of our own conduct is of this kind,
> unpremeditated yet not involuntary.
>
> (Ingold 1996: 185)

In practice we regularly communicate in organised ways even when not fully conscious that we are doing so – through gestures, for example, smiles, or sounds that
are not necessarily verbalised (the two children in Figure 1.1 for example). Indeed

the processes of communicating can, in E. T. Hall's words, 'occur simultaneously on different levels of consciousness, ranging from full awareness to out-of-awareness' (Hall 1966: 4). Or consider the empathic sharing of sympathy or of irony during a multi-sided conversation using not just words but also tone of voice, movements, touches, or facial expressions: not all verbalised but certainly not random, accidental nor without purpose. We do not have to posit the existence in every case of consciously formulated mental intentions to appreciate the many purposive and patterned ways in which we humans communicate.

Behavioural impact or active interconnection?

A contrasting approach is to see communication in terms of its effect on the behaviour of others. Very different from a focus on meanings or mental models, this is found especially (though not exclusively) in studies of animal communication where behavioural interpretations perhaps seem more obvious than cognitive ones. It typically refers to 'effects', 'responding appropriately', 'affecting another organism', or 'modifying/altering behaviour'.

Such accounts sometimes present the process as mechanical: the initiating communicator's actions result in direct changes in the communicatee's behaviour. Narrowly behaviourist models that imply simple one-way 'impacts' have their snags, but in general this perspective is illuminating in turning attention to *action* and to people's interconnecting in the world rather than inwards to the mind. It also encourages us to look to the actions and mutual influences of *all* those taking part.

Coordinating the activities of those involved can be one aspect, something that comes out strikingly in some animal communication studies. Flocking among birds or schooling by fish depends not on single prominent signals, but on tiny movements through which the participants subtly affect each other's actions.

> The flock or school can wheel and twist about, all the members sticking closely together and all seeming to turn at just the some moment. Here, surely, is communication, and of such a complex sort that we humans, looking in from the outside, may need slowed down film or videotape to see what is going on.
>
> (Dawkins 1995: 72)

Among humans too, there can be multiply interacting participants, if usually in lesser numbers. All the flows of mutual influencing can be relevant, perhaps differing for each individual or at different points in time, including the small but not unimportant mutual acts and adjustments that occur during communicative processes. Recall the three-way conversation at the start of this chapter and imagine how it might have proceeded. All three individuals are actively participating but affecting each other in different ways as they overlap not just in speaking but also through their active expressions of attentiveness (or not . . .), claims to turn-taking, interruptions, or continuing feedback, also through gestures, non-verbal sounds, positioning or touch. The communicating is jointly created through the active but varying input of all three participants in real time, but the mutual effects are subtle, multiple and differentiated rather than once-for-all 'impact'. The participants co-construct the process and, in turn, each other's actions and experiences.

If communication involves a degree of mutually effective interaction, the corollary is that the participants need to some extent to share recognised patterns of action and experience to make affecting each other's actions practicable at all. The resources they use for this will need to be explored later. They vary greatly, from relatively standardised devices recognised – to a degree – over wide spans of space and time (certain systems of writing, for example, pictorial representation or architectural display) to more fluid conventions observed in particularistic settings. There may be wide discrepancies between the participants too – hostility and mis-understandings are familiar features of human interaction after all – or little more than a shared acceptance that active and mutually experienced interconnection is possible. That itself is a far from trivial point, however. It rests on some recognition by human communicators of their shared human-ness and with it of the possibility of affecting each other's actions and experiences.

Evolutionary narratives or comparative perspectives?

Evolutionary perspectives, finally, offer a different but equally influential set of approaches to communication. The basic framework is a powerful and persistent one: a narrative account both of the evolution of species in general and of the specific development of human beings and human society. It appears in a number of diverse, if related, forms.

One influential version comes in the evolutionary psychology that has become so popular in the last decade or so. The human brain, together with many traits of present-day human behaviour, can be explained by its evolutionary adaptation. This neo-Darwinian approach continues the intellectual tradition, manifested also in sociobiological and cognitivist writings, of looking to the physical or biological features of our evolution for an explanation of our current characteristics. Humans are to be understood in terms of their genetic make-up or, in the recent analyses, of the evolutionarily adapted constitution of their brains.

In this view the computational mechanisms of the human brain derive from its evolution in early prehistory. When humans came down from the trees and, so it goes, adopted a hunter-gatherer livelihood, the neural connections in the brain adapted to meet these conditions. It is these which shape present-day human patterns such as women's and men's differential mating strategies, conflict between the sexes, parenting and kinship customs, social stratification, rape, aggression or altruism. The features developed in pre-agricultural times are still with us, traits shared by all human beings – 'information-processing devices that exist in the form they do because they have solved specific problems of survival or reproduction recurrently over the long course of human evolutionary history' (Buss 1999: 64).[12]

This approach has caught the imagination of many, seeming to open a window onto the long processes of human development and of how we have come to be as we are. It is also highly controversial. To its critics its methodology is suspect (is the 'evidence' from prehistoric 'hunter and gatherer societies', for example, anything more than speculation or backwards projection from the present?). Equally pertinent for the understanding of communication, it offers a thin and reductionist model of human-ness, with its cognitivist presupposition that the essence of a human lies in the brain and its computational mechanisms. Human beings, together with their communicative resources and practices, are approached not in terms of present-day interactions or cultural specifics, let alone their creative processes of interconnecting with each other, but by reference to the supposed constitution of the brain laid down at some far-off time in prehistory. This approach contrasts sharply with that taken up in this volume.

Some of the work on animal communication has also presupposed an evolutionary framework, though not necessarily of the kind just described. Darwin himself wrote observantly about the bodily expression of animal emotions – Figure 4.1 on p. 96 is drawn from his 1872 analysis – and many accounts of animal communicating have been inspired by Darwinian concepts. But as will emerge in Chapter 2 and later, recent animal studies now often focus less on long-term evolutionary causes or explanations about sexual competitiveness or survival, but combine more open-ended comparative perspectives with detailed investigations of communication among specific species or groups. The ethologist W. J. Smith stresses cooperation and negotiation – not just competition – and the importance of context and circumstances, where communication is 'forged in the linking of different individuals' (Smith 1997: 31). Such comparative work puts human communication into a wider setting.

A more open approach is also evident in recent approaches to the social and the biological, now increasingly seen more as continuum than dichotomy. A model of gene–environment interaction is superseding the older mutually exclusive opposition between 'nature' and 'nurture', seeing them instead as both going on at the same time. The recent collection on *Nonverbal Communication. Where Nature Meets Culture*, for instance (Segerstråle and Molnár 1997), explores both the many ways that cultural capabilities are biologically grounded and how humans, like other animals, develop biological capacities for social purposes. This is not too far from the underlying approach in this volume. Cultural variability must indeed be a significant part of any comparative study of human communication, and any wholesale reduction to biological universals or narrow evolutionary imperatives is to ignore the human ingenuities and diversities which are among the facts of human communicating. But neglecting our biological resources is also to miss something important. As a species, humans have developed wonderfully diverse modes for communicating whilst sharing certain basic biological foundations which both facilitate and limit our powers to do so.

Within this comparative perspective we can sidestep the evolutionary narratives and instead see human modes of communicating in the light of those among other animals. Recent research is increasingly revealing the surprising extent and subtlety of communicative processes among all kinds of animals, challenging older ideas about the limited abilities of non-humans. This is true not just for the primates, traditionally the focus of interest, but for a much wider range, from insects to birds, spiders to mammals. Animals draw on combinations of communicative modes, suitable for their own environments, lifestyles and bodily potential. Between them they utilise movements, colours, squeaks, taps, whistles, calls, smells, strokes, pushes, body positioning, plumage, echo-sounding, scratch marks, vibrations, odour deposits – to name just some. Amidst these many resources it is illuminating to note those relied on by the human species and how these both overlap with and differ from those among other animals. If each species develops its own unique mix, humans are no exception, one species among many.

Other evolutionary themes too crop up in some analyses of communication. Many again evoke those powerful images of human progress 'upwards' in both biological and social terms – mythical charter for the present supremacy (or so it is assumed) of humankind. One major account focuses on human communication, seen as the final achievement for which earlier and lower forms were merely the incipient stages. Here the attainment of human *language*, either through gradual development (the most common tale) or in some sudden dramatic event (Bickerton 1996), is portrayed as *the* crucial evolutionary step by which humans became differentiated from animals – 'the quintessential human attribute' (Pilbeam in Jones *et al.* 1992: 4). Through this we emerged as intelligent beings capable of symbolic and rational thinking, leaving behind – more or less – the emotional, gestural, non-rational and non-verbal forms of animal communication.

This account of the crucial link between verbal language and human-ness is near-universal in both academic analysis and popular wisdom. 'The hand, the brain and tools produced for a purpose, were important steps in our development', says a recent textbook on communication, 'but only with language did we become really human' (Rosengren 1999: 28). Norbert Elias presents language as responsible for 'the fundamental difference between human and animal societies' (Elias 1991: 114) while Esther Goody adopts a similar line when she sees 'the ratchet that led to the emergence of incomparably greater hominid intelligence' as likely to have been 'closely related to the gradual emergence of spoken language' (1995: 1). This is the standard approach of anthropology course-books; 'the crown jewel of human communication is language', and 'language' is, quite simply, 'the essence of our humanity' (Womack 1998: 168; Keesing and Strathern 1998: 26). Such assertions are legion. Verbal language, especially in its 'rational' and referential capacity, is *the* unquestioned mark and fulfilment of true humanity.

These assertions are less solidly founded than often supposed. Debates still continue about the interpretation of the archaeological and biological record. One might also question how far this evaluation of human language is the result of direct evidence, how far shaped by other factors: pleasantly speculative 'just-so' stories, tautology (only humans can have *human* language after all), a touch of complacent humano-centrism, or even perhaps intellectuals' unwitting privileging of their own linguistic expertise. A Lockean ideology of the referential nature of language implicitly underpins many such assessments – but this too, as we saw, is only one interpretation. The view of human-ness as founded in verbal language and in linguistically defined 'rationality' is not only itself controversial but also arguably a limiting model of humanity and hence of human communicating.

Similar accounts are also extended to the more recent history of human communication. In the grand narratives of modernisation, verbal language is the key to objectivity, science, individual enlightenment and rational thought, leaving behind the more 'primitive' involvements with ritual, tradition, magic or emotion. The continuingly recycled 'great divide' theories posit a radical contrast between societies with 'oral' as against 'literate' modes of communication. From this perspective the story of humanity is of an upwards path which reaches its final destination in the emergence not just of literacy but of the alphabetic writing systems favoured in the west. Here again we have a controversial model of human-ness – and, it could be said, a parochial and west-centred one. The spotlight is on the verbal/linguistic, the foundation for historic divides in human evolution ('orality' as against 'literacy') – a narrow basis for such sweeping and value-laden distinctions which, once again, deny the importance of other communicative channels. Equally widespread is the related assumption that the writing systems developed in the west, above all alphabetic forms, represent the pinnacle to which graphic communication had ultimately been tending: other attempts are clumsy, incomplete or undeveloped, at best 'proto'-writing, as against the destined triumph of alphabetic script. This goes so deep in western thought and educational practice that it is hard to challenge. But in comparative perspective it looks less plausible and, as will emerge in Chapter 5, cannot be taken for granted.[13]

At the root of many of these ambitious evolutionary models lie on the one hand images of separation and of ranking and on the other particular views of what it is to be 'fully human'. Some are visions of how humans came to be separated from other animals, above all through language. Other versions (not least that projected in the 'Varieties of mankind' picture, Figure 1.2) depict the gradual victory of modern western civilisation over inferior and less evolved forms elsewhere; the 'fully human' virtues of rationality, science and intellectual thought are again linked to linguistic communication systems, here principally writing and, in particular, alphabetic systems and (western-style) printing. Underpinning most of these accounts is a cognitively led view of both language and humankind, dividing not only humans from animals but 'pre-literate' from literate. But this tale of the upwards move of humanity into its 'true' fulfilment of linguistically explicit rationality is no longer unchallenged. Recent writings across the humanistic and social science disciplines, not least anthropology, now increasingly explore the role of emotion and expressiveness as universal features of human life, querying the assumption that humans are, or ever could be, purely cognitive, verbal and rational creatures. And we now increasingly appreciate that linguistic expression in explicit propositional and linear form is itself only one special case in the context of the many practical activities and bodily experiences of human beings – 'look, sound, feel, smell, taste and so on' (Bloch 1991: 193, 194).[14]

Grand evolutionary narratives, with their ethnocentric and humano-centric evaluations, are now widely questioned. But in the field of human communication they have remarkable tenacity. Differences there certainly are – between humans and other species, between different human cultures and historical periods, between differing groups and individuals. But as far as communication goes these can often be better appreciated by non-evaluative and, as it were, lateral comparison than by these value-steeped and hierarchically ordered teleological tales. Similarly with the roles of language and cognition in the definition and study of communication. That verbal language, spoken and written, plays an important part in human communicating is incontrovertible and it will figure extensively in the pages that follow. But it is unwarrantable to assume either that language, especially in the referential guise in which this is often envisaged, is unquestionably the 'highest', the primary, or in all circumstances the most important form of human communicating, or that the prime function of communication is to process information. In the final analysis, a rounded view of human-ness has to include more than brains, print or verbally articulated meaning, and go beyond self-congratulatory assumptions of evolutionary divides between ourselves and others.

Communicating – a multiple, relative and emergent process

These varying perspectives on communication have clustered round certain recurrent issues on which analysts take divergent positions. There are the sticky questions of how far communication has to be fully conscious and/or verbally explicit; in what ways it takes place between or among participants (straight-line transmission? exchange? mutual influence?); what is essentially involved (messages, meanings, mental representations, symbols, systems of signs, social processes, collective interacting . . . ?); how far and in what sense it involves influence or impact on others' actions; whether modes of communication mark the divisions between human and animal, or between 'modern' and 'primitive'; and, finally, the issue that crops up again and again, the centrality or otherwise of cognition and verbalised expression. The above comments on such issues have hopefully contributed to delineating the position in this volume. It could be summarised somewhat more directly by saying that communication is here taken to be a dynamic interactive process made up of the organised, purposive, mutually influential and mutually recognisable actions and experiences that are created in a variety of modes by and between active participants as they interconnect with each other.

This formulation naturally carries the ambiguities and opacities of any attempt to encapsulate a complex and controversial notion in a relatively short form of words. It is certainly not intended as a forever definitive account. But it does take a stand on the interpretation and relevance of certain issues that recurrently feature in contrasting approaches to communication. Three aspects could do with further comment.

First, it lacks the sharp focus of some definitions and, fuzzy at the edges, cannot provide an unambiguous distinction between communicating and other forms of human behaviour. Its breadth and apparent impreciseness are in fact positive properties. This is a 'bundle definition'. In other words, 'communicating' is not one single once-and-for-all thing which you either have or don't have, but a bundle of features, themselves graduated rather than absolute. A process that can be described as communicating may be more, or less, purposive, organised and conscious; more or less mutually influential or recognisable; work simultaneously or sequentially on multiple levels; develop and change during its temporal process; draw on relatively standardised systems or on less widely agreed or only partially shared conventions; and involve more, or less, explicit interacting among the enactors who (to different degrees and in different ways) participate more (or less) creatively in the process and at greater or lesser temporal or spatial distance from each other.

Communication in this view is a relative process with multiple features each of which may in any given case be present to a greater or lesser extent – a multidimensional spectrum of acting and experiencing, not a bounded entity. And just because the spectrum *is* multifaceted the boundaries between communicative and non-communicative action are not absolute. Perhaps all human action involves some degree of communicating, but in some cases only minimally. Other cases are clearer, with a strong input from all the elements mentioned. In other cases yet again, some may be clearly in play, others weak or absent. It is a multifaceted matter of degree.

This relative quality is also relevant for what has proved a difficulty in many theories of communication – a consistent framework for both personal small-scale interaction and communicating across space and time. The perspective here might appear better for close embodied interaction than for more distant situations. But human communication *does* also take place over distance (this too being a matter of degree) in organised, purposive and (more, or less) mutually recognisable ways. It may be mediated through material artefacts rather than in tangible bodily co-presence but still involves human interconnecting through, for example, pictures, books, buildings or, more recently, auditory records. What M. D. Anderson aptly calls 'the picture book of the churches' (1971: 81ff) is one good example of the communicative use of material artefacts lasting well beyond the immediate moment, terrifyingly illustrated in the 'doom paintings' of mediaeval Christian churches (see Figure 1.4). As explained in later chapters there are indeed multiply

diverse resources through which people interconnect across generations and between different cultures and geographical areas as well as nearby, doing so with a greater or lesser degree of active and creative involvement. It is not an all or nothing matter.

A second point may seem too obvious to need stating: humans use a *variety* of modes to connect with each other. This is another way of emphasising the point, repeatedly made above, that human communicating is not confined just to one mode. Humans draw on manifold resources. There are not only the direct actions of people's bodies – a versatile and marvellous resource indeed, from frowns or bows to sign languages and dance – but also the multifarious sum of human-made media like clothing, books, calligraphic systems, sculptures, textiles, paintings (of 'doom', 'human varieties' and much else), musical instruments, recording devices, set-piece performances, fragrances, broadcasting systems, computer screens and an infinitude of others. Humans have used all these forms to interconnect both face-to-face and at a distance. These resources and the ways we use them are the focus of the later chapters.

Finally, the phrase '*as they interconnect with each other*' is crucial. Communication is a dynamic and emergent process: a dimension of human activity not a separate entity. This emphasis on 'mutuality' and 'interconnectedness' may give an unduly harmonious and optimistic impression (a reasonable criticism of some pragmatist approaches). But looking to the modes through which humans actively interconnect need not carry assumptions about whether this is done in a friendly, hostile, self-interested or self-sacrificial manner (to mention just some possibilities), any more than we can assume that human interconnections always end up to the benefit or mutual understanding of the many rather than few. The focus here is on the process

---

Figure 1.4 Teaching of heaven and hell: the Doom painting, Chaldon
This twelfth-century painting (now restored) in the Church of St Peter and St Paul, Chaldon, Surrey uses evocative images to convey messages of Christian salvation and the terrors of rejecting them. Through the centre the ladder of salvation stretches from deepest hell to highest heaven, symbolising the cross by which sinners can be redeemed, with Christ above in glory. On the right is its contrast, the tree of the fall with the serpent in its branches. Clouds divide the painting horizontally. The naked souls below are pulled off by demons, bitten by a dog and pitchforked into a boiling cauldron; to the right demons torment sinners and hold a bridge of spikes for dishonest tradesmen to cross. Above, Christ triumphs over hell and Satan lies prostrate, transfixed by Christ's cross (right); on the left St Michael weighs souls in the balance and the devil tries to weight them down towards hell, while innocent souls are taken upward by angels. The pictorial layout enables the juxtaposition of hell and heaven, doom and salvation, intermingled with subtle and powerful imagery, again in a more immediate and compelling way than could be achieved by spoken or written enunciations of theological doctrine; it combines flexibility of interpretation, accessible in varying ways to educated and uneducated alike, with 'an impressive affirmation of belief' (Anderson 1971: 128, also, for this painting, 126–7). (© Crown Copyright, NMR)

of human interconnectedness not its 'good' or its 'bad' effects in any given case. To go back to Birdwhistell's phrase, communication can indeed be understood as the 'dynamic aspect of human interconnection' (1968: 27). It is found in the actions and experiences created by and through people as they interact, affective no less than cognitive. It includes interacting at a distance as well as bodily co-presence at a given temporal moment, and not just messages transmitted from one party to another but all the multidimensional contacts going on within and among groups of people, all the emergent processes through which people mutually – and to multiply varying degrees – interconnect with each other. This is a wide perspective on communication, and, in consequence, on humanity. It enlarges the scope beyond information-transfer and linguistic articulation to encompass all the modes exploited in our active human sociality.

This book cannot pursue all the multiple practices, contexts and functions of human communicating. It focuses on just one aspect: the variety of modes developed and exploited by humans as they communicate and the resources that they draw on in doing so. But the wider framework sketched above forms the background to this account of the astounding and extensive resources through which human beings, to a degree and in many different ways, manage to interconnect with each other.

2 How can we communicate? The basic resources of humans and other animals

Communicating may indeed be fundamental to our social existence – but that still leaves the questions raised at the outset. How is it that we can reach out to others beyond ourselves? And what resources are available to humans – and other animals too – for managing this remarkable feat of actively interconnecting one with another?

At the most basic, we could consider first the world into which we are born and in which we live. Life itself depends on the power to process external sources of energy and earthly living creatures turn the sun's energy to use, either directly as with plants, or processing it through ingested food. Plants regulate slowly developing growth processes but animals often do something more with this energy: they can move, and sometimes relatively rapidly too, transporting themselves from place to place and moving specific parts of their bodies. Humans and other animals exploit this crucial resource of movement in a huge variety of ways to interact actively with each other and with the world they live in.

Whether dwelling in air or in water, active by day or by night, in the tropics or the temperate zones, living creatures inhabit a world full of resource and movement – currents and winds that carry sound, smell, or touch; light to enable and activate vision; physical terrains and seascapes with their obstacles as well as avenues for effective locomotion; the atmosphere with its pressure pulses, the source of touch and sound waves through air or water. Their precise relevance varies by species and with the properties of different environments. Light for example is a rich resource for most terrestrial animals, among them human beings, but less so in the dark or in water; there communication through sound is often more prominent. But whatever the variations, the interactions between living beings are ultimately enacted through the exploitation and complex combinations of these fundamental earthly resources.

There are also the resources of the living organism itself. Animals exploit their bodily endowments in a wide variety of communicative activities. They create visible shapes, colours, distances, movements; produce sounds; emit smells; make contact through touch or movement. They move around, communicate through posture, locomotion, or size, and in some cases manipulate and create material objects. Sea creatures interconnect through sounds, insects lay down chemical trails, rabbits and moles send vibrations through the ground, and birds create visible nests as well as songs – just a small selection of the astonishing range of animal communicating.

Humans similarly exploit the conditions of the world and the capacities of our human bodies. We use light and the faculty of vision in multifarious ways. Sound waves and audition too – we listen to vocalised utterances and much else too. Touch and movement play their part, far more than often recognised. And humans have also created arts and artefacts to harness both their bodily and their external resources to their purposes: textiles, sculpture, pictures, scripts, tombstones, drumming, dress, public architecture . . . all form part of the resources that human beings have developed in so many different ways to aid their active interconnection. The underlying resources, in our bodies and our external environment, may be relatively simple to state. But the variety of ways humans build on them is remarkable indeed.

Getting a handle on these multifarious human resources is far from simple and runs quickly into problematic issues. The terminologies commonly used for the resources of communication are multiple too – 'senses', 'faculties', 'modalities', 'channels', 'media', 'material culture', 'capacities', 'skills', 'discourse', 'codes', 'arts', 'intelligences' – all with their own controversial baggage. No wonder there have been diverse approaches to trying to capture these multiplex resources. Since each casts some light on one or another dimension of human interaction, it is worth considering some of the categorisations which have shaped studies of communicating. With their own strengths and weaknesses, they yet serve to illuminate something of our manifold human resources.

The human senses

The first framework that immediately springs to mind is the familiar one of 'the senses' – 'the faculties of perception or sensation' in the *Oxford English Dictionary*'s definition. The fivefold list in Box 2.1 was probably at one time learned by every English-speaking schoolchild and is repeated in innumerable children's books – a long taken-for-granted classification, securely founded, as it seems, in our bodily reality.

Box 2.1 **'The five senses'**

Sight
Hearing
Smell
Taste
Touch

This is one way to think about our resources for communicating. It usefully widens our perspectives beyond the audio-visual, avoids over-emphasising cognition and language, and in part underlies later chapters of this volume. It also focuses attention on our bodily – rather than mental or aetherial – involvements in our communicating. To put it more grandly it reminds us of the body as 'the nexus where biology meets culture, where the individual meets society . . . the medium through which self is engaged with other . . . a reference point for our isolation and for our connection' (Roseman 1991: 179).

But this list of senses is not as unproblematic as our childhood learning makes us suppose. It is certainly not self-evidently complete. Modern scientists (and some earlier ones too) identify bodily faculties like balance, pain, hunger, weight or bodily position which might equally be classed as sense organs. Classical and pre-modern writers sometimes made 'speech' one of the senses, a human ability like sight or hearing – a view re-emerging in cognitive representations of speech as hard-wired 'instinct' or innate natural ability, our 'language organ' (Chomsky 2000: 4, also Pinker 1994). The distinctions are also less clear than appear at first. There are many connections between smell and taste (some classifications collapse them into one) and at one level hearing and touching merge. Classifications in other cultures do not always accord with our fivefold division either. The Nigerian Hausa have one word for sight and another for 'hearing, smelling, tasting and touching, under-standing, and emotional feeling, as if all these functions formed part of a single whole' (Ritchie 1991: 194).

Even the fivefold list itself has been variably presented. There have been many different treatments and allegorical representations of the senses in European literature (see Vinge 1975, also Rindisbacher 1992: 6ff). Sometimes the fivefold list is comprehensive, matching the organs through which humans and other animals 'perceive external objects and changes in the condition of their own bodies' (to quote the *Oxford English Dictionary* again); but elsewhere it means 'bodily' faculties as opposed to 'higher' faculties of 'intellect, spirit etc.' (*ibid.*). Older evolutionary hierarchies commonly associated the 'bodily senses' of smell, touch and taste with the 'animalistic' nature of 'primitive peoples' in contrast to the sight and hearing of 'civilisation' (Classen 1997: 404ff).

Human cultures vary in their treatment of the senses. The earlier general theories about differing cultural balances between the senses (Carpenter and McLuhan 1960, McLuhan 1964, Ong 1967) have been followed by more detailed ethnographic studies of specific cultures and historical periods.[1] The West African Songhay for example emphasise hearing and 'conceive-perceive the world as constructed on an acoustic scaffolding' (Howes 1991: 10) while Steve Feld's *Sound and Sentiment* (1990) shows the Kaluli of Papua New Guinea as in some ways ranking sound above sight (see further in Chapter 3 below). Work in the anthropology of the senses takes particular interest in this 'ratio of the senses':

> Western societies are overwhelmingly dependent on visual and verbal faculties
> for their experience of the world. But different societies use and combine the
> senses in different ways and to different ends. What is the world like to a cul-
> ture that takes actuality in less visual, more gustatory or tactile, auditory or
> olfactory terms than those to which we are accustomed? What is the impact of
> other 'sensory ratios' on the life of the mind and the emotions?
>
> (Howes 1991: blurb)

In such studies the sensory classification, problematic as it is if taken as the final
word, provides an illuminating framework for comparative analysis, not limited to
verbal or visual skills but also taking in hearing, touch, smell and taste.

One problem about taking 'the five senses' as basic to our communicative
resources is that they seem closely associated with 'perception', implying perhaps
mere passive reception. But the senses can also be pictured not as neutral physiological receptors, but as active channels for interpretation, communication and
constructive world-making with human beings moulding the processes of perception as they formulate their experience and differentiate selectively within it. This
view of the senses envisages perceiving as a learned and creative process, humanly
constructed rather than mechanically received and subject to differing formulation
among different cultures and different individuals – an approach that could also be
applied to communicating.[2]

The fivefold sensory classification takes us a long way. Less solid and transparent
than it seems at first, it yet reminds us of the range of bodily activities which
humans undertake and remains one important basis for understanding varieties of
communication and expression. But in another way it gives only a limited pointer.
Movement and space are often significant in our communicating but both they and
our use of external objects would be easy to overlook if we focused solely on the
senses. They utilise the senses, certainly. But they also in certain ways take us
beyond them and, as we will see, need to feature in any full account of our resources
for communicating.

'Non-verbal' expression

If verbal language is not the only mode of human communicating, then we have
need of terminologies and categories pointing beyond this. A number of frameworks have in fact been developed specifically for the analysis of 'non-verbal'
resources. One influential classification is that of the human 'nonverbal communication system' under the heading of 'primary nonverbal codes' or 'modes of
expression' by Burgoon and Guerrero (1994: 124ff, 165ff).[3] This is summarised
(slightly adapted) in Box 2.2.

***Box 2.2* Seven non-verbal modes of expression**

Proxemics (structuring and using space to communicate)
Haptics (using touch to communicate)
Chronemics (using time)
Kinesics (visual aspects of bodily movement)
Physical appearance (carrying messages to others)
Vocalics (vocal as opposed to verbal aspects of speech)
Artefacts (both as message vehicle and influencing other codes)
                    (after Burgoon and Guerrero 1994: 125, 165–7)

This gives another handle for identifying our communicative resources. It supplements the fivefold sense classification by reminding us of the role of human-made material objects ('artefacts') and the importance of movement and of space. 'Proxemics' draws attention to our communicative uses of space, patterned processes which can be effective indeed even when below the level of consciousness (see Chapter 4). 'Kinesics' covers the many ways we communicate through gestures, facial movements and bodily positioning. The two girls in Figure 1.1 provided one illustration, further examples are the Italian gestures pictured in Figure 2.1 (others come in Chapter 4). If there was some ambiguity over the possibly passive connotations of 'the senses', there is none here. We are unquestionably dealing with actively deployed, observable and purposive human processes.

There are limitations to set against its strengths. *Non*-vocal sound gets no mention but should surely be there (think of clapping, whistling, knocking, and of sirens or drums). Communication through smell is similarly absent: an elusive subject certainly but not one to omit totally. The focus furthermore is on live interpersonal interaction, with little or no allowance for distance communication.

More radically, 'non-verbal' is itself a contentious term. It has long been useful in challenging the misconception that words constitute the whole of communication. But even in doing so it risks privileging the verbal by defining other communicative modes by its absence; 'the verbal' is implicitly the norm while 'non-verbal modes' can too easily be pictured as merely secondary adjuncts to speech. A further assumption has sometimes seemed to follow: that 'non-verbal' expression is something unitary, a separate domain independent of verbal communicating or classifiable under some single term like 'body language'. This is to drastically simplify our actual practice. As pointed out by writers on language and social interaction (among others), gestural and vocal actions are often integrated rather than autonomous, and verbal and non-verbal communicating 'usually produced in a highly coordinated fashion': they are not distinct domains (Sheldon 1999: 157, also Kendon 1994, McNeill 1992, 2000). Positing a special realm of

Figure 2.1 Communicating through hand and head
Illustrations from Andrea de Jorio's classic 19th-century account of Italian (Neapolitan) gesturing. He explains them as: 1. Silence; 2. Negative; 3. Beauty; 4. Hunger; 5. Teasing; 6.
Hard work, tiredness; 7. Stupid; 8. Squint, be untrustworthy; 9. Deception; 10. Astuteness
(explanations by de Jorio, as translated in Kendon 2000). Some may be recognised as in
some places still accepted forms (from Andrea de Jorio *La mimica degli antichi investigata nel
gestire napoletano,* 1832, Plate XXI).

'non-verbal expression' has led to unfounded generalisation about this supposedly separate form: the medium for emotional and relational rather than cognitive communicating, for example, or comprising 'lower', 'animal' forms in contrast to the 'higher' and more 'human' achievement of language. Even if the assumptions behind such value-laden suppositions were acceptable, the fact remains that the resources covered by the term 'non-verbal' are diverse and complex in the extreme. It can only be misleading to bunch them together as a distinctive communicative mode.

But if generalised categorisation of 'the non-verbal' proves unhelpful, its sub-categories illuminatingly highlight facets of communicating absent from the sensory perspective. While not entirely escaping the negative connotations of 'non-verbal', the taxonomy in Box 2.2 avoids blanket generalisation precisely because it identifies a series of different dimensions. Elements from this illuminating framework will recur extensively in later chapters.

'Multiple human intelligences'

The concept of 'multiple intelligences' formulated in Howard Gardner's influential *Frames of Mind* (1983) gives another revealing viewpoint. Gardner queries the common assumption that there is just one kind of 'intelligence', capturable and measurable along a single scale. Instead, he urges, there are several different and relatively autonomous human intellectual competences (Box 2.3).[4]

Box 2.3 The multiple human intelligences

Linguistic
Musical
Logical-mathematical
Spatial (often, but not necessarily, visual)
Bodily-kinesthetic
Personal intelligences
                    (based on Gardner 1983)

Such a listing challenges the assumption that in charting human communicative resources we should be looking only for one kind of skill – one, furthermore, particularly associated with linguistic and logical reasoning. Rather, Gardner holds, *all* these 'intelligences' deserve serious consideration, arguing among other things from exceptional individuals like *idiots savants* and autistic children who have extraordinary achievements in one domain while retarded in others. He points out that these domains are developed differentially both by different individuals and within different cultures and illustrates how each can be deployed in both heightened and more ordinary ways. Thus he starts his discussion of linguistic intelligence with poetic composition before going on to more mundane cases, and presents dance, mime and athletics as examples of bodily-kinesthetic skills. In contrast to much psychological writing, Gardner is alive to cultural variation in the practice and ranking of these 'intelligences', at the same time highlighting an aspect often downplayed in anthropological studies by combining the idea of generic human potentialities with the actuality of differential individual achievement.

Gardner's focus is on 'mind' and 'intelligence', rather than on experiencing or acting. Aspects of his neurobiological arguments are controversial, especially where linked to 'modularity' theories with their focus on the structures and computational systems of the brain – a notably cognitive and controversial approach to communicating (for varying versions see Fodor 1983, Hirschfeld and Gelman 1994, Sperber 1996). Gardner's own approach is far from narrowly mentalistic, however. He speaks of the 'domains of potential intellectual competence' which individuals can develop – 'know-how' rather than 'know-that'. Intelligence is not just something 'that occurs between your ears, but something that you do publicly' (Gardner 1983: 284, 68–9, Davies 1996: 18).

This provides yet another framework for approaching our variegated resources for both distant and face-to-face communicating and the multiform arts through which these can be formulated. One could argue about the specific list and some of its implications but the general perspective again takes us beyond the traditional focus on language or rationality, enlarging our appreciation of the multidimensional nature of human action and capacities.

'Media', artefacts and human-made arts

Another way of envisaging human communication and its resources is to consider the technologies and material forms that humans have developed and used in their processes of interconnecting. These are more significant than one might conclude from many accounts of communicating.

'The media' is a much-used phrase nowadays. It proves a somewhat elusive concept however. It often means the 'mass media', usually press, radio and television but also sometimes the cinema, recordings of popular music and some computer-mediated forms. Earlier writers took a less limited conspectus, as in McLuhan's view of the media as all 'the extensions of man' (1964). In wider historical sweeps, broad distinctions have been drawn between writing, print, and electrical media, with the recent addition of electronic computer-based media; sometimes the 'oral medium' of speech starts off the series. Yet other writers use 'media' to refer to concrete forms like coins, maps or graffiti. The magisterial *International Encyclopedia of Communications* lists under 'media' nearly thirty forms of varying levels of generality, including sculpture, photographs, motion pictures, murals, radio, television, books, maps, stamps, portraits, writing and telegraphy, but the list does not seem to be intended as a systematic or comprehensive one (Barnouw *et al.* 1989, vol. 4: 365). 'Media' and 'medium' are not exact technical terms and will continue to be used, by myself as well as others, in both broad and more specific senses.[5]

The general idea is nevertheless an illuminating one. Humans' interconnectedness is achieved not just through the direct contact of people's bodies but also through external forms – media in the widest sense. People can interact by 'mediational means' (Scollon 1999: 153). This is not just a matter of journalism, television or computer communications, the often assumed meaning of 'the media', for, as Scollon continues, 'virtually everything is a medium or may be a medium for social action' (1999: 153). This 'mediation' may be in the form of other human beings, sometimes a conventional and routinised part of performance. 'Mediators' such as poets and priests or the 'speakers' of West African Akan chiefs communicate in mediational performances on behalf of others (Bauman 2001); so in less formalised settings do many others. But it also often takes place through the use of material objects and technologies, from clothes to seals, tactile maps to scented letters. Even the land around us can be a medium in communicating. Among farming families in northern England

> The material world mediates in the forging of bonds between men, between husbands and wives, between parents, grandparents and grandchildren, bearing silent but visible witness to the webs of interconnections which necessarily tie each to another and about which little needs to be said [in words].
>
> (Christensen *et al.* 2001: 76)

This 'mediational' dimension is now attracting increasing attention (see references above, also Silverstone 1999, Streeck 1996, Tracey 1999: 3). It is further supplemented by the spreading work on material culture and on 'artefacts' – the many human-made forms which, we will see, are an important part of human communicating.[6]

This raises two issues that will keep surfacing throughout the later discussion. First, these material media of various kinds are often surrounded by clusters of uses and practices which in themselves present accepted options and constraints for communicating. Such conventions form an important dimension of our communicating. At the same time we have to remember that no medium, from stone pebble to written page, ultimately communicates in its own right, but only as it is used and interpreted by human enactors. The millers' knots of Figure 2.2 would mean nothing to most people; but for those involved this particular medium and the way it was used formed a precise and economical form of communication which in its actual context exactly met the participants' requirements. Similarly the little weights of Figure 2.3, once used in Ghana to weigh gold, could convey a meaningful commentary on human experience – when they were used and understood in this way.

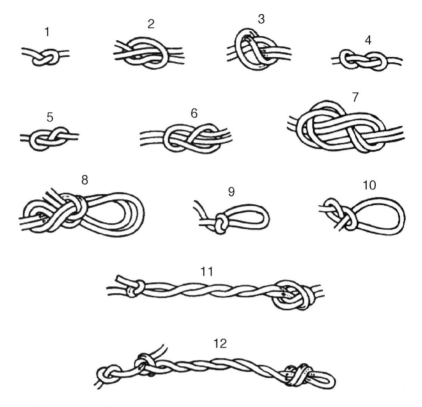

Figure 2.2 Knots that declare the measure

German millers used an efficient system of knots to inform bakers of the amount and type of milled flour in their sacks – 'knot writing' as Menninger terms it (1969: 255). 1–7 above: 'Knot-numerals' showing amounts: 1, 2 (two variants, both shown), 5, 10, 20 and 60 measures respectively (intermediate numbers being combinations of these); 8–12: Loops and tufts indicating type of meal: hog-mash, rye, barley, 1st- and 2nd-grade wheat flour (sketch and description in K. Menninger, *Number Words and Number Symbols,* 1969: 255–6, Fig. 90, by permission of Vandenhoeck and Ruprecht Publishing Company).

We need to balance the fact that objects do not communicate of themselves with the practices by which human beings on occasion organise them as effective communicative tools, perhaps to do just that.

Second, the apparently straightforward distinction between external media and those more directly located in the body turns out to be far from clear-cut: more a matter of degree than an unproblematic opposition. 'Intrinsic' and 'extrinsic', 'embodied' and 'exosomatic' – such terms are illuminating up to a point but involve continuities and social shaping as well as contrasts. Perhaps the very lack of exactness of the term 'medium' has its uses, reminding us yet again of the multiplicity and relativities of our communicative resources. As Schiffer says in *The Material Life of Human Beings,* 'human life consists of ceaseless and varied interaction among people and myriad kinds of things . . . called "material culture" or, better, "artifacts"' (1999: 2). These human-used things, interacting and interwoven with our somatic resources, will feature extensively in this volume.

Elaborated arts such as music, dance, pictorial art, mime, sculpture or perfumery have been extensively developed in human societies. These provide a further route into appreciating the range of human communicative resources. The long recycled debates about 'higher' as against 'lower' arts or the meaning of 'Art' need not concern us – in any case the creativity involved in human communicating and experiencing means that sharp divisions between 'art' and 'non-art' are near-impossible to draw. More helpful is the plural term 'arts', understood in the broad sense which shades into crafts and the locally recognised practices that pertain to them. These cover more than the so-called 'high' arts like portraiture, ballet or illuminated manuscripts, but can equally embrace the arts of house styles, canoe making, painted rickshaws, drum signalling, oratorical gesture, ritual touch, or the studied deployment of fragrances in sacrifices.

Certain of these are at times recognised as heightened forms, valued, expert or specialist performances or products in themselves, and sometimes associated with an explicit cultural aesthetic or with specialist institutions, like the contemporary English 'colleges of music', the expert traditions of Indian dance, mediaeval Irish bardic schools, the poetic 'schools of learning' in Polynesia or the expert mediaeval artists who planned and created the doom paintings or stained glass windows pictured in Figures 1.4 and 10.4. Or they may be recognised more in the act and the experience – in 'everyday aesthetics' (Forrest 1988) and in the 'prosaics' as much as the 'poetics' of communicating (in Morson and Emerson's term, 1990). There are often implicit but more or less agreed conventions for telling personal stories, for performing and experiencing music in particular settings, for quilt makers in the American mid-west, for the movements learned and deployed by Venda dancers in southern Africa (Blacking 1967, 1985), or even for small children engaged in what Gardner (1980) percipiently terms their 'artful scribble'. Another way of putting this would be to speak of 'communicative genres' (Luckmann 1995) or of the shared conventions about appropriate audiences, styles, formats, performance modes or channels by which, in Becker's terminology (1982), people operate within different art worlds. '*Some* repertoire of [communicative] genres will be found in all societies', as Luckmann points out (1995: 181). Their variety illustrates yet again the multifarious ways that modes of human expression are valued and practised throughout the world and the role of human creativeness in developing and deploying this multiplicity of communicative resources.

There have been many ways of classifying these manifold arts, from the spheres of the nine Greek muses, the mediaeval *quadrivium* and a multitude of other local taxonomies, to the comparative accounts by anthropologists and others which often differentiate visual and plastic arts (usually the prime focus), verbal/literary arts,

Figure 2.3 Ashanti goldweights
Among the innumerable material objects which humans construct and utilise in communicating are the tiny brass weights used in southern Ghana to measure units of gold dust in the nineteenth century and earlier, cast in both geometric form and as miniature representations of creatures and situations from local life. They not only weigh gold but also, in material form, communicate wry, ironic, and reflective commentaries on life. Some are also associated with proverbs or stories. The crossed crocodiles joined at the stomach convey the futility of individuals trying to snatch for themselves what should be for the good of all – the separate heads nonsensically competing even while sharing the same stomach. The snake-and-bird figure recalls the story of how a bird refused to repay a loan – but, as happens in life, was finally caught (Copyright © The British Museum).

music, and dance. Dewey's *Art as Experience* proposes a rough distinction between the 'automatic' and the 'shaping' arts – that is, between those that 'have the human organism, the mind-body, of the artist as their medium and those which depend to a much greater extent upon materials external to the body' (1934/1958: 227). We might query his term 'automatic', again raising the intrinsic/external issue: body-centred arts too are purposive and culturally shaped. But, though all such classifications are ultimately elusive and relative, even the attempts to formulate them extends our appreciation of the fantastically rich resources for human communication and their variety of expression through (relatively) external artefacts and organised collective activities. Humans turn to their purposes not just a small collection of concrete 'media' but a vast range of human-created forms and activities.

The channels of animal communication

The complex range of human communicative resources, then, can be looked at on many levels. We can enlarge our grasp of them still further by returning to the question of animal communication. Its relevance lies not in those analyses which would explain human communication by its earlier evolution or draw sharp distinctions between animal and human communicating. Rather, it directs us to resources that human beings, more or less, share with other members of the animal kingdom, setting the modes of human communication in wider perspective.[7]

Non-human animals have often been pictured as essentially automatic and involuntary. But with our widening knowledge of the ingenuity and variety of animal communicating this model is now thoroughly in question. Animals exploit their communicative resources not just for the purposes of sexual attraction and competition which once formed the principal focus of interest but to convey, for example, friendly greetings, indications of mood or intentions, hostility, territorial boundaries, boastful self-display, or information about some outside object or activity such as food, danger or a friend's approach. They open and continue negotiations; avoid confrontation; organise mutual spacing; keep in touch when dispersed over distant terrain or waters; recognise nestmates, friends, kin, strangers, potential mates, or members of distinct classes; claim or accept leadership or specific social relationships; cooperate in raising offspring; deceive (yes, that too); maintain sociality; dispute but also cooperate; and many many other things. And, like humans, other animals too can produce individual innovations and deal flexibly with new situations.

Both humans and non-humans modify their environments in ways relevant for their communicating. Some animals communicate not only by their bodily actions or appearances, but also through physical marks and extrinsic objects outside themselves. Dogs mark out their territory by urine, other animals by faecal piles or scratches on tree trunks. Primates use material objects to communicate hostility or attack, throwing stones and other objects to frighten off enemies or brandishing vegetation in display or threat. Birds communicate (among other means) through constructing nests and displays. Bowerbirds are famous for the wonderful bowers and courts that the males build, decorating them to attract the females' attention with highly coloured fruits, flowers and shiny objects, sometimes changing the flowers daily for months on end – 'carefully inspecting each blossom as he puts it in place, shifting its position if he is not satisfied' (Collias and Collias 1984: 82); some bowerbirds paint their bowers with a secretion that they make from fruit pulp, bark, chewed green vegetable matter or charcoal and apply with their beaks (Collias and Collias 1984: 79ff). Palm cockatoos break twigs off trees, shape them into drumsticks and use them on resonant hollow logs in their courting (Gray *et al.* 2001: 52, also Wynn 1994: 135ff on 'non-human tools').

Our understanding has been further enhanced by recent studies of animals who, like humans, live and operate in groups. The auditory communication of Kenyan vervet monkeys is one justly famous example (Cheney and Seyfarth 1990, Griffin 1984: 166ff). These monkeys use three distinct calls to warn each other of danger. One reports the approach of a leopard or other large carnivorous animal, a different call indicates a martial eagle, yet another a large snake. Taking cover in thick vegetation is the way to evade an eagle, but climbing a tree is best for escaping from a leopard, moving onto the thin branches where the heavier animal cannot follow – so getting it right may be a matter of life and death. For a snake they first locate it by standing upright, then move away. These monkeys also use a series of grunts with differential meanings for varying social contexts and purposes. As Cheney and Seyfarth conclude:

> Like the primatologists who study them, vervet monkeys observe social inter-actions and draw generalizations about the types of relationships that exist among individuals. The monkeys also use sounds to represent things and com-pare different vocalizations according to their meaning.
>
> (1990: 312)

The intricate signalling systems used by weaver ants are equally striking, though expressed through very different channels. The ants live in social colonies with a complex division of labour and communication between members is essential. Worker ants forage for food at some distance and when they find a good source return to the nest for help to gather it before other animals remove it. They report its location to fellow-workers by lateral head wagging and mutual antennae touches as well as by laying down odour trails from the nest to the food. At times these for-agers are threatened by other insects. They release alarm pheromones (chemical signals) and if they cannot repel the attackers themselves again return for help, jerk-ing their bodies back and forwards to communicate the need – a different signal. The recipients repeat the same movements to yet other workers, thus conveying specific information about something the communicators themselves had not been exposed to directly – an effective form of chain communication eventuating in the rapid recruitment of a large number of defenders (Griffin 1984: 170–3).

The elaborate patterns of avian singing have also been the focus of much recent research. This has revealed how the communicative systems of some birds include both notable individual creativity and complex, culturally diverse, song traditions which have to be gradually mastered by young birds (Kroodsma and Miller 1996). Experiments with birds' ability to learn and use human language have also produced some remarkable results. The shining example is the vocal African grey parrot 'Alex', the subject of intensive and rigorous study over many years (Pepperberg 1993, 1999, among many other publications). Alex can use English words to refer to objects, shapes, colours and numbers up to six, as well as to request, refuse and quantify objects. He can ask for more than eighty different objects, including ones out of sight, and use words accurately and effectively for actions and for properties such as colour, shape and material as well as purposeful phrases like 'Come here', 'Wanna go [to some place]', 'Want Y [some thing]', 'I'm sorry', and 'No!' .

Overall there is now a much greater understanding of the complexity and sophis-tication of animal communicating. The once-standard contrast between the cognitive, culturally mediated and planned communicating of humans as against the involuntary, instinctual or emotionally driven interaction of other animals has been eroded from two directions. From the one side the pre-eminently rational model of humans is by now open to question. From the other, recent studies of animal behaviour have been increasingly exploring cognitive issues, querying older assumptions about the limited abilities of non-humans. And it is not just humans, it seems, who can be said to have 'culture'. Other animals too develop particular practices and innovations and pass them on to others. One famous innovation was introduced fifty years ago by a young Japanese monkey who pioneered the practice of washing sweet-potatoes to clean off the dirt, soon copied by her mother and her peers, then other members of her community. It is still followed by their descendants today (de Waal 1999: 635). There are also the distinctive traditions of songbirds, established and inherited in particular areas and different from those elsewhere. Humpback whales from the same breeding area similarly sing the same songs, slowly changing from year to year, whereas whales from different oceans have completely different songs (Gray *et al.* 2001: 53). Equally significant is the comparative summary of long-term field studies which charts the distinctive cultural repertoires of different chimpanzee communities in different regions of Africa (de Waal 1999, Whiten *et al.* 1999). All in all, it seems that, to take Irene Pepperberg's words, 'Animals have capacities that are far greater than we were once led to expect' (1999: 327–8).[8]

So if we regard communication as essentially a purposive, organised and mutually recognisable process in which individuals actively interconnect with each other, there are good arguments for using this of non-human as well as human animals. No one could of course deny that there are differences between the communicative processes of, say, worms or shellfish and those of human beings. But recent research and analysis is revealing continuities rather than absolute divides, challenging the humano-centric focus of earlier approaches. The sharp qualitative break between human and non-human animals once taken as self-evident now seems less convincing.

This provides good reason to turn to comparative studies of animal communicating for possible frameworks for analysing human communicative resources. One regular feature of these studies is particularly pertinent: that of the channels for animal communicating. A widely used classification is summarised in Box 2.4.

Box 2.4 Main channels for animal communication

Sight – visual channel
Sound – auditory channel
Smell – olfactory/chemical channel
Touch – tactile channel
Vibration – seismic channel
Electric fields – electrical channel

Here we have another set of categories through which to capture and illuminate human communicative resources. To an extent it overlaps with the fivefold sensory framework, sharing some of its strengths and limitations. But it differs not only in its specific categories but also in building on extensive empirical research set in a comparative perspective (not limited to humans) with a focus on modalities used for action and interaction rather than on receptive sense organs.

These channels are widely and actively used in animal communication. The ethologist W. J. Smith comments that 'every sensory modality (except possibly thermoreception) that detects external events has been involved. One result is enormous diversity: the signals of animal communication have been elaborated in many and often unimagined ways' (Smith, W. J. *et al.* 1989: 69). That they are exploited differentially by different species of animals will be no surprise given differing bodily capacities and environmental resources. The range, in fact, is astonishing. Some animals communicate through sounds made by rubbing parts of themselves together or beating on outside objects, others through processes associated with respiration. Many insects use smell in versatile ways not open to human beings; lovebirds touch bills to show non-aggression during greetings; skunks issue warnings by their powerful stink; rabbits thump the ground to alert others to danger; titi monkeys indicate friendly relations by intertwining tails; mammals use threatening stares to see off their opponents or play-gestures to show amicability; female fireflies flash their lights so the males can find them; bees use waggle dances to share information about food. In one spider species the male plucks a special rhythm on the (larger) female's web to announce himself and his intentions – crucial communication indeed, to avoid being taken for prey and devoured. Both human and non-human animals convey messages to each other through movements of the head, eyes, or limbs, through posture and orientation, touches, noises, movements towards or away. Others use vibration: sightless moles communicate by vibrating the earth, insects send ripples across the surface of the water. Certain tropical fish living in muddy waters where visibility is poor create an electric field around themselves, a signal which goes around obstacles and is detectable even in murky conditions. Through this they can communicate with others nearby – they live in groups – a channel for conveying threats, submission or sexual information and for wooing females in 'an electrical courtship song' (Goodenough *et al.* 1993: 577).

These are merely a few examples from the vast range of animal communicating. Each species has its own unique repertoire which its various groups and individuals exploit and develop as they interconnect with each other. But overall the same basic modalities occur again and again. They give yet another handle on our communicative resources, modifying and in a way challenging the fivefold sensory framework.

These communicative modalities also seem to have some recurring characteristics; these too may have some bearing on our communicative resources and how we take them up. Their detailed relevance in human communicating must be left till later chapters, but the summary in Box 2.5 (pp. 50–1) can start us off, drawn from recent comparative work on animal communication.[9]

In practical terms we take much of this for granted in our everyday practice even when, as with many other recurrent patterns, we are not explicitly conscious of their existence. In fact we see their operation all around us. I could instance the clever behaviour of our two cairn terriers. These dogs know well how to pressurise us, communicating by tail-wagging, particular postures, moving purposively towards the door or (the hungrier one) dancing towards the kitchen at supper time – but they also know that their visual signals work only so long as they are in sight. If they are outside and want to be let in, they turn to the acoustic channel, each with their preferred strategy: one scratches noisily on the door, the other barks gently just outside it. Sound does not last long so if nothing happens they try again. They know too that nearness is essential for tactile communicating, through a soft paw or lick, and that this can work even in the dark – like the urgent nudge from the bedside when they come upstairs unbidden in the night. They use similar tactics with other dogs but there, unlike with humans, engage in yet further communication through smell and by the deposit of long-lasting smelly urine.

Parallel strategies are used by humans, exploiting their own biological and social potential in the context of the human ways of life. We may seldom if ever think consciously about the strengths and limitations of sight but in practice know and use them well. Vision is a wonderful resource for rapid communication within reasonably close conditions. It is effective even when it is noisy, well suited to the human terrestrial and diurnal way of life (it works best in air and daylight), good for conveying a range of dimensions, and easy to locate precisely. We have found ways to exploit this long-lasting potential of vision in our creation of visual objects and their usage in communicating. But we also know in practice that it works less well in the dark and that we cannot see or be seen around obstacles or at great distances. We know a lot about audition too. Sound is no sooner produced than it vanishes, unlike the longer-lasting sights, and its exact location is not always easy to pinpoint. But we exploit its capacity to span long distances, to overcome visual obstructions, and attract rapid attention in both light and dark. Olfaction is something we use less, but we are certainly experienced in the qualities of touch. We are aware that it is (mostly) only effective over short distances and does not last. But we also know from experience that tactile communication is close, fast and effective, can on occasion be exercised secretly, works in the dark, is quickly locatable and can override impossibly noisy conditions: a good channel for members of a close-living gregarious species.

A summary of this kind should not be taken as a definitive list of each channel's properties nor imply automatic results from their usages. We need to balance the constraints and opportunities that tend to be characteristic of different channels with an awareness of the varied and creative ways they are in practice used in specific contexts. For humans as for other animals these modalities represent resources

Box 2.5 Some characteristics of the main channels of animal communication

	Auditory	Visual	Tactile	Chemical/olfactory	Seismic*	Electrical
Speed	Fast (but slower than vision)	Fast	Fast	Varies, but usually slower than auditory or visual	Fast	Fast
Spatial range	Long-distance (through both air and, especially, water)	Medium-distance (weakens with distance)	Near-distance	Long-distance, specially in air/water currents (but varies)	Long-distance (further than auditory signals)	Short-distance
Duration, persistence	Short (doesn't linger, disappears without trace)	Duration varies (and can be manipulated)	Short	Mostly long (but varies); fade-out mostly slower than auditory or visual	Short	Short
Effectiveness in noisy conditions	Poor	Yes	Yes	Yes	Yes (?)	Yes
Effectiveness round obstacles	Yes (also effective in limited visibility)	No (has to be *seen*, less effective in darkness, water)	Yes within limits (touch needs to be physically possible); effective in dark	Yes	Varies: good underground but seismic ripples may be affected by obstacles	Yes

	Auditory	Visual	Tactile	Chemical/olfactory	Seismic*	Electrical
Ease of locatability	Medium	Good	Good (even in dark)	Varies; usually harder than visual, auditory or tactile	?	Good
Complexity	High (variety in e.g. volume, pitch, melody, beat, also bandwidth, frequency; varied ways of producing)	High (large variety of signals e.g. brightness, colour, shape, movement)	Medium (variety of both simple and complex messages possible)	Recent research seems to be revealing much more complexity than assumed previously	Variety of forms (e.g. underground, ripples, webs)	Low

Note:
*The seismic channel is not always distinguished separately (it overlaps into touch and perhaps audition) and has been less extensively studied.

which may or may not be exploited and manipulated in particular directions. There is room for enquiry as to whether and how far humans have found ways both to maximise their benefits and also, perhaps, to break through some of their limitations – a point to return to in later chapters.

The communicating human animal

Just as every species has its own specific repertoire of communicative channels and the morphological resources to exploit them, so too do human beings. Our human capacities to exploit a selection of these modalities also form part of our resources.

Humans walk upright, on two legs. This is sometimes traced to long-gone times when, it is said, 'men came down from the trees' and learned to walk on two legs. Whatever the truth of that origin tale, bipedalism is a crucial characteristic of the human species, directly relevant for our communicative abilities. There is the near vertical position of the human face with its intricate facial musculature (a versatile and much-used communicative resource), and the prominent position of our eyes, often one of the first features noticed during personal encounters. Equally important is the human hand. Walking on two not four legs frees our hands from locomotion, allowing us to employ them for a large variety of purposes: not only for gesture and touching but also for tool-using and for making and utilising a vast range of communicative media, from pictures, textiles or stone inscriptions to illuminated manuscripts, musical instruments and computers. The distinctive make-up of the human hand is relevant too, with its flexibility of movement and twist, the capacity of thumb and first two fingers to work as a unit, long opposable and robust thumb, broad finger pads for grasping, and a palm stabilised for gripping and supporting. All this enables fine, precise, flexible and controlled movements. The production and use of external artefacts is not unique to humans but has certainly been developed to a particularly high degree among them, much used in communicating – and this largely depends, directly or indirectly, on our human hands.

Another crucial resource is the human visual power. Some capacity to respond to light is widespread among animals, but developed in many different ways. Reptilian vision detects nearby movements of both prey and predators in daylight, some birds of prey have remarkable distance vision (better than humans), owls (again unlike humans) can perceive infrared light, while some mammals have eyes well adapted for darkness or dusk. Primate vision is sometimes said to have developed amidst the brightly coloured flowering plants of the arboreal phase of evolution. Whatever its origin, it is certainly a much-used resource for maintaining contact and facilitating interaction. Humans have stereoscopic vision and the human eye is a powerful instrument for detecting, among other things, movement, size, shape, distance, depth, texture and colour. Vision has its limitations (see Box 2.5), but all in all is a flexible and much-used resource in human communicating.

Many animals move parts of their bodies so as to communicate through sounds. Among many terrestrial mammals including humans this is through vibrations of the vocal cords. We resemble many other mammals in converting the airflow from our lungs into acoustic energy, but the specifically human form of larynx, tongue and lips also enables the production and differentiation of a great diversity of sounds: a foundation for the extensive human use of vocal speech. Paralleling this, hearing is another critical human capacity. Humans can both make and hear a remarkable variety of sounds, discriminating in terms of, for example, volume, intensity, pitch, melody, duration, timing, or timbre. On the other hand the range of frequencies detectable by the human ear cannot match the infrasonic capacities of elephants and fin whales at the one end nor, at the other, the ultrasonic sounds used by bats or porpoises; nor do humans match the mimicry and auditory recall of many birds. But it is basic to human interaction nonetheless and, as will appear in Chapter 3, audition is extensively used in human communicating.

Olfaction is perhaps little exploited for communicating among humans compared to some other animals, in part no doubt related to our upright posture and way of life. But humans are still capable of discriminating many thousands of smells and may perhaps have the potential to expand the role of olfaction in the future. Touching is arguably more important and has a firm foundation in our human anatomy. Humans have a large expanse of skin and the tactile sensitivity of the many touch receptors on the body are significant both for communicating through direct touch and for exercising our manual dexterity. The hands are especially sensitive for touching and manipulating – here again our upright posture facilitates their use.

The relatively large size of the human body is perhaps also relevant. This not only aids vision and visibility but enables the movement and manipulation of large and heavy objects – significant for producing the many artefacts used in communicating. The human power of relatively rapid movement is significant too, a resource for touching, making sounds, attaining the locations for seeing and being seen, and manipulating people and objects. We can move parts of heads, hands and limbs in kinesic communicating as well as the postures and movements of our bodies as a whole. Humans can move from one place to another and, though less far or rapidly than some other species, travel self-propelled across space – the background to much of our communicating.

The size and structure of the human brain might also be added to the typically human resources for communicating. These would certainly feature conspicuously in many accounts, especially those stressing human rationality or envisaging the brain as *the* human cognitive organ which sets humans at the evolutionary pinnacle of living creatures. But there are grounds for asking whether the brain should take quite so prominent and unquestioned a place. Not only are the simplified narratives about human cognition themselves under scrutiny, but recent researchers on animal communication have come to query the arguably dated assumption that the size (at least) of the brain is so crucial. They have uncovered the impressive capacities of birds, for example, their brains so much smaller than – and differently structured from – those of humans, and, even more different, those of insects (see Pepperberg 1999: esp. 8ff, Griffin 1984: 170ff). Or take the brilliantly deceitful communicating of certain tiny spiders who use both stealth and aggressive mimicry to deceive their intended victim as they enter its web after a long-planned and complicated detour to stalk their prey (Wilcox and Jackson 1998). When they started their research, the last thing the investigators expected was that they could one day be seriously discussing cognition in a spider, or facing the challenge of understanding how 'an animal with so little in the way of a brain can nevertheless do so much' (Wilcox and Jackson 1998: 428). The particular size and structure of the human brain may indeed have some relevance but, it seems, we can no longer take this as self-evident.

Amidst all our rich resources there are lacks and disadvantages too. Humans seem not to have the seismic receptors used to such good effect by some animals and unlike most birds are not equipped for rapid self-propulsion over far distances in the air with the vantage point that this gives. Humans detect sounds only within a limited range of frequencies, see poorly at night compared to some nocturnal animals, and make little use of vibration. Their faces are distant from the ground, making the use of smell less feasible, and they lack the electrical organs through which some fishes communicate.

The significance of all these characteristics lies less in the separate human features, many of them differing only in degree from those of other animals, than the overall combination. It also rests in how they are *used* – the ways in which human beings have exploited and developed these biological potentials in keeping with their way(s) of life: in the main gregarious, diurnal (mostly operating by day), ground-dwelling (not arboreal or aerial) and terrestrial (land not water). Added to this is the human capacity – found indeed among other animals but arguably not to the same extent – to innovate creatively and, to a degree, to transmit their innovations to others both through co-present interaction and through the production of often long-lasting artefacts. Setting human beings in the perspective of communication among other animals enables us both to understand the illuminating continuities and to see where the particular human combination is specific and distinctive.

From a comparative perspective, then, it could be said that human animals typically emphasise audio-visual rather than tactile-olfactory channels and are biologically well equipped to do so. This conclusion, though broadly valid, is also perhaps a little over-simplified. As we shall see, olfactory and tactile modalities too play a role in human communication. It would also be wrong to make a parallel assumption that non-human animals all rely principally on touch or smell. Many make extensive use of sight and hearing – here again there is no sharp break between humans and other animals. But it is true that both audition and vision represent particularly rich and versatile resources for human communicating, with a secure base in the morphology of the human body. They will appropriately form the subject of much of the discussion in Part II of this book.

Our complex bundle of resources

Human resources for communicating, then, are both complex and variegated. In view of their multilevel and multidimensional spread, we have to look for them in several areas rather than capturing them in a single unilinear list. There is the long tradition of 'the senses' as modes of perception linked to receptive bodily organs (from some viewpoints also a matter of active experience, cultural construction, and positive action); the non-verbal modes of expression; multiple 'intelligences'; the human arts and media; the channels of animal communication and their typical features; the physical resources of the world we live in; and the resources of our own human morphology.

None of the classifications in this chapter can be taken as the final word. Not only are there disagreements as well as overlaps among them, but insofar as the categories are clear in the first place they emerge in varying ways – and with different strengths and limitations – in different contexts. What they can do between them, however, is to sensitise us to the *many* ways in which humans interconnect and the resources which they both draw on and create in so doing – an overlapping conglomeration of senses, arts, media, intelligences, practices, artefacts, channels, our earthly and environmental resources, and the biological capacities of the human body.

It will be clear that, no more than in any of the lists above, have I found here a definitive way of distinguishing or delimiting the modes of communication. Indeed though the following chapters focus in turn on separate modalities, in practice these are typically interdependent and intertwined, a point to return to in the concluding chapters. But as a way to get started I will be drawing on various permutations of the categories above (especially those around the modalities of animal communication and the uses of human artefacts), taking these not as definitive typologies but as ways into appreciating the amazingly rich and variegated array of intermingled resources that humans use in their interconnecting.

Part II

Channels of communication

3 The sounding world and its creation

Audition is one good place to start. Sound is widely used among living creatures, going far back, it seems, in the long evolution of animals. It is one of the first senses to which we become alive: we hear sounds even in the womb and from their first hours humans use the auditory channel to declare their existence and interact with those around them. Through sound we actively assert our presence and draw notice from others, and we also formulate and learn our own identity from hearing the very sounds we ourselves make. Here we have a fundamental resource which human beings exploit in manifold ways to create and maintain contact with each other.[1]

We may picture the world as made up of sights – the visible things and events around us. But whether we consciously recognise it or not, human beings also indubitably live in a world of sound. There are the sounds of nature – of water, wind, birdsong, animals, trees, earth, fire, air; of our built environments – of cobbled, tarred or mud streets and vehicles running on them, city squares or hedged fields, the contrasting sonic qualities of thatched cottages, colonnaded temples or concrete high-rise buildings; the sounds from our own bodies – heartbeats, breathing, footsteps, clothing, movements, shouts, sighs. We seldom give our full attention to these 'soundscapes', to adopt Murray Schafer's evocative term (1977), but they make up the multiplex sonic experiences through which humans live, and form as objective a part of the environment for human communication as does the undoubted existence of visible objects.

The role of sound is often underestimated. It is still a common assumption that it belongs to primitive layers of the human make-up, linked to emotion rather than the 'higher' cognitive faculties, and that abstract language and perhaps sight are pre-destined to supersede this older auditory mode. Western philosophers from Plato onwards have mostly ranked sight above sound and the triumphs of western science are commonly linked to vision not audition. Many analyses have of course been made of music and of speech, unquestionably examples of auditory communication. But the focus is usually less on their acoustic quality than on their cognitive import or, indeed, their visible aspects (words as written, notes in a printed score). It is not often that the *sonic* features take centre stage. With a few exceptions (referred to as we proceed), sound has seldom been extensively considered as a significant dimension of human communicating.

The romantic tradition (for example in Herder's writings) might seem to offer an alternative viewpoint with its challenge to rationalist models and celebration of the sensory aspects of language and role of sound. But many versions of this approach themselves implicitly promote similar assumptions, glamorising sound as something of 'the other' – that is, of cultures 'far away and long ago' or, alternatively, of emotions buried deep within the self. Here again it seems natural to conclude that sound has little serious role in the communication of today.

The tide may be turning however and, for a variety of reasons, the importance of sound is starting to be taken more seriously. This is reinforced, too, by critiques of self-confident Enlightenment evaluations and a growing appreciation of non-western experiences. Sound is still often devalued in studies of human communication and culture but our 'auratic forms of experience' (Bull 2000: 194) are perhaps becoming more recognised as one significant dimension of human interaction.[2]

This chapter follows up this sonic dimension, taking it for the moment as the main focus (later we will need to look at a wider mix of modes). This should give some idea of our human auditory resources, of how humans operate with the constraints and options offered by this channel of communication, and the range of strategies they have developed for utilising and extending it.[3]

The sonic resources for animal communicating . . .

The resources we exploit in our sonic communicating are to be found both in the intrinsic resources of our own bodies, some shared with other animals, and in a range of human-made instruments and other artefacts. Starting with a brief look at the auditory capacities and practices of animals can set these human resources in perspective.[4]

To be relevant for communication, sounds must be *heard* and there are various devices for this. Marine animals receive underwater sound via air-filled spaces or solid structures through which they detect fluctuating pressures. Bats use ultrasonic frequencies for 'listening in the dark', while some insects' receptors are precisely tuned to the frequencies of calls from their own species. Terrestrial vertebrates and insects have ears of one kind or another, membranes which, like the tympanum of the human ear, vibrate in response to fluctuations in external pressure.

Animals (including humans) *produce* these hearable sounds by forcibly vibrating some part of their anatomy: rubbing bits of their bodies or beating things in the environment, also, common among vertebrates, utilising their respiratory organs. The sounds vary greatly. Insects – versatile producers of sounds – make stridulations by scraping themselves. Locusts pull legs across forewings, crickets and grasshoppers use hind legs against wings or wings against wings, cicadas scrape a stiff plectrum against their protuberances. Other animals click bits of their external skeletons or whistle through emissions of air. Beetles knock heads against surfaces while bats 'see with their ears' using high-frequency signals to navigate and detect targets through echolocation, as well as other sounds to communicate with each other (Popper and Fay 1995). Birds not only vocalise (see below) but also communicate by clapping their beaks, drumming them on trees, and scraping or vibrating their feathers. Similarly with some other animals: rattlesnakes frighten potential attackers by shaking their rattles, porcupines by rattling their quills, and beavers warn each other of danger by slapping the water with their flat tails. Many animals use sounds produced by air passed through some bodily organ. Bull alligators and red deer roar to attract mates and warn off rivals, while choruses of frogs call loudly to distant females.

Birds are great vocalisers, using air expelled from their lungs through a syrinx. Many songbirds learn to sing in the same way humans learn to speak, beginning with a 'subsong' stage just as human babies babble. They go on to develop large repertoires, often with both local dialects – learned song traditions – and new songs arising from their own individual creations and improvisations. Their rhythmic variations, pitch permutations and note combinations sometimes resemble those of human composers, retaining the same melody with a change of key or countersinging in matched melodic canon (Gray *et al.* 2001: 52). Male nightingales sing about 200 discrete and distinguishable types of song each with its own prosodic features, both as solos and in complex interactive dialogues. The nightingales use them in a variety of social settings to advertise their territory, countersing with others, or attract mates, varying the singing to the occasion (Todt and Hultsch 1996). Other birds exploit their vocal resources differently, but commonly use them for, among other things, sounding alarms, keeping contact with other flock-members both individually and generally, courting, indicating distress, sexual communication, cooperating, fighting, warning off rivals from a nesting territory and recognising neighbours. There are occasions for display, pre-dawn serenades, and formalised vocal interactions with others. Avian communication has been described as, in all, 'one of the most evolved and sophisticated communication systems known' (Hailman and Ficken 1996: 136).

Many mammals make sounds by vibrating vocal chords, flexible membranes worked by expelling air from the lungs. The exact mechanisms for producing these vocalisations vary but overall enable a great variety of amplitudes, frequencies and intensities. The extent and flexibility of this vocal communicating among certain animals is far greater than was once appreciated. We are of course well acquainted with the growls, barks or whines of dogs or purring of cats. But these are only small examples amidst the huge diversity of vocalised sounds, used variously by many kinds of animals to draw attention, warn of danger, threaten, fight, attract mates, submit, keep contact with others, welcome, negotiate, make friends, engage in play and a host of other purposes. Tigers have an elaborate vocabulary of vocalisations, using growls, grunts, mewls, roars and chuffs (affectionate greetings) to keep in touch (Morgan 2001: 16). The extraordinary range of vocal calls between elephants is also now starting to be recognised. Using an intricate communication system of trumpets, snorts, screams, barks, roars, cries and at least thirty distinct forms of 'rumble', East African elephants reinforce bonds between friends and relatives, keep contact, reconcile differences, jointly care for offspring, form coalitions and advertise their sexual state, identity and rank within the multilayered network of relationships in which they live and cooperate (Kigotho 2001: 19, quoting Joyce Poole). Many monkeys and apes have distinct calls for different purposes, like the differing 'isolation peeps' of squirrel monkeys or the distinctive 'coo' calls and vocal alarms for different dangers recognised by Japanese macaques (Ploog 1992: 18, Marler *et al.* 1992: 69ff). Cheney and Seyfarth's field studies of vervet monkeys (see pp. 45–6 above) document the distinctive sounds used to convey differentiated information about objects or events in the external world. 'Like humans, [the monkeys] classify calls not just as physical entities but as sounds that *represent* things' (Cheney and Seyfarth 1990: 15).

In water sound travels more efficiently than it does through air whereas vision has limitations. It is not surprising, then, to find that audition is extensively used by aquatic animals. Underwater listening devices can now access the huge amount of noise in the 'unsilent sea' (Morton and Page 1992: 33). Crustaceans use their external skeletons to make clicks and stridulations, snapping their claws or scraping their antennae against ridges on their heads. Hundreds-strong lobster groups in the North Atlantic keep together through their constant rasping noises, changing pitch and pace to communicate danger and using yet other sounds as mating calls. Fishes produce sounds by snapping bones, grinding teeth or fins, or air sac vibrations, and male seals sing complex songs with patterned sequences of notes during the breeding season. Cetaceans like dolphins, porpoises and whales are famous for their whistles, squeals, clicks, squawks and flatulences, produced as territorial advertisements, defence calls, courting, and social contact, some of them audible over hundreds or perhaps thousands of miles (Hopp *et al.* 1998: 230). The songs of humpback whales (the best studied) are complex indeed, lasting around 10 to 30 minutes and with structures similar to human songs. They use rhythms, sequences of themes based on patterned musical notes not unlike human scales, and refrains that form rhymes: 'these marine mammals are inveterate composers' (Gray *et al.* 2001: 52, also Tyack 1998).

. . . and their human uses

Humans do not have access to the full range of auditory resources found across the animal kingdom as a whole. We cannot hear all the frequencies that are (between them) exploited in animal communicating, and generally lack resources like the avian syrinx, bats' echolocation or cetacean capacities for underwater sounding.[5]

But a surprising number of the auditory devices discussed above *are* in fact also exploited by humans – once again there turns out to be more continuity between human and non-human animals than is often realised.

We humans, too, strike together parts of our bodies to make sounds, especially our hands. We regularly utilise the auditory device of clapping to attract notice, communicate the need for haste, or convey appreciation or congratulation. Clapping can be important in music-making, arguably the leading form of percussion in African music, outstripping drumming (Ottenberg 1996: 73). Like other animals, humans too make noises by beating objects in the external environment. We tap with hands or fingers to convey impatience, thump and knock hands or feet against surfaces to communicate irritation or announce our presence. We use strumming, scraping, and finger snapping to draw attention, fist pounding to convey anger or emphasis, and communicate by tongue clicking, thigh slapping, teeth grinding, or lip smacking.

Like some other animals, human auditory communication makes extensive use of respiration. Whistling uses controlled emissions or intakes of air for communicating. Sometimes it carries explicit meanings, as in whistled signals among scattered walkers or male 'wolf whistles' for pretty girls; in certain types of terrain it is used for long-distance communication. In other contexts it can be a subtle but effective way to establish contact and communicate feelings.

> The whistler does not talk, yet he communicates . . . [and] communicates too in a very specific way with his fellow man. With a whistle he implies all sorts of inner moods, motives, and thoughts . . . the meaning of the whistle cannot be definitely pinned down, so that the whistler is safe from criticism, discovery, and punishment. He can get away with expressing a whole range of feelings – hate, disdain, coolness, nonchalance, pity, and tenderness – by whistling.
>
> (Ostwald 1973: 66–7)[6]

The breathy exclamations sometimes written as 'whew' and 'ha' are further small examples, and humans regularly use sighing, gasping, snorting or sniffing in their communicating. Between them such sounds can convey multifarious meanings, from disapproval, amazement, affection or relief to salute, summons, suffering or frustration. They initiate and maintain contact and bring human beings to each other's notice. And as has come out in a series of studies, controlled or sudden silence is another effective, and essentially sonic, medium for communicating (Bauman 1983, Burke 1993, Davies 1988, Jaworski 1993, Peek 1994).

The sounds that, like many other terrestrial animals, humans produce through vibrating their vocal chords have more varied powers than is often remembered: cadence and song as well as speaking. Consider the diversity of communicating that can be accomplished through shouts, shrieks or moans; non-verbalised exclamations, acknowledgements and warnings; yodelling; singing and humming.

Laughing is an important communicatory device too, surprisingly overlooked in many analyses. So are sobbing, weeping and moaning, vocalised forms used widely throughout the world. Even the shortest of lists points to an extensive variety of sounds, usable for a host of situations and purposes.

Overlapping and interacting with these instances comes the human deployment of vocal chords in speaking – vocalisations characterised by the organised inter-mingling of multiplex acoustic features. In this form of auditory communicating humans have built up complex conventions for producing and distinguishing audiovocal patterns of a much greater range than that deployed, for example, by vervet monkeys. Humans spend many years after birth in mastering these, gaining the physiological control to utter and differentiate the sounds and practising the locally recognised auditory patterns for structuring them. The skills they eventually develop make human vocalised communication an astoundingly effective, versatile and multifunctional resource for both speakers and hearers (something to which we must return in the next section).

So far the coverage has mainly been confined to sounds that are, more or less, produced directly by or within the human body. But this is not the end of it. As we have seen, animals sometimes go beyond their own bodies and make sounds by interacting in some way with the external environment. Human beings do this to a marked degree, utilising a diversity of external objects and human-made artefacts.

Humans have found ways to amplify their vocal productions, for example, by using both natural and manufactured instruments, from conch shells to loudhailers and microphones. Noises made by tapping, thumping or banging are enhanced or modified by external objects. The scrape of chairs on the floor signals time to move and the rattling of cups in an adjoining room announces either a mealtime or a subtle request for assistance. Human beings have also long understood the prin-ciples of creating sounds by blowing across tubes, striking stretched membranes, or vibrating strings, and have developed a huge variety of sound-producing instruments activated by strumming, plucking, rubbing, bowing or beating.

An extensive range of communicatory sounds can be effected through these means. Striking of gongs or bells, or blowing whistles, horns or sirens commonly demarcates time periods, issues commands, or communicates warnings. Percussion – striking with hands, feet or external implements – is a widely used human form of sound production, utilised for multiple communicative purposes: announcing, celebrating, coordinating people's movements, inducing trance and religious fervour, commanding silence or attention, confirming a decision, confer-ring authority, and marking out a particular act or situation as 'special'.

Human-made instruments are also employed for highly specific messages. Lighthouses had distinctive warning sounds, commands passed by bell from bridge to ship's engine room, and North American train drivers exchanged secret personal messages on their whistles (Schafer 1977: 81). Elaborate communication systems are sounded out by European post horns, French village bells or African drums.

Acoustic messages are conveyed through beeps on computers; strikes, chimes and ticks on timepieces; automatic warning signals on trains; and synthetic human speech by various technical devices. Sounds can be communicated over great distances too not only by amplifiers and loudspeakers but also, more extensively, by telephones, radio or computer. Furthermore sounds can now be stored and transmitted through a variety of mechanical or electronic means, greatly extending the spatial reach of human auditory communicating.

All this again depends on the capacity to hear, and, more than this, to discriminate. Sound is complex indeed, and the ear has to detect a wide range of properties, from variations of volume, pitch, rhythm, intensity, speed, tone, cadence or timbre to direction, distance or alternations of sound and silence. We need to recognise varying modulations and tones of voices, noises made by hands or feet, combinations of instrumental tones and rhythms, or complex intertwinings within musical ensembles. Humans have to some extent developed exosomatic techniques to help our listening – ear trumpets, hearing aids, stethoscopes as well as the range of distance-covering technologies – but essentially audition remains centred on our human ears.

Like other animals, humans have to sort out and interpret the sounds they hear. We recognise the voices of those we know and love, interpret the slightest of hesitations or wryness in a voice over the telephone, and even in a jumble of noises 'prick up our ears' at the sound of our own name. As McAdams and Bigand point out in their *Thinking in Sound* (1993), even the most powerful computer program could scarcely cope with the versatility and skill of human acoustic comprehension:

> Imagine for just an instant . . . the array of information and set of procedures with which it would be necessary to endow a computer so that it could distinguish a violin from a flute in polyphonic music, extract an alarm signal from the sonorous background within which it is embedded, grasp the connection between a theme and a musical variation, analyse by simply listening to the noise of a car a problem with the engine, detect an inhabitual sound in the beating of a patient's heart.
>
> (McAdams and Bigand 1993: v)

The sounds we attend to and discriminate are not just the result of passive reception from the external environment. The changing acoustic patterns of the sea are harkened to in particular ways in a fishing village for example. So are noises made by sheep or cattle among farmers, the aurally evocative sounds of mallets beating barkcloth against an anvil in Polynesian islands, or the ring of church bells marking the boundaries of the mediaeval Christian community. Our soundscapes are moulded by cultural experience as well as individual circumstances for we screen out some noises while valuing and attending to others. In a measure, we ourselves make the sonic worlds in which we interact.

Like many other animals, then, we humans produce and hear noises made by the body either itself or in interaction with an external surface and sounds made through our breath and vocal chords. We also extend our embodied resources through external instruments and technologies. Humans, in all, have a vast range of acoustic resources which they can turn to practically any of the manifold purposes with which human living is concerned.

The arts and organisation of acoustic communication

Our uses of communicative sound are all in one sense organised and creative – actively produced and heard according to human-constructed conventions. But there are also cases where the human uses of audition have been elaborated in spectacularly versatile and systematic ways.

The elaborate development of human vocalisation is a notable case. This includes the patterns of the singing or intoning voice – some see these, together with cadence and melody in general, as the bedrock of audiovocal communication (see for example Fernald 1992, Gray *et al.* 2001). Overlapping and intermingling with this is communication through spoken language, arguably among the greatest of human creations.

One way of grasping the vast scale of this communicative achievement might be to cite the huge number of languages developed by human beings: five to six thousand are said to be spoken in the world today together with the many others from the past (Crystal 1997: 286–7). Their numbers, variety and versatility are indeed astonishing. We need to be cautious about taking such figures too literally, however. To picture 'languages' as separate entities works reasonably well for *written* systems (formulations with some degree of permanent and distinctive visibility), but the auditory processes of *speaking* do not divide up so easily. Certainly speakers from widely separated cultures are unlikely to share most of each other's conventions; but among more closely interacting people(s) the acoustic patterns can merge into each other. 'Separate languages' may well be distinguished as much by political, economic or educational markers as by the sounds of people's speech. Norwegian, Danish and Swedish are regularly classed as distinct languages, for example, belonging to separate nation states and with their own published grammars. But in practice their spoken dialects merge into each other in much the same way as those of speakers from contrasting parts of the British Isles who are counted as having the 'same language' (English). Many linguists would now question the older model of languages as distinct and homogeneous entities with their own abiding structural characteristics (see for example Bloomaert 1999, Hymes 1996: 67, Simpson 1994).

Acoustic communicating through the voice is in fact a flexible process rather than fixed system. Even within what might be labelled the 'same' language, there are differing registers, in-group sounds, specialist pronunciations, situational conventions, creative innovations, melodic contours, changing patterns, regional accents, group or class diversities, and individual sonic nuances, all of which different participants may pick up on in different ways. And then there are combinations and permutations of these elements too, differing 'speech communities', changes over time. We are dealing with a multiplex and infinitely creative process of human interconnecting based on (more or less) shared acoustic patternings, rather than the automatic application, as it were, of a permanent and definitive set of ready-made units.

It may seem stating the obvious to remark that this vocal communicating relies on sound and hearing. This needs emphasis, however. The human voice is an extraordinary auditory instrument which can be played and heard in multiple and subtle ways. It can produce infinite numbers of distinctive sound combinations differentiated by specific uses of (for example) teeth, lips, tongue, nose and palate. It can differentiate along a spectrum of rhythm, pitch, tempo, timbre, tone quality, phrasing, melodic and other musical elements, pacing, volume, intensity, breathiness, roughness, low and high registers, vibrato or plain delivery, abrupt or sustained phrasing, silences . . . only some of its powers.

Analysts of language have in the past played down these sonic qualities of speech. Grammarians traditionally focused on written forms, philosophers emphasised the referential and abstracted role of language rather than its situational performances, educationalists and intellectuals ranked literacy above oracy, linguists looked to texts rather than action or experience. Any sonic dimensions of human communication, we might gather, are merely secondary while the central reality lies in abstracted writable elements, the 'words' (these in turn often implicitly defined as units differentiated within alphabetic writing). But this model is no longer self-evident. The emphasis in many circles has shifted towards the analysis of people's actual practices – conversations and communicative interactions rather than abiding structure, prescription or text – and the ideology of language as autonomous and non-contextual increasingly recognised as merely one among several possible approaches. Sonic dimensions of prosody like rhythm and cadence have always attracted some interest but linguists now pay them more explicit attention and include other features like length, accent, stress, tone, and intonation; grammars now more often consider phonological dimensions. All this has awakened greater awareness of the *sonic* qualities of speech: normal, essential and regularly utilised features of human vocal communicating.[7]

In practice we know this well. We need only think of a simple utterance like 'Don't worry, it's *quite* all right'. It is bland in written form. But the acoustic resources of the human voice and a speaker's purposive projection of it as, say, a crossly spoken phrase with a particular intonation, tenseness and clipped pronunciation can communicate not reassurance but anger, cold disapproval and rejection – likely to be well grasped by all parties who hear it. As Ostwald put it in his perceptive *Semiotics of Human Sound*:

> The color of the voice, nasality, tremulousness, breathiness, and other accompanying sounds transmit the emotional tone of the message. For example, the words *I feel fine*, uttered by a disturbed patient, can be entirely misleading unless the listener correctly perceives the depressive quality of the voice. People also emphasize certain of their words and phrases by barks, bangs on the table, swoops from one vocal pitch to another, or a peculiar accent, to bring out the emotional implications.
>
> (Ostwald 1973: 40–1)

We make constant and sophisticated use of such sonic features. It is more than just 'emotional tone'. Commands, questions, sympathy, assertiveness, warnings, anticipations of coming to a close or yielding the floor to another speaker – these are all communicated at least in part by the *sound*. Crucial aspects are conveyed by an ironic, sarcastic or mock-quoting tone, a mournful, droning, hesitating or low-pitched voice, or a breathy and excited delivery. We alter the whole communicative context if we switch from a light, high-pitched and rapid presentation with wide ranges of pitch and dynamics (an 'innocent'-sounding style that disclaims responsibility) into the solemn, low-pitched and measured pace that conveys a mature sense of responsibility (Truax 1984: 36). The relationships between people are communicated and reinforced through the multiple sonic qualities of their vocalisations, not just through their words.

> Guarded language, carefully controlled pitch range, and absolute rigidity of tempo and dynamics in a speaker may make us skeptical of what the person says. We 'read between the lines' that the person is self-protective and anxious to avoid personal involvement, particularly that of an emotional nature. Bureaucrats in particular perfect this style of voice when repeating the 'official' policy of others to avoid taking responsibility.
>
> (Truax 1984: 36)

As communicators we are adept at deploying and interpreting these and other acoustic subtleties.

If the multidimensional uses of sound are always important in vocal interaction, their detailed deployment differs in different traditions. Learning unfamiliar forms of vocal communicating, whether the register for a particular situation or group, a dialect, or a 'foreign language', is not just a matter of 'vocabulary' but of learning its (more or less) recognised acoustic conventions. These may be elaborate indeed. *Pitch* sometimes plays a prominent role. In Chinese it is a crucial marker for differentiating meanings; so too in Thai, Zulu and many West African languages. Yoruba speakers in West Africa sometimes say it is easier to understand someone who gets the tones right and other things wrong than the other way round, and there and elsewhere tonal patterning is a recognised element of poetic prosody (Finnegan 1992: 96ff). Pastaza Quechua speakers of Ecuador use 'sound-symbolism' to convey moods of catastrophe, futility, normalcy, beauty, lightness, and buoyancy . . . the forcefulness and even viciousness of a movement; the tediousness of a pro- tracted effort; the remorseless working out of natural processes of decline, decay and death; and the naturalness of the bizarre and the unexpectedness of what is most normal. Besides their affective significance, sound-symbolic adverbs have considerable performative potential for 'filling out' relatively abstract grammatical concepts such as durativity and completiveness with semantically specific portraits of actions, events, and processes.

(Nuckolls 1996: 276–7)

Or again, take the subtle onomatopoeic expression and sound symbolisms that have been noted for many African languages, especially their rich acoustic system of *ideophones*. These little sonic particles add vividness to both story-telling and every- day conversations – concise images-in-sound which directly portray elements such as distance, gait, ways of doing things, even smells and tastes (elements which out- siders might not otherwise perceive as auditory). The sound of someone walking in high-heeled shoes is evocatively and economically conveyed by *peswa-peswa* (Thonga), for example, a drunkard's gait by the acoustic image *tlikwi-tlikwi* (Thonga), light flickering on a cinema screen by *nyiri nyiri nyiri nyiri* (Shona), while *ntrr* is the sonic image of birds flying upwards in the sky or the high flight of an aero- plane or missile (Zulu). In the Ijo *Ozidi Saga* from Nigeria the sexy breasts of the witch masquerading as a young girl go *yereke yereke* 'all yearning and yielding' (Okpewho 1992: 94–5).[8]

These multifaceted acoustic qualities are not just secondary attributes but them- selves an inherent part of the auditory communicative process. In subtle and variegated ways human vocalisers actively draw on this infinitely versatile auditory resource, one which can be attuned to different circumstances and people, even 'heard' differently by different participants. Each sonic usage is unique to each communicative interaction and yet shaped by a degree of shared resonances and conventions. Its enactment goes far beyond matters of propositional reference. John Hull remarks from his experience of blindness on 'the amazing power of the human voice to reveal the person' (1997: 18) and as Bruce Smith points out in his perceptive analysis of sound in theatre, 'the object the audience hears in a human voice is character' (1999: 245).

This acoustic versatility is one side of the coin. But, on the other, it is also strik- ing that human beings have been able to forge acoustic conventions with enough endurance and acceptability to enable a huge range of purposive communication between people in many places and periods. Some non-human animals have indeed developed complex and flexible vocal processes for communicating, but humans seem to have taken it to a notably high degree. The range and complexity of their accepted vocal conventions is extraordinary.

This is emphatically not just a matter of 'grammar, syntax and vocabulary' (the traditional focus) but also of mutual conventions, shared more, or less, among the various participants, which may involve all or any of the sonic qualities mentioned above, and, as well, expectations about audiences' sound-making or the appropriate deployment of single, overlapping or other combinations of voices. All human vocal interaction relies on some combination of conventions relating to such acoustic features. Some have relatively narrow recognition, practised mainly within fairly small numbers of people. Others are widely spread, current over large areas of the world.

Certain acoustic conventions are more standardised, with applications relatively independent of their context of use ('relatively', because context is never totally irrelevant); they can also, to a degree, be combined and recombined with other sonic units and refer to abstract as well as concrete and immediate matters. Defining these communicative conventions in terms of 'words' or 'symbols' does indeed capture one important dimension. But there are also all those other sonic features like intonation, volume, speed, rhythm, intensity and style of delivery generally, as well as 'paralinguistic' vocalisations like sobbing or laughing. These too can be highly patterned, acoustic conventions which themselves have to be learned. We need to note *all* these sonic dimensions, and sometimes the (expected) 'background' noise too, not just the writable 'words'. Here is a subtle intermingling of individually sounded and -heard creations, of specific context, and of patterns which are more or less enduring and agreed with others. In its capacity to draw on auditory resources in this versatile mix of ways, human vocal interaction makes up a remarkable, highly flexible and enormously far-ranging human-created tool for sonic communication.

These acoustic elements of human vocal interaction can also be yet further marked out in specially heightened ways. There can be artful patterning even in apparently 'common and everyday' utterances of course, interwoven perhaps with pun, wit, onomatopoeia, proverbial expressions, or elements of narrative: there is no absolute divide. But there is also the undeniable fact that the human voice is also used both in (more or less) entextualised and crystallised forms and for staged performances, explicitly recognised as such – 'a specially marked, artful way of speaking', as Bauman and Briggs put it, where 'performance puts the act of speaking on display – objectifies it, lifts it to a degree from its interactional setting and opens it to scrutiny by an audience' (1990: 73, also Bauman 1977). There are the many forms of oratory, sermon and prayer; lament and love song; judicial sentencing, school boasts, or after-dinner tales; rock lyrics, rap, or political protest songs; sung or intoned church services; panegyric, epic and dance song; and all the manifold spoken and sung verbal genres found so richly throughout the world.

These artistic and specialised genres of the voice deserve some notice, for their extent and sophistication are often not properly appreciated. Some are relatively simple – or simple at first sight but still, like the 'minor form' of rhythmic or tonal riddling found in many places in Africa, resting on subtle sonic interchanges. West

African Mosi word-games, for example, depend on clever interchanges of tonally patterned phrases, taxing the cognitive and auditory ingenuity of the players (Kawada 1996: 47–8), and throughout Africa proverbs, praise names, even salutations and farewells often have artful sonic patterning. And then there are the high-flown panegyrics and great oral epics of the past or present, performed through the arts of the speaking, intoning or singing human voice in solo or dialogue, sometimes with instrumental accompaniment. In many cultures the arts of oratory are the focus of particular elaboration. Shorter oral forms too display their own artistic conventions, from the Beatles songs or 'miniature' Somali love lyrics to the unwritten poems of the Gilbert Islands (Kiribati) composed by the solitary reflective poet and performed by rehearsed mass choirs in thronged public ceremonies. Laments are widely found too, probably a universal genre of human interaction. In Caucasian Georgia, to take just one example, laments draw on elaborate stylistic conventions. They are performed in spoken or sung pulse units (lines) with crying sounds, voice changes, drawn-out sighs, voice modulations, slowly falling intonational contours with integrated peaks, and expressive lexicon together with constructed dialogue, multiple address and vivid imagery; the emotion is deeply felt, but managed and communicated through the artful conventions of the genre (Kotthoff 2000, 2001).

Earlier assumptions would have it that unwritten vocal forms were essentially crude and lacking in artistry, to be sidelined as 'traditional' or 'tribal'. But it is now clear that in both past and present many of these performed oral genres partake of the poetry and creativity that we associate with literature. Indeed unwritten acoustic arts can be all the more creative precisely because their enactors can call on the diverse range of acoustic subtleties noted above as they engage in live performances to and among active participants. There is often one lead voice, but other voices too may contribute to the complexity as duet, dialogue, overlap, backing track or responsive chorus, linking the participants into a multiply performing group. We have here a set of extraordinarily developed art-ful forms of human communication, widely practised throughout the world in both past and present, which relies on the portable vehicle of the human voice and on the enactors' ability both to hear this in accordance with locally recognised conventions and to take part in the sonic action themselves.[9]

Human-made instruments too are at times the centre of elaborate specialisation, sometimes alongside the human voice, sometimes sounding independently. The European post horn had special sounds to report the type of mail being carried (express, normal, local, packages) or to announce arrival, departure, distress, or the number of carriages and horses, giving the changing stations advance notice of their needs (Schafer 1977: 47). French village bells had traditional local forms for making announcements, often varying by parish: the widely understood hurried and uneven clang of the warning tocsin, but also the specialised rings for weddings, baptisms or deaths. In one locality three peals on the large bell meant a boy's baptism,

Figure 3.1 West African drums
Drums and drumming run through much communicating in West Africa. There are many different forms, played in multiply diverse contexts – for announcements, messages, rituals, dance, drama, praise and much else. This figure shows just two: left, announcement drum outside a government building in northern Sierra Leone in the 1960s, used to publicise particular times, occasions and duties; right, a Yoruba drummer in Nigeria prepared to sing and praise (Photographs: David Murray).

two on the smaller bell that of a girl; in another a married man's death was announced by three strikes of the great bell, a married woman's by three on the second bell, and a third bell used for the unmarried (Corbin 1999: 159, 164, 192). These auditory systems work even where vision is limited. Foghorns travel over misty seas, drums penetrate dense tropical forests, and hunting horns or army bugles allow people to keep in touch even if dispersed over a wide terrain.

The so-called 'drum languages' are especially effective for conveying acoustic messages across space, found in many places throughout the world, from Africa and Amazonia to Oceania. These mostly exploit the capacity of the human ear to hear fluctuations of pitch and/or rhythm over distance, whether through drum beats, whistles, horns, or vocal yodelling. In West and Central Africa drums sound out patterns of contrasting pitches which are heard as speech tones; or rather, to put it more precisely, as the longer poetic phrases conventionally used in this form of communication. Among the Congolese Kele, for example, the words for 'manioc', 'plantain', 'above' and 'forest' have the same tones, but drum communications avoid ambiguities by transmitting longer phrases like 'the manioc which remains in the fallow ground' or 'plantain to be propped up'. 'Money' is drummed as 'the pieces of metal which arrange palavers', 'month' as 'the moon looks down at the earth'. Births, marriages, deaths, hunts or wrestling matches are announced through this drum system (for further examples and discussion see Carrington 1949, Finnegan 1970: 481ff, Sebeok and Umiker-Sebeok 1976).

Drummed communicating is prominent on ceremonial occasions. In West Africa, announcing and praising through drums is a kind of panegyric poetry, practised by experts as a specialist and complex art. In Ghana, a poetic salute was drummed out as the chief entered:

> Chief, you are about to sit down,
> Sit down, gracious one.
> Sit down, great one.
> Chief you have plenty of seating space.
> Like the great branch, you have spread all over this place.
> Let us crouch before him with swords of state.
> Chief, you are like the moon about to emerge.
> Noble ruler to whom we are indebted,
> You are like the moon:
> Your appearance disperses famine.
>
> (Nketia 1963: 147)

The communicating is overwhelmingly sonic, heightened by the stirring and public mode of delivery and conveying by loud and distance-reaching sounds the glories of authority.

These examples are already merging into the forms of musical communication so widely found among human beings. Debates about 'the definition' of 'music' are beyond my scope here, except for pointing out that the commonly made distinctions between musical and spoken communication ('music' and 'language') are hard to maintain in any absolute terms, both because of the great diversity of taxonomies in different cultural traditions and because the deliberate deployment and recognition of tone, rhythm and melody are unquestionably features of spoken expression too. But if we take 'music' in the broadest sense of patterned sound characterised by the deliberate deployment and recognition of such acoustic features as tone, rhythm and melody, then music is a notable dimension of many forms of human interaction. Song, chant, lament, rhythm, and melodically contoured speaking are common modes of human interconnection, performed in a whole series of ways – not just via the audience–performer separation characteristic of certain types of western classical music but also the more engaging call-response or audience-participation modes found so widely throughout the world. These and similarly patterned sounds can construct their own special atmosphere and contexts of interconnectedness, often transcending or amplifying more referential meanings and playing at the least an equal part with 'words' in the communicative process as a whole.

Musical communicating is often expressed through the human voice. But other sounds are used too, both separate and intermingled. There is a vast range of human-made instruments where sounds are ingeniously created by air, by string(s), by the body of the instrument itself, by a stretched membrane, or by electrical means. These are sounded in manifold combinations and situations. They add lustre to events, celebrate rituals and delight their participants. They are often a prominent dimension of auditory communication on religious and public occasions – Limba or Yoruba drumming, gamelan orchestras, Orange flute and drum processions in Ulster, Chinese opera, folk guitar singers, rock gigs, Indian raga, the great oratorios of western classical music and a host of other performances. In Malaysian healing rituals the medium's song is 'the conduit through which the spirit guide emerges and communicates' and sound plays a key role in personal and cosmological transformations (Roseman 1988: 813). These arts too form part of human auditory resources. Indeed many would regard such musical forms as among the great glories of human communication.

No more than contextless 'words' can 'musical sounds' communicate on their own. But humans have made use of them, turning their patterned usages of sound to a whole series of organised purposes in keeping with their ways of life and social ordering. As with spoken language referential meaning is sometimes in play, but often just as one aspect in a spectrum that shades imperceptibly into shared bodily experience (more or less shared, that is), emotive ambience and sonic association. John Blacking would go further, following Schutz (1951) in seeing the role of music as central to human interconnectedness, with 'some kind of tuning-in relationship . . . at the heart of all effective (and affecting) social interaction, [as] people organize their bodies in mutually agreeable and intelligible ways without the need to rationalize' (Blacking 1991: 68).

None of all these acoustic arts are free floating, unrelated to other aspects of the human social order. As a powerful channel for human communication, sound is not only widely exploited in human cultures, it is also organised and regulated both in its more specialist overt forms and in the informal, often unnoticed, ways in which people communicate acoustically every day of their lives.

Some controls are explicit. The interest of authority in regulating noise was a familiar part of life as far back as the ancient Sumerian *Epic of Gilgamesh*, the prelude to the flood.

> In those days the world teemed, the people multiplied, the world bellowed like a wild bull, and the great god was aroused by the clamour. Enlil heard the clamour and he said to the gods in council, 'The uproar of mankind is

intolerable and sleep is no longer possible by reason of the babel'. So the gods agreed to exterminate mankind.

(Sandars (transl) 1964: 108)

More recent governments too take pains (if in less drastic fashion) to control acoustic communication and its media – the range of legal restrictions on particular sounds is well illustrated in the bye-laws of the city of Bern (see Box 3.1).

Box 3.1 Some seventeenth- to twentieth-century bye-laws controlling sound in the city of Bern, Switzerland

Based on data from the municipal archives (as reported in Schafer 1977: 190, a selection only).

Year passed	Bye-law
1628	Against singing and shouting in streets or houses on festival days
1661	Against shouting, crying or creating nuisances on Sunday
1743	For respect of the Sabbath
1763	Against noisy conduct at night and establishing regulations for night watchmen
1784	Against barking dogs
1788	Against noises in the vicinity of churches
1878	Against noises near hospitals and the sick
1879	Against the playing of music after 10.30 p.m.
1911	Against noisy music, singing at Christmas and New Year's parties and against unnecessary cracking of whips at night
1914	Against carpet-beating and noisy children
1918	Against carpet-beating and music-making
1927	Against noisy children
1936	Against bells, horns and shouting of vendors
1939	Against excessive noises on holidays
1961	Against commercial and domestic noises
1967	For the preservation of quiet on Sundays

It is not just noise in general, of course, but its form and context. During the early development of polyphony in the fourteenth century, the Pope tried to ban the new forms:

> Semibreves and minims and . . . notes of small value . . . voices incessantly running to and fro. . . . Devotion, the true end of worship, is little thought of, and wantonness, which ought to be eschewed, increases. . . . We straightly command that no one henceforward shall think himself at liberty to attempt those methods, or methods like them in the . . . Offices, and especially in the canonical Hours, or in the solemn celebrations of the Mass.
>
> (1322 decree, in Wooldridge 1929: 295–6)

The Council of Toulouse in 1590 expressly prohibited the 'ringing of bells in any church before those of the Cathedral or of the mother church had given the signal' (quoted in Corbin 1999: 98), part of its claim to the mastery of airborne sound; in France a cathedral was allowed five to seven bells, lesser churches two or three, and there were bitter and continuing battles between religious and municipal authorities for auditory control. The sounding of the loudest instruments is commonly reserved to those in power.

Implicit conventions can be powerful too. When and how to speak or keep silent, or who has the right to sound in what situation and in what manner, are not random matters. Members of certain groups may or may not make particular sounds in given contexts, and the expected ways of speaking both limit and extend individuals' vocal communicating. At the teacher's or the ruler's voice others must fall silent. 'Children should be seen and not heard', it used to be said, and I still recall the text displayed in my first school telling us that a woman's voice should be 'soft, gentle and low'. Acoustic conventions can be disputed or altered too: witness the current conflicts over the sounds of mobile phones in 'public' yet personal space, or the empassioned battles over new musical styles of which the fourteenth-century papal reaction to 'semibreves . . .' is only one example.

Many roles and situations have their implicitly regulated acoustic forms, from disc jockeys, auctioneers or readers of broadcast shipping forecasts to newspaper sellers, Georgian lamenters, and Yugoslav epic singers. Becoming a member of an occupational or professional group often means adopting their patterns of sound-making, part of the way they project themselves and their messages. As Ostwald points out, it is often possible to identify clergymen, lawyers, teachers, and other professionals from their voices alone, and

> Special privileges about sound-making are given to some occupations. Bell-ringers, organists, cantors, and priests have the right to intone the sounds of religious worship. Clowns and acrobats are permitted to entertain their audiences with raucous and impolite noises. Policemen carry big sticks and loud whistles. Singers and musicians who belong to the proper union can provide the noise for public meetings. Bandleaders and prompters can dictate the beginning

and end of sound-making. Trumpeters, announcers, and hosts raise curtains with sounds.

(Ostwald 1973: 33–4)

Specific genres and settings for acoustic communication are regularly governed by (relatively) shared and culturally specific conventions. Even where these are below the level of conscious awareness they form an influential dimension structuring our ways of communicating. In churches the notes of the organ and the building's sonic ambience mark the division from 'secular' space outside and set the frame for the gathering's interaction, just as in certain pubs the familiar noises of customers, glasses, low-raftered rooms, wooden tables and specific musical instruments mould the expectations and experiences of their participants. When two individuals in a noisy street move together into close acoustic space their conversing takes on a different quality. Or recall the Limba initiations in Sierra Leone (Chapter 1) where the ritual was acoustically marked by specific genres of drumming together with the singing, clapping, shouts and other voiced sounds from the crowd. These sounds both defined and constituted the publicly communicated rite of validating the transition from boyhood. The sonic setting shapes people's communicating. To quote Ostwald again:

> The blend of noise at a cocktail party, for example, creates an atmosphere, one of impersonality. There are tinkling glasses, jumbled voices, and soft music. . . . With the background noise of the party . . . statements like 'How are you' are taken as greetings, not questions. In another setting the words would have a different implication. In the psychiatrist's consultation room, for instance, atmosphere is provided by a muffled silence. This, plus other cues of privacy, prepare the patient to respond to 'How are you?' with a detailed recital of his personal problems.
>
> (Ostwald 1973: 41)

Here the nature and combination of sounds act together to define particular situations and, far from being 'mere' context, are themselves part of the communicative process. Their (culturally specific) resonances are actively in play. The rustle of clothing, resonances of engine noises or splashing oars, sonic ambience of an intimate interchange in an enclosed alcove, tuning-up before an orchestral concert, multiple yells of football supporters amidst the sounds of ball, kicks and whistles, or a speaker's ringing tones in an echoic building – in all these the participants' interactions and experiences are in part formulated through aspects of sound. As radio broadcasters and sound recordists know well, sonic features are not additional extras but essential dimensions of the process of communication itself.

As Ostwald implies, we need to take account of the complex 'blend of noise'. In vocal communication, for example, multiple sonic dimensions are in play. We may picture human speech as made up of 'words', units transcribable on a written page. But we know in practice, even if we forget in theory, that when we communicate through speaking we depend not just on these (writable) units but also on the swirls of sonic sequences and combinations from intonation, volume, pacing and silences; from people's sniffs, sighs, giggles or voiced hesitations; from the inter-acting sounds and rhythms of 'listeners' as well as 'speakers'. Sonic dimensions are not irrelevant even in forms of communicating which at first seem non-auditory, like reading or writing. Think of the hushed (but not soundless) atmosphere of a great library, helping to shape the reader's and writer's approach to the visible pages; reading aloud at Victorian bedtimes; non-lettered migrants dictating to letter-writers on the West African coast; the sonority of church Bible readings; or, even for solitary students in the quiet of the night, the sonic ambiences of wind or distant traffic, the ticking of a clock, scrape of pen, tap of keys, or rustle of page. In other words *all* the sonic elements produced and experienced among people may shape their interaction, not just those privileged in certain ideologies as being what 'really' matters.

Communicating through sound is thus not just a personal and ad hoc matter, but inevitably linked into local situations and specific social, economic and political arrangements. This affects how sound is formulated and used: the occasions open to various classes of participants, the sounds valued or prohibited, the speakers or hearers authorised or not authorised, the battles over patronage or control, and the often unspoken but nonetheless powerful sonic structuring of people's experiences. These variegated conventions both regulate auditory communicating and at the same time offer human beings an amazing wealth of developed sonic arts through which to further their interconnectedness.

Sonic creation and experience in a wealth of cultures

Our uses of audition are not the same everywhere and humans have exploited this rich diversity of communicative resources in multiple different ways. This point deserves some attention. It takes some effort of imagination to realise that our sonic environments and practices are not just part of the 'natural' world nor an unchang-ing backdrop to human affairs, but developed through human action in specific historical circumstances as people select, interpret and attend to the sounds they make and hear. There is also the question of whether there are broader distinctions between different types of societies in their treatment of sound: the 'modern west' perhaps against other cultures of the past or present?

A few examples can illustrate some of the diversities. The first comes from the Kaluli people of Papua New Guinea who have developed sound and sound symbol-ism to a high degree (see Steven Feld's ethnographic accounts in (among others) 1986, 1990, 1995, 1996). The Kaluli live in remote settlements scattered through the tropical rain forests of the Great Papuan Plateau, a forest environment in which they cannot see far. They depend greatly on sound to assess such features as height, depth, distance, and location. 'Kaluli must and do depend on their ears', Feld explains, 'and . . . this dependency is elaborated into artistic/expressive forms and aesthetic ideologies' (Feld 1986: 22). Sound is central in Kaluli experience, extending not just to their music but to their cultural system as a whole.

> They locate distance, hunt, reckon space, and cycles of seasons and daily time by sounds. The Kaluli language is enormously rich in onomatopoeic and iconic devices, and Kaluli claim that the tones of their scales come from bird calls; they sing with, to and about birds, cicadas and waterfalls; they have an elaborate taxonomy of sounds based on water metaphors and these are utilized as theoretical concepts to explain and discuss music.
>
> (Feld 1986: 21)

Sound figures prominently in Kaluli cosmology for birds and humans are transformations of each other, experienced through their voices. Visible and invisible reality is transcended and linked through the production and perception of sounds. Kaluli invoke the symbolism (and actuality) of birds or waterfalls in their imaginative encapturing of the world: composing a song is like 'having a waterfall in your head', and Kaluli often compose and sing sitting by a stream where, they say, 'the flow of water fills their minds with ideas' (Feld *et al.* 1991). The aesthetics of song are strongly linked to water, and onomatopoeic words evoke the sounds of swirling waterpool, bubbling creek, splashing waterfall, water flowing through rocks, or the sprinkling of mist rising from white water.

The reality of auditory experience and imagery for the Kaluli comes through with vivid immediacy in the audio-recording *Voices of the Rainforest* (Feld *et al.* 1991) which conveys a Kaluli day's sonic experience. As the day's soundscape unfolds we hear, with the Kaluli, the natural rhythms of the forest and the songs and drumming of the Kaluli themselves. It starts with early morning sounds – buzzing insects amidst wet mists and dripping leaves, then the dawn voices of myriad birds, their calls overlapping and interacting; then on through the work and sounds and songs of the day; the singing and relaxing by gently flowing creek waters; again the swelling of bird voices; the drumming sounds of a rainstorm beating on thatch in cross-rhythms with insects and frogs; ceremonial drumming and song assimilating the intensely emotional pulsations of the *tibodai* bird's voice and its evocations of a dead child calling through the drum for its father, moving its participants to tears. Finally the creatures of the 'inside night' are heard as owls and eerie insects join their voices until the morning sounds begin again.

> It's a never-ending and dense soundscape. And with it Kaluli sing along and beat out their own rhythms using the primal percussion of bamboo and palm canes,

stone pounders, machetes and axes. . . . [They] think of themselves as 'voices in the forest'. They sing with birds, insects, water. And when Kaluli sing with them, they sing like them. Nature is music to Kaluli ears. And Kaluli music is naturally part of the surrounding soundscape.

(Feld *et al.* 1991)

All Kaluli interaction takes place in this multilayered soundscape and the far-reaching sonic evocations through which they experience the world – an acoustic epistemology.

Other anthropological studies have similarly been revealing the special value some cultures attach to acoustic communication and the individual lines on which they exploit this. Researchers in South America have been particularly eloquent on this. Seeger's account of the Brazilian Suyá Indians shows their emphasis on hearing and speaking (not vision) as key social faculties (1981: 83, 86). For them, the height of oral expression lies in song, and music underlies their construction of social and conceptual relationships (Seeger 1981: 86, 1987). The Brazilian Kalapalo also hold a 'musical view of the universe' (Basso 1985) and their ritual performances are centred on sound – a 'powerful mode of communication . . . the experience of a unity of cosmic forces, developed through the unity of sound formed by creative motion' (Basso 1985: 243).

Through sound symbols, ideas about relationships, activities, causalities, processes, goals, consequences, and states of mind are conceived, represented, and rendered apparent to the world. It is through sound that cosmic entities are rendered into being and represented by the Kalapalo . . . in a veritable musical ecology of the spirit.

(Basso 1985: 311)

Among the West African Songhay sound is the foundation of experience. In the local healer's words to the anthropologist Paul Stoller, 'without sight or touch . . . one can learn a great deal. But you *must* learn how to hear or you will learn little about our ways' (Stoller 1984: 560). The sounds of sacred musical instruments link Songhay of past and present, auditory presences that transform people morally, politically and magically. Their musicians and healers have to *hear*. They learn how sound links the inner and outer worlds, the visible and the invisible, the tangible and intangible, for 'outer and inner worlds interpenetrate in . . . a world in which sound is a foundation' (1984: 563). For the Songhay sound structures the world, a dimension of experience with its own existence.

Alain Corbin's striking account of bells in the nineteenth-century French countryside (1999) reminds us that it is not only in non-western cultures that sound can play a deeply significant role. These French village communities could not live without their bells and in the early nineteenth century were ready to spend more on reconstituting peals destroyed in the Revolution than on relieving poverty or promoting education (Corbin 1999: x). Bells were the focus of village identity and the occasion for innumerable passionate struggles over both the bells themselves and the authority to ring them.

> Possessing a peal of bells was a prerequisite of modernity in a society increasingly subject to haste but as yet without any other means of transmitting information instantaneously.

> The bell was also the voice of authority and the means by which public announcements were made. It prevailed over rumor because it alone could mark what was new in the sea of truth.
>
> (Corbin 1999: x)

Bells were not the only instrumental sounds employed in local communication. But they dominated public auditory space to a degree it is almost impossible to exaggerate. Their sounds drowned all others: 'within aerial space, over which it still held a monopoly, the bronze voice, falling from above, hammered home the injunctions of authority; it called to mind the . . . system of norms' (Corbin 1999: x–xi).

The types of bells and ways of sounding them had specific uses, marked by well-understood conventions within local areas, and, as well, by deeply symbolic resonances. The distinctive tocsin strike sounded the alarm for fire, flood or external attack, and recognised bell combinations broadcast information about major events in personal life cycles and solemnised rites of passage – 'a sort of auditory certification' (Corbin 1999: x).

> The bell called upon listeners to foregather. It summoned people to religious services and punctuated their most solemn moments. It called them to prayer, and sacralized its auditory territory. The theologians of the Catholic Reformation ascribed to it the power to open a path for the good angels from heaven and ward off the creatures of hell. It was the bell that announced festivals on the eve of their celebration, and the proclaimed collective rejoicing. It imparted a rhythm to the ordinary functioning of the community. As an auditory synchronizer, the bell told its listeners when the market had opened, when the tax collector had arrived, when a flock had set off for the mountains, when the wine harvest was declared, when the community's bell was present, or when the work on the roads had recommenced. As a consequence, a subtle auditory rhetoric was developed. A bell had to have its own language, which varied from one commune to the next.
>
> (Corbin 1999: xi)

In some settings, then, it seems that sound is very specially valued. Studies like those above enlarge our appreciation of the auditory resources and symbolisms exploited

Figure 3.2 Village bells across the French countryside
Now as in the past the church and its belltower dominate the traditional hilltop villages of France, where farmers and winegrowers live in the heart of the village and go out to work the surrounding fields. Bells still call the hours and half-hours and still peal for morning and evening services, sounds audible from a couple of kilometres away across the hills. Reminders about completing official forms, announcements of festivals and entertainment, or requests about lost property, are heralded by a brief burst of accordion music, followed by an official voice, 'Allô, Allô . . .'

in human communication.[10] They also raise more general issues. It has been forcibly argued that together they present a challenge to deeply rooted western assumptions. Stoller uses the Songhay case to mount a strong critique of western epistemology, contrasting the Songhay approach to sound with the emphasis on the eye in western thought and citing Zukerkandl's argument (1958) that the 'gaze' of western thought has ignored the dimension of sound (Stoller 1984: 560). Parallel points are now being made by scholars from many disciplines. The modern west, it is argued, has privileged vision and verbal-cognitive conceptual models at the expense of the acoustic dimensions of human experience and action. An examination of this complex set of arguments must be postponed until Chapter 5, where it can be considered in the light of the later discussion of visual communication, but two immediate points can be made now.

First, whatever the comparative sensory 'ratio' (if indeed that can be measured), sound is in practice prominent in contemporary western communication. Consider the auditory signals of sirens, gongs, bells; our shouts, cries and sighs; the formative sound-ambiences of buildings, streets or mountains; chimes and ticks of clocks, pipping of electronic computers and calculators; the subtle uses of microphones; the massive proliferation of sound in modern cities, from traffic signals to mobile phones; and of course the hugely influential acoustic processes of vocal interaction through personal conversations, public address systems, market cries, songs, storytelling, oratory – the huge and diverse range in which the human voice is used. In the last couple of centuries, furthermore, humans have in fact extended their auditory communicating through telephone, wireless, film, mobiles, audio-recording and 'virtual' sound-making. Now as in the past human beings use sounds to manipulate and manage social interactions 'whether these involve conversation, intrigue, seduction, entertainment, education, or other mutual activities' (Ostwald 1973: 41). An extensive reliance on acoustic communication is emphatically not just something of 'other cultures' far away or long ago.

Generalisations about broad cultural variations also miss a second point: the detailed multiplicities and changes at any one time, including in our own current practices. The treatment of sound does not always stay the same in any given group nor is it always operated in the same way by all its individuals or sections. One possibility is indeed that a series of developments may now be flowing together to result in greater use (or anyway awareness) of audition in the contemporary west. The performance genres of music emerging over several decades together with audio-recordings, microphones and wider circulation of non-western musics have all provided a counter to the traditionally valued visual (or written) dimensions of music. They have certainly increased our sensitivities to its *sonic* qualities – voice, timbre, rhythm, performance and active participation. As Van Leeuwen suggests:

> In contemporary popular music, sound matters more. Key singers and instrumentalists develop their own, immediately recognizable styles of singing and playing, and, thanks to recording, these can now become part of the language of music and be imitated and transformed by countless others. Saxophones can be soft and mellow, or tense and strident, sound like a hoarse whisper or a foghorn in the mist. Voices can be soft, smooth and well oiled, or rough, raspy and cracked. And singers as well as instrumentalists use a large repertoire of howls, wails, groans and other vocalizations.
>
> (Van Leeuwen 1999: 127)

Broadcast, telephone and computer technologies have similarly encouraged a fuller appreciation of sound, while personal stereos and, more recently, mobile phones have become a regular feature of both street and home life. There have been effects from the 'oracy' move in schools, 'communication skills' in business and higher education, and the challenges (albeit ambivalent and shifting) to 'the written word'. As in the famous 1990s British Telecom advertisements, it has become 'good to talk' – not just on the telephone but in schools, therapy, customer relations and the 'enterprise' culture (Cameron 2000).

The situation is complicated, however. New technologies simultaneously highlight the visual, and in any case specific role(s) of sound are differentially taken up – and no doubt always have been – not just on differing occasions but by different generations, interest groups or occupations. Just as in the demoting of sound said to have resulted from the spread of print or from cheapening newspaper and book production, so too with more recent developments – the complexities are unlikely to be captured by a single measure.

A generalised calculation of 'sound' versus 'sight' blurs internal changes and variations. The communicative roles of sound are indeed exploited and conceived differently in different human environments, and are as open to change and to conflicting and differentiated usages as any other aspect of culture. But this is a matter of multiplex and specific practices rather than a monolithic continuum with cultures dominated by sound lying at one end and the visual and verbal west at the other.

The limits and versatilities of audition

Does sound have particular implications for human communicating? The general strengths of audition as a communicative channel are commonly said to include its spatial range, relative rapidity, effectiveness in conditions of limited or obstructed vision, and its great variety (see the summary in Box 2.5 on p. 50 above). On the other hand sound does not linger, its location is often hard to pinpoint, and it can be drowned out by other sounds.

Human beings certainly make good use of the complexity and variety of sound. As we have seen, sounds can be produced and communicated in an immense diversity of ways not only across the animal kingdom in general but also by the human species: through vocalisation; by other bodily movements, such as beating, blowing, scraping; and by deploying an astonishing range of external materials and instruments. The multiple properties of sound can be exploited with almost infinite subtlety: volume, pitch, melody, tempo, rhythm, frequencies, duration, harshness, intensity or stress – to mention only some – and the human ear is attuned to discriminate them. They are drawn on in multifarious ways, interacting with specific institutions, expectations and epistemologies, and with differing environmental conditions and the demands of different situations.

The most obvious uses of audition come among humans interacting together at a specific place and time (for example through vocal interchange between two or three people within easy earshot of each other). But human communicating also happens – or might be desired – over much larger geographical and temporal distances. So how is the auditory channel placed for the perennial human issues of communicating across time and space?

The spatial range of audition is crucial here. To a greater degree than vision or, even more, than touch, sound travels. It can be heard across long distances both on land and, even more, through water. This quality is extensively exploited in human communicating. It is useful even for short distances. We call out, and are heard, from one room to another, knock on doors or floor, snap fingers or clap hands to attract a waiter's attention across the room, whistle to our friends or dogs during a walk in the woods – all more effective than using vision. The same distance-conquering capacity – but more so – is utilised in street and market cries, the muezzin's resonant call to prayer, church towers in France (and not just France) and the ringing of school bells. Shrieks and shouts carry across the intervening space, sailors call across the water. As mainly land-dwelling creatures, humans cannot easily match the huge distances across which aquatic animals transmit their sounds, but they have nonetheless developed manifold skills to extend the distance-carrying potential of the human voice. Echoic chanting in large buildings, calling across wide valleys, processional song in the open air, the aerially transmitted tocsin, and

Figure 3.3 The sound of Islam through the bush: mosque in northern Sierra Leone
Tall slender minarets with their open balconies provide effective vantage points for the wide distribution of sound as the muezzin calls the faithful to prayer. Like the upstanding French belltower of Figure 3.2 but in a very different cultural setting, their height and prominence facilitate auditory communicating over the surrounding area, here amidst the huts, tin roofs and palm trees of northern Sierra Leone (Photograph: David Murray, 1964).

public oratory ringingly declaimed to a large audience are merely some of the multifarious examples. And those with the power to do so have created larger structures to enhance the carrying powers of their voices and instruments, from high bell towers and minarets to pulpits, platforms and daised thrones.

Very much longer distances are possible too, for humans have created a multiplicity of external instruments to supplement the span of the immediate human voice. Post horns transmit signals through the countryside, sirens sound across a city, drum messages travel through expanses of forest or mountain. Brass bands in the streets, explosive sounds of fireworks, ships' horns and lighthouse bells across the sea – all depend on the capacity of sound to communicate across distance. And electrical and electronic technologies enable transmission of sound over ever greater distances through telephones, radio, television and computers as well as by ultrasonic means through the sea. It is not just a matter of overcoming distance but also of manipulating it. People organise the sounds they make to suit the intended spread of their communicating. Contrast the low-voiced intimate interaction between two close participants with a ringing declamation to a massed audience or resonating drums across the forest, integrating scattered listeners – whether they wish it or not – into shared acoustic space. By its nature sound, more than vision, can be actively directed to define communicative space and those participating in it.

Closely related to sound's spatial power is its capacity to go around obstacles – not perfectly, but better than vision – and to travel even in conditions of limited visibility. When we want to communicate with someone out of sight we call out. We utilise this property of audition by knocks at the door, ships' foghorns, communication in the dark, acoustic signals through dense forests, or church bells ringing out to peasant farmers in the remoter fields and pastures of the French countryside. It is exploited too in the practices of talking, story-telling, singing, or instrumental music on unlit evenings. Relatively poor visibility is not an uncommon setting for human communicating and here sound offers both an alternative and a supplement to sight. Vision mostly gives us the skin of things, the surfaces that can be seen and measured. Sounds and hearing take us around and inside.

Time is another problem again. Unlike smell or vision, sound does not linger and once produced it disappears without trace. We are well acquainted with this impermanence in our acoustic communicating – both advantage and disadvantage depending on your situation. Spoken promises, whispers in the dark, the secret tapping out of a morse message, or ambulance sirens through the streets leave no tangible record. Nor do telephone conversations, warning bells, or even the most magnificent of auditory performances whether by great orchestras, public orators or village story-tellers – the sound dies leaving nothing behind. It enables secrecy, flexibility and informal interactions that would be different if articulated into fixed visible form.

Humans beings have also attempted devices for – to a degree – extending these vanishing sounds. One strategy is to try to capture certain aspects of audition in another medium, for example in writing or in the variety of systems for encapsulating and communicating musical sounds in fixed visual form (Figure 3.4 illustrates the notated tradition of western classical music, but there are others too, among them the earlier western system visible in the fifteenth-century missal in Figure 7.2 and the Japanese directions for vocal performance in Figure 10.3). Then there are the technologies developed over the last century or so enabling the relatively permanent storage and reproduction of sound – or rather, since recording is a creative rather than merely mechanical process, of particular formulations of sounds. It might be argued that current technologies now allow sound to conquer time; maybe space too since audio-recordings can be transported in physically durable form. This would go too far: the sounds when replayed still die equally quickly on each occasion. But these are certainly now important human-created artefacts which up to a point circumvent the short-lived nature of auditory communication.

Allied to the ephemerality of sound is the successive nature of auditory communication. One sound *follows* another. We utter and hear words one after the other and not all at once, play through a musical performance over a period of time, listen to the unfolding of a story in order. Unlike vision, audition is sequential: in marked contrast to a picture, sounds come in turn rather than simultaneously.

This has implications for human communicating. The time-specific nature of audition makes it an apt tool for the sequential marking of events in both real and imagined time. It facilitates temporally ordered communications like vocal greetings, musical performances, and a wide variety of oral literary genres; drives on the time-ordered stages of rituals; and meets the needs of that recurrent form of human communicating, narration. Hearing much more than seeing captures 'the dynamics of things coming into being over time' (Wulf 1993: 10 as translated in Van Leeuwen 1999: 195). The human creators of sounds build temporal sequences through subtle sonic reorderings – alternating different vocal timbres or combinations, varying rhythms or intensities, sequential changes of loud/soft or sound/silence, different acoustic interactions with audiences at different times. These temporally framed sonic forms of communicating, realised in a wide range of complex formulations, are immediate and *event*-ful in a very different way from visual communication.

We should not exaggerate this 'single-strike' quality of sound, for the human ear is marvellously able to detect and select from a number of concurrent sounds. Conversations involve overlapping speakers, we are all experienced in hearing several things at once, and the human arts include deliberate combinations of sounds in vocal and instrumental performances. Up to a point we can hear several sounds simultaneously – hence the importance of taking note of *all* the sonic dimensions of our interactions. But only up to a point. One sound can overpower others or, alternatively, itself be drowned out. We know in practice that speaking extra loudly or penetratingly can dominate or break into a conversation, on the same principle as the local vicar who cheerfully encourages parents to bring children to church with 'don't worry, they won't disrupt the service – *I* have the microphone!'. As

Figure 3.4 Western musical notation: 'the Hallelujah chorus'

Western classical music commonly uses a system of abstract symbols to convey sequences and combinations of sounds, showing their temporal ordering and relationships by spatial layout and positioning. This is (a visual version of) the opening bars of a chorus in Handel's *Messiah*, a much-performed work in the English choral repertoire with manifold associations for performers and audiences through both biblical references and the familiarity of the musical sounds and their enactment. The written score, though a guide to performance and in the western classical tradition sometimes pictured as equated with it, does not encapsulate all the actual performance practices, like specifics of dynamics, timing, balance, timbre, breathing, emotive force or vocal delivery – these cumulatively vary in each performance. Such scores remain a *visual* and necessarily incomplete representation of an auditory (and bodily) performance (reproduced from a choral singer's copy of *The Messiah* (London, Novello and Company, about 1902), in private possession).

performers or speakers we try to hush other noises to gain attention for our own sounds. The struggles over bells between mayor and priest in the French country-side were no coincidence, for those in positions of power commonly seek to control sound and silence so that the dominating noises are their own. Again and again the instruments for transmitting the loudest sounds – drums, bells, cannons, blazoning trumpets and, more recently, microphones – are associated with the occasions of the powerful, the most piercing way to dominate the sound-carrying air and the means of auditory communication.

The difficulty of hearing too many sounds at once also throws light on chang-ing usages. In the streets of eighteenth-century European towns tradesmen's cries and songs were commonly used for advertising their wares; but with the contin-uous clamour from traffic, industry and broadcast sound, visual street signs are now more effective for informing passers by (Schafer 1994). The sounds of French bells became less prominent with the increasing spread of household clocks, newspapers and a more effective postal service, and their earlier monop-oly of aerial sound has now been surpassed and neutralised by the sounds of aeroplanes (Corbin 1999: 97, 214).

At the same time its immediacy still makes sound an effective and rapid way of commanding notice. People clear their throats or bang with a gavel to draw atten-tion to the auditory communication about to follow. Sound is a good resource not just for maintaining contact with others but also for initiating it, and attracting attention acoustically is part of everyday experience. It is especially effective with sudden and abrupt sounds. Telephone rings command our response, players call out to team-mates, loudspeakers, sirens and gunshots sound insistently to control crowd movements. Sound is useful even where vision plays some part too: things can only be seen if people are looking, and a sound-transmitted signal can direct inter-est and activate sight. As among other animals, sound is good for warning or announcing. Bicycle bells or car horns do so in the streets, and sudden shouts cap-ture urgent attention. The passage of time is often signalled by sounds too; the chimes of a clock tower or buzz of an alarm clock convey a more immediate mes-sage than the quiet signs on its face. In the same way drum beats and other vocal or instrumental sounds not only celebrate the entry of a personage but focus people's attention on it more speedily and directly than vision on its own could manage.

This capturing property of sound is all the more effective precisely because we have little defence against the dominant sound of the moment. To things seen we can shut our eyes; but there is no easy way for us to close our ears. The 'wrap-around' invading quality of sound is the more pervasive because of the spacial ability of sound, going round corners and surmounting obstacles. So auditory com-munication is especially effective for incorporating and marshalling people. One of its fortes lies in coordinating rhythmic movements like marching, processing, danc-ing, working on the assembly line, or the active experience of jointly participating in musical performances.

Sound is the more encompassing because of its physical reverberations. Rhythm and tempo have effects in the body, and can change the heartbeat, respiration and adrenalin of the participants. Music, it has been suggested, is experienced with the whole body (Blacking 1976: 110–11) and sound can be hypnotic and exhilarating, drawing people inescapably out of themselves and into a common communicative ambience. Its effects lie not just in the sounds themselves, however, but also in their symbolic and experiential associations. Some are experienced as carrying deeply emotive resonances, moving experience from the mundane to the transcendental or whipping up the passions of a crowd – the violent sounds of tocsin, whistle, gun or drum have accompanied not a few battles and massacres. Acoustic sequences in rituals actively engage the participants and the affective associations of sound are widely utilised in creating active and emotive co-experience. The mind-binding and body-moving effects of drum-beats have often been noted, and sound, especially rhythmic sound, is widely used to alter consciousness and mobilise participants into one coordinated whole, a capacity widely used, among other purposes, to induce spirit possession or ecstatic trance. Walter Ong claimed that sound incorporates, pours into the hearer: 'When I hear . . . I am at the center of my auditory world, which envelopes me, establishing me at a kind of core of sensation and existence' (1982: 72) – a touch romanticised perhaps, but still a telling contrast between vision and hearing.

Shared sonic experience has often been regarded as a key vehicle in creating and enacting human community. It can create *communitas* in ritual enactments, moving participants from the mundane into a joint transmundane experience, and draw people together in light-hearted gatherings too. Ottenberg describes the shared somatic states brought about among the singing clapping chorus in Limba songs and story-telling (Ottenberg 1996: 121) and the rhythms of a jazz performance can similarly join the participants, if only for a moment, in shared reverberation. And though it is over-simple to dub sound as the special vehicle of 'emotion', there is no doubt of the affective impact of a skilful musician's or orator's acoustic artistries; Jesse Jackson's political oratory drew its hearers into a kind of total engagement and emotional identification where they '*felt* he must be "telling the truth"' (Tannen 1989: 195). Audiovocal interchanges between priest and congregation in religious services bring people together in joint sonic-somatic enactment, while the active singing of a national anthem, the frenzied slogans of a protesting crowd, 'call and response' interchanges – all these can for a time gather participants into one.

Such sonic enactments are perhaps at their most intense when time and space dimensions coincide – when people are present at one place, one time. But even over time and at a distance they are not without effect. Physically scattered people are gathered into auditory union through the sonic symbols of piety or through political chants and slogans sent out through the air or broadcast over the public media, while the fans' active sonic-somatic involvement in their favoured music in audio-recordings or via the web holds some element of shared experience across temporal or spatial separation. Schutz saw the heart of social interaction as lying in a 'mutual tuning-in relationship, the experience of the "We", which is at the foundation of all possible communication' (1951: 92). In Van Leeuwen's more succinct phrase (1999: 197), 'listening is connection, communion'.

Sound carries very special overtones. Its particular combination of temporal and spatial properties gives it a unique role in human communication, opening opportunities for individuals' interactions, enhancing the potential powers of those who in one way or another control acoustic space, and gathering people into a shared communion. It is true that we must beware the temptation to romanticise sound or identify it with 'lost' cultures of the past: the human uses of sound are too variegated to make easy generalisation possible. Furthermore the bodily and emotional penetration of sound illustrated above is not intensively deployed in *all* acoustic settings: there are plenty of off-handed and less fraught auditory occasions as well. But equally we should not ignore the deep resonances of auditory communication, a key resource in human sociality.

Any full account of human communication must include some appreciation of this human involvement in sound and its creative resonances in human action and experience – constrained in some respects but infinitely rich in others. Humans are noisy creatures, as Ostwald puts it (1973: 20), and one way we assert our existence is through our acoustic actions and responses. The organisation and experience of human interaction is full of sound. We find it in our sonic environments and the ways we create and react to them; in the everyday experiences of human living, varying as these do through space and time; in the elaborated political, ritual or artistic uses of sound (and abuses too some might say); in sonic artefacts in their great variety, and the music, speech or other sounds for which they are vehicles; in the multifaceted sonic dimensions of vocalised and embodied interaction in conversations, announcements, verbal art and ritual enactments. Communicating human beings have long exploited and created myriad forms of this wonderfully versatile resource of sonic action and experience, and sound continues to provide a rich complex of resources through which (for good or ill) people interact, sound out their experiences, join together and in profound ways reach out to one another as individuals and groups.

4   Shaping the sights: vision and the communicating body

We live not only in a world of sound, but a world of sight too. When newborn we may use sound more immediately than sight but our multiple visual capacities are thenceforward developed in a big way. We are surrounded by sights: landscapes, seascapes, cityscapes; mountain or desert vistas; street and interior scenes; the detailed architectural and spatial settings for human life; gardens, forests and vegetation with their multifarious colours; the unending products of human manufacture; living creatures of diverse kinds; and, not least, other human beings. All these and more play a part in our visual world. Through our power of vision we apprehend their shape, size, colour, movement and distance. We manage and interact with this seen world, and, within it, with other living creatures and especially other human beings, selecting and creating the sights for visual communication through our own bodies and our material creations.

Because sight is so taken for granted in human life it is easy to overlook its extensive role in our communicating. The visible world is just around us, it seems, so familiar that it can be hard to see the many contexts in which we use vision in our communicating. But the range is huge. Consider the communicative powers of facial expression, eyes, gestures, posture, or clothing; of illuminated manuscripts, tapestries, carvings, buildings, film, photographs, computer screens; the visible displays and performances of dance, procession, ritual; the visual interaction between individuals or groups which enables them to carry out joint tasks of work or play or conflict; the systems for communicating through flags, semaphore, maps, diagrams, sign languages, books.

All this depends on vision. Even if we limit ourselves to pictorial images (only one part of the full story, as we shall see):

We are bombarded with pictures from morning till night. Opening our newspaper at breakfast, we see photographs of men and women in the news, and raising our eyes from the paper, we encounter the picture on the cereal package. . . . Leaving our house, we pass billboards along the road that try to catch our eye and play on our desire to smoke, drink or eat. At work it is more than likely that we have to deal with some kind of pictorial information:

photographs, sketches, catalogues, blueprints, maps or at least graphs. Relaxing in the evening, we sit in front of the television set, the new window on the world, and watch moving images of pleasures and horrors flit by. . . . Picture books, picture postcards and colour slides accumulate in our homes as souvenirs of travel, as do the private mementos of our family snapshots.

(Gombrich 1996: 41)

The examples would be different at different times and places. But whatever the details, sight seems everywhere a fundamental and versatile channel for communication, the basis for human interconnection through a huge range of both embodied and external sights.[1]

This discussion of vision covers two chapters. After a brief comparative overview, this first chapter considers the communicative uses centred on the human body, the next the more externalised arts and artefacts. This is of course an artificial division (the familiar issue of the contrasting yet interlocked 'intrinsic'/'extrinsic' dimensions of communication): the 'visible body' is no less the site of human shaping – and in culturally diverse ways too – than the 'external' visual arts. But the field to be covered is so large and yet coterminous that we have to start somewhere even if the divisions are not altogether satisfactory. The two chapters end with some comment on the role of vision more generally and the controversial issues this raises.

Vision in animal and human communication

The prime origin of the light that makes vision possible is the sun. A few luminescent creatures generate lights themselves and humans have produced some forms of artificial light. But essentially it is the sun's light that enables the infinitude of reflections and transmissions of light from objects in the world, and humans and non-humans alike use this light to see objects, surfaces, living organisms and events.

Most animals have light receptors of one kind or another, used and functioning in a great variety of ways. These vary from the human eye's capacity to distinguish form, colour, size, movement, distance and depth to little more than the differentiation of light and dark. Some animals form images – vertebrates, some molluscs, and most insects and spiders. Insects have 'compound' eyes rather than a camera-like single lens, especially good for perceiving movement. Some birds have extremely sharp vision, notably the visual acuity of hawks as they detect and swoop on their prey from long distances. Not all animals distinguish colour, however, and relatively few animals share the binocular vision of humans.

Almost all freely moving diurnal animals use vision in their communicating. It enables them to get information about their environment, move around it, and interact with other living organisms; few rapidly moving large animals function without it. They can use their bodies to produce visible signals, crucial for visual communicating. They create 'sights' (if I may put it that way) by moving into or out of sight, changing posture or direction, altering bodily shape or demeanour, moving portions of their anatomy. Vision in communication is not just a matter of seeing but also tapping the powers of mobility to produce communicative sights.

This is worth emphasising, for on the face of it vision seems very different from audition. We accept that sounds depend on active making and hearing whereas sights seem 'just there', part of the abiding external world. There is something in the distinction, and no communicative channels are exactly commensurate with each other. But there are parallels too. Using the visual channel depends on the capacity of both humans and other animals not just to 'perceive' objects and events, but also to *create* sights, just as they create sounds, by their own actions and by how they use and interpret them in communicating.

Other characteristics of sight are worth recalling too (see Box 2.5). Vision allows rapid transmission – faster than sound. It combines both durability and (if the visible object moves out of sight) rapid and near-immediate fade-out; sound by contrast always disappears rapidly. Sights are easier to locate than sounds, and, again unlike audition, vision is effective in even the noisiest of conditions: visual signals work amidst the din of a seabird colony, just like our well-tried recourse to lip-reading and gesture in noisy parties. It enables rapid and exact extraction of spatial information, facilitating fast adjustments to the environment (like avoiding others in a crowded street); many elements furthermore can be actively searched by the eyes in a way not really possible with the ears. Vision tends to be a simultaneous rather than, like audition, a sequential channel. It is also a complex one enabling the communication of multiple dimensions such as brightness, shape, movement or in some cases colour.

For something to communicate visually it must also be *seen*. Viewers have to direct their eyes towards it, actively look, be within unimpeded 'eyeshot'. This has implications for communicating. The need to look physically towards a sight may demand certain stances or movements, limiting or precluding other actions (another contrast to audition). Vision, furthermore, is easier to block out than sound. The sight is ended abruptly if the prey eludes its pursuers, a friend moves out of vision round a street corner, or a viewer looks away. Visual signals weaken with distance, so far-off sights are progressively less effective and to work at all have to be bolder and simpler. Overall their effective spatial range is normally less than for audition. In general the bigger the better for both seeing and being seen; very small creatures, unlike humans, often rely more on other channels.

Sights cannot go round obstacles or, like sound, penetrate poor viewing conditions. Urban buildings, high grasses, dense vegetation, crowds, partitions, darkness – all interfere with visual communication. Birds in dense vegetation often utilise audible rather than visual contact, just as someone communicating from outside a closed door must either make a noise or move through into sight. Diurnal animals make the greatest use of vision – those who, like humans, are active during the day rather than the night. During the hours of darkness, or in fog or gloom, even largely visual creatures may turn to auditory or tactile means. Some species are able to use vision effectively in gloomy conditions, however, and a few nocturnal creatures or those living in the deep ocean or in dark caves make their own light; humans have in addition extended their visual scope through forms of artificial lighting.

Visible signals diffuse widely, making it possible to communicate visibly to many recipients at once: an advantage in some situations but also sometimes drawing unwanted attention when a sight intended for one viewer is detected by others. Vision thus has implications for concealment as well as display. In the colours of some male animals there is a trade-off between conspicuousness (to communicate to females) and inconspicuousness (to avoid predators); it sometimes fits the differing interests of both prey and predators *not* to be too visible. Vision can also be manipulated to allow private communication, for since sight cannot go round obstacles, creatures can screen themselves from others' view.

Vision allows viewers to take in complex or multiple sights simultaneously; in contrast to the typically sequential nature of audition the 'whole picture' can be seen together.[2] But some elements may fade into the background or be so taken-for-granted as not to be noticed, so visual communicating may also involve highlighting specific elements to draw attention, making particular use, for example, of colour, contrast, movement, intensity or size.

Animals exploit these characteristics of visual communication in diverse ways.[3] Mostly they make direct use of bodily appearance and action. Animals living in groups constantly monitor each other's behaviour by observing their body postures, movements, glances or in some cases facial expressions. Social animals can coordinate their behaviour by this means and keep in well-informed and discriminating contact with their fellows. Visible bodily properties like colour, plumage or shape, or appendages like antlers, ear tufts, tail adornments or erectable crests can convey differential visible messages about, for instance, species, size, age or sex. Bodily appearance can be manipulated too. Some male lizards enormously extend their dewlaps, at other times hidden, to demarcate their territory or woo a female. Courting peacocks or turkeys display their tails in wonderful fan shapes, zebra finches fluff their feathers as an appeasement signal, and bicheno male finches ruffle their plumage to accentuate their black and white markings and impress females. Other animals make themselves look bigger to frighten predators or attract others, as in the huge extra size achieved by male frigate birds in courting. Blue tits spread their wings wide and hunch their shoulders to look larger and more threatening to anyone disturbing their nests.

Bodily movement and positioning are commonly used to communicate. Particular stances and orientations can convey, for example, friendliness, hostility, playfulness, receptiveness, dominance, aggression or appeasement. We are probably all familiar with the way dogs communicate their friendly or aggressive intentions by their appearance – Figure 4.1 gives one example. Gulls use an upright position, wings forward, bill downwards to convey an intention to attack, a crouching posture for submission. Moving nearer or further away can visibly indicate an offer of courtship, non-aggression, fear, cooperation or competition, reinforced further by the animal's orientation, rapidity or gait. Animals know well how to exploit the interruptible property of vision to remove themselves from sight behind physical barriers as well as how to use their movements and stances to produce 'sights' of themselves, visible far beyond their own bodies, interacting visually with others across space.

Animals also communicate by moving specific parts of their bodies according to the understood conventions of different species or situations. Limbs, tail, fins or hands are particularly used – prominent and visible features. Apes make a 'begging gesture' with palm upward to ask for food while Siamese fighting fishes display complex visual threats by spreading their fins, turning broadside to their opponent, and beating their tails, at the same time showing flashes of bright colour on tail and body. Some species, including humans, particularly utilise head and eyes – facial expression, mouth positions, direction and intensity of gaze, display of teeth, and head movements. A prolonged look can intimidate or provoke. A stare from a subordinate will make a dominant male monkey attack; non-aggressive cats on the other hand blink to show their stare is not hostile when they gaze at other cats (or humans). Among humans, similarly, both eye contact and looking away can 'say' something.

Animals exploit the capacity of sight to take in several things at once. Elaborate displays with multiple visual dimensions appear in courtship rituals, like mandarin ducks' combination of plumage, gestures and dancing. The threatening dog communicates by a multiplicity of near-simultaneously visible signs, from type and speed of gait, orientation, head carriage and teeth display to the lie of the hair, position of tail and ears, and glare of the eyes.

Figure 4.1 Darwin's visually communicating dog
The dog uses posture and movement, including tail, legs, head, mouth, ears, eyes and hair, to communicate, first, a hostile approach, second a friendly and playful one (from sketches in Charles Darwin, *The Expression of the Emotions in Man and Animals,* 1872, pp. 52–3).

Some animals make some use of extrinsic visual communication – that is, of visible materials or artefacts separate from the body. Chimpanzees brandish sticks and throw objects in aggressive displays and a number of animals mark their territory by faecal deposits, possibly a visual as well as olfactory sign. Others signal their claims or their presence by leaving visible scratches on trees. Some make piles of earth, others build nests, dens and other constructions which convey the makers' presence, ownership, and perhaps attraction to potential mates. Visual display is also important in the elaborate stages that male bowerbirds create to charm their females, with sticks piled around a tree fern, a moss platform at the base, and colourful mounds of blue, yellow and green fruit (Smith *et al.* 1989: 69, 71).

Humans use many of the same strategies as other animals. We too interact by creating and observing sights through bodily shapes, orientations and movements, and use our bodies as a frontier and visual stage for interacting with others. Like all species, we have our own characteristics. We live not in water but in air – a good medium for vision – and like other diurnal animals mostly sleep at night and operate during daylight (supplemented by some 'night vision', by star- and moon-light, and by some use of artificial light). The make-up of the human eye means we see not only shape, structure, movement, colour, distance and depth but also features like texture, brightness/shade, subtly differing colours, contrasts, solidity, edges, and degrees of distance. Depth perception is aided by our stereoscopic vision, merging images from two eyes set at the front of the head: three dimensional sights are important in human communicating. Humans can detect distant objects and events, but have a narrow cone of clear vision and less developed peripheral vision than some other animals: the need for selective attention to sights has a biological as well as cultural basis. Human central vision is extremely powerful, however, equalled by few other animals and surpassed only by some flying insects and birds.

Like other animals, humans move and manipulate their bodies so as to create the sights used in visual communicating. All the visible areas of our bodies can be brought into play (but no tails . . .). Human facial musculature is exceptionally developed and our upright position and forward-looking eyes make subtle facial expressions highly visible. The relatively large size of our human bodies is also a good base for both seeing and being seen. As two-legged animals, we do not need our forelimbs for walking and, as we will see, exploit our upper limbs to amazing effect in gesturing systems.

Human beings make particular use of external media in their visual communicating. It is true both that some other animals make some limited use of exosomatic devices and that the 'intrinsic'/'extrinsic' contrast remains somewhat simplistic. But it is nevertheless indisputable that human manual dexterity, aided by the development of manifold tools and machines, has enabled the creation of a remarkable range of visual arts and artefacts and that, more so than other animals, these form a prominent dimension of human visual communication.

The visible human body

Let us start with communication directly through people's bodies – bodily movements, postures and appearances. These very real elements in human communication have often been downplayed, one result perhaps of our preoccupation with verbal language. But in practice we take serious account of them every day whether in face-to-face interaction or through our visual assessment of people via distance media like film or television. Even when not fully aware of it, we have nevertheless learned to use and interpret them in subtle and effective ways. These bodily processes are often multimodal. But the prime channel is very frequently the visual one, based in our capacity to *see* for ourselves the shapes, structures, colours, postures, orientation and movements thus created through the body.[4]

Like many animals, we make special use of our heads and faces – the communicating children in the earlier Figure 1.1 will have been nothing unfamiliar. The eyes take a notable part. Not just the organs of visual reception, they are also themselves active players in our communicating. In his classic account of visual interaction Simmel comments that:

> The union and interaction of individuals is based upon mutual glances. This is perhaps the most direct and purest reciprocity which exists anywhere. . . . The totality of social relations of human beings, their self-assertion and self-abnegation, their intimacies and estrangements, would be changed in unpredictable ways if there occurred no glance of eye to eye.
>
> (Simmel 1924 [1908]: 358)

Even brief eye-contacts in a crowd can introduce an element of direct personal interaction. 'The Look' brings an awareness of another as a being with consciousness and intentions (Kendon 1990: 51) and we have doubtless all had the experience of someone's fixed gaze mysteriously drawing our attention. It can be used to *reject* as well as start off social interaction. A waiter can refuse to let you 'catch his eye'; and when pedestrians or motorists want to ensure their own right of way against others, one strategy is 'to avoid meeting the other's eyes and thus avoid cooperative claims' (Goffman 1963: 94). The eye is often envisaged as a kind of 'pipeline into our psyche', which we may try to obstruct to prevent others seeing into us too directly (Applbaum *et al.* 1973: 117). Levin speaks more romantically but with some truth of the 'intertwining of gazes', where seer and seen, seeing one another, 'cannot avoid an involuntary, organismic acknowledgement of their primordial kinship' (Levin 1988: 333).

Looks do more than just initiate mutual interaction. They also themselves actively communicate. Hostility, anger, affection, welcome, accessibility, amusement, reserve, suspicion, embarrassment, boredom or love – all can be conveyed through the eyes. We exchange rueful, resigned or mocking glances, communicating with a light-touch subtlety that can seldom be achieved by deliberate words. During face-to-face social engagements we carefully maintain 'an eye-to-eye ecological huddle', as Goffman puts it, 'maximizing the opportunity to monitor one another's mutual perceivings' (1963: 95). As among other animals, stares can communicate invitations, threats or challenges, even a rapid warning to someone out of line, while the differential statuses of varying participants can be acknowledged – or claimed – by an 'open' gaze, lowered eyes or short glances.

Looking often goes along with verbal communicating. Their mutual gaze enables participants to express and regulate emotion and share in organising the process. A speaker may direct a sustained gaze at a listener when about to come to an end, indicating an anticipated exchange of speaking roles. Speakers often look at listeners while speaking fluently, monitoring their attentiveness, but keep control by looking away during more hesitant speaking or at the start of a lengthy utterance, not just to concentrate on organising what is to come next but to forestall interruptions.

The communicative manipulation of gaze is controlled by culturally specific patterns, with the practices varying according to the particular group, status, role or gender. The Navajo, for example, avoided 'the direct open-face look in their eyes' and froze if looked at directly, while the habit of showing respect by looking down, said to be characteristic of American black children, was taken as lack of attention by their (white) teachers (Hall 1974: 104). E. T. Hall pointed in the 1960s to misunderstandings between English and American speakers because each was unsure whether the other was listening and understanding. The reason, he explained, lay in their eye behaviour: 'The Englishman is taught to pay strict attention, to listen carefully. . . . He doesn't bob his head or grunt to let you know he understands. He blinks his eyes to let you know that he has heard you. Americans, on the other hand, are taught not to stare' (Hall 1966: 134).

It is not just the eyes. To quote Simmel again, the expression of the face is 'the first object of vision' between one person and another:

> Our practical relations depend upon mutual recognition, not only in the sense of all external characteristics, as the momentary appearance and attitude of the other, but what we know or intuitively perceive of his life, of his inner nature, of the immutability of his being, all of which colours unavoidably both our transient and our permanent relations with him. The face is the geometric chart of all these experiences.
>
> (Simmel 1924 [1908]: 359)

We actively use visible facial expressions in both verbal and non-verbal interactions, made possible by our extensive capacity – partly shared with other animals but developed in ways specific to humankind – to move our head and its separate muscles: scalp, cheeks, mouth, eyebrows, nose, lips, chin and neck. Think of smiling, frowning, grimacing or wincing; lifting the chin in defiance or determination;

screwing up our eyes or wrinkling our noses; raising eyebrows in greeting; and using our faces to communicate pleasure, welcome, joy, fear, pain, shock, attraction, shyness, embarrassment, sympathy, attention (see also Box 4.1). Some of these probably occur in broadly similar forms throughout human communicating but in their finer detail and the forms of enactment there is great variability.[5] One could mention the highly effective but varying patterns for conveying humour, cynicism or commiseration. Facial expressions communicate far more than we mostly realise. Sometimes indeed we might prefer to conceal what they only too clearly convey to others, as with blushing, pallor or facial rigidity. Other expressions, such as most of those mentioned just above, lie more within the deliberate (if not always fully conscious) control of human actors.

Box 4.1 Using our faces to communicate

This lists some visual facial expressions widely recognised as communicative, based on an account focusing on recent English-American non-verbal communication (Burgoon and Guerrero 1994: 158). There are many others, sometimes appearing in more personal and fleeting forms.

Anger	Brows drawn and lowered, lips either tightly pressed together or slightly squared, hostile stare
Disgust	Wrinkled nose, lowered brow, upper lip raised, chin raised
Happiness	Smiling, raised cheeks, dimples, eyes crinkle at corners
Sadness	Frown, lips parted, inner brow raised, brows drawn together, gaze aversion
Surprise	Raised brows, slightly raised open eyelids, white of eye shows above iris, open mouth

---

It is not just a matter of relatively static expressions but also how they change. Sequential phases can be subtly created by narrowing the eyes, a re-directed gaze or an increasingly 'glazed-over' look. Participants in face-to-face exchanges watch each other's faces, alert to react to the unfolding interaction – this is a mutual not a one-way communicative process. Changing expressions visibly and rapidly communicate speakers' attitudes to different phases of their own utterances, a listener's developing empathy in an exciting narrative or sorrowful tale, successive stages of doubt, persuasion, surprise, or delight, or the joint establishing of agreement or of hostility. This continual visual interaction plays an important part in formulating the process as it happens. Even when, as often, some words are not fully heard, the visible expressions carry the listener through (it is not just overt lip-readers who watch speakers' lips). All this helps to formulate the mood and atmosphere, that crucial dimension of our actual processes of communicating. 'The face is the most important non-verbal channel', in Michael Argyle's assessment, 'particularly important for expressing emotions, and attitudes to other people' (1988: 121). Far from just transmitting fixed once-and-for-all messages, facial expressions create subtle and emergent processes of dynamic communication over time.

The head too is brought into play. As among many animals but with the additional prominence of its human elevated position, the head's highly visible movements are apt for communicating either on its own or coordinated with speech. Shaking and nodding it indicates 'no' and 'yes' in many west European countries (but not everywhere), while specific versions of head nods, tosses and dips are often used in both greetings and more extended conversations. Again the process is usually a dynamic one as the participants continue (or, equally communicative, cease) to convey attentiveness, interest or empathy by moving the head in acknowledgement. Head movements can refine what is being said – like the coaxing head-tilt when the vocalised words alone might be taken amiss – or reinforce it; head movements with a spoken invitation to approach are very different from those for an aggressive 'Go away!'. Visual communicating through our heads and faces forms an important and versatile part of human face-to-face interaction.

We also use our limbs extensively for communicating visually. Inviting others to take a turn in speaking can be indicated not only by facial expression but by relaxing a foot, extending a hand or altering a stance. Foot tapping can send signals, so can leg movements. Most important of all are our upper limbs, extensively used in human visual communicating. This brings us directly to gestures and gesturing, something developed to an extraordinary degree in human communicating. Its detailed discussion will be postponed until a little later, however, for though gesturing with the hands and arms must be counted one of the most important aspects of bodily visual communicating and it is indeed rather artificial to omit it for the moment, it needs to be treated at greater length, below.

Our ways of walking communicate too. As Mauss pointed out many years ago (1979 [1935]: 100–2), *how* people walk is a learned and culturally variable process. It can certainly convey the walker's specific role and status. We are familiar with – and draw conclusions from – a nurse's brisk approach, a teacher's way of moving round the classroom, soldiers' various traditions of marching or a worshipper's way of entering a church. In Homer's *Iliad* heroes walk with long powerful strides, impressing the enemy with their prowess. We read subtle messages from someone's gait both at a given time and as the situation unfolds: sequential messages of, for example, annoyance, pleasure, haste, relaxation or mutual attraction.

Figure 4.2 'The disappointed ones'

In this painting (*Die Enttäuschen*, 1892, oil on canvas, 120 × 299cm) the Swiss artist Ferdinand Hodler depicts vividly how people's postures can 'speak', conveying their disappointment and all the feelings and attitudes that go with it (Kuntsmuseum Bern, Staadt Bern, Inv. Nr. 0249).

Like other animals, we also use overall posture, orientation and demeanour to communicate either on their own or in conjunction with other channels. Think of the messages conveyed by, for example, a threatening and challenging stance; turning one's back; postures expressing sympathy, boredom, joy, emotional closeness, embarrassment, detachment, disapproval or fear; stances marking subordination, subservience, friendliness, aggression, disregard or command. The forwards- or backwards-slants of our bodies are part of our communicating, so too are contrasting 'open' or 'closed' postures, or a sideways lean (Bull 1987). Ferdinand Hodler's painting 'The disappointed ones' (Figure 4.2) brilliantly captures the way that someone's whole comportment can communicate.

Many parts of the body are often simultaneously involved – not just facial features, head and limbs but also the tilts and movements of the trunk. It may be below the level of explicit consciousness, but we regularly engage in conventionally patterned movements; conveying annoyed acceptance by shrugging our shoulders and moving the rest of our bodies to suit; impatience by moving irritatedly from foot to foot; sympathy or love by hugging. Coordinated body movements subtly communicate differing degrees of confidence, doubt, warmth or disbelief, as the communicative process develops. Together they can show pleasure and surprise in giving and hearing some unexpected good news; mutual attention and support during an interpersonal conversation; and fear, aggression, welcome, sexual attraction, or changing degrees of agreement or disagreement.

Our knowledge of visual communicative conventions is what makes mime and silent films so effective and visible body movements remain an essential dimension in contemporary film or television even where audible speech is used too. Silent 'one-act plays' are common features of everyday experience too:

> Imagine four people in a supermarket, using *only* their facial expressions and body movements, saying the following:
>
> A: 'I only have an apple and a milk carton, and I'm in a terrible hurry. Maybe you'd let me slip in front of you.'
>
> B: 'Hell, no. I have to wait my turn. Why shouldn't you?'
>
> B to C: 'These people are all alike.'
>
> C to B: 'I know, isn't it a nuisance?'
>
> D to A: 'Here, you can get in front of me. I'm not in that much of a hurry.'
> (Applbaum *et al.* 1973: 109)

We also regularly use bodily appearance and bearing to classify people and mark differentiation, drawing on culturally specific conventions about appropriate movement and demeanour. As Adam Smith observed of the eighteenth-century nobleman:

His air, his manner, his deportment, all mark that elegant and graceful sense of his own superiority, which those who are born to inferior stations can hardly ever arrive at. These are the arts by which he proposes to make mankind more easily submit to his authority, and to govern their inclinations according to his own pleasure: and in this he is seldom disappointed.

(Smith 1976 [1759]: 54)

The seen movements between teachers and pupils or doctors and patients communicate and regulate their relationship (Woolfson 1988). And just as authority is frequently conveyed by an erect walk and upright head, so acquiescence and recognition of that authority may be communicated by a cowering or bending gait, or by bowing, kneeling, crouching or prostration. Visible actions do indeed sometimes speak louder than words and our learned ability to create, see and act on them forms a crucial and amazingly flexible resource for our human interconnection.

These embodied sights already take us a long way into our human ways of communicating. But we also have the additional communicative resources of our spatial positioning, our gesturing – that wonderful human art – and our bodily displays. Although this means leaving some threads dangling in this discussion of the dimensions of the visibly communicating body, each of these topics needs some further treatment on its own.

Seeing spatial relations

Like those of other animals, human bodies have a localised presence and their interactions take place in space. We depend on the eye's power to discriminate not just distance but also the spatial relations between participants (and other objects) within the field of vision. Our capacity both to see these spatial relationships and to create them through bodily movements is a far-reaching dimension of human communicating.

At the simplest level vision is crucial in helping us navigate in space, including the far from simple task of spatially interacting with other moving people. A truly impressive process of feedback and mutual interplay between individuals enables us, usually without conscious awareness, to work together in a crowded office, avoid bumping into other family members in the kitchen (mostly), or, using mainly visual cues, steer down a busy street. But there is more to it as well. Our corporeal presences and co-presences in particular places not only form an inescapable dimension of human interactions but are also regulated by complex communicative conventions about just how people should locate their bodies in relation to one another. These spatial conventions are subtle and multiplex indeed, a proxemic system amounting to what has been called a 'silent language'.[6] They organise our communicating to a much greater extent than usually recognised, working together with the other visual processes discussed in this chapter.

People communicate through the distances and positions they take up during interpersonal encounters. In human interactions a person's space is not coterminous with the edges of the body, for individuals have 'bubbles' around them whose violation they regard as intrusion. E. T. Hall compared this to the 'flight distance' in other animals, the distance an animal likes to keep between itself and potential predators:

> A lizard can be approached to within six feet before he flees, an antelope to within 60 feet, and an alligator takes off at 150 feet. Man himself carries with him a number of hidden zones that elicit different responses as boundaries are crossed. The behavior appropriate for each zone . . . and the distances to each boundary are all a matter of culture, learned early in life.
>
> (Hall 1960: 42)

These 'proxemic zones', as Hall terms them, form concentric spaces around people, fitting culturally specific conventions about the appropriate type of communicating allowable within it. Since we are often unaware of these spatial patterns even when we actively and regularly deploy them in our own communicating, their relevance can best be introduced by an example (Box 4.2).

Box 4.2 Spatial conventions in interpersonal communicating: an American example

This is based on E. T. Hall's description of proxemic zones in mid-twentieth century American communicating; while the principles are probably widely applicable, the specific conventions vary cross-culturally (adapted mainly from Hall 1966: 110ff, see also Hall 1959, 1974).

Intimate distance
Presence of other person unmistakable (even overwhelming), high multisensory interaction. Narrow field of vision.
Close
> Physical contact actual or highly possible: muscles and skin can communicate, including pelvis, thighs, head and (possibly encircling) arms. Direct contact through olfaction and radiant heat; little vocalisation except relatively involuntary sounds. Great detail seen but narrowed and blurred field of vision. Regarded as appropriate distance in love-making, mother–infant interaction, wrestling, comforting, protecting and physical fighting.

Far (six to eighteen inches)
> Not direct bodily contact, but hands can reach and grasp extremities. Some effect of olfaction and body heat, vocalisation very quiet. Close

vision without sharp focus. Appropriate distance for intimates in private, but intrusive or hostile for non-intimates (if unavoidable in crowds, intimacy denied by rigid posture and avoidance of eye contact).

Personal distance
The 'small protective sphere or bubble' (Hall 1966: 112) that individuals keep around themselves.
Close (one and a half to two and a half feet)
   Can reach and touch with extremities. Casual speaking style. Clear vision of other's features, including three-dimensional qualities and texture; mutual visual feedback possible. For close interactions between people with accepted personal relationship.
Far (two and a half to four feet)
   Personal interaction 'at arm's length', just outside easy touching distance. Little or no olfactory or thermal contact; moderate voice level. Clear mutual view including facial details. Common in personal conversation: can communicate personal interest without the commitment of touching.

Social-consultative distance
Beyond the limit of physical domination (i.e. the distance where someone can 'get their hands on you'). Omnidirectional hearing, wider field of vision. Moderate voice level, conversations audible up to twenty feet.
Close (four to seven feet)
   Eyes take in more of the body, good mutual views of head and upper trunk. Common distance for working together or casual social gatherings.
Far (seven to twelve feet)
   Participants need to see each other, moving heads or bodies to avoid obstacles and keep eye contact (necessary for maintaining communication at this distance). Social interaction can be avoided by bodily orientation, screens or withholding eye contact (at lesser distances social recognition more or less mandatory). Appropriate for more formal social or business interaction.

Public distance
Here it becomes easier for participants to break off or evade communication.

Close (twelve to twenty-five feet)

   Clear vision of more than one person but without fine detail of skin or eyes; greater visual scanning of body/ies feasible. Loud voice, more formal speech. Well outside sphere of personal involvement.

Far (twenty-five feet or more)

   Visual signals amplified or exaggerated; subtler facial expressions and movements no longer visible. Greater projection of voice, usually slower, more deliberate. Thirty-foot zone regularly set around important public figures. Appropriate for public communication, e.g. between actors and audience, priest and congregation, lecturers and students. Mutual interaction between participants as individuals increasingly perceived as minimal.

As Box 4.2 indicates, human interactions in space are often multisensory, especially the most intimate. But vision is almost always important and in less close encounters often the predominant channel. People pay careful visual attention to where they and others place themselves in relation to one another, and a great deal about their relations overall, as well as their intentions or feelings at particular moments, is conveyed through both their initial positioning and their successive movements around their shared space. As Lebaron and Streeck comment:

> Human interaction and communication involve space in multiple ways. . . . Participants in interaction must perform spatial manoeuvres to secure their visual and auditory access to one another, to keep each other informed about their mutual involvement, and to regain the attention of those temporarily distracted. Participants also mark off their interaction from the surrounding world to make it an event with its own integrity and licenses for participation. Participants 'formulate' with their bodies the specific context or 'definition of the situation' that they hold during the successive 'frames' of their interaction. And together they reorganize their configuration when the theme, topic, or definition of their encounter changes.
>
> (Lebaron and Streeck 1997: 2 [omitting citations])

Thus two people talking – or even just mutually looking – at a distance of around two feet from each other are recognised by both themselves and others as engaged in the kind of communication only possible between those who know each other well: the spatial setting is itself part of the communicating. A non-intimate taking a position within this space would be interpreted (and probably intended) as explicitly intrusive, even threatening. A wife can step 'inside the circle of her husband's close personal zone with impunity. For another woman to do so is an entirely different story' (Hall 1966: 113). Since greater distances are seen as appropriate for less personal and public interaction, any infringement in itself carries a message. The progress of mutual communicating can likewise be signalled by shifts in bodily orientation and spacing, with a gradual increase in mutual intimacy or status-recognition, for example, or claims being quietly rejected by withdrawal. Similarly people conducting a formal transaction mark this by a 'social zone' distance, but when business is concluded may turn to chatting about more personal matters, mutually indicating this by moving closer. Here too the spatial dimension is part of the communicating and of the communicators' unfolding intentions and relationships.

Proxemic conventions are learned not innate. Small children create embarrassing situations through ignorance of adult spatial norms – wandering into spaces where they are not welcome, invading a high-status visitor's personal zone, or keeping their distance from someone they are supposed to kiss. Culturally diverse patterns can lead to misunderstandings. According to E. T. Hall (1966: 112) the Russian 'social zone' was smaller than the corresponding American one; so Russians were thought intrusive and pushy by Americans, Americans as stand-offish by Russians. But even within the same country, spatial conventions can differ in different groups, areas, even families and individuals – unspoken but acted upon. These 'silent communications' (Hall 1966: 6), conveyed largely through the visual channel, may be as salient as more explicit printed or spoken messages.

The use of space has been most studied in one-to-one encounters, but it is clearly also relevant for communicating within groups. The layout of participants, distance individuals take up from each other, orientations of their bodies – all are factors in the communicating process. People's seating arrangements partly shape their interchanges, not least their access to easy eye contact, the visibility of their own gestures, or their vantage point on changing postures. Those who want to affect the tone or hierarchies of a meeting move round the chairs beforehand; a chairman's position at the head of the table or a potential antagonist facing him can add special force to their respective pronouncements. Together these dimensions of space and movement visibly reinforce, enrich, discriminate and qualify our communicative processes. We are well accustomed to interpreting these proxemic elements in others' interactions, both live and in filmed depictions, and ourselves make active use of them.

The bodily appropriation of places is relevant too. Moving into a particular space can signal the start or development of a particular communicative phase – taking the chair at a meeting for example or moving up to the altar at a church service. It conveys something if a teenager sits in 'the father's chair', a newcomer usurps the best view in a shared office, or a back-row violinist moves up a rank. Merely occupying a particular space or moving into, through, or out of it can carry visible messages to others, while encroaching onto someone's territory can be taken as insupportable and hostile invasion, from explicitly combative conflicts between rival gangs to the disputed streets claimed by processions in the north of Ireland. And in a wider context 'emotional communities', in Hetherington's phrase (1998), create and 'perform' complex symbolic spaces to express and convey their identity.

We recognise relative age or status by spacial positioning. People signify deference by standing further away from someone they regard as superior and move closer to peers (and those they like) than to those who are older or younger. Burgoon and Guerrero observe that one can tell the relationship of subordinates to their boss or students to their teachers by how they approach: those of lower status stand in the doorway, others walk up to the desk (1994: 127). The space between performers and audience, preacher and congregation, commander and ranks – all have meanings within given cultures. There are designated pews for special families in some churches, or separate areas in many contexts for men and women, children and adults, high and low, initiates and non-initiates. The 'rightful placing' of people according to status is part of the ordering of courtly or ecclesiastical life which it is a serious act to reject.

Spacing is often prominent on public and ceremonial occasions, where the positions and movements of bodies in space are in a way 'symbolic resources used to represent the ritual order' (Lebaron and Streeck 1997: 2). Think of the placing of people in processions, or the spatial ordering during marriages and funerals. Even the hidden messages in the seating plan at a formal dinner can arouse chagrin because of implicit but influential conventions about the placement of honoured guests. People's roles on specific occasions are signalled visibly by their location: stewards towards the edges or back, receptionists and door-keepers behind a desk and at entrances, judges on the bench (differently placed from jury or litigant), policemen at intersections, public speakers on a dais at the front and audience below.

Understood within the parameters of local conventions, these and the many comparable proxemic processes are indeed visual forms of communicating to which we are accustomed to pay attention. We have learned to utilise them both subtly and economically, without the necessity for spoken or written words.

Movement, gestures and 'sign languages'

Movement is a major strand in our communicating. This is partly related to one of vision's limitations: that things can fade into the background or become too familiar to be noticed. The human eye is alert to movement, however, so this is an effective means for attracting visual attention at a particular time or place. Waving, standing up, raising a theatre curtain, hoisting a flag or making a movement towards someone to begin a conversation or take a turn at speaking are all well-tried ways to start off a communicative phase. In addition, few if any human acts of communicating lack a temporal dimension; we are dealing not with once-and-for-all messages but processes over time. Here our movements play a large part. These are now drawing increasing interest, often under the general head of 'kinesics' – the study of visible bodily movements in communication.[7]

This brings us, then, to the great subject of gesturing. The terms 'gesture' and 'gesticulation' are actually somewhat ambiguous – most frequently used for hand and arm movements but also sometimes encompassing other bodily movements too. It is in truth near-impossible to separate off hands and arms: as we have seen already, their movements often go along with those by eyes, face, head, legs and the body as a whole. A narrow definition of 'gesture' and 'gesticulate' is unrealistic. But at the same time the main focus of most of what follows will indeed be on the arms, hands and fingers. These are of outstanding importance in human communication, prominent and visible parts of our bodies which we deploy in a great manner of ingenious and subtle ways. The two-legged upright human stance facilitates their free and rapid movement and they are among the most flexible and extensively developed tools for embodied visual communicating.

Human gesturing takes diverse forms – there is no universal 'gesture language' – and it varies greatly in its degree of standardisation and explicitness. At one end of a rough continuum comes the (relatively) non-conscious gesticulation that co-occurs

Figure 4.3 The farmer's indignation
One of the tableaux by Gaetano Gigante with which Andrea de Jorio illustrated his account of Neapolitan gesturing. As he explains it, the farmer has caught the young woman with a bundle of corn and angrily accuses her of stealing it, with a threatening gesture. She has thrown it down and is tearfully and pitifully pleading her innocence (someone from another farm gave it to her . . .). Her mother's arm-positions repeat the denial and their bewildered innocence. The farmer's companion, unconvinced, suspects that the tearful ingratiation will eventually soften the farmer's justified indignation; rather than saying so aloud he uses the Neapolitan gesture for 'He's being duped' (see 9 in Figure 2.1) (from Andrea de Jorio *La mimica degli antichi investigata nel gestire napoletano*, 1832, Plate XIV).

with speaking, at the other specialised forms such as dance, mime, and the marvellous array of more systematised 'sign languages'. All deserve attention as established forms of visual communication.

The farmer's indignation in Figure 4.3 gives one vivid example of the common practice of people gesticulating while they speak, fitting their actions to occasion and purpose: Andrea de Jorio's comments, summarised in its caption, bring out what is going on and how effectively the four are using visible movements to communicate. It is true that we do not make gestures every time we talk, nor is gesturing the same in all cultures or situations, but some gesticulating is an extremely frequent feature of human speaking. It takes place near-spontaneously as we accompany what we say by visible hand and arm movements (often of course along with gaze and other bodily movements, especially shoulders). We use hands to describe the visual characteristics of some object or action, add force to what is said (like the actors in the farming mini-drama), signify modesty, anger, irony or humour – familiar communicative actions we encounter every day. Gestures have advantages over speech in regulating and enriching interaction among speakers. Someone can actively and economically request a turn at speaking or comment on what is being said by visual means without interrupting the auditory flow. A potential speaker can foreshadow what they want to say and the speaker currently holding the floor hint what they are planning next (Streeck and Knapp 1992: 12ff). Sometimes gestures override what is – apparently – being communicated vocally. R. A. Hinde recalls how he learned as a young researcher to watch his boss's little finger. Once this started to tap on the desk, the movement would spread through the other fingers to his hand, then his arm, and 'it was better for me to leave the room before the pounding on the desk stage was reached' (Hinde 1975: 108).

This kind of gesturing is in part individual and idiosyncratic. At the same time even here there is some degree of formalisation and it works because it draws on (more or less) shared conventions. Shaking a fist, pointing, beckoning, nose thumbing, or holding up a hand to stop someone are quite explicit. But, as David McNeill points out in his brilliant *Hand and Mind* (1992), even with less explicit gestures there are some underlying patterns (1992: 12ff). Speakers employ gestures as 'iconic' when they mimic an action they are describing vocally and thus make it more vivid (gripping something and bending it over for example), or as 'metaphoric' where the pictorial content presents an abstract idea or category rather than a specific object or event. 'Deictic' gestures point to something, not just objects in the physical world but also abstract ideas *as if* they had a physical locus. The deceptively small gestures McNeill terms 'beats' – as in beating music – reveal a speaker's conception of the discourse as a whole, marking meta-levels or temporal discontinuities. 'Cohesives' on the other hand spell out the continuities: they integrate different parts of a speech by repeating the same gesture in different places to emphasise a recurring theme, well exemplified in politicians' speeches (McNeill 1992: 16). Gestures point to concepts as well as physical objects, anticipate what is to come, set the scene, clarify the salient points of a narrative or an argument, or orient the speaker and listener to overall functions of discourse.

> Often these functions are shown more clearly in gesture than in speech. Gestures exhibit such narratological features as voice, perspective, narrative distance, and narrative level; they are able to show what is significant in the immediate context and exclude what is irrelevant.
>
> (McNeill 1992: 217)

We may seldom think of our gestures consciously, but in practice, it seems, we use them with great efficiency, economy and sophistication to cover a surprisingly wide range of communicating.

In many cases speaking and gesticulating are so closely intertwined and co-synchronised that some analysts see gesture and vocal language as a single integrated system rather than two separate processes supporting each other. In this view both equally form 'part of the speaker's ongoing thought process' (McNeill 1992: 245, also Kendon 1997, Streeck and Knapp 1992). The two function in different ways, however. Vocal speech is rich in the sequential and linear properties of audition, gestures more akin to images with their 'gestalt' and simultaneous visual quality. To quote McNeill again:

> [Gestures] are closely linked to speech, yet present meaning in a form fundamentally different from that of speech. My own hypothesis is that speech and gesture are elements of a single integrated process of utterance formation in which there is a synthesis of opposite modes of thought – global-synthetic and instantaneous imagery with linear-segmented temporally extended verbalization. Utterances and thoughts realized in them are both imagery and language.
>
> (McNeill 1992: 35)

Principles of this kind may well underlie many forms of gesticulation, but the detailed conventions vary in differing traditions and genres. Their diversity as well as their importance comes out in the practical dangers of not recognising gestures in foreign countries (including those for insults!). The facial expressions and gestures of different languages, cultures and groups are not necessarily the same. It was said of Mayor La Guardia of New York that one could switch off the television sound and 'know from his gestures whether he was speaking English, Italian, or Yiddish' (Thomas 1991: 6), while to assimilate to American culture immigrant Italians and East European Jews had to change not just their spoken language but their gestures too (Efron 1972). Actors learn the bodily movements for a 'typical' Frenchman, upper-class Englishman, Sicilian or Russian while, in lighter vein, we have all heard of the Italian who had to remain silent because it was too cold to take his hands out of his pockets (for further examples see Morris *et al.* 1979, Kendon 1997: 115ff).

Gestures also vary over time. In western Europe conventions changed with the Reformation and with the Puritan disapproval of lavish gesturing (Hibbitts 1995, Burke 1997b: 60ff; for earlier changes, Schmitt 1991). New kinds of gesture replace the old or are used in different settings and with different accoutrements. A seventeenth-century Quaker text rejects the 'fond ceremonies' of worldly honour with their 'foolish windings, turnings, crouchings and cringings with their bodies', and recommends instead 'giving the hand, falling on the neck, embracing, kissing . . . [as] more infallible demonstrations of true honour, than those dirty customs [bowing, curtseying, doffing the hat]' (quoted in Bauman 1983: 46–7). The details changed, but gesturing in the broad sense was still used to communicate.

All gestures rely on some degree of shared agreement if they are to be effective, but some are organised in more articulate and conscious forms than others. The patterned gestures of southern Italians present one notable case: 'the "bundle of pictures" that a "traditional southern Italian" usually carries in his hands' (Efron 1972: 123, also Kendon 2000). A few examples are given in Figure 4.4, but there are many others. Highly conventionalised gestures of this kind sometimes become relatively stabilised within particular groups and cultures and persist over time. We can employ gestures without speech to convey agreement, negation, greeting, farewell, command, disapproval, dismissal, defiance, sympathy, insult, obscenity or congratulation. The degree and detailed formulation of such gestures vary in different traditions and situations, but overall this is a widely used resource, one that it is easy for people to recall and use. Semi-standardised gestures are less interdependent with speech than many of those discussed so far. In some situations they can be used on their own, effective for both open and relatively secret communicating (Figures 4.4 and 4.6 give examples).

Conventions for embodied visual communication are often more explicit and self-conscious where they link into potential conflicts over differing values or power. Manuals of etiquette and manners lay down the proper gait, direction of gaze, orientations and gestures for different situations and statuses – 'proper' that is from the viewpoint of the compilers. Mediaeval novices had to give up 'secular' gestures and adopt the correct motions for monks (Schmitt 1991: 69) and most organised religions prescribe postures and gestures which symbolise and regulate religious experience or communicate the nature of particular acts: postures for praying, meditating, blessing, reading the scriptures or expressing penitence. Deeply felt political or religious controversies have focused on movements of the body, again exemplified in the Quakers' refusal to bow, curtsey or observe 'hat honour', or in the religious schisms over whether two or three fingers should be used for blessing in seventeenth-century Russia (Burke 1997b: 61). Heated arguments about handshakes might seem trivial, but in the Dutch Republic 'shaking hands and other "nonsensical minutiae" were . . . as important as matters of state. In diplomatic circles they even *were* matters of state' (Bremmer and Roodenburg 1991: 179).

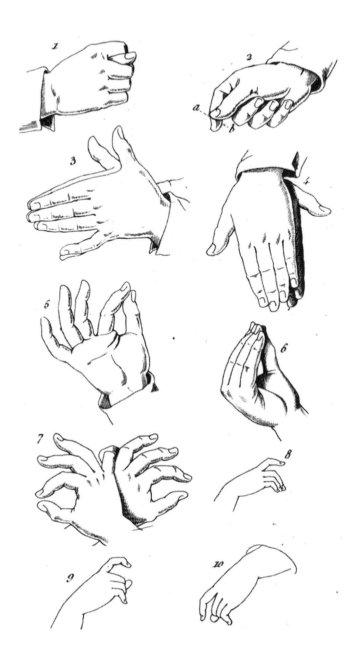

Figure 4.4 Italian hand gestures

Widely recognised hand shapes in Italian communication, again from Andrea de Jorio. His explanations (based on translation in Kendon 2000) are: 1. The 'fig' hand (various meanings, differentiated by facial expression, among them obscene insult); 2. Money (enumerating coins); 3 and 4. Stupid (often commenting behind someone's back); 5. Love, affection

Gestures often have an explicit and studied role in ritual, especially (though not exclusively) in the absence of a tradition of written record. In royal coronations, papal enthronements, acts of homage or saluting a senior officer, the transfer or acknowledgement of authority is communicated through visible gesture. Rites of passage are performed through visible bodily movements. People throw earth on a coffin at a burial or recognise the conventionally prescribed gestures during a wedding, communicating the ritual enactment as memorably to those present by visible gesture as by words (sometimes perhaps more so). When we shake hands on a contract or ceremonially hand over something to its new owner the transfer is often conveyed through symbolic bodily movement as much as or more than by words. Gestures can define legal meaning. Raising one's hand or touching the Bible shows that an oath is being sworn: in the Bayeux tapestry Harold is shown swearing an oath of allegiance by touching relics (Figure 4.5). It is 'a sort of semiotic shorthand, alerting people not only to the fact that something of legal consequence is happening but also to the precise legal nature of that "something" . . . the swearing of an oath'; mediaeval gestures of homage acknowledged that the vassal was legally bound while the lord in turn placed his hands over his vassal's to demonstrate his dominance within the feudal relationship (Hibbitts 1995: 63–4). Visible gesture enables communication across linguistic and educational divides.

> Unlike writing, gesturing is something that virtually everyone does and can do. Gesturing does not take years to either learn or interpret. It is usual, simple, and comprehensible to the point that it even transcends speech (making it an instrument that can bridge linguistic as well as educational gaps – a capacity that proved particularly useful in the Middle Ages, when formal law was frequently articulated in Latin or some other language that the common people could not understand).
>
> (Hibbitts 1995: 66)

Among the explicitly articulated gestural systems are those of classical oratory (see Graf 1991). Cicero wrote of the 'language of the body' (*sermo corporis*) and there were many textbooks for orators. Quintilian's treatise in the first century AD considers not only voice but also posture and dynamic gesticulation, emphasising the importance of gesture in conveying emotion and persuading the audience. It

---

(fingers together then separated), asking (kept together); 6. Asking (more pressing than the previous), kissing (starting at mouth then turning and opening the hand energetically to 'throw' the kiss to someone); 7. Dissembling (fingers look like a crab which walks sideways – just like someone's conduct); 8. Finger-snap (various meanings, again differentiated by face or bearing, including joy, acclamation or disdain); 9 and 10. Scorn, offence (from Andrea de Jorio *La mimica degli antichi investigata nel gestire napoletano,* 1832, Plate XX).

Figure 4.5 Swearing an oath

In this scene from the eleventh-century Bayeux tapestry (panel 17), Harold touches two chests of relics as he swears to support William of Normandy's claims to the English throne – not that his oath was kept, as is depicted later in this dramatic embroidered history of the Norman invasion of England. Harold's gesture visibly demonstrates his act of swearing an oath, as also do the presence and posture of those witnessing it (The Bayeux Tapestry – eleventh century. By special permission of the City of Bayeux).

gives systematic instructions about moving parts of the body from head to feet and for manipulating the toga, so as to create the desired impression on the audience. The hand is pre-eminent:

> The hands may almost be said to speak. Do we not use them to demand, promise, summon, dismiss, threaten, supplicate, express aversion or fear, question or deny? Do we not employ them to indicate joy, sorrow, hesitation, confession, penitence, measure, quantity, number and time? Have they not

power to excite and prohibit, to express approval, wonder or shame? Do they not take the place of adverbs and pronouns when we point at places and things?
(Quintilian *Institutio Oratoria* XI, 3, 85–7,
transl. Butler 1922, vol. 4: 289, 291)

Though not always so minutely described, similar oratorical arts are found widely throughout the world. They make studied use of gestural conventions, from the dignified yet dramatic movements of West African orators with their subtle manipulation of outer clothing, to treatises for princes in early modern Italy or the professionally honed techniques of contemporary politicians to sell themselves and their policies on television.

Moving further along the continuum between the more and the less standardised and articulate forms of gesture brings us to the highly formulated and explicit systems. Some are used just for certain purposes, limited circumstances or small specialist groups or occupations. Others, however, constitute extensively developed and articulated systems, widely used and recognised among large numbers of people, such as deaf 'signing' or the 'sign languages' of Aboriginal Central Australia where standardised movements are used to communicate visually as part of an organised system. Different forms have been developed in different cultures and historical periods – far more than is often appreciated. Some are fully, or nearly fully, independent of vocal speech, others bear some relation to it. There is often particular emphasis on the fingers, hands or arms but here, as often, it is impossible to make sharp divisions and other parts of the body are quite often involved as well.

Classifying these systems is scarcely easy, not least because here again there is a continuum in the degree of standardisation and codification, with overlaps rather than sharp divides. However, the summary in Box 4.3 can at least give some idea of their range – extraordinary systems which have generally received far less attention than they deserve. Following the boxed overview a few brief examples will then have to suffice to give some flavour of their variety.[8]

Box 4.3 Systems of communication through visible bodily movements

These examples represent only a selection of the systems developed and used over the centuries. The classifications broadly follow those in Kendon (1988) which, though not necessarily either comprehensive nor fully distinct, form a convenient basis for indicating the range.

Standardised forms of visual signing
Limited to specific settings or with relatively small numbers of codified gestures (not an autonomous mode of discourse).

In specific contexts (often occupational), especially where difficult or inconvenient to communicate through sound, or where visual signs can be detected further away than vocalisation; for example in:

Auctioneering, broadcasting, cinema and other ushering (signalling availability of seats), crane operation, diving, fire fighting, horse-racing (signalling the current betting odds to the bookmakers), lorry driving, marshalling aeroplanes, sawmills, stock market transactions, surveying, sports umpiring, team interchange on the playing field.

In communicating confidentially with selected participants, unknown to others. Overlaps with the above, also examples such as:

Casino staff (discreet communication between croupiers and supervisor about problem players etc.); drug peddlers; hunters (visual signals less likely to alarm prey); street gangs; fellow members of secret or forbidden societies (e.g. Chinese Triad society).

For specific purposes

Finger counting, finger spelling.

Performance and religious systems, for example

European classical ballet; Indian and Chinese theatre; Hindu dance drama (extremely elaborated, but used only in its specific context); Buddhist symbolic hand language (*mudra*).

Sign languages
Autonomous or near-autonomous modes of discourse, with large and flexible vocabularies of codified gestures.

Primary sign languages: full communicative systems, without reference to auditory speech, used especially by deaf people and varying in different countries; for example:

American sign language (ASL); British sign language (BSL); similar sign languages in many other countries (different in each) e.g. Brazil, China, Denmark, Finland, France, Holland, Italy, Japan, Norway, Russia, Sweden, Switzerland, Thailand etc. (also sometimes local dialects within these countries).

Alternative sign languages: developed for special contexts by people who use or have used vocal language in other contexts:

Australian Aboriginal peoples – many systems in North Central Desert; Plains Indians of North America; married women in Armenia (not allowed to speak in in-laws' presence); monks following rule of silence (Cistercians, Cluniacs, Trappists).

Recently devised sign languages: overlap with both the above, worth noting separately merely as having been recently developed (or adapted) for specific purposes; unlike primary sign languages, mostly based in verbal speech or writing:

Finger spelling; 'signed English'; 'manual English'; 'makaton' (for people with learning difficulties or acquired impairments).

The visual system used in the sawmills of Oregon and British Columbia is an example of the many occupational systems: highly developed in its own sphere but otherwise of limited circulation and coverage (summarised in Kendon 1988: 408). It started as a way of coordinating tasks in conditions where spoken signals would be inaudible, but then developed into a complex system in which workers could exchange jokes, news about sporting results, and bits of gossip. Others are less elaborate, but still make effective use of a range of visual gestures. In the din of the Stock Market floor, a racecourse, a public auction, an orchestral performance or a football pitch, vision works better than audition. Sometimes people can see each other but are out of effective earshot, as with crane operators, traffic policemen or broadcasting producers and performers. Skin divers, similarly, are unable to transmit sounds easily but need to exchange rapid and unmistakable signals. In other cases, certain people wish to communicate without drawing the attention from outsiders that would be attracted by vocal speech (for some examples see Figure 4.6).

Using fingers to communicate numbers is another useful device. These systems of visible counting, of which there are several, are codified in the sense that different units can be used separately with unambiguous meaning and also joined in varying permutations. The Romans had a complex method for showing numbers from 1 to 10,000 on the fingers of both hands – a form of 'finger-writing' as Menninger terms it (1969: 201) – also used as a kind of practical commercial language in mediaeval Europe, transcending linguistic and cultural divisions; an illustration can be found in Figure 10.1. In Arabic and East African markets a system of finger enumeration similarly enabled commercial communication between people of different languages while a more limited but comparable system was used in the Chicago cattle market (Menninger 1969: 214, Zaslavsky 1973: 238ff). The example from northern Tanzania in Box 4.4 illustrates the complexity combined with clarity that can be achieved by such systems.

Figure 4.6 Some standardised gestures
Recognised gestural signals where sight is more effective than sound. Top: directing aero-planes on the ground. Middle: signals by producers to performers in broadcasting – film sequence coming up; tape all right now. Bottom: in skin diving – trouble (with my ear); let's go up; air supply; OK (John Hunt).

Box 4.4 Finger counting among the Arusha, northern Tanzania

One hand is used (usually the right). The overt distinctions between (for example) 6, 60 and 600 may seem small but the order of magnitude is normally clear from the context (based on Gulliver 1958: 259ff)

1	Forefinger extended motionless, other fingers lightly curled in palm
2	Forefinger and 2nd finger extended, moved scissor-like with 2 fingers brushing against each other

3	Ball of forefinger on top of thumb, tip of 2nd finger between 1st and 2nd joints of forefinger; 3rd and 4th fingers curled out of way
4	Forefinger and 2nd finger extended, 2nd finger on top of forefinger
5	Clenched fist, tip of thumb protruding between forefinger and 2nd finger
6	Tip of thumb to tip of 3rd finger, and brought down sharply several times with clicking of nails
7	2nd finger rubbed down inside of thumb several times
8	Palm flat, fingers together and extended, thumb straight; whole hand moved up and down slightly
9	Nail of forefinger on ball of thumb to form circle, other fingers extended
10	Begins like 9 then forefinger shot forward to pointing position, other fingers lightly curled up
11–19	Begins with 10, followed by 2nd number (similarly with 20, 30 etc.)
20	Fingers and thumb extended, fingers then slapped down to base of palm and extended 2 or 3 times
30	As for 1 but with slight twisting of wrist
40	As for 8 but with slight twisting of wrist
50	Thumb between forefinger and 2nd finger, 3rd and 4th fingers extended, slight twisting of wrist
60, 70, 80	As for 6, 7, 8 but repeated several times
90	As for 9 but wrist slightly twisted and shaken
100	Fist loosely clenched then fingers shot out, splayed apart
200	Begins with 100, then pause, then forefinger and 2nd finger extended motionless
300, 400, 500	As for 3, 4, 5 with twisting of wrist (whereas 3, 4, 5 are motionless)
600, 700, 800, 900	As for 6, 7, 8, 9 but with vigour so whole hand involved
1000	As for 100, repeated 5 times
2000	As for 100, repeated 10 times

Dance too uses visible movement to communicate.[9] Here, as John Blacking put it, the logic may defy verbal description and even the participants may not be capable of putting it into words, but the dancing may still have its own coherent and structured system where the participants are 'actively sharing a nonverbal mode of discourse' (Blacking 1985: 67). Sometimes performances are linked to known stories or values, enacted visually through the dance so even without any explicitly codified system their conventional force may still be clearly recognised. Kalabari 'Tortoise masquerades' in south-eastern Nigeria, for example, are 'a wonderfully concentrated distillation, in the gestures of the dance, of a character whose portrayal is normally spread through a vast corpus of story' (Horton 1967: 237). Similarly the complex and superlatively controlled arm movements of south Pacific Tongan dances performed by serried rows of uniformly moving dancers are 'a visual extension and enhancement of sung poetry . . . projected into visual form', used to praise and honour gods and chiefs as well as to celebrate events, people and places (Kaeppler 1993: 1 and ff). Military marching and displays – a kind of dancing – have their own effectiveness too. Through massed movements of drilled human bodies they can convey the ideologies of marchers, organisers and spectators to communicate and reinforce multifarious evocations of power, group-confidence, pride or menace.

Some dance traditions employ articulate and codified systems, especially in narrative or representational dance genres. The highly stylised movements of classical ballet and mime are familiar examples but there are many others. Religious hand symbols are extensively used in Buddhism, each symbolising a doctrine or experience such as an event in the Buddha's life (Denny 1987: 463), a system which runs through ritual, iconography, dance and drama and is also used in teaching. In Hindu dance dramas (as in Figure 1.3, p. 22 above) the system of communicative movements is as elaborately developed as in some primary sign languages with gestures representing abstract concepts as well as concrete objects. They have been described in similar terms to written language with its

> repertoire of phoneme-like elements of movement, position and handshape which combine according to rules of formation into units comparable to morphemes. These in turn are assembled within the performance to create units that are analogous to units of discourse.
>
> (Kendon 1988: 408)

Even more comprehensive are many of the 'sign languages': so called because they constitute autonomous or near-autonomous modes of discourse with large and flexible vocabularies made up of codified gestures. Unlike the (relatively) limited forms above, these are systematic, comprehensive in their coverage (insofar as any language can be so), and in principle adaptable for any kind of circumstance or user.

'Primary' sign languages are systems in their own right, communication modes independent of, and unrelated to, vocal speech. The best-known examples are those used in communication with and among the deaf, for example the current British sign language (BSL). These rich and complex systems are now found throughout the world. Families sometimes develop their own idiosyncratic versions and individuals invent new signs, but in general sign languages in the full sense are current and intelligible within whole countries (like spoken languages, they can have their own dialects, however, and contrary to what is sometimes believed there is no one universal sign language). These systems contain the resources to communicate a full range of meanings using a gestural-visual rather than vocal-auditory channel.

The main focus is on signs made by the hands and arms – shapes, locations, movements and orientations – but eyes, face and head often play some part too. Grammatical functions like tense, aspect, negation or verb/noun discrimination, together with subtle meanings and extensions, are conveyed simultaneously by, for example, varying the sign or sign combination slightly, use of eyes or face, or body orientation. Some signs are clearly arbitrary, but, in contrast to most vocal language, there can be some iconic basis (i.e. some kind of relation between a sign and its referent) – although what is seen as 'iconic' of course varies in different traditions.

In the past 'deaf languages' have sometimes been pictured as by definition less complex or subtle than communication using the vocal-auditory channel. At times they have attracted outright hostility, perhaps because they implicitly challenge or bypass the spoken modes of the dominant majority. There continue to be passionate controversies about the merits of signed language as against 'oralism' (speaking plus lip-reading) in the education of deaf children. But it is now more widely appreciated that gestural systems such as the American or British sign languages are full languages in their own right, in that they communicate independently of sound and speech and have their own complex syntactic and morphological structures and poetic forms. They can be – and are – used not just for everyday information and emotional interaction, but also for complex and abstract notions. It has become accepted practice in many large religious gatherings and scholarly conferences for the spoken proceedings to be simultaneously translated into one or more sign language(s). For some, signing carries its own glories as 'an embodiment of [the deaf] personal and cultural identity' (Sacks 1991: 125).

These sign languages share one problem of visual communicating: they cannot operate if sight is obstructed. But they also have advantages over the vocal channel. They function unmolested by the noisiest of conditions and can communicate with more simultaneity than the sequentially uttered sounds of speech.

> Whereas, in speech, linguistically significant units can be organized in temporal sequence only, in the kinesic medium forms may be constructed which contrast in their spatial organization, as well. Furthermore, the instrument of sign language expression, the body, has a number of spatially separated parts which can be used as articulators, simultaneously. Linguistically significant expressions can be constructed that, all at once, involve the head, action in the face and bodily orientation, as well as the hands.
>
> (Kendon 1988: 6)

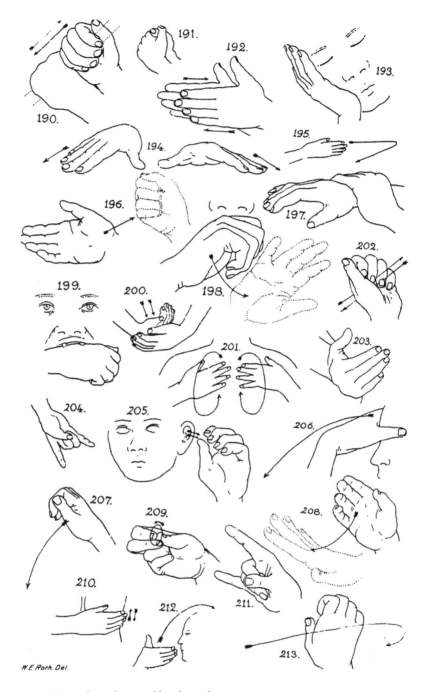

Figure 4.7 Australian Aboriginal hand signals
Aboriginal hand signs, recorded by Walter Roth in the late nineteenth century, were used to depict specific objects such as animals (a rich variety), plants, and manufactured articles;

Users of these signing systems often find them of the greatest subtlety and versatility, contrasting their evocative and vivid qualities favourably with those of spoken communication.[10]

'Alternative' sign languages are systems which, though in themselves extensive, are used only in special contexts and by people who, though competent in vocal language, need to avoid speech for religious or social reasons. In one region of Armenia, for example, a married woman was not allowed to speak in the presence of many of her husband's relatives; the corollary was their use of a complex sign language. European monastic sign languages were similarly developed in mediaeval times to deal with the rule of complete or partial silence among Cistercian, Cluniac and Trappist monks (see for example Umiker-Sebeok and Sebeok 1987). Versions of these are still practised.

The Aboriginal peoples of central Australia created highly complex alternative sign languages for use in certain ritual situations. Women must remain silent as a sign of mourning, sometimes for as long as two years after a husband's or mother's death, and communicate through an elaborate system of signs. Not just something of the past, older women sometimes choose this, even when not in mourning, where it is inconvenient or tiring to speak – signing enables messages to be sent over longer distances and with less effort than vocalising (Kendon 1988: 457). Signs are also used where people are some distance apart and it is inappropriate to talk loudly. Women who are angry sometimes switch into sign language; they also use it in gossiping and to exchange information about their symptoms when waiting in a clinic (Kendon 1988: 90–1). Though mainly a women's communication system, men too use sign language in parts of central Australia, especially during male initiation ceremonies.

Another well-documented but contrasting set of examples are the alternative sign languages of Native American peoples in the great plains of North America. Their use in oratory, story-telling and public performances as well as for everyday communication was plentifully documented by European visitors from the sixteenth century onwards. As the different groups in the Plains area came into greater contact following the introduction of the horse in the seventeenth century, a largely shared sign language emerged, enabling communication across language boundaries, with a range perhaps approaching that of primary sign languages.

Formalised systems such as these are both extensive and little recognised in most

---

number, location and direction; interrogation; various states and conditions; and abstract ideas. Roth translates the hand shapes and movements here as follows (using his original numbering): 190, 191, 192 Fire; 193 Sleep; 194, 195 Swimming; 196 Grasp, catch hold of; 197 Grasp, steal; 198 Eat, food; 199, 200 Anger, intention to fight; 201 Sickness, sick person; 202 Sickness, lie down, sleep; 203 Sickness, seriously sick person; 204 Sickness, moribund, a corpse; 205, 206 Forgetfulness, loss of memory; 207 Yes, all right; 208 No, negation; 209, 210 Good (person or thing); 211 Bad (person or thing); 212 Ghost; 213 Water-sprite (from Walter E. Roth, *Ethnological Studies among the North-West-Central Queensland Aborigines*, 1897, Plate X).

Figure 4.8 Lean Wolf's complaint
'Four years ago the American people agreed to be friends with us, but they lied. That is all' – a protest in sign language by the chief of the Hidatsa Indians, Dakota Territory, when he visited Washington in 1880. The signs, which included movements as well as poses, were translated by Garrick Mallery in 1881 (pp. 526ff) as: 1. 'White man'; 2. 'With us'; 3. 'Friend, Friends'; 4. 'Four [years]; 5. 'Lie'; 6. 'Done, finished: that is all' (from Garrick Mallery, *Sign Language among North American Indians Compared with that among Other Peoples and Deaf-Mutes,* 1881, pp. 526–8).

accounts of communication. Some (perhaps in some senses all) were created by deliberate and systematic planning, such as versions of the deaf signing languages, the sign language 'makaton' (recently developed for communicating with 'mentally handicapped' people), and some of the monastic and occupational systems. For all we know, other sign languages, such as the 'alternative' forms of Australia or North America similarly owed much to individual initiatives. But inherited and learned transmission among actively participating communicators clearly plays a part too, developing and realising these remarkable gestural systems over many years.

These elaborate systems are by no means self-evidently inferior to the auditory medium of speech. And even the less formalised and systematic forms of gesturing with which we started this section have their own unique and sophisticated place. It is certainly hard to imagine the intricate subtlety of human interaction taking place without some deployment of this rich resource of humanly controlled visible movement: 'this old, efficient, and beautiful technology of communication' (Streeck 1994: 266).

The shaped and adorned body

Moving now to another dimension of somatic visual communication we come to the modifications and adornments of human bodies. We interpret others in part by their physical appearance, and take account of visible features like hair arrangement, skin, facial (and other) cosmetics and physical marks. A few physical characteristics such as stature, skin colour, sex or bone structure are relatively unchangeable: they are interpreted in some traditions as communicating crucial or highly emotive information nonetheless and people have sometimes tried to exploit the relatively limited scope for modifying them. In most other respects, however, there are vast possibilities for manipulating the communicative resources of the visible body.

The deliberate shaping and ornamentation of the body is a widespread feature of human culture. There is traditional Chinese foot binding; ear, nose or lip piercing; hand removal as an enduring punitive sign; treatment of the teeth; the strenuously achieved tiny waists or slimness valued by certain groups or the fatness admired by others; tattooing and scarring – all can be used to convey messages to others about an individual's commitments, propensities, gender or status.

Scarification is one example. Branding can communicate the holder's enslavement or criminal status. More often scars are visible signs of an individual's achievement or position. The Brazilian Suyá honour adult men who have killed enemies by parallel horizontal cuts on their legs, arms, chest, back and shoulders, and vertical ones on their buttocks and lower back – marks for all to see, signalling their prowess and status (Seeger 1981: 82–3). Among the Nuer of the southern Sudan, prominent forehead scars marked those who had completed the rigorous initiation into full male adulthood. Their brows were cut to the bone in six cuts from ear to ear, scars that would remain for life (Evans-Pritchard 1940: 249). There are many parallels, all the more visible if clothing is relatively scant and the body with its markings extensively visible.

Tattooing is another common form. A recent study documents its use in Roman times, early modern England, the Renaissance, Victorian Britain, India and Russia, illustrating the diversity of people displaying this form of bodily marking: Christians, convicts, deviants, aristocrats, entertainers, lovers, pilgrims, sailors, serfs and soldiers (Caplan 2000). It is developed to a high degree of sophistication in Japan. In contemporary western cultures it has been used to celebrate personal presence and beauty, signal particular minority attachments, or make a statement of protest or threat – sometimes all of these at once. As Sue Benson points out in her reflections on contemporary Euro-American 'inscriptions of the self', now sometimes a complex art form, tattooing is also used for projecting and incorporating images of the self: a kind of 'montage of my life', 'a private diary', and a way of memorialising those loved and lost so as to 'remember my friend in a way that is now part of me' (Benson 2000: 246). Pacific peoples have also devoted much effort

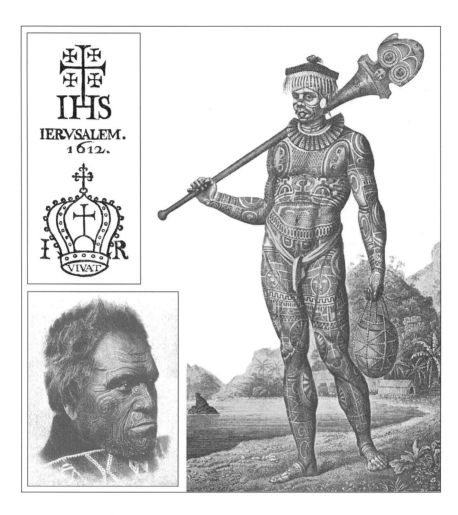

Figure 4.9 A trio of historic tattoos

Left, above: In his memoirs (1640) William Lithgow describes these striking tattoos on his arm as 'The Armes of Jerusalem' and 'King James his foure Crownes'. He visited Jerusalem in 1612 and a local Christian 'did ingrave on our several Armes . . . the name of Jesus, and the Holy Crosse; beeing our owne option, and desire: and heere is the Modell thereof. But I, decyphered, and subjoined below mine, the four incorporate Crowns of King James, with this Inscription, in the lower circle of the Crowne, Vivat Jacobus Rex: returning to the fellow two Piasters for his reward.' The marks visibly asserted his religious and political affiliations (from engraving in William Lithgow *Totall Discourse of Rare Adventures and Painefull Peregrinations . . . in Europe, Asia and Affrica* 1906 [1640] facing p. 252). Left, below: A Maori chief in the late nineteenth century. More than just personal adornment, facial tattoos conveyed the air of disdain and defiance then expected of chiefs in the agonistic ethos of Maori society (from H. G. Robley, *Moko or Maori Tattooing*, 1896, Frontispiece). Right: Marquesan tattoo (late eighteenth- or early nineteenth-century). Marquesan tattooing was characterised by its spectacular visual design over the body as a whole (as elaborate as many

and artistry to the complicated arts of tattooing where the skin acts as symbolic form. In these hierarchical Polynesian cultures tattoos are often connected with social ranking, produced and worn with the greatest visibility and care (see Figure 4.9). As Alfred Gell puts it in his aptly titled *Wrapping in Images*, 'the social skin is the support or vehicle for the expression of social relations . . . a means of creating and marking social differentials and establishing social identities' (1993: 24, 121; for a complementary view, Thomas 1995: 99ff).

People can also convey much about their status, affiliation, gender, situation or disposition through the application of colours, patches or other decoration to their faces (sometimes other parts of the body too) and by treating their teeth and nails. There is the clown's exaggeratedly coloured visage, the painted faces of Peking opera, or the cosmetics considered appropriate for differentiating particular social roles and settings (see Brain 1979, Ebin 1979, Gröning 1997). Even relatively minor signs of this kind can carry important visible messages but some are developed in remarkably elaborate and explicit ways.

In parts of Papua New Guinea, to take one example, people's decorated bodies are seen as presenting their true inner selves (Strathern 1979). Michael O'Hanlon's *Reading the Skin* explains that the Wahgi people's main artistic elaboration lies in the adornment of their bodies and 'skin' (they are without elaborate architectural, ceramic or sculptural traditions:

> In English, the notion of 'adornment' suggests the superficial, the non-essential, even the frivolous. We often think of adornment as an artificially added layer concealing what 'really' lies beneath. The Wahgi concept is rather different. For them, the decorated appearance is more often thought to reveal than to conceal. Far from being frivolous, adornment and display are felt to be deeply implicated in politics and religion, marriage and morality.
>
> (O'Hanlon 1989: 10)

For them body decoration plays a central role, developed especially in their great 'display' occasions. They mark out these festival and martial rituals through the visual media of hair arrangements, head-dress, paint, colour, and special accoutrements. The men decorate themselves with special clothing and adornments, donning arm and head bands, shell and fibre ornaments, bulky aprons, impressive bird plumes to top their head-dresses and in some cases enormously complex wigs and painted display

---

contemporary art tattoos), divided into recognised zones and iconographic patterns with their own specialist terms and carrying mythic and cosmological imagery. For European readers at the time such pictures also often conveyed particular visions of the South Sea Islanders as fierce warriors or, alternatively, as 'children of nature' (from K. Von den Steinen, *Die Marquesaner und ihre Kunst*, vol. 1, 1925, p. 90).

boards. They go to the greatest pains to decorate their faces, applying charcoal, pork fat, and red and yellow paints. A specialised vocabulary distinguishes the variegated processes: painting in dots or spots; scoring a line of paint along or across a given facial feature; applying paint at an angle or zigzag; using paint to surround or 'dig out' a facial feature such as the eyes. Metaphorical terms describe the design elements with names like 'water pool', 'bird's foot' and 'lizard's foreleg' (O'Hanlon 1989: 92–3).

In common with other writers on this area, O'Hanlon regards Wahgi display as essentially 'a system of communication' (1989: 17). Their visual adornments communicate images of strength and well-being. In the Wahgi setting of shifting alliances and hot rivalries, they make visible political statements to intimidate rival clans, frighten enemies, assert their strength, change the perceptions of events, or assert claims to land and power. They embody information about crucial moral relationships, authenticated visually on the skin. In Wahgi terms, the 'skin appears bad' if there is dissension within the group, but if united 'their skin is like fire smoke. Their fighting goes well and they go out to beat down the enemy. . . . The charcoal on their bodies really smokes and their skin sparkles' (quoted in O'Hanlon 1989: 126). As Morphy comments more generally on this form of bodily communicating:

> The painted and decorated artist is not making a [linguistic] statement 'I am fierce', rather he is creating an image of fierceness, power, and group identity that is integral to the presentation itself. The body painting works not only as communication to others but on the person's self, creating an image of power that is palpably *felt*.
>
> (Morphy 1994: 666)

Hair is well placed for visual communicating. Dreadlocks, oiling, wigs, straightened or dyed hair, shaven or tufted heads – all can indicate, or be interpreted as indicating, the affiliations or intentions of their wearers. Confining the hair, hiding it or dressing it in a specific way is often an outward sign of a particular status or of accepting the obligations of particular religious groups. So too is wearing it loose or uncut. Carefully constructed coiffures can visually assert prestige or aspiration, seen in extreme form in the gigantic erections of the 'bigwigs' of the eighteenth-century French court. Beards are often a prominent mark of religious, chiefly or senior status, and various meanings have been attached to the presence, absence or specific shape of facial hair. The visual messages to fellow members of particular groups or cultures cover a wide communicative range, providing information about people's stages in the personal or family life cycle or visibly asserting or imposing affiliations related to religion, gender, age, gang or interest-group.

Ornaments too say something about the wearer. Wedding and engagement rings are a prime example in western cultures: not just attractive adornments but also telling us about the wearer's status. So do crosses or crucifixes with their Christian connotations, badges of particular organisations, necklets with Koranic inscriptions, or coloured ribbons giving information about their wearers' armed service. In contemporary English culture earrings worn by men are interpreted in specific ways, while in West Africa the sex of even the smallest girl baby is immediately conveyed by her earrings. Ear- and lip-discs among Central Brazilian Suyá declare their wearers' life-stage, and as people age 'the design of their ornaments changes and they assume different roles' (Seeger 1981: 82). The ornaments also mark their identity as Suyá, for these highly visible ear- and lip-discs unambiguously distinguish them from their neighbours.

This leads into the subject of clothing – not such a large step after all for, as Eicher and Roach-Higgins comment:

> The dressed person is a *gestalt* that includes body, all direct modifications of the body itself, and all three-dimensional supplements added to it. . . . Only through mental manipulation can we separate body modifications and supplements from the body itself – and from each other – and extract that which we call dress.
>
> (Eicher and Roach-Higgins 1992: 13)

What people are wearing affects our judgement of them. People's attire can mark particular roles, life-stage, gender, achievements, or group membership – or, at any rate, be interpreted by its observers as so doing. Clothes can carry clever misinformation too, as when people dress misleadingly to disguise themselves or wear clothing suggesting a status or profession to which they are not entitled. Transition from one life-stage to another commonly involves a change of clothes, whether through ceremonial enrobing (as in graduation or coronation rituals) or as a continuing sign of the new stage thereafter. Female converts in Africa for example were once expected to cover their breasts, visibly confirming their Christian status. The prominent display or suppression of 'traditional' clothing often plays a part in formulating (or denying) ethnic self-consciousness. Gandhi insisted on locally produced cloth – 'the fabric of Indian independence' – as a way of asserting and marshalling Indian national identity in opposition to British colonial rule (Bean 1989). Clothing is in fact widely used in asserting, accepting, presupposing or even rebutting specific personal, political or religious claims.

The clothing of the head is often particularly important. This high, central and extremely visible part of the attire frequently publicises religious, status or gender affirmations. The 'crowning achievements' of African arts of dressing the head have drawn particular notice:

> From ancient Egypt to the present, Africans have regularly invested this 'head-work' [hats, caps, diadems, crowns and hairstyles] and its permanent or ephemeral products with heightened value. Certain headdresses can recall founding myths or historical episodes. Hats and hair styles can celebrate the achievements of individuals or glorify an office.
>
> (Arnoldi 1995: 9)

The diverse head coverings of Muslim women convey something about their wearers' affiliation or situation, and the distinctive head-dress for men who have made the pilgrimage to Mecca visibly marks their religious achievement. English monarchs are crowned and Hausa leaders turbanned as visible signs of assuming their authority and the doffing or resuming of head gear can declare both status and gender recognition. This flexible and prominent resource of the head is widely used

> to express and explore shared and deeply held cultural beliefs and values towards ethnicity, gender, life stages, status and authority, occupation, and social decorum. . . . As a material 'language' hats and hair styles can be put on, and taken off, manipulated, and invested with an aggregate of meanings depending on how and in what contexts they are put into play.
>
> (Arnoldi 1995: 13–14)

Other items of apparel can be significant too. In contemporary Britain men are still sometimes excluded from certain formal occasions if not wearing ties – conveying the wrong image. Scarves, shawls, veils or belts can be interpreted as visual signs about the wearers or help to define specific occasions: veils in weddings for example or gun belts in 'country and western' gatherings. Wearing a mask can convey, variously, anonymity, disguise, transient role-changing, romance, intimidation, playfulness or the outward signs of superhuman spirit power – and do all these things more effectively than any attempts to convey them by words. Other visible accoutrements too can declare something about the wearer. One need only mention episcopal crooks, dark glasses, monocles, fans, sceptres, batons, wands, watches, briefcases or stethoscopes.

The fact that clothing is so visible gives it very immediate communicative force. As Barnes and Eicher point out, the clothed body means that 'visual communication is established before verbal interaction even transmits whether such a verbal exchange is possible or desirable' (1992: 1). We have probably all noticed on occasion how someone's clothing influences how they are treated by, say, a waiter, receptionist or passers-by in the street. Clothing is accepted as a mark of the wearer's status, work, age, cultural identity or even appropriate participation in a specific occasion. Gender is communicated through clothing, something which may itself have strong resonances with the culture's social and symbolic system. Consider the colourful appliqué panels – *molas* – which Panamanian Cuna women make and wear. These are not only a continuously visible sign of a Cuna woman's 'hard work, ability, creativity, and individuality' but also an outward mark of the sexual division of labour and of power. At Cuna meetings the (male) chiefs chant and their interpreters explain the chants, while 'the women listen, wearing their best *molas*, and making new ones' (Sherzer and Sherzer 1976: 31, 36). 'The clothed body', as Perani and Wolff put it, 'is essential to the projection of the social self by expanding the "vocabulary" of the body and visually reinforcing social roles' (1999: 1).

Some individuals and groups of course labour under greater constraints in their choices than others. But these visual messages do not necessarily depend on great arrays of different clothes or on the 'culture of consumption' sometimes said to be characteristic of the present era. There is always some opening for display. West African women for example are famous for clever re-arrangements of a single head-tie to signify differing dispositions and intentions on different days, while even the apparently concealing veils among Rajasthani married women with their covered faces can be subtly manipulated to convey multiple messages about the wearer's status and demeanour (Lambert 2001: 60). In all parts of the world, we can be sure, people 'dress to impress' and 'to look the part' (Keenan 2001).

Sometimes the role of clothing is highly formalised and explicit. Carefully planned attire is often a prominent feature of ceremonial occasions, while in many parts of Africa whole groups sometimes deliberately don identical clothes to communicate their loyalty to a particular family, association or political party (Perani and Wolff 1999: 29). Particular roles or statuses are marked by special clothing, from the leopard skins worn by priests among the otherwise near-naked Nuer to the deliberate costuming of prisoners, schoolchildren, nurses or police officers. In street feuds as well as on the sports field contrasting clothing visibly signals both friends and opponents. This explicitly identifying power of clothing was well recognised by the city of Harvard's law in 1993 forbidding anyone in the city to 'knowingly use, display or wear colors, emblems, or insignia' that communicated the wearer's gang membership or sympathies (DeVito 2000: 139).

Contravening the accepted 'dress codes' can carry strong messages, sometimes making people consciously aware of what before they had merely presumed or bringing some underlying dispute to the surface. Someone turning up to an event in attire classed by others to be ostentatiously 'wrong' can be taken to present a visibly disruptive challenge to the accepted order – witness the furore over the 'disrespect' conveyed by the then leader of the Labour Party Michael Foot when he attended a national cenotaph ceremony in duffel coat, not formal suit. Contrariwise copying the appearances and attire of 'significant others' – political or religious leaders, say, admired peers, saints, film stars – can carry symbolic meaning for those who would emulate them. Clothing can be organised in versatile ways to make particular points. The Amazonian Ashéninka are notably skilled in the deliberate manipulation of clothing. They regard their handmade cotton tunics (cushma) as *the* sign of their identity and existence, 'a symbol of the Ashéninka perception of themselves as in possession of their own cultural and social universe' (Veber 1996: 173). But they also use this costume deliberately, donning it for self-presentation in Amazonian political gatherings but changing into western clothes for visual 'impression management' when bargaining with settlers, knowing they get better terms when not wearing Ashéninka garb (Veber 1996: 174–6).

Clothes can also be effective visual signals in cultures and situations where ranking matters. Sometimes there are explicit rules about who can wear what. Some companies have dress codes for employees which in effect visably communicate their place in the hierarchy while differential ranks in armies and other highly hierarchical organisations are signalled by distinctive uniforms, an immediate sign of the wearer's position. In fifteenth-century England the permissible clothing for different social classes was prescribed by law. The clothing-reform act in Edward IV's reign, for example, decreed that 'no knight under the rank of a lord . . . shall wear any shoes or boots having pikes or points exceeding the length of two inches, under the forfeiture of forty pence' (quoted in Morris 1977: 217).

In religious contexts too clothing can be a deliberate communicative tool, identifying members of religious orders or conveying both overt and symbolic allegiance. Think for example of the attire for Christian nuns, for orthodox Jews or, among certain groups, for Muslim women, together with the religious symbolisms these embody. Clothing carries particular significance among adherents of minority or proselytising religious groups such as seventeenth-century Quakers, contemporary Amish communities in America, or the twentieth-century Christian missionaries whose converts' acceptance of particular dress codes (especially female) visibly demonstrated their religious status. The correct dress was of crucial importance for members of the South African Zionist church. The women wore a striking attire of white robes, green tunics and white headscarves, uniforms held to be infused with power and to encase their wearers like a shield. These uniforms distinguished them from others in the over-crowded areas where they lived, prominently declaring their religious identity and commitment (Comaroff 1985: 203ff). Linda Arthur rightly notes that:

> While a person's level of religiosity can not be objectively perceived, symbols such as clothing are used as evidence that s/he is on the 'right and true path'. . . . We wear our identities on our bodies and our bodies are used by religions to visually communicate world views.
>
> (Arthur 1999: 1, 6)

Having started with the body, we have now moved into areas which extend beyond it. Clothing shades into textiles, ornaments into the three-dimensional and plastic arts. There is no dividing line. Even in the earlier sections of this chapter we had to go beyond the body itself – for 'the body' never really is just 'itself'. One reason is of course that its conceptualisations vary in different traditions – the body schemas of the Yucatec Maya for example are very unlike those of the English (Hanks 1996: 249ff) – and a separation between 'internal body' and 'external world', so to speak, is scarcely a cultural universal. It will also by now be clear that even the subtleties of facial expressions, let alone gestures and the more standardised visual systems, are all human-made – they are 'embodied' but not a-cultural.

Furthermore many material artefacts are at times shaken, waved, swayed or otherwise moved as part of our proxemic and kinesic communicating, and as we have just seen the dressing and ornamentation of our bodies adds yet further dimensions. But if there is no sharp divide between intrinsic and extrinsic forms of communication, it is nevertheless worth noting that we have increasingly been dealing with visible signs that are relatively external – a bridge therefore into the focus of the next chapter on the human-made artefacts so much used in our visual communicating.

Our embodied visual resources

Visible bodily movements, spatial positionings and the shaping of the body are sometimes brushed aside as if belonging to some earlier stage in human communication, now somehow outmoded or superseded by the quintessentially human art of verbal language. This viewpoint seriously underestimates the communicating capacities of our bodily acts and appearances. Most human beings deploy their bodies extensively and subtly to communicate visually with each other just about every day of their lives, not to speak of the truly remarkable sign languages and other gestural systems discussed earlier. It is extraordinary that many accounts of communication give so little attention to these wide-ranging bodily resources used so creatively, not only to amplify verbal interchange by forms with their own unique qualities, but also at times to transcend it.

Recent developments are perhaps extending our appreciation of these somatic communicative arts. As Hibbitts remarks, video and computer technology is now making gesture 'readily recordable, transmissible, and (in virtual reality) simulable . . . potentially permanent and independent of physical co-presence' (1995: 74–5). The same might be said of the reproduction and distance-transmission of movement, spatial relationships and bodily appearances more generally. This is not a totally new phenomenon. Telescopes, eye glasses and other optical devices had already extended the range of human vision and thus of our visibly communicating bodies; in any case this form of visual communication is not just a matter of co-presence, for we have long used and interpreted it in pictures and three-dimensional representations and, more recently, in photographs. But facial expression, gesture, and bodily spacing and appearance are now becoming increasingly communicable over wider spans of both time and space. We are skilled in interpreting even the smallest eye movements or eyebrow changes on close-up faces on television, the body movements of real and fictional personages, the actions we see on film and video. We recognise the communicative force of these embodied movements and spatial presences across distance as well as creating them ourselves.

It might seem that in starting with the body we have been dealing with the more 'natural' and fundamental elements of visual communication. And it is certainly true that our intrinsic biological resources link us with the visual communicative strategies of other animals. There is also a sense in which the body is a 'natural' symbol, as Mary Douglas put it (1966, 1973). But this is far from implying that we have here reached some unchanging bedrock of communication, far less something lower on the evolutionary scale or less fully human than other communicative forms. Our corporeality is indeed in one way basic to us all. But it is also the site of great elaboration, a rich communicative resource adapted in myriad ways as a tool in human communicating. Comaroff rightly states:

> The 'natural' constitution of human bodily forms give[s] it enormous potential for symbolic elaboration and representation – of structures in space, of processes in time, and . . . of the interrelationship of the two.
>
> (Comaroff 1985: 8)

To adapt Schiffer's term, people are themselves 'macroartefacts' (1999: 42). The body with its adornments, movements and spacing everywhere provides a visual stage and surface which humans organise to project themselves and their commitments. It is infinitely variable and subtle, with many depths and intricacies, but also a familiar and easily tapped part of our everyday communicative interactions. The manifold displays, movements, placings and modifications of the visible body in all their complexities are no less human or less creative than those other human-made arts and artefacts to which we must now turn.

5   Creating and sharing sights: human arts and artefacts

As well as the sights in and from their bodies, human beings also fashion external visible objects, from monocles to pictures, from house decoration to print. The body is itself a work of art and there is of course no sharp line between the embodied arts of the last chapter and the constructed sights less directly located in our bodies. But we do need to take special account of the striking human practice of creating prolific external arts and artefacts, linked perhaps to our visual acuity, tactile efficiency, and the upright posture which gives our hands their freedom.

There seems no end to the manifold human-made objects and arts we use in visual communication. Textiles, carvings, pictures, dwellings, furniture, utensils, books, scripts, graphics, films, photographs – we grow up surrounded by constructed visible objects, both flat surfaces and three-dimensional forms. Many seem a taken-for-granted part of the environment and it is indeed true, as Danny Miller points out (1994), that a distinction between 'artefactual' and 'natural' is scarcely easy to draw. But so many of the objects we see and use every day are unambiguously created by human act and design. Their specific forms and applications may vary across the innumerable historical eras and cultures of the world. But all human beings have experience of living in a visible world of human-constructed artefacts which between them figure substantially in our lives.

The communicative significance of these human-made materials is now being increasingly recognised. Physical objects are being taken more seriously as media for human interaction, with a greater awareness of the intricate and influential ways that material artefacts are linked into human affairs. Recent analyses of remembering emphasise that it is not only through verbal arts that we maintain social memories but also through the materiality of monuments and of visible and tangible objects (Fabian 1996, Forty and Küchler 1999, Kwint et al. 1999). Historians and others supplement their study of texts by considering pictorial and spatial communication systems or the role of visible objects in the symbolic or iconographic systems of particular groups. As Schiffer justly comments in *The Material Life of Human Beings*, 'artifacts participate in virtually all human communication' (1999: 89).

The sight of objects

What then are these arts and artefacts that we create and use in visual communication? No list could cover them fully, but the range runs from buildings, architecture and the shaped environment through plastic and three-dimensional arts like carving, basketry, weapons and other implements, ceramics, jewellery or furniture, to cloth and to the manifold pictorial and graphic forms, among them photography, heraldic designs, writing, the notations for music and movement, and the moving images of dance and of film . . . and that is only to scratch the surface, merely a quick and unsystematic reminder of (some of) the staggering variety that humans have produced, distributed and utilised as part of their collective human life.

All these forms have multiple dimensions of course – tactile or auditory, often, as well as visual; but it is fair to say that in our communicating their visual properties are often particularly significant. We *see* these pictures, street signs, houses, tombs, crosses, dances, written pages, and have learned to apply our visual capacities so as to appreciate not only their shape, size and distance in both two and three dimensions, but also their texture, depth, structure, materials, physical relationships and colour, in both their simultaneous immediacies and their sequences over time. And when we wish to affect others by means of such objects, it is often their *sight* that we bring prominently into play.

Visible objects provide a shared backdrop to our lives and through their visual conventions and imageries directly colour our interactions. Even the landscape which to outsiders may just appear a fact of nature is experienced and shaped through human – and varying – construction rather than just passively perceived. Visual images are often to the fore in these 'cognitive maps', sometimes entwined with complex but diverse symbolic linkages between identity and the concepts and experiences of place. Cityscapes, seascapes, deserts, even particular hills or streets carry their own associations. In Carey's words, 'Place is no empty substratum . . . it is an already plenary presence permeated with culturally constituted institutions and practices' (1996: 46).[1] Here as in other fields human interaction is moulded by people's lived experiences, from their varying perceptions of the heavens or of the human face – shaped in part by current pictorial conventions – to shared visions of the nature of humankind. The taken-for-granted imageries and visual preconceptions with which people see the world help to structure their actual processes of communicating.

Against this background any of the multifarious material forms in the human world can on occasion be actively utilised in human interconnecting. They can be used to communicate about, for example, social relationships, status, personal and group identities or aspirations, political claims, ideologies, values, symbolic ground rules, or religious commitments. All this can take a variety of forms, from the unspoken but nonetheless effective roles of the built environment or everyday decorations to the more systematically arranged media of maps, pictographs and visible writing systems. The field is too vast to do more than dip into, so a few examples will have to suffice to illustrate our human usage of this great and varied array of visual resources.

One issue needs to be recalled briefly first. Clothes, houses, flags, printed pages, paintings and other visible human products do not communicate of *themselves* but only as and when they are selectively – and variously – used and interpreted as such by human beings. The religious uniforms or the ornaments mentioned in the last chapter, Ashanti goldweights (Figure 2.3) or the Laughing Buddha of Figure 5.1, are not themselves communicative, only as formulated and organised in particular human experiences. It is tempting to assume that we always know what specific objects 'mean' or that an interpretation acceptable to one group – or to the analyst – must necessarily be shared by everyone. Often indeed they are surrounded in given cultural settings by commonly understood practices and associations. But human uses of visible objects are typically multiplex, and to imply that they carry

Figure 5.1 The Laughing Buddha
One of many Buddhist statues near Lingyin Temple (Hangzhou, China), carved in the rock between the tenth and fourteenth centuries. It gives one recognised representation of the Buddha, popular throughout China, material token too of a particular viewpoint on the world. He stands for happiness, prosperity and long life, 'the Buddha of the future' and 'the loving and friendly one' who can foretell the future and (specially if his belly is rubbed) bring good luck. In a couplet dedicated to him 'His belly is big enough to contain all intolerable things in the world; / His mouth is ever ready to laugh at all snobbish persons under heaven' (Photograph: David Murray).

some unmistakable or uniform code or meaning is unwarranted, at best over-simplified. We need to proceed cautiously, looking to accounts rooted in specific ethnographies not just to generalised analyses (hence the number of short examples and illustrations in the discussion below). But, that said, it does indeed appear that visible objects are often actively and purposively utilised in human communicating – and to a greater extent and over a wider range than has often been appreciated.

The 'obvious' case might seem to be a page carrying written words. This is certainly one good example of the human use of a visual object for communicating, one that will reappear later in this chapter. But it can also be a misleading model, especially if its strong associations with concepts of linearity and cognition are taken as the norm, for in one sense it is no different from other uses of visible objects. As with them, it only becomes relevant for communicating as and when *used* as such. An unread un-noticed page does not communicate on its own. Nor can it be used effectively unless shared conventions (more, or less, shared that is) enable people to see it in particular ways – ways which may well vary with differing groups and situations. It is the same with other cases. Whether it is a matter of writing, of pictures, or of other material objects, their use in communication is rooted in human-made conventions and in the active processes of human interconnecting.

Many visual objects are not inscribed with writing. But that is not to say that they have to be a less rich resource for human communication. This rather obvious point, clear to all who have studied human uses of pictorial images, has too often been obscured by the value attached to the written word in western educational practice. Banners, pots, geometrical designs, rugs, sticks, carvings or the embodied philosophy of the Buddha statue – these too are on occasion utilised as visual vehicles for human communicating. The conventions for their usage are sometimes less tightly articulated than the formulations of visible writing. But then – the theme of this volume – the processes of human communicating are emphatically not confined just to words.

Take something so mundane as a fence. Fences are often useful devices for physically confining or separating, but they can also be visible signs on the ground for communicating boundaries and dividing different groups or practices. In Papua New Guinean gardens, fences certainly keep pigs away from sweet potatoes. But they also classify the spheres of pigs and of gardens and visually signal the bounds of private gardens (Barnard and Spencer 1996: 545, Sillitoe 1988). The practical and emotive connotations of these visible markers of exclusiveness have resonated through many cultures and periods, not least in the enclosure of land for private ownership or colonial administration. Fences were a central issue, for example, in the long efforts by the Native Affairs Department of the Northern Transvaal to control and divide the land in the late nineteenth and early twentieth centuries. Their aims of precise land measurement, private ownership, and permanent visible boundary marks fitted ill with traditional ideas of land use. Isabel Hofmeyr describes how local residents of the over-crowded chiefdom saw the erection of fences both as barriers cutting off their accustomed routes to water and other resources and as part of the whites' takeover of the land by putting their marks on it. 'The wire' was the crucial sign, set up to 'enforce dispossession and make private property a reality' (Hofmeyr 1993: 77). Once erected, fences became not just visible markers warning off outsiders and sanctioning private possession but prominent tokens of new bureaucratic and literate ideologies. 'The fence embodies the reality of the boundary and . . . writes it permanently into the earth' (Hofmeyr 1993: 77).

The built environment, like the landscape, can be a potent resource for visual communication. Houses, public buildings, and city layouts are all highly visible dimensions of people's lives, settings where political or symbolic meanings can be expressed and reinforced. They can remind dwellers of their history, their identity and their differentiations, not through words but visually. The locale of power or nature of social divisions are visibly incorporated in fortified castles, public edifices, street furniture or contrasting city quarters, memories and evaluations carried in the presence and siting of war memorials, while mosques, temples or churches declare the values of spiritual authority with their visual display. In mediaeval Europe the Christian church played a leading role in conceptualising space and organising territorial divisions imbued with sacral meanings such as the cemetery, parish, and church buildings (Rosenwein 1999). When power changes hands the signs on public edifices often change to send different messages; new regimes remove their predecessors' statues and previously prominent monuments lose their place.

Dwellings, too, are more than just places for people to reside or find shelter and are often used to display both shared symbols and differential statements about their dwellers. Some houses visibly communicate the authority and wealth of their owners through their setting, architecture or adornment; pre-eminent examples are royal palaces or the precisely conveyed signs of rank in the ornamentation of some Chinese buildings. Subtle points about their inhabitants are communicated by the location of dwellings or by lace curtains, open verandahs, front doors, flowers, garden furniture, flags or shrines. In sixteenth- and seventeenth-century Norwich the city's power structure could be viewed in the visual mnemonics of street furniture, not least in prominent house fronts. One Christopher Jay erected carvings of Samson and Hercules on his doorstep:

> Fellow members of the educated urban elite, and a substantial proportion of more humble inhabitants of the city, would have known what Jay was saying in making this installation. As they walked past these imposing sentries they would have recalled the immensely popular tales of Hercules, those sermons on Samson . . . [recognising] Jay's implicit assertion through his street furniture that he and his like were the strong men who undertook stupendous labours on behalf of the city.
>
> (Morgan 1999: 190)

This kind of visual statement is not confined to the past. In *The Meaning of the Built Environment* (1990), Rapoport describes new communities in California whose residents had little money left after buying their houses, often not enough for adequate furniture. Even so they invariably put in front lawns and maintained them; these not only communicated the dwellers' adherence to a particular image of group identity, but also 'certified the worthiness of the individual to inhabit the particular area' (Rapoport 1990: 129–30).

The house and its objects enshrine and perpetuate family memories while its internal layout marks out areas for people with specific characteristics or separates the more and the less public spaces. In many South Asian houses gender roles are symbolised in divisions between women's food-preparing spaces and the more public realms; likewise among the Papua New Guinean Kwoma the separated areas for men and women convey and visibly reinforce a recurrent local theme: men ceremonially and spatially at the centre, women at the periphery (Bowden 1992). Mongol tents had complex spatial rules, the designated places for both objects and people acting as visible markers of their strict ranking system and division of labour. The rank of each category was explicitly communicated through physical separations within the tent and a guest sitting in the wrong place could incur a heavy fine for insulting his host (Humphrey 1974). In our own homes we may not make precisely those divisions, but we still know the meaning of visitors 'making themselves at home' if they take possession of a space usually reserved for the permanent residents.[2]

The layout of buildings and other arenas for human interaction encapsulates and conveys social divisions and activities, in homes, schools, or public offices alike. The rake of a long lecture theatre structures pedagogic communicating differently from a wider single-level room while the physical layout of a church conveys the expected separation or, it may be, integration of clergy and laity, at times a matter of heated congregational and theological dispute. Diane Sidener's contrast between a high Episcopal Church and a Friends Meeting house in Philadelphia (1987) makes a similar point. The spatial character of each building expressed and formulated people's weekly experience of their shared worship. The cruciform layout of the church, with its division between nave (where the congregation must sit) and chancel (for the choir and sanctuary), together with the plentiful inner architectural features marking these spatial distinctions – all encouraged a prime visual focus on the altar and on the intermediary role of the clergy. Worshippers experienced and used the symbolically imbued areas of the church as they moved to interact with the clergy in the sacred space near the altar during the act of communion. The square room of the Friends Meeting house was signally different, with its inward-facing benches and lack of decoration. Its visual focus was the empty space in the middle, a visible sign of the Quaker belief in seeking inwardly for the Spirit and in the communion of every person direct with God. In these buildings, as in many other cases,

Figure 5.2 Street signs
Visible signs have commonly been used by shops, trades and inns to publicise their services.
Top: Baker and wine merchant, Pompeii (70 AD). Below: Two jolly brewers (Banks's Bills
1770), Nag's head tavern (Cheapside 1640) (from J. Larwood and J. C. Hotten, *The History
of Signboards*, 1866, from Plates I and II).

> social interaction is conducted in places that are symbolically preordained:
> buildings, zones, locations, as well as objects and their locations, embody
> social-symbolic order. . . . Interaction contextualizes itself within histories of
> material symbolic practice and contributes another chapter to it, by reinscrib-
> ing material culture.
>
> (Lebaron and Streeck 1997: 2)

Cloth (and fabric more generally) is another highly visual medium for communication, remarkably elaborated throughout the world in a great variety of forms
and settings. It offers a flexible and portable resource, a surface which cries out for
decoration in the form of colour and design, and though not without other sensual
qualities is above all a strikingly visual object. These features of cloth have been
exploited extensively through the centuries to create abstract, graphic and pictorial

design, from American Indian blankets or the colourful patternings of Middle Eastern and Asian carpets to embroidered personal and religious motifs or domestic patchwork quilts, mnemonic embodiments of the origin and meaning of the patches. The personal input into stitching and weaving is itself sometimes a vehicle for individual expression, even in circumstances of otherwise little overt power, a visible and socially acceptable means of formulating their makers' own 'story' not in words but through a created visual artefact.

Cloth is much used for visually commemorating and conveying particular views of the past and present. Tapestries are displayed to depict and celebrate famous individuals or events, while throughout Africa specially printed cloths commemorate independence anniversaries, educational and health programmes, visiting dignitaries, festivals, popular musicians and the birthdays of important people (Perani and Wolff 1999: 30). The iconography of altar coverings communicates and reinforces symbolic images for the faithful; so do T-shirts of musical bands and their fans. Flags too are spectacular signs of political alignment, dissent or triumphalism. The passionate quarrels in Northern Ireland are a familiar example, where flying the British Union Jack or, alternatively, the Irish tricolour is to make a prominent and divisive political statement. Flamboyant embroidered banners were commissioned in the early twentieth century by Canada's Governor-General to mobilise the spirit of Empire and strengthen ties between Canada and Britain. They depicted Saint George, the patron saint of England, visually advertising the values of 'Englishness' and of Empire (Salahub 1999).[3]

Some relatively autonomous and explicitly articulated systems are based on visual materials. There are semaphore systems, flags at sea, and (with more limited purposes) traffic lights; also, for more distant communicating, human uses of fire, heliographs and visible material signals, for example through beacon relays over many hundreds of miles or the eighteenth-century 'mechanical telegraph' (other standardised systems need to be considered among the pictorial and graphic categories treated in the next section).

More often perhaps material objects are interwoven with other forms of communicating. Clothing and other accoutrements are exploited as part of gesturing, speakers brandish sceptre, document, weapon or other exhibit as exemplars, adding visual emphasis to their arguments, someone picks up a pen or book to signify the end of an interview. Stories are recounted not just through spoken words but also through dynamic visual enactment, like the Australian Aboriginal sand-drawings (see below pp. 154–6) or the string figures that encapsulate narrations in South Pacific islands. In mime, dance, film and theatre, visible 'props' are part of the performance, just as the circuses of classical Rome used moveable scenery, hidden lifts, and pulleys to present changing scenes of palm groves, rocky hills, pavilions and displays of Asian and African animals, impressing the thousands-strong audiences with the empire's far-flung successes (Owen 1999). In a less spectacular but still vivid way, George Fox's journal depicts a seventeenth-century Quaker making a symbolic and prophetic communication when she 'was moved to go to the Parliament that was envious against Friends [Quakers] and to take a pitcher in her hand and break it to pieces, and to tell them that so should they be broken in pieces, which came to pass presently after' (quoted in Bauman 1983: 87).

This last example reinforces the point that material artefacts do not have to take particular forms – 'representational' or otherwise – to act as a medium for communicating. Almost anything can be used as a 'present', for example, signifying (among other possibilities) affection, gratitude, ingratiation, tribute or a new status, so long as it is presented following the accepted conventions and in the appropriate setting. Showing off a new bicycle by riding it down the street can assert pride, handing over a pen to someone recognises his superiority, sending and receiving a Christmas card mark a continuing social relationship. Everywhere people make use in their variegated ways of visible physical objects to communicate. The 'ornamentalism' of the British Empire functioned through manifold material forms to display and communicate the images of social hierarchy that interconnected the imperial world (Cannadine 2001). The distinctive decorated sticks of the Ethiopian Oromo visibly demarcated their users' life-stages and symbolically 'ground man to the reality of his being . . . link to the present and his past' (Kassam and Megerssa 1996: 164). The Ashanti miniature goldweights in Ghana evoked proverbs (Figure 2.3) and Ponam Islanders in the Pacific laid out their history and organisation through ordered displays of food – visual maps of the village (Carrier and Carrier 1995). Flashing colours and special costumes are a powerful dimension of dance, carnival or public procession, while the sight of approaching military vehicles or armed personnel can convey an unmistakable threat. The sight of sacred objects like cross, chalice, or Bible carry profound meanings for devotees in religious services; so too does the solemn carrying or lowering of coffin or shrouded corpse in funeral rituals. All over the world precious valuables link people together through public displays and exchanges. In short practically any visible object can be utilised on occasion. Beadwork, decorated pottery, baskets, carved surrounds, cars, relics, pianos – all are at times brought into play as visual assertions of particular claims, the outward sign of personal presence or allegiance, or a host of other purposes.

So rather than producing more examples here, let me conclude this section by simply saying that everyone will be able to think of their own favourite cases of using human-made objects to communicate. For as humans we are all well experienced in employing visual artefacts to assert or deny particular viewpoints, make religious or political statements, express and encapsulate personal stances, and reiterate, qualify, reject or subtly alter relationships. All this and more is made possible by the multiplex and sophisticated human capacity for creating and using visible sights.

Pictorial and graphic sights

A slim line divides the previous examples from what could be broadly termed pictorial and graphic forms. These too are part of human material culture. Extremely
important in human communicating, they demand some direct discussion on their
own.

As so often the terminology is unsettled. 'Pictorial', 'graphic', 'icon' and
'image' are all used in both generic and more specific senses which variously include
or exclude the others. Here I follow some writers and, perhaps, common usage in
making a rough division among them: 'graphic' mainly for more stylised and syn-
copated forms, mostly two-dimensional and sometimes combinable into larger
visual communication systems such as written scripts; 'pictorial' generally for less
condensed or standardised visual forms, especially (though not only) those of a representational nature; 'image' and 'icon' mostly as less specific terms overlapping
these categories, but with the former tending more towards the 'pictorial' end of
the continuum, the latter towards the 'graphic'. However, none are clearly distinct
categories with precise meanings, and ultimately it is impossible to make a sharp
break between them.

The same applies to the line between 'representational' and 'non-representational'.
How people 'represent' what they see is a relative matter, affected by the visual systems they have grown up in, whether the Christian, Buddhist, Hindu or Australian
Aboriginal traditions, the rich geometrical symbolisms of Islamic art, the differing
conventions before and after the development of perspective, or the deeply felt aesthetic and personal associations of cattle colours among Nilotic peoples (Coote
1992). Pictorial conventions and people's visual experiences are mutually intertwined. The contrasting depictions of birds in Javanese batik illustrate vividly how
the taken-for-granted 'realism' of one tradition can seem mere superficiality or lack
of competence in another: what looked like 'naturalistic' images to European eyes
were seen locally as less like 'real' birds than the highly stylised spiralling forms created by Central Javanese artists to represent the true 'essence' and 'feeling' of birds
(Boow 1988: 96ff, Layton 1991: 164). Maori carvers who seemed to outsiders to
give a far from accurate and balanced representation of the human body were not
trying to imitate anatomical features but depicting other qualities of ancestral and
mythic beings (Firth 1992: 20). In the same way the places, groups and ancestral
tracks represented in paintings among the Australian Aboriginal Yolngu are mean-
ingless to others but communicated with precision to those familiar with the
myth-steeped interpretations of the initiated (Morphy 1991, 1994: 665–6).[4]

Issues about blurred boundaries and cultural diversities remain, but it is still clear
that pictorial representations – or forms in some way experienced as representations – provide a powerful and extensively used resource in human communicating.
Paintings, friezes, religious icons, photographs, statues, even English pub signs
visibly display religious cosmologies, political powers and contests, the personalities

of great or humble, and the ironies and beauties of the human world. Colour, shape and balance variously add to their depth. In both two- and three-dimensional formats and both still and moving images, a vast array of pictorial sights are utilised throughout the world in ways that amplify, qualify and transcend words.

Thus newspapers and pamphlets use pictures to sharpen and summarise the accounts more laboriously or clumsily conveyed in their written texts, and advertisements often project their messages through pictorial effects – 'a picture is worth a thousand words', it is said. The painted representations of Australian landscapes, with their gradual move away from nineteenth-century English images, reflect and communicate crucial changes in images of Australian-ness in ways it would be hard to express so effectively (if at all) in words. In Bangladesh decorations on rickshaws communicate people's world views, illustrated in the elaborate and carefully worked example in Figure 5.3. They use a series of evocative images to show film stars, scenes of nature, and modern buildings imbued with national sentiment like the Parliament and monuments to martyrs of the war of independence. Pictures of mosques predominate, above all the Taj Mahal, conspicuous

Figure 5.3 The painted rickshaw
Meticulously painted decorations on Bangladeshi rickshaws convey people's vision of the world. Scenes of flowers, birds and animals present their owners' and pullers' appreciation for the 'beautiful, useful, potent wonders of nature' (Glassie 1997: 37) (Hutchison Picture Library).

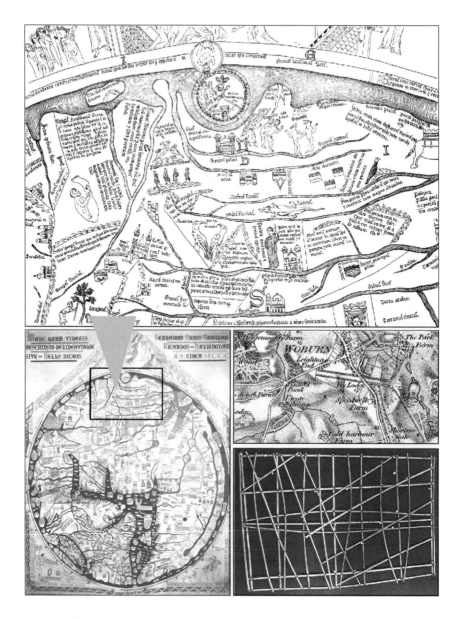

Figure 5.4 Contrasting cartographies

There are many ways to encapsulate and reinforce particular visions of the world. Above and below left: *Mappa Mundi*, a thirteenth-century map of the world on vellum (a sheet of 64 × 54 inches) portrayed from a Christian perspective with Jerusalem at the centre, the east at the top and Christ in Majesty at the summit; the detail shows the Garden of Eden in a round island within the encircling ocean and Adam and Eve with the forbidden fruit, then, to the right, their expulsion from Paradise; other drawings illustrate human life and history, the marvels of far-off lands, peoples, and fabulous beasts (Copyright © The Dean and Chapter

signs of the faith of both owners and pullers: 'the symbol of our Islamic heritage' (Glassie 1997: 37, 29).

'Historical' pictures communicate particular views of the past – and hence formulate understandings of the present too. Examples are legion. The embroidered Saint George on imperial banners is one. So too are the political murals of Northern Ireland (exemplified in Figure 6.1), pictures of the Protestant 'King Billy' on his mythic white horse at the famed Battle of the Boyne, or the many reconstructions of the past in film or television. A set of paintings from Shaba in south-eastern Zaire (now Democratic Republic of Congo) illustrate the same point, richly ironic and allusive works from the 1970s by the local painter Tshibumba. He wanted to create a particular viewpoint on the history of Zaire, to 'make us think' about the present as well as the past (Fabian 1996). Religious paintings of the Christian Madonna – and many other subjects too – exhibit and perpetuate long-standing cosmologies about the nature of human life, of birth and of death. Graffiti too, like paintings on buildings, can act as a pictorial language which for those in the know make unambiguous partisan statements, mark out gang territories or sectarian allegiances, express anger or threats towards opponents, or at the least convey a visual mark of the artist's active existence in the world. Even photograph albums embody and communicate particular views of the nature of a family and its relationships.

Maps and charts are further visual artefacts through which humans share their experience and formulation of the world, at the boundaries of graphic and pictorial form. As illustrated in Figure 5.4, cartography is shaped by culturally specific conventions both about the 'important' features of the world and the visual devices for encapsulating them; as Delano-Smith and Kain say, 'maps are drawn on a blank surface, not with a blank mind. They represent points of view, not simply a physical viewpoint' (1999: 6). This is evident in early Chinese or Babylonian maps, for example, the religious formulations conveyed in the *mappa mundi*, or the maps of nineteenth- and twentieth-century Europe which celebrated the civilising vision of European culture spreading around the world (Wintle 1996). Particular viewpoints underlie even the famous 'Underground' map of London, and are asserted in value-laden charts of property rights, nation states or imperial sway, or, in a different vein, in contemporary pictorial maps communicating the historical or artistic wealth of a locality to tourists and residents. And then there are the Inuit (Eskimo) carved coastline maps and the striking navigation charts used by Pacific voyagers, like the

---

of Hereford Cathedral and the Hereford Mappa Mundi Trust). Centre right: From first edition of English Ordnance Survey one-inch to the mile map, 1834, clearly marking routes, settlements and physical features (Photograph: John Hunt). Below right: Marshall Island stick chart used by Pacific voyagers; the rectangular grid probably shows the open sea, the shells the relative position of islands, and the curved sticks the wave fronts (precise details are debatable) (Copyright © The British Museum).

Caroline Islanders' pebble diagrams of the star compass and the Melanesian 'stick chart' directional aids (Gladwin 1970: 128ff, Aveni 1986, Lock and Peters 1996: 826–7: an example is given in Figure 5.4). Whatever the specific patterning, maps act as vehicles through which their makers visually communicate and reinforce particular world views and ways of apprehending reality.

There will be more to say about pictorial representation, but let us first take up the specific case of graphic signs. This is to move along the continuum towards more standardised and codified visual forms: to the relatively succinct and stereotyped visual designs, that is, which can be used to convey economically and directly a wide range of claims, values, events and ideas through their visible shape, structure or colour. Primarily (though not exclusively) two-dimensional and used more on surfaces rather than in the round, these graphic symbols shade into the pictorial examples given earlier. They can be characterised nonetheless as taking a more explicit and standardised role in organised communication than the artefacts and pictures considered so far.

Examples come from many periods and directions. We can think of the early Christian 'fish' symbol, the swastika, CND badges, mandala, regimental signs, devices on shields, and marks of ownership from farmers' brands on livestock to the imprint of a personal seal. Authorship or authenticity are conveyed by silver and gold hallmarks, printers' signs, trademarks, or watermarks for fine paper or treasury notes. Symbols for clouds, rain or sun show weather patterns on television or in print; heraldic signs declare family pride and allegiance. The American hobo language used visual signs to tell later arrivals 'you can camp here', 'unsafe place' or 'bad dog'. Sometimes graphic signs are linked together into complex displays, as in the Maya calendar (Figure 5.6), the historical annals on buffalo skin used by the Dakota Indians to record the year's most important event (Figure 5.9) or the complex wiring diagrams or engineering blueprints of today. Two-dimensional graphic devices display and communicate quantity, space, cause and effect, scale, parallelism, multiplicity, musical sounds, bodily movements, personality, or scientific discoveries . . . and so on and on: 'a sparkling and exuberant world' (Tufte 1997: 9).

Graphic forms are a notable feature of contemporary living, their pictorial facets highly stereotyped and standardised. They appear in electrical and fluid-power diagrams and schematics, as 'icons' on computer screens and in cleaning labels sewn into clothes. We use them for road signs, both raised aloft and inscribed on the surface itself, for company logos, for numerals, and as internationally understood signs to carry information about, for example, exits, gender-differentiated toilets, first aid, information points or telephones. They are a fast-growing part of computer communication. Here, as so often, the visual symbols override language differences and communicate more directly than written words.

Conventionalised graphic forms can serve complex mnemonic and recording functions. Incised marks on clay date far back into the past and tallies such as notched sticks have been used through many periods to indicate the numbers of, for example, animals hunted, stores needed, length of time, debts or contracts. Up to the twentieth century German millers used a system of knots to mark the amount and variety of milled flour contained in each sack – more three-dimensional than those discussed so far, but working on the same lines (illustrated earlier in Figure 2.2). Tally marks are far from the crude attempts at measurement that is sometimes supposed. The English treasury relied on them for centuries, with matching notched sticks marking payments (the treasury kept one stick, the creditor the other), and until 1826 used notched sticks to keep records of taxes and other income (Menninger 1969: 223ff, 233, 236).

This links to the important role that graphic signs have played in scientific and mathematical communication. The visual symbols for numerals are one notable and highly sophisticated example (see Menninger 1969, also Coulmas 1996: 357ff, Daniels and Bright 1996: 795ff). Their long history covers many different forms but there are remarkable continuities too, for here again visual forms can be used to communicate irrespective of language or generation. There are the numerals in the impressed clay tablets of early Mesopotamia, the varied Chinese, Roman, Hindu-Arabic or Maya systems for numbers, and the visible signs for particular known or unknown values such as x, Σ, π. Other graphic notations link numerals and similar

Figure 5.5 A sampler of graphic symbols
Top: Christian 'fish' symbol; sign of CND (Campaign for Nuclear Disarmament); peace dove; frost/snow, air-conditioning; symbols for male/female. Middle: Recycling (both on goods' labels, showing their recyclability, and on disposal boxes); road sign (set above); company logo and sign (McDonald's); 'Information' point; company logo and sign (BP, with 'green' and soft overtones); petrol. Below: Hobo signs – 'Good for a handout', 'Kind-hearted lady here', 'Food for work'; fluid power symbols – electrical hand valve (gate), temperature switch (John Hunt).

signs together and show their relationships, using conventional symbols such as the decimal point, = , +, and %, or relative positioning and placing. A huge diversity of materials and artefacts are used to display visual numerical information, from coins, stone or paper to clock faces, calculators or telephone dials. Visual equations, formulae and models are a key characteristic of modern scientific communication and discovery; 'the diagram is special in its ability to render the invisible visible' (Owen 1986: 156). Put another way:

> Ability of the eye to apprehend structural relations at a glance lies behind the utility of many kinds of graphic representation, in science as elsewhere, in contrast with verbal description that would be not only excessively wordy but perhaps incapable of simultaneously indicating spatial relations between objects.
>
> (Drake 1986: 153)

For engineers and designers likewise 'sketches and drawings are the basic components of communication' (Henderson 1999: 1). As with pictures, these diagrams, charts and similar graphic representations do more than just short-circuit words; for some purposes they communicate more directly. Here then is another set of visible resources which humans can utilise to organise and display multifaceted data – which 'envision information in order to reason about, communicate, document, and preserve . . . knowledge' (Tufte 1990: 33).

These many graphic signs offer flexible human-made resources for formulating and conveying in visible form some dimension of the world or of human life. Their use goes far back in human history and despite their variety and, in some cases, only ephemeral and limited applications, some have been both long-enduring and current over wide areas. Throughout the world coins, stamps, treasury notes, official letter heads, advertisements and computer screens carry succinct visual images well understood by their creators and viewers – or at any rate, as exemplified in esoteric formulations like the Maya calendar of Figure 5.6 or some current computer displays, by users with particular backgrounds or positions. New software is now providing additional scope for sophisticated graphic display (see discussions in Harris 1999, Henderson 1999). Not the least of their advantages is that for those acquainted with their conventions and contexts – and sometimes this means very large numbers of people – they work independently of verbal language. Computer icons, hallmarks, numerals, tally marks and other graphic signs – all can on occasion transcend linguistic divides.

The graphic and pictorial forms exemplified so far have mostly possessed that characteristic feature of visual objects that, unlike the sequences of auditory communication, they are basically seen with immediacy and simultaneity (basically – in practice the eye may scan through a complex presentation or focus on particular elements). This has both costs and benefits. A visual display enables people to grasp

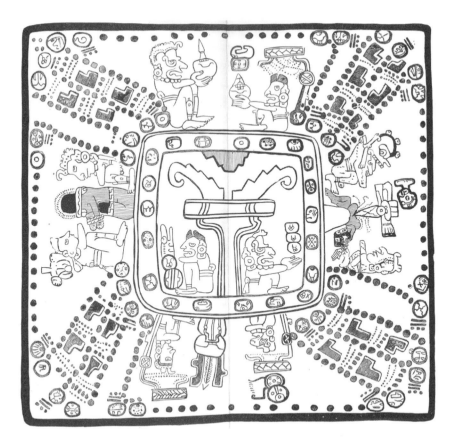

Figure 5.6 Maya calendar
Ancient divinatory calendar or cosmological almanac as recorded in one of the few folding
bark-paper books that survived from pre-Columban Maya culture (their hieroglyphic writing is now at last being deciphered). In a band encircling the two central figures under a tree
are the symbols for the twenty days of the Maya month and, further out, for the four car-
dinal directions, while a continuing line of dots represents the 260 days of the year and their
various cycles; in the top (east) sector a god holds the glyphic symbol of the sun (day,
time). The elaborate Maya calendrical system provided a means of recording cycles of years
which extended over many centuries, with an accuracy and spread far greater, it seems, than
anything of that period in the 'old world' (from *Madrid codex* (*Cortesianus*) as reproduced in
Cyrus Thomas, *Notes on Certain Maya and Mexican Manuscripts*, 1884, Plate II).

relationships 'at a glance', often with greater effectiveness and immediacy than
through words. Juxtapositions, contrasts and parallels come vividly through in
forms like the 'varieties of mankind' and the 'doom painting' shown earlier (Figures
1.2, 1.4), the two styles of preaching in Figure 5.11 below, or the many diagrammatic displays of scientific or statistical displays. On the other hand the fixity of
graphic and pictorial visual representation contrasts with the more dynamic and

sequential nature of sounds and is in itself less obviously capable than audition of embodying change or development.

Human beings, however, have also constructed ingenious ways of using graphic or pictorial forms to convey sequences of ideas or events over time. It is worth pausing to note two main strategies for achieving this: activated temporal sequences and spatial succession.

The first enacts the sequential process in real time: the dynamic revealing (and withdrawing) of sights matches the temporal or logical unfolding of the communication. This proceeds in much the same way as in the 'sign languages' described in Chapter 4. The 'sand stories' narrated by Aboriginal Walbiri women in central Australia give us one striking example. This graphic-cum-gestural system, extensively documented by Nancy Munn (1973), repays some longer consideration.

To tell the stories a woman smoothes out a small space in the sand, then narrates the tale through an interplay of graphic notation and gestures, accompanied by a singsong verbal patter. The vocal input is often minimal and the story carried mainly by gestural and graphic signs. The narrator marks successive graphics in the sand, presenting them in sequence following the temporal flow of the narrative with their positions reflecting the spatial arrangements of the tale's actors and objects. She builds up a single graphic scene by a succession of marks without rubbing out those already drawn in the sand; one layer is sometimes drawn on top of another. So a character in the story may first be shown sitting and eating, then lying down to sleep. Successive 'scenes' are divided from each other, however, each erased before the start of the next one; 'a graphic story develops through the continuous cycling of scenes in the manner of a movie' (Munn 1973: 69). The graphic signs are thus closely related to the speaker's bodily actions but at the same time detached from the body, 'objectivated outside the speakers and listeners in a concrete spatial field that forms the visible focus of their interaction' (Munn 1973: 87).

The narrators regularly use around a dozen basic graphic elements, each representing a general category with a range of meanings (see Box 5.1). The specific application is made clear by the context:

> Two or more straight lines partly enclosed in an arc representing a bough shade are always actors lying down in camp and not objects. Narrative context or verbal commentary may provide the information as to the identity of these actors. If one line is considerably smaller than the other, it is a child and the line beside it a woman.
>
> (Munn 1973: 68)

The sequential scenes use subtle combinations and elaborations of these graphic elements, to depict, for example, love affairs, fights, emu hunts, a man's transformation into a snake, or immoral behaviour such as incest followed by its punishment.

At the story's end all its people are often pictured coming together and going into the ground. The narrator draws a circle and shows the actors' path lines converging onto it; if a death precedes the ending, the paths are directed into the open end of a U shape.

Box 5.1 Graphic elements in Walbiri sand story vocabulary

(based on Munn 1973: 65–7)

Basic element	Category	Range of meanings
	Elongate, non-mobile objects	Spear, fighting stick (if non-upright), digging stick, actor lying down, animal lying stretched out, fires flanking each side of shade
	Straight movement of actors, trajectory of object	Actor in motion – walking, running dancing; spearing
	Dancing movements (men's or women's)	Actor(s) dancing
	Footprints of actor moving along	Actor walking, dancing
	Prone actor, body more curved than in straight sign above	Actor lying on one side, asleep
	Curved implements	Boomerangs
	Curved place markers, surrounding or defining area where actors can sit or lie	Bough shade or shelter, line or grove of trees
	Place marker for trees only (usually depicting shade in which kangaroo lying)	Grove of trees
	Enclosure for living	Hut
	Static actor	Actor sitting
	Striated or crumpled place on which actor can rest	Creek bed, blanket, 'bed'
	Oval hollow containers	Food or water scoop, baby carrier, shield, spear thrower, oval 'bed', hollow in ground for sleeping
	Closed roundish items or encircling non-directional movement	Nest, hole, water hole, fruits and yams, tree, hill, prepared food, fire, upright fighting stick, painting material, billy can, egg, dog (when curled up in camp), circling (e.g. dancing around) or any encircling object

Note: arrows indicate movement

Unlike some other graphic systems Walbiri signs are short-lived with no permanent record; each scene is obliterated in turn and thus no more time-resistant than the gestural and verbal signs that accompany it. The narrator creates 'a kind of visual punctuation of the total narrative meaning . . . fleeting graphic images of [the story] as part of the narrative process' (Munn 1973: 69, 87). These link to the Walbiri visual system more generally, with its expression in men's and women's designs, dreams, religious symbolism, and the complex graphic imagery associated with the totemic ancestors. The graphic forms enter into Walbiri imagination and experience as a kind of 'visual language', organized 'not simply in a linear way following speech sequence as is characteristic of a script, but also as images in pictorial arrangements' (Munn 1973: 87).

That particular system is distinctive to Walbiri culture (though not without partial parallels in other Australian traditions). Other cases use different formulae for the same basic strategy of visually displaying sequences over time. Animated cartoons do much the same thing, presenting visual images in temporal sequence. So too do films, videos and sequences of computer-generated images.

In the second strategy a series of separate visual representations are set into more or less permanent form, spatially ordered so that the eye can travel over each in turn. The observer's active scanning plays a large part in creating the succession, rather than a temporal structure imposed by the generator. Thus we can look through a sequence of photographs telling a story, narratives portrayed in comics, chronological series of historical maps, flow-charts on paper or computer screen, or the ordered sequences of written scripts. Friezes and paintings tell stories in religious buildings and elsewhere, often through juxtaposed pictorial representations of a whole series of events, sometimes selecting just one or two to evoke a known narrative sequence; so too with the saint's exploits portrayed in the multiple panels of the St William window in York Minster (Figure 10.4) and the dramatic episodes of the Norman invasion in the sequentially ordered frames of the Bayeux tapestry (Figure 4.5). Illustrations for the Indian *Ramayana*, like that pictured in Figure 9.4, have similarly been termed a 'sequential art form', comparable to the comic strip and the cinema in telling a story pictorially (Williams 1996: 4–5). The Assyrian narrative sculptures from the Nineveh Palace now displayed in the British Museum are another striking example, wonderfully depicting the experiences of men and animals in King Ashurbanipal's royal lion hunt in the seventh century BC (Figure 5.7). In one sequence the lions are released from a cage and shot at. One climbs onto the king's chariot and is held off by the attendants so the king can have the kill. Then the death agonies of the lions follow in realistic and gruesome detail. The series ends with a libation following the royal success.

The same strategy for communicating development through spatial ordering comes in graphic conventions for representing musical sounds. There is the well-known notation system of western classical music, where pitch, duration, dynamics and structuring are represented by sequences of abstract graphic symbols together

Figure 5.7 From an Assyrian tale of a lion hunt
An episode from one of the sequences of seventh-century BC narrative sculptures from the Nineveh Palace depicting King Ashurbanipal's lion hunts. The king attacks one lion while another leaps at his spare horse from behind; in the next episode (not shown here) he has killed both lions (Copyright © The British Museum).

with their spacing and positions on the staves, well illustrated in the singing score for Handel's 'Hallelujah Chorus' (Figure 3.4) or the notes in the Missal in Figure 7.2; parallel but differing in details are the visual contours in Buddhist 'pictures of sound' where undulating lines depict vocal or melodic sequences (Ellingson 1986: 302), musical indications alongside verbal words in Japanese Noh performance texts (Figure 10.3) and the alphabetic letters and associated marks of the tonic sol-fa system. All depend on visually displayed sequences, where sequential spatial distributions on a surface link to chronological or logical development. Standardised notations for dynamic bodily movements are less established but do occur, for example systems for indicating oratorical gestures and mnemonic notations for fifteenth-century European social dances. Several competing choreographic systems have been developed over the last couple of centuries, again based on sequences of graphic symbols. Some are recognised and practised within certain specialised communities, such as the notation of Figure 5.8, even if none has attained unchallenged currency (for further examples see Daniels and Bright 1996: 855ff, Sassoon and Gaur 1997: Chap. 9).

The two strategies – dynamic presentation in actual time and successive series of fixed sights in space – are not totally distinct. Nor is the logical or temporal development of spatially sequential sights always presented in the left-to-right direction which seems the 'natural' paradigm to readers of alphabetic scripts, for visual sequences of temporal events, ideas and causal relationships can also come in vertical columns or in circular, spiral and parallel orderings in space. Scientific diagrams rest on the trained eye's capacity to detect causal relationships in many different formats, not excluding three-dimensional models. But whether in overlapping or relatively distinct forms, both strategies represent creative ways in which human

Figure 5.8 Notating movement: the Benesh movement notation system

A recognised system for representing human movements in fixed visual form designed by Joan and Rudolf Benesh in the mid-twentieth century. The system is most widely used for the recording and reconstruction of dance, but also has applications in other fields such as physiotherapy. It transcends linguistic divides and enables an accurate three-dimensional representation of the movements, positions and directions of the limbs, head, hands, feet and body. The changing body actions are plotted in a series of notated frames along a five-lined stave (one stave for each dancer), with details of rhythm, phrasing and dynamics immediately above the stave, direction, location and travel below. The particular positions and movements of the dancers shown here (Tamara Rojo and Daniel Jones) are captured in one form

beings have exploited the potential of vision while to an extent breaking free of some of its constraints.

The strategy of fixed visual representations ordered in space is notably exploited in human writing systems, a topic to which we can now return. It is not in fact a large step to move on to the graphic forms linked together into relatively larger systems. Pictorial and graphic means of communicating are intertwined rather than representing some evolutionary progression *from* one *to* the other, and the self-evident distinction once presupposed between 'writing' and other visual systems no longer seems an easy one to draw.

The overlap between graphic and pictorial forms is well illustrated in Sumerian clay tablets, Egyptian hieroglyphs, Chinese ideograms and Maya glyphs. These work with stylised signs that have some pictorial dimension, used to represent specific notions or things and often presented in highly illustrated settings. The balance between a more pictorial slant on the one hand and graphic syncopation on the other varies in different systems. The long-lasting and highly standardised Chinese script relies on a large number of ideographic characters with some pictorial base but an emphasis on stylised graphic aspects. In some pre-Columban Mesoamerican systems the pictorial dimension is more to the fore. Thus Aztec pictorial histories use serialised images to produce a narrative with 'the images working together to tell who, what, where and when' (Boone and Mignolo 1994: 52). The basic stories and names were widely known across the region and the visual images and associations could tell the tale pictorially rather than verbally.

Graphic-cum-pictorial systems where the visual images work relatively independently of spoken language are sometimes described as 'semasiographic' forms of writing (Boone and Mignolo 1994: 15ff).[5] The relation between the visual symbols and the ideas or relationships they convey is sometimes a matter of relatively arbitrary coding, but also at times more inclined to the pictorially representational (elusive though that concept remains). Many of the graphic signs and notations mentioned earlier could similarly be classed as semasiographic, their formulations not rooted in the sounds of speech – our system of numerals for example, music and dance notations, or graphic representation in mathematics and science. So too, if in a more scattered way, can individual 'iconic' symbols like those in Figure 5.5 above, and the more complex combination – more graphic-pictorial signs than writing perhaps? – used in the striking Dakota 'winter count' of Figure 5.9.

Other forms of writing are more closely linked to the sounds of speech, commonly described as phonological or glottographic systems. Here, as in western alphabetic scripts, the graphic signs are arbitrary shapes standing for sounds which

---

in the photograph (not part of the notation) and, in another, in the central section of the notation below (Benesh Movement Notation © Rudolf Benesh, London 1955, courtesy the Benesh Institute, London. Photograph © Patrick Baldwin).

can be put together in near-infinite series of different combinations to convey verbalised meanings. The scripts embodying them are of many kinds, based variously on syllabic, consonantal or alphabetic signs, displayed on many different surfaces or as three-dimensional objects, and produced by many different tools. Alphabetic writing is just one variant but currently a powerful one: versions of it have circulated for centuries in the west and have wide currency in the world today, deeply entrenched in modern social arrangements.

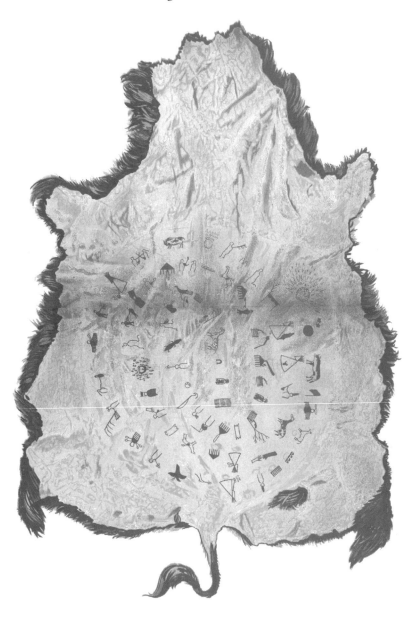

These sound-related writing systems between them make up rich, standardised and versatile visual resources for human communication, both in the present and stretching far into the past. They are not quite as simply differentiated from other systems as may appear at first sight, however. Phonological systems are sometimes described as 'visible speech'; but in practice no writing system is – or could be – an exact or full replica of vocal speaking. Even if all the subtle acoustic features noted in Chapter 3 were reproducible in a visual medium (and they are not), the standardised format of writing depicts only an approximation of the inevitably varying pronunciations and vocal delivery of speakers even at one period, let alone over generations or centuries. As Derrida memorably put it, 'that particular model which is phonetic writing *does not exist*; no practice is ever faithful to its principles' (Derrida 1976: 39 – italics in original); the relations between spoken sounds and their graphic reproduction vary but are never unproblematic. Further, even apparently phonological scripts contain elements which have no direct relation to spoken words. In alphabetic texts, for example, we pay attention to visual indicators like

Figure 5.9 Lone-Dog's winter count
One of the 'winter counts' of the Dakota Indians (Native Americans), painted by a man named Lone-Dog in black and red colours on a buffalo robe, depicting the annals of 1800–1871. A striking interweaving of graphic and pictorial representation, this historical record contains 71 signs, one for each year, covering (among other things) deaths in battle, diseases, horse stealing, dances, wars, successful hunts, white soldiers and traders, peace-making, and a solar eclipse. A full explanation of all the signs is given by Mallery (1893: 266–87); a few are explained below, starting just below centre with winter of 1800–1 and moving spirally anti-clockwise.

1800-01 30 Dakotas killed by Crow Indians (heavy black lines depict Dakotas killed by enemies)	1801-2 Smallpox	1803-4 Dakotas stole curly-haired horses from Crows
1805-6 8 Dakotas killed by enemies	1813-14 Whooping cough	1819-20 Foreign trading store built
1824-5 The chief's horses all killed	1825-6 Flood on Missouri river, many drowned	1828-9 Lodge built by white man
1839-40 Dakotas kill village of Shoshoni Indians (arrows stick in tent)	1840-41 Dakotas make peace with Cheyennes	1851-2 Peace with the Crows (exchanging pipes for peace smoke)
1867-8 Flags from Peace Commissioners. Dakota Treaty 1868	1869-70 Solar eclipse (sun in black, stars red)	1870-71 Battle, Crow fort surrounded

(from Garrick Mallery, *Picture-Writing of the American Indians*, 1893, Plate XX).

position on the page, direction, spatial relationships between different signs, marks indicating punctuation or structure, lines, and sometimes colour, intensity or size. Tufte again reminds us of the proliferation of non-verbal elements in contemporary print: 'Charts, diagrams, graphs, tables, guides, instructions, directories, and maps comprise an enormous accumulation of material. . . . Tens of trillions of images created and multiplied the world over every year' (Tufte 1990: 9).

The differences between the varied forms of visual communication commonly classed as 'writing' are thus relative only, certainly not the pure and distinctive categories implied in earlier classifications, far less distinct evolutionary stages. Both pictographic *and* phonetic elements appear in differing combinations and balances, as in the Chinese script, Egyptian hieroglyphics or the hieroglyphic Maya system (sometimes referred to as 'mixed' systems, as if this was somehow not quite natural). Alphabetic and other phonological systems exploit semasiographic as well as phonetic principles. Picture, idea and sound intermingle.

The preoccupation with delineating clear-cut typologies of writing was doubtless partly rooted in the long-held paradigm of alphabetic (western) systems as *the* pinnacle to which other types were leading, the most effective, versatile, and truly developed form of communication: both 'simple' and 'transparent'. Diringer reflected a widely held position when he asserted that 'the alphabet is the last, the most highly developed, the most convenient and the most easily adaptable system of writing. Alphabetic writing is now universally employed by civilized peoples' (1968, vol. 1: 13). This teleological model still casts a shadow, one reason perhaps for the relative lack of interest in the more semasiographic systems – those where, as in Mesoamerican pictographic scripts or musical notations, the graphic system 'communicates meaning directly', independent of language (Boone and Mignolo 1994: 15). But far from being 'outdated', a semasiographic dimension is pervasive in the contemporary world. In the Chinese system, used by a large proportion of the world's population, one major element is the visual representation of ideas, 'stylised drawings of things in combination with one another to convey ideas' (Brown 1998: 17). Being relatively independent of sound it can be read by all literate readers throughout China and beyond, even if their spoken languages differ. Indeed a notable feature of semasiographic signs generally is their power to transcend linguistic barriers by communicating visually across a whole region – or more. They are crucial in modern science at every level, from advanced research to introductory science textbooks where written text is increasingly displaced by non-verbal visual presentation (Kress and Van Leeuwen 1996: 30). Numerical notation and diagrammatic display are all around us, and as Sassoon and Gaur suggest, 'computer generated iconic communication' might increasingly transcend verbal languages (1997: 7). Their potential for international communication may be all the more significant nowadays in what is said to be an increasingly global and multicultural world, enhanced by the technologies of transferring images across space through scanning and faxing.

Writing is often thought of as a linear form, structuring communication in a single direction, in contrast to the multiple and simultaneous qualities of pictorial display. There is certainly something in this, but the distinction can be over-stated. Not only is this not in practice the only way that people read,[6] but written scripts at times partake both of the simultaneity more typical of pictures and of additional possibilities outside the apparent sequential constraints. No diagram is surely needed here, for the very format of this book already – and typically – exemplifies it. Even if we disregard pictorial elements (large omissions!), we must note the complex relationships represented by spatial layout and by other links to and within the text: white spaces within and around the page, paragraph indications, bold and italic print, indents, page numbers, and special layouts for 'prelims', first pages, notes, bibliography and index. In some printed works parallel columns, marginal annotations, 'running heads', footnotes and illustrations can all appear within a single page opening. End notes, diagrams, maps or figures render the text multiplex rather than single. The threefold format of Greek or Latin editions is familiar to classical scholars: original text at the top of one page, translation facing, and the foot of each page covered with dense notes and commentary. And, as Michelle Brown points out, the principles of computer hyperlinking were long anticipated in

> the rubrics of complex liturgical volumes [which] display an awareness of the concept of 'hyper-text', whilst the 9th-century audience of the influential Carolingian Utrecht Psalter was well able to mentally 'click on' a detail of its images, relate it to a passage of text and provide a raft of underlying exegetical interpretation, foreshadowing electronic applications of intertextuality.
>
> (Brown 1998: 90–1)

Written forms are thus visual artefacts with multiple visual properties involving more than just the graphic codes for the 'words' or 'letters' focused on in traditional classifications of writing. Other visual components play a part too, such as the materials used, their spatial presentation, colouration, size or overall shape. Visible signals indicate, for example, direction, proportion, or type of communication, and even within the 'same' writing system, different layouts, shapes, calligraphic styles, colours, three-dimensional structures and settings, placings or pictorial ordering all at times make their visual point. In their concentration on just selected aspects, scholars too often downplay these other substantial visual dimensions.

Sometimes the 'pictorial' dimensions blend in with graphic signs and assume comparable importance. In Maya or Egyptian forms it can be hard to see where picture ends and writing begins. And then there are all those pictorial decorations in scripts, from pin-figure drawings or kisses in personal letters to the arts of medi-aeval illuminated manuscripts or Asian calligraphy. The colours and forms in the Book of Kells or Lindisfarne gospels, or the illustrations in modern children's books are scarcely secondary to the words. The same applies in Chinese and Islamic calligraphy where *how* it is depicted can be as valued as the content, perhaps more so – Figure 5.10 gives one elegant example. Even in less consciously art-ful forms a whole series of visual elements (not just the written 'words') contributes to how we actually communicate through the multiplex visual media labelled as 'writing'.

We end up then with something of a continuum not only among types of writing but also among all the many pictorial-graphic forms of visual communication. Tufte is right that 'to envision information – and what bright and splendid visions can result – is to work at the intersection of image, word, number, art' (Tufte 1990: 9). Images enter into alphabetic scripts, visual icons mix in with 'writing'. And where exactly should we draw the line between, say, Aztec pictorial histories and mediaeval stained-glass narratives of a saint's exploits or a sinner's doom? The

Figure 5.10 Calligraphy and picture: a Chinese fan
The visual artistry and pictorial qualities of Chinese calligraphy are displayed in this beautiful example of integrated writing and picture, painted as a personal gift 'in the fierce heat of the summer of 1929 . . . to fan the summer heat away'. The calligrapher's seal is on the left, and the calligraphy 'in the style of Yuan dynasty scholars' flows together with the painting (in private possession, reproduced by permission of David Murray. Photograph: John Hunt).

boundaries between 'writing' and 'non-writing' are blurred and what emerges is the overlap between pictures, images, graphics and scripts.[7] As Roy Harris insists:

> From a technical point of view, writing is an extension of drawing, or more generally of graphic art, if we subsume under that term the whole gamut of forms of colouring, carving, incision and impression of surfaces which writing employs. . . . *Writing* was originally merely a term designating the process of scoring or outlining a shape on a surface of some kind. . . . Ancient Egyptian had one word meaning both 'writing' and 'drawing'. Similarly, the Greek verb γράφειν ('to write') originally meant in Homer 'engrave, scratch, scrape'. . . . Writing stands at the basis of the picture just as much as the picture stands at the basis of writing.
>
> (Harris 1986: 26, 29, 156)

In these abounding graphic-pictorial systems humans have developed a wonderfully versatile visual resource for communication, capable of being turned to so many of the multifarious purposes of human interaction. In its manifold forms writing is in constant use throughout the world – though not by everyone and not equally every-where, for like other media they are embedded in human social institutions. We draw on this resource extensively to encapsulate and communicate knowledge and experience in a (relatively) permanent form which can to an extent transcend both space and time and, to a degree and in some cases, bridge cultural and linguistic dif-ferences too. Materialised through a series of visible and multiplex forms, our use of this essentially visual resource exploits the capacity of the human hand to inscribe, and the human eye to analyse, a vast range of visual dimensions and to deploy a combination of them in our communicating.

Mostly we do not know the specifics of how these graphic-writing systems were started: the unidirectional narratives recounting their origins and diffusion through the millennia are surely over-simplified. But people are certainly capable of creating writing systems and a number of new ones have been deliberately invented over recent centuries. Indigenous scripts using alphabetic, syllabic or pictographic forms were devised for several African languages in the nineteenth and twentieth centuries, for example, 'remarkable', in Coulmas's assessment, 'for their originality and pre-cision in the transcription of sounds' (Coulmas 1996: 4). Some achieved a certain currency, especially in religious and esoteric contexts, and the names of their local creators are sometimes known.[8] No doubt similar processes obtained in other times and places. Many systems were also presumably built up and gained wider cur-rency (or were imposed) over time, though this is not to say that individual human genius had nothing to do with it. Whatever the details, these complex visual systems did not spring up of themselves nor grow by some impersonal process of natural selection or teleological evolution (as some accounts still imply) but – even more amazing in fact – were and are created and activated by human beings.

These pictorial-graphic systems, finally, are themselves only one category among the many material things that humans have developed in the past and present and pressed into use in their communicating. The range of human visual artefacts is indeed remarkable, created in both two- and three-dimensional forms and going far beyond anything we know of organised visual communication among other animals. A large part of human interconnectedness lies in this exploitation of vision, creating and using these visual artefacts – material, pictorial and graphic – in our communicating.

We should go further too, to note the overlap between gestural systems and graphic-pictorial communication. Recall the graphics of Walbiri sand stories, partly gestured and relatively impermanent, and the outstanding Native American development of both gestured and pictographic systems. Chinese speakers trying to differentiate between people with identically sounding names often use fingers to sketch out the lines of their written characters in the air while two-dimensional illustrations of finger-counting systems like that in Figure 10.1 freeze gestures in fixed and stereotypical form. In all this where is the great divide between standardised bodily movements and graphic representation? Certainly there are stark contrasts between the extremes but the boundaries merge. Gestured writing, graphic gesticulation – all are examples along the continuum of ingenious ways that humans communicate by mobilising the channel of vision to create and focus attentively on specific and relatively standardised visual sights.

The roles of vision in human cultures

Vision has many strengths as a mode for human interaction and it should be no surprise that collective human life involves such extensive use of both material and embodied sights. Indeed, as has been pointed out by blind people, the 'normal' human world is conceptualised and organised as dependent on vision. In some ways more accessible than sounds, sights can be seen simultaneously by many people and from multiple viewpoints. We can visually convey rapid and widely seen messages to numerous people at once – but can also do so in secret or silent ways without the explicit commitment of vocalised sound, as in the cautious looks or gestures between potential lovers before any spoken declaration. A complex channel, vision is perhaps even more open to differentiated personal usage than sound, enabling people to select those elements in which they are interested or to note features which others had perhaps not intended them to observe. Whether through the visible body, portable visual artefacts, art forms, architectural styles, pictorial conventions or culturally approved arrangements for movement and space, vision is regularly implicated in the formulation and communication of shared cultural symbols, all the more powerful through apparently being uncontestably 'there' in the visible world. Visual artefacts can be long-lasting and for this reason are of the greatest importance for communicating over space and time – witness the communicative roles of built edifices, of sculptures, frescoes and pictures, or of books and other artefacts carrying the visual medium of writing.

But a thing has to be *seen* if it is to work in visually communicating. Humans are adept at obstructing or preventing vision, sometimes unintentionally, sometimes with deliberation. Human-made conventions regulate people's appearances, accoutrements, movements and access to materials – and thus to how these may be used to communicate. There are rules about how and where people *look*, from unspoken restrictions on the direction or intensity of gaze by particular categories of people, to customs about where people may go and therefore whom and what they may see and visually interact with. Interposing barriers between people or cutting off particular people from specific sights are effective devices for controlling visual communication. So too is removing people from the vicinity – that is, from sight – or ensuring better views for some than others: think of guards on high towers, one-way mirrors or controlled lighting. The 'hidden city' in Beijing, theatre curtains, shut doors to private rooms, guards to official buildings, blindfolds, partitions, prison gates, limited access to printed books or, as in many cultures, to the specialised arts needed to decipher writing – all are ways of restricting admission to specific sights and hence of regulating communication.

Vision is much used in marking out differentiations between people. In similar ways to the bodily appearances described in Chapter 4 visual artefacts too can be used to assert the status quo. The regalia of power are embodied in dominating and long-lasting architectural and engineering edifices; likewise in royal art and governmental buildings set up in central and conspicuous places. Vivid displays depict the glorious successes of the rulers, from ancient Egyptian portrayals of the crowned Pharaoh receiving his foes' submission or the Assyrian king's hunting triumphs to recent government posters. Maps can be another effective vehicle of authority, documenting and disseminating specific political or religious viewpoints – hence their description as the 'science of princes' (Harley 1985: 281).

But vision can also be used to challenge commonly accepted symbols or arrangements. It is sometimes a merit, that unlike the active and attention-attracting production of sound, visual media can work silently and underground; in other cases their easy visibility is part of their appeal. Cartoons, graffiti or tattoos cock a snook at established authority, while the portable visual media on which writing is often inscribed have been utilised not just as tools of the powerful but for individual and localised expression or organised divergence from otherwise dominant views. Personal access to the Bible is commonly held to be one crucial – and democratising – element in the Reformation. But pictures, too were, effective. Popular visual propaganda for the German Reformation, like that in Figure 5.11, included vivid woodcuts showing the 'Papal Beast' identified with the Beast of the Apocalypse, or presenting the Pope enthroned as a demon in hell. Their antagonists portrayed a seven-headed Luther or Luther-as-Winesack (Scribner 1981). In this huge array of illustrated broadsheets, picture books and woodcuts, the pictures were arguably as compelling as the more often cited printed word.

Visible artefacts, movements and events are pervasive in human lives, used in

human communication in a vast range of settings, everyday as well as consciously art-ful. But as with audition, certain visual aspects are also at times singled out for particular specialisation or emphasis. In sculpture, painting, architecture and dance, the visual elements of movement, display or action can be heightened and developed with particular intensity. There are the cultivated displays of Chinese gardens; the specialised dance arts of Asia; the ceramic arts developed in many areas and ages throughout the world; schools of painters, sculptors and landscape designers; the manifold arts of the illuminated manuscript and the book; Benin royal art; Javanese shadow puppets – and all those other visual arts too numerous to list. There are the explicit traditions of artists, carvers, dancers, costumiers, weavers, potters, smiths, house-builders, film-makers, architects and, not least, the expert audiences and co-creators who interact with them.

Writing is a visual art-form too. Amazingly elaborated products and processes surround the spectacle of writing with its calligraphers, artists, illustrators, binders and printers. Books, miniatures, scrolls, pictures, carving – writing is visually displayed in all these forms and more. It is attached to the arts of architecture and painting; appears on pyramids, monuments, churches, mosques; and interacts with the scintillating material arts of the manuscript and the book (see for example Manguel 1996, Tonfoni 1994). European illuminated manuscripts are justly famous, but the diverse calligraphic arts of the east are equally striking. For over two thousand years calligraphy has been the supreme Chinese art: not just a matter of technical skill, delicately though that was nurtured, but of rich personal expression – 'calligraphy *is* the person' (Stevens 1996: 247). There is also the wonderfully complex artistry of Islamic calligraphy. Writing is a divine gift from Allah and, with pictorial representation of the human or divine form discouraged, calligraphy is the

---

Figure 5.11 'True and false preaching'
This mid-sixteenth-century woodcut by Lucas Cranach the Younger is characteristic of visual propaganda during the Reformation in Germany. Using popular visual images of the time it damns the Catholics and lauds the reformers, at the same time teaching the Gospel messages which lead to salvation. In the polemical treatment in the right half we see a monkish Catholic preaching without a Bible, pointing downwards to the clergy below, and listening to the devil blowing into his ear; bottom right the Pope sits amidst coins and money bags selling indulgences, and the scene is set by fat monks, signs of folly and dissipation, and an air of doom; from above God sends fire and brimstone while St Francis vainly intercedes. In the 'true religion of Christ', by contrast, the evangelical preacher, identifiable with Luther, speaks from the open Bible with words from the Acts of the Apostles, inscribed on the pulpit, and points upwards through a textband to the symbolic lamb, the risen Christ, and onwards to God. The crowd, laity not clergy, listen attentively or enact the rites of sacrament and baptism. The two scenes display a series of theological, moral, social and political contrasts in a manner that it would be hard to convey so economically or with such immediacy in written or spoken words (for fuller commentary see Scribner 1981: 201ff) (© Kupferstichkabinett, Staatliche Museen zu Berlin – Preussischer Kulturbesitz. Photograph: Jorg P. Anders).

main vehicle for visual art. It adorns 'nearly everything in the Muslim world: books, coins, ceramics, brocades, buildings, furniture, rugs, garments, belts, hats, funeral shrouds, pills and other forms of medicine, and even skin' (Stevens 1996: 244). Colour, shape and arrangement distinguish the multiplicity of scripts, each suited to particular contexts. They may be presented as much in decorative even pictorial form as in the simple linear format we often associate with writing – see the striking example in Figure 5.12. Here Islamic calligraphy

> take[s] the written sign and alter[s] its form and decorative style by changing the treatment of line. This plastic form simultaneously serves both the meaning of the actual statement and the composition of images, of letters that are recreated as image. The actual meaning of the statement here becomes secondary, so that the imagined reader is like a dreamer awakened, whose vision is woven within a context of art.
>
> (Khatibi and Sijelmassi 1995: 7)

Figure 5.12 The Shahadah: a calligraphic declaration of faith
Calligraphic representation of the Islamic Shahadah (Declaration of Faith): 'There is no god but Allah and Muhammad is his messenger'. It is written in the form of turrets from right to centre with the left half a near mirror reflection and the name Muhammad in the separate square at the middle of the base of each half (Courtesy Kenneth Cragg and the Institute of Islamic Studies, Rawalpindi).

There is a further point about human visual communication, specialised and everyday alike: the *durability* of many visual artefacts. It is their (relatively) long-lasting nature that enables these visible objects to be used for communicating over time and at a distance. A sight can, it is true, be removed from someone's vision instantaneously. But, unlike audition or (up to a point) smell, it can also endure in fixed visible form over long periods of time, accessible (at least in principle) in a whole series of different 'sightings'.

This is a highly significant feature of human communication. Certain non-human animals make some use of external visual objects. But humans have developed a vast range of visual communicative resources in relatively permanent forms which, like pictures, statues, inscriptions, buildings, tombs, stained glass, and photographs, can be used to communicate at a distance and over time. Some artefacts furthermore are highly portable, enabling communication not just over time but also over space – think of paper, bark, papyrus, jewellery, coins, flags, pottery, textiles, even up to a point the adorned human body. The staying power of human-made visual artefacts similarly plays a part in constructing and maintaining human memory. Some visual arts, like tombstones, ancestor shrines or war memorials are explicitly mnemonic or memorial. Others, like a seal, sacred object, inscribed weapon or suitably produced written document, are used to signify continuity or validate a claim. But even cases less deliberately planned for specific communicative purposes such as buildings, pictures, furniture, maps, paintings, heirlooms, written manuscripts and printed books can serve as visual evocations of the past, offering resources through which humans formulate, validate and communicate their awareness of their own continuities and identities. All are essentially visual artefacts with the potential to endure over both time and space.

These general characteristics of vision, then, are widely exploited in human communicating. Not all human beings share exactly the same attitudes to visual expression, however, or emphasise the same visual objects or processes – cultural and individual specificities have their place too. Their visual environments also have differed over the centuries and throughout the world. Some are full of palm trees, the blues and greens of deep sea and lagoon, canoes, fish and fishing equipment, brilliant colours of dance dress, nets and shell-decorated arts; others of large public buildings, interior decoration, street lights, books, or the visual iconography of flamboyant religious architecture; others again dominated by the restricted vision of forest terrain or by a world of fields, agricultural implements, cattle. In crowded city streets the *sight* of fellow humans may be more salient than auditory and tactile contacts (or so Simmel (1924) suggests), and artificial lighting may affect the specific usages and availability of visual objects. Our visual environments, artefacts and all, both vary across time and space and form a far from neutral frame within which human communicating is formulated.

Equally important, vision is selective and sights and seeing shaped by people's situations and interpretations. Hidden as well as acknowledged conventions mould what we learn to see and produce. From an early age children produce 'artful scribbles' moulded by cultural patterns (Gardner 1980), while orthographies are not transparent, as often assumed, but culturally prescribed visual systems that children have to *learn* (vividly demonstrated in Kress 2000). So too with learning how to 'read' the visual representations of music, the specific properties of maps with their varying conventions in different historical contexts, or the varied human gestures for 'no'. From the specifics of gestural expressions or colour imagery to the decoration on a canoe prow or spacing of photographs in an album, different groupings have their accepted patterns for what they create and see and for how they regulate and use their sights in communicating. Something of central interest to one group or individual may simply not be noticed by others, and in this sense take no part in their visual communication. In urban settings the shape, horns or colouring of cows are of little moment but for the Nuer people of the twentieth-century southern Sudan they carried deep symbolic meanings: 'their social idiom is a bovine idiom' (Evans-Pritchard 1940: 19). Likewise the symbolic associations of black, white or red vary enormously in different cultures and are used to contrasting communicative purposes. What is seen and *how* it is seen depend both on individuals' attentiveness and on the frameworks set up through the preconceptions and organisational arrangements of varying human groups.

Because the channel of vision is highly complex it can be exploited in many different and changing ways. Even within what might appear 'the same' cultural tradition, visual practices can vary both internally and over time. Sometimes changes are linked to new intellectual concerns, sometimes to technologies, trade routes, or power balance. The invention and application of paper or of telescopes, Chinese and western print technologies, the development of perspective, images reproduced through woodcuts, photography, film, and specific forms of text processing – all affected the visual resources humans could draw on at various points in time and space.

Some scholars go further. They posit far-reaching contrasts between cultures, in particular seeing the modern west as radically different both from other cultures of the world and from its own earlier history in the central role it accords to vision. Writers like McLuhan (1964) and Ong (1967, 1977, 1982) suggested that the privileging of vision over sound came about with alphabetic literacy and, especially, with print: 'an eye for an ear' (McLuhan 1964: 91). Foucault describes sight gaining dominance over smell (1970: 132–3) while Lowe's *History of Bourgeois Perception* argues that 'a new perceptual field, constituted by typographic culture, the primacy of sight, and the order of representation-in-space' was superimposed in the seventeenth and eighteenth centuries over the earlier emphasis on hearing and touching (Lowe 1982: 13). This set of ideas has become established theory in many circles. It is now widely assumed that vision and its associated practices hold a privileged position in western culture, a position, furthermore, that the expansion of the west has progressively imposed on other cultures.[9]

There is something to be said for this analysis. It rightly challenges the ethnocentric assumption that the particular mix of communicative resources with which we are most familiar is either universal or ipso facto superior. Just as the New Guinean Kaluli discussed in Chapter 3 were specially attentive to sound, so, too, different cultures have developed sensitivities to differing communicative forms. The conditions of human life have varied over the ages and throughout the world, even within different groups in the same era: there are variations in people's differential access to artificial light, for example, living arrangements, visual (and other) technologies. The precise forms of communicating are indeed likely to vary rather than follow one uniform paradigm.

It is also undoubtedly correct to draw attention to the role of vision in recent western culture. Visual artefacts are plentiful and complex, much used in our communicating: clothing, graphics, buildings, film, television, advertisements, public spectacles, pictorial representations, written media. Vision was crucial to the history of western science, where sight distances observer from object and provides a basis for objectivity. In medicine likewise the earlier attention to smell was replaced by opening the body to visual scrutiny and control. Indeed, as Hewes summed it up some time ago, modern science depends on

> reducing data and relationships from almost all domains of the natural world to visible patterns – to graphics of one sort or another. In genetics, for example, the earliest breakthroughs came not only from being able to observe and draw the phenomena of mitosis and meiosis, but from the discovery that the new aniline dyes could be used to stain and make visible what therefore come to be called *chromosomes*. Later, in the Watson–Crick era, understanding of the structure of the critical DNA molecule came from analysis of X-ray crystallographic photographs, and then the actual construction of three-dimensional models of the elusive molecule. To an overwhelming extent, science has advanced by finding means to *visualize* relationships and events.
>
> (Hewes 1978: 17)

Visual imagery underpins western philosophy, it seems, and Rorty plentifully illustrates 'the domination of the mind of the West by ocular metaphors' (1980: 13, also 162–3, 376, Poteat 1974: 177–8). Perception is commonly envisaged (sic) in terms of *visual* perceiving and our everyday speech is full of visual metaphors – viewpoint, see, appear, insight, observe, envisage, picture, perspective, the mind's eye. . . .

But the matter is somewhat more controversial and complex than usually recognised in the now familiar generalisations about the privileged role of vision in 'the west'. One complication is that *several* 'revolutions', 'turns' or 'paradigm shifts' are cited, and from different dates. There are the supposedly far-reaching changes from oral/aural to visual culture attributed to writing and, in particular, alphabetic writing and western printing (as in McLuhan 1964, Ong 1982 and their followers).

Other analysts, however, (notably Ivins 1953, Jussim 1983) see the technologies for processing exactly-reproducible images as equally if not more revolutionary in bringing new approaches to visual communication. For the latter part of the twentieth century we hear of the 'visual' or 'pictorial turn' associated with film and television and, alongside new computer technologies, eventuating in the 'increasing centrality of visual culture . . . mediated through the image technologies of advanced communication in modern societies' (Heywood and Sandywell 1999: xi, see also Barnard 1998: 1, Evans and Hall 1999: Introduction, Mitchell 1994). Then there are the 'regimes of surveillance' where, it is argued, 'the hegemony of vision', unlike the innocuous ocularcentrism of the past, is compounded by the worst tendencies of modernism (Foucault 1977, Levin 1993: 2ff). We read, too, of the postmodern shift to visual impacts, spectacle and the triumph of the 'simulacrum', as fleeting images replace texts (Baudrillard 1988, Evans and Hall 1999: Introduction). 'Postmodernism', it is sometimes claimed, 'is visual culture', and 'human experience is now more visual and visualized than ever before' (Mirzoeff 1998: xi, 1999: 1). Whatever the detailed evidence for these various trends, the matter is clearly one of multiple and differentiated historical processes taking place at different periods and in a range of situations, rather than some uniform 'visual bias of western culture'.

   'The west' is also an imprecise term that smoothes out variations both internally and over time and space. Its temporal and geographical boundaries seem to gain solidity only when contrasted with mythical 'others'. Some commentators furthermore focus so wholly on recent visual media that they overlook the co-existences of auditory and tactile channels, thus minimising the complexity of historical changes over many centuries. They also downplay the role of visual communication both in non-western cultures and at earlier periods of western history before the so-called 'Gutenberg revolution'. But as Frances Yates (1966) vividly describes, the amazing ancient arts of memory operated through the organised recall of visual images, a skill with a long history in the west before being downgraded (arguably) by the contending visual medium of print. In mediaeval Europe sight was in fact often ranked first among the senses. The 'Doom painting' of Figure 1.4 or York Minster's St William window (Figure 10.4) are examples of the churches' spectacular use of visual images; and late mediaeval European culture, with its stress on 'seeing' and 'salvic display', has been justly described as 'intensely visual' (Scribner 1981: 3ff).

   It is no more justifiable to lump together all 'non-western cultures' than to over-generalise about 'the west'. Even where high value is accorded to sound or to touch, it does not follow that visual communication has to be unimportant. Further, it could be argued that cultural traditions in which heavy restrictions are placed on vocal speaking are (in *that* respect) *more* visual than others – recall the remarkable (visual) sign languages developed in certain Australian Aboriginal groups or mediaeval monasteries as alternatives to speech, and the impressive gestural systems of

Native America. Among the Native American Apache, pictured depictions play an important role in their interchanges, and their conceptions of language and of thought are cast in 'pervasively visual terms' (Basso 1996: 84). To propose a one-dimensional contrast between 'the west and the rest' that associates vision with the first and audition or olfaction with the second is to fall again into the simplistic and romanticising prejudices encouraged by outdated binary stereotypes.

It would be more accurate to say that *all* human cultures in one way or another make extensive use of visual communication, but that there is a multifaceted spectrum of differing contexts and forms in which this rich channel is actively exploited and emphasised. Particular historical trends are indeed relevant, not excluding the last two centuries, but both changes and continuities are multiple and situational rather than once-and-for-all shifts along a single axis or some simple opposition between contrasted cultures or eras.

All in all, visible actions, displays and artefacts play a major role in human communicating, made possible by the power of the human eye to take in such variegated features as shape, colour, size, movement, structure, distance, spatial relationships, direction, depth and texture. Vision is an outstandingly versatile and multiplex channel, and it is scarcely surprising that it is used in a host of varying ways by human beings. We see and create sights of huge variety and complexity – always dependent on some degree of shared recognition, but sometimes also amazingly standardised and articulated, current over wide areas and times. There are striking continuities too, not just in iconographic patterns developed among specific groups and applied to many different spheres of their visual expression and action, bodily and artefactual alike, but also between forms of human visual action that are often discussed and classed separately. There are overlaps between pictorial, graphic and gestural forms; between surface-inscribed graphics and three-dimensional artefacts; and between all these and the visual signs and decorations of our bodies both in embodied presences and in their representations in pictures, photographs, film and sculptures. To discuss these independently – still worse, try to divide them into some rank order – is to play down the remarkable subtlety and ingenuity of our manifold human history of visual interconnections.

Vision is widely used by many other animals too. But humans, it can be said, are notable for the extraordinary development of their visual communicative forms – not only through their somatic sights, partially shared with other animals, but also, and most strikingly, through their many visual arts and long-lasting artefacts. Through them we have developed resources to communicate not just in the embodied moment, though that too is important, but also to a degree across the divides of space and time.

6   Sensing the odour

We now come to modalities with a much lower profile in studies of human communicating: smell and touch. It is understandable that vision and audition, so important in human interaction, should attract the prime attention. Smell and touch furthermore are not easy to study. Their precise application and relevance are even more elusive than those of sight or sound and insofar as organised processes of tactile and olfactory communication are detectable among humans, they are often below the level of conscious awareness. But the potential resources offered by touch, smell and, perhaps (overlapping with smell) taste, certainly deserve to be considered. As will emerge, both smell and, especially, touch play a much greater active role in human communicating than often recognised.

Smelling and tasting: resources for human communicating?

Smell has often been rated low in western epistemologies. In earlier assessments it was associated with the 'lower' emotions, the 'natural' and the 'animalistic' rather than the truly human. Kant's 'On the five senses' (1798: sections 15–23) puts smell unambiguously at the bottom:

> To which organic sense do we owe the least and which seems to be the most dispensable? The sense of smell. It does not pay us to cultivate it or to refine it . . . besides, the pleasure coming from the sense of smell cannot be other than fleeting and transitory.
>
> (Kant 1978: 46 [1798: section 22])

From the eighteenth century on, European travellers believed that a reliance on smell was characteristic of 'savages', unlike the sight and hearing cultivated by civilised beings – a view that still holds some sway (for further instances see Classen 1997: 404ff). In this evolutionary framework smell was typical of man's animal nature, something that modern cultures and individuals progressively outgrow.

A very different approach is adopted in recent analyses of smell, notably in comparative studies by anthropologists, psychologists and cultural historians.[1] They point to how the practices, concept and evaluations of smell, or of particular aspects of smell, are socially constructed – a matter of culture rather than biology. Human babies learn to experience smells in culture-specific modes. Furthermore the apparent suppression of smell in contemporary culture, both in people's ideologies and in the practical realities of everyday life, is only one, historically contingent, approach to smell. The 'deodorisation' of modern western society by increasingly eliminating individual and public smells through personal deodorants, 'air fresheners' and cosmetic/pharmaceutical preparations is neither a necessary mark of 'progress' nor universal. Smelling, like vision and audition, is learned, conceptualised, experienced and ordered differently in different social worlds and at different points in history.

A series of studies have documented the different and sometimes more explicit roles that odour has played elsewhere. Constance Classen describes the smells of antiquity: the scents pervading households, banquets and baths, the 'pomp and perfume' of public entertainments in classical Rome, the aromas of religious ceremonies, and the sensitivities to fragrance imbuing Latin literature (Classen *et al.* 1994: 13ff). The Latin poet Martial evoked the perfume of a lover's kisses through a series of scent-drenched images:

> The scent of an apple as a young girl bites it, the fragrance that comes from Corycian saffron, the smell of a silvery vineyard flowering with the first clusters or grass that a sheep has freshly cropped, the odor of myrtle, of an Arabian harvester, of rubbed amber, of fire pallid with eastern incense, of turf lightly sprinkled with summer rain.
>
> (Martial *Epigrams* 3, 65, trans. Bailey 1993, vol. 1: 249)

Classen conveys the stunning mixture of sweet and disgusting smells characterising mediaeval and renaissance homes and public spaces: the stench of excrement and death, pomanders to combat plague, perfumes and scented flowers to cover obnoxious smells or beautify the body. Noxious odours were a source of fear, both cause and symptom of death and disease, and smell played a significant part in medical diagnosis. Alain Corbin's vivid account *The Foul and the Fragrant* charts the terrible stenches and putridity in pre-revolutionary France. He describes the nineteenth-century preoccupation of the bourgeoisie with removing foul and detrimental smells from public and private life; 'they were obsessed with pestilential foci of epidemics. To escape this swamp of effluvia, the elite fled from social emanations and took refuge in fragrant meadows' (Corbin 1986: 230). This came to mark a radical change in western attitudes to smell, a 'perceptual revolution, precursor of our odorless environment' (Corbin 1986: 229).

The contrasting olfactory experiences and 'osmologies' described in such studies suggest it is worth questioning the ethnocentric assumption that the olfactory channel is necessarily of little relevance for human communicating – or, at any rate, for truly 'human' or 'modern' communication. They might also make us more sensitive to unnoticed ways in which we too make use of olfaction.[2]

Gustation is also worth considering. Food and drink are clearly important in human culture.[3] Shared meals – commensality – provide a focus for human gatherings and hence, as Simmel among others points out (1997 [1910]: 130), for regulated and communicative sociality. Food transactions and classifications can symbolise and enact social relationships, and markers of identity, status, life-stage, caste or religious affiliation are often enshrined in requirements to eat (or avoid) particular foods, rules about their preparation and distribution, or conventions about how and with whom you can eat. Food often has a role in delineating and enacting gender relations (Counihan and Kaplan 1998, Counihan 1999) while Jack Goody's study (1982) of the highly differentiated cuisine of Eurasia in contrast to Africa suggests an intricate link between food, hierarchy and social organisation.

That eating can carry deeply felt symbolisms as well as nutritional substance is well illustrated in Piero Camporesi's account of food and fantasy in early modern Europe, *Bread of Dreams*. He draws an awesome picture of the everyday imaginative life of ordinary people, 'in a state of almost permanent hallucination, drugged by their hunger or by bread adulterated with hallucinogenic herbs' (Camporesi 1989: blurb). Bread marked the life–death divide – a matter of necessity, indeed, but also of deep cosmic potency and Christian imagery.

> Bread – a polyvalent object on which life, death and dreams depend – becomes . . . the culminating point and instrument, real and symbolic, of existence itself . . . the nutritive function intermingles with the therapeutic, . . . magico-ritual suggestion with the ludico-fantastical, narcotic and hypnotic.
> (Camporesi 1989: 17–18)

For another era and continent Lévi-Strauss (1970) found profound symbolic meanings in the 'culinary triangle': deep-seated concepts of 'raw', 'cooked' and 'rotten' were formulated in traditional Native American myths and underlay their ordering of the world. As with seeing and hearing, the human ability to taste also forms the basis for complex technologies and art forms. Cookery everywhere has its recognised conventions, whether as everyday practice or high art, and the provision and tasting of food or drink figure prominently in ritual contexts; in the Japanese tea ceremony it is the central focus. Food and wine are fundamental in the Christian sacrament of communion, and alcoholic or narcotic drinks a common ingredient in social and religious rituals.

Such studies of taste and of smell provide an indispensable background, alerting us both to the cultural organisation of smell and taste and to their often underrated significance in human interaction. Can we conclude that these too are among the key modalities of human communication?

Gustation is especially elusive – necessary, pleasing and often highly cultivated feature of human experience though this is. Certainly food and drink play a large part in human interaction and, like any other tactile and visible objects, can be used in the process of communicating. But does it follow that gustation is the modality being actively drawn on here? Often, I suggest, it is through the visual, tactile and perhaps auditory experiences associated with preparing, classifying, displaying or consuming food and drink rather than the gustatory channel as such that humans can communicate.

But perhaps we can identify a system of agreed 'codes' carried by particular tastes, bringing them directly within our communicative processes? Some scholars certainly believe so. Sweet or sour, raw or cooked, the arrangements of menus, dietary systems, the structure of meals – all these have in fact been interpreted as coded. There have been enticing studies, mainly from structuralist and semiotic perspectives, of tastes as mythological codes embodying universal problems of existence, and of how to 'decipher' the codes of both ordinary and ceremonial meals (Lévi-Strauss 1970, Douglas 1975: 249ff, 1982). These raise the familiar issue of disentangling how far these 'meanings' are legislated by academic analysts rather than experienced by participants. Further, it often seems less a matter of *tasting* than of visual or perhaps olfactory sharing. As with other human arts and artefacts, meanings and symbols can be sought and found in meals, menus or drinks just as they can in buildings, ornaments or facial expressions – but it does not follow that it is through the *gustatory* channel that these meanings operate.

In a striking passage Simmel points to a special property of eating or drinking: that even while the gathering in which it takes place contributes to sociality, the process itself is inevitably individual.

> Of all the things that people have in common, the most common is that they must eat and drink. And precisely this, in a remarkable way, is the most egotistical thing, indeed the one most absolutely and immediately confined to the individual. What I think, I can communicate to others; what I see, I can let them see; what I say can be heard by hundreds of others – but what a single individual eats can under no circumstances be eaten by another.
>
> (Simmel 1997 [1910]: 130)

He is right – at least in the sense that, despite the traditional five-sense western classification, tasting does not provide the same basis for active and shared participation as seeing, hearing, touching or even, as we shall see, smelling. For this reason, and even though food and drink are rich topics in themselves, I have decided, controversially perhaps, not to explore gustation as a communication channel here in any direct way (it does of course emerge indirectly from time to time through its close connection with smell).

Olfaction is different. Smell can be shared, long-lasting, extended beyond a single body, and a vehicle for distant communication. Animal studies recognise olfaction as a key communicative channel and have explored how odours are detected and shared between individual organisms. These provide an illuminating comparative perspective on our human resources. So rather than dwelling longer now on the recent studies of changing olfactory conceptions and practices – the backdrop rather than main focus here – let us go first to a brief account of animal olfactory communication before returning to our human uses of smell.

Animal uses of smell

Many living creatures get their knowledge of the world from the chemical properties of events and objects. Smell is widely used among insects, reptiles and mammals. Species as diverse as elephants, lemurs, beavers, ants, moths, minnows, snakes and snails sense chemicals in the world around them, and many animals communicate through actively sending and receiving chemical signals in the form of smells.

These pheromones (chemical signals) can be transmitted through both water and air and also deposited on external objects. Olfactory signals are sent out from scent glands on the animal's body, situated variously in the ano-genital region, armpits, face, feet, lips or back. They are deployed in an extraordinarily wide and complex series of ways in animal communication and come in many different forms. As specific chemical compounds, each has a real physical existence with its own physical properties.

Animals employ smell for many purposes. It is used for recognising individuals, fellow-members of the same family, group or species, and characteristics like gender or rank. Mammals identify each other through subtle differences in body odour. Mice emit chemical signals which communicate not only individual and group identity but also their genetic relatedness, social status or dominance. The familiar patterns of face-to-face or nose-to-tail sniffing of dogs are found in varying forms among many animals, using smell to recognise, greet, avoid and interact with others or to convey complex information about relationships and group membership.

Olfactory communication also occurs between unacquainted or potentially competitive animals. Smell offers a low-risk means of assessment that avoids the commitment of direct bodily contact, and can be used to indicate non-hostile intentions and greetings as well as to threaten and defend. The dominant males of many species utilise olfactory signals for self-advertisement while the skunk's notorious stink warns predators to keep their distance. Some fishes indicate aggressiveness by emitting pheromones, greenflies send out a warning scent if attacked, while ring-tailed lemurs signal their competitiveness by rubbing secretions from their forearms onto their huge tails then waving them to waft the smell to their rivals.

Scent marks define territorial boundaries or identify a particular presence in the area. The animal uses smells from bodily products like urine, faeces or saliva, or rubs secretions onto objects from its scent glands. Male deer put smells onto trees from a gland near their eyes to tell other bucks of their presence, and lemurs rub branches with their hindquarters, foreheads or hands. Dogs make their presence known by urine deposits and bushbabies urinate on their hind feet which they then rub with their hands. Rhinoceroses mark territory by piles of faeces carefully deposited round the edges to warn off encroachers. Some New World monkeys can identify species, sex, agonistic status and individual from scent marks. Such olfactory signals work even in the bodily absence of the sender, and often persist over time. Their intensity, furthermore, can tell how long ago they were deposited.

Olfaction can thus be a highly effective channel for communicating at a distance. Snails, snakes and bees among others exploit the long-lasting nature of certain pheromones by laying down scent trails for their fellows to follow. Smells indicate sexual receptiveness (or the opposite) and among many species individuals emit far-travelling smells which members of the opposite sex detect and follow to find the sender. Certain moths are famous for using smells to advertise for mates. The female silk moth releases a minuscule quantity of the pheromone called bombykol from a pair of glands on her abdomen. This is wafted downwind and males several miles away receive it through receptor hairs on their antennae. In good wind conditions it can be detected 'much farther away than could any sound or visual signal produced by such a tiny animal. The male is supremely sensitive to that exact chemical and flies upwind to home in on the female and start his courtship' (Slater 1986: 67).

Olfactory communication is especially important among social insects such as ants, wasps, bees and termites who depend on complex communication systems to organise their cooperative existence. They use it to mark their home range, alert others, attract sexually and signal an alarm, as well as for the recognition and discrimination of kin and nestmates. When honeybee foragers locate a source of food they mark it with scent from a gland in their abdomen to show others the site, exploiting the capacity of smell to communicate at a distance since it lingers even in the absence of the emitter. Similarly ants lay scent trails to show others the way to and from food. Pheromones form the key communicative device for coordinating the complex tasks that have to be managed in these highly differentiated societies: 'Thousands of individuals that must continually be guided, instructed and encouraged in the many activities required to maintain an elaborate community' (Agosta 1992: 80).

Olfaction has many advantages as a communicative channel. It is true that smell travels more slowly than sights and sounds, at least over short distances; and unlike them cannot be changed rapidly. It can sometimes be hard to locate and (for some a disadvantage) to conceal. On the other hand darkness is no problem and physical barriers less obstructive than for sight. Olfaction is not constrained by an animal's size – it is used by elephants as well as by insects – but is perhaps especially valuable for the very small where vision and audition may be less effective. Smells can spread readily in all directions and over long distances, particularly when assisted by currents of air or water. Some pheromones are volatile, good for short-term purposes like warning of danger; others have the capacity to persist over time and can be detected months after having been left on a surface: useful for marking boundaries or food sites and for communicating even in the depositor's absence. In ways which are only beginning to be fully understood, olfaction turns out to be an unexpectedly rich and complex resource, widely used by living creatures both for immediate interaction and for communicating over space and time.[4]

Olfaction and human communication: the odorous body and its ordering

Despite all these advantages, humans make less use of olfaction, it seems, than many other creatures. In the human upright posture our smelling organs for detecting chemicals – our noses – are well away both from the ground and from the genitals of co-members of our species, and their small size and position on shortish necks make them less flexible and extendable than those of some other animals. In addition, though we have relatively well-developed scent-producing organs, comparable to those of chimpanzees and gorillas, humans apparently exert relatively little control over purposive emissions of smell. The human nose can in fact discriminate many thousands of odours but we have a very limited vocabulary for noting and differentiating them. When we try to describe smells we seldom employ olfactory classifications as such but instead refer to the context or to the *thing* being smelled – the smell of a rose, of newly cut grass, of sewers, of sweet potatoes being baked, of manure in a Chinese peasant farm, of the seashore, of fresh bread. As McKenzie put it: 'Smell is speechless . . . We never name an odour; we only say it has a "smell like" something or other' (McKenzie 1923: 60, 59). Smells are elusive to identify or define; nor are they measurable in the same way as sounds or sights. They are continuous rather than discrete, without edges or precise beginnings or endings.

These are real constraints and humans tend to turn to auditory, visual or perhaps tactile channels to fulfil purposes for which some other animals use olfaction. Nevertheless we make more use of the olfactory channel in our communicating than is often recognised, both through human bodily scents and in the extrinsic olfactory products, discussed later, through which humans deliberately exploit the communicative potential of smell.[5]

Smell is, first, part of the persona, one channel through which people present their unique individuality to others. Everyone, it appears, has their own personal odour. Dogs recognise human individuals by their smell, and so too, it seems, do some – perhaps all – humans. This is often below the level of awareness and scarcely easy to investigate, but there does indeed seem to be evidence that it plays a real part in human interaction. Mothers and young babies recognise each other's distinctive smells and olfaction is one channel through which they bond as individuals (Kellman and Arterberry 1998: 74). Some blind people are particularly alert to people's individual odours. Certain experiments also suggest that at least some people can use smell to differentiate gender or to identify clothes worn by themselves, their partners, or other family members (Doty 1981: 355ff). As Russell concluded his classic account in *Nature*: 'At least the rudimentary communications of sexual discrimination and individual identification can be made on the basis of olfactory cues' (1976: 521). Someone's individual smell is one facet of their personal signature.

This personal odour is in one way a natural property of the individual; but it is also processed and manipulated. There are effects from diet, disease and physical environment, and also the deliberate addition of externally applied perfumes (see below). The practices of organising the body also play a part. Since the main human scent glands are in the anal-genital regions, the face, the scalp, the umbilical region and, especially, the armpits, their impact is affected by the treatment or removal of body hair, by the direct application of various cosmetics and by type of dress. Even without conscious intent, this personal scent forms part of personal presentation. Sometimes it is dramatic. Schleidt (1992) notes a recurrent 'dominance display' among American males: raising their arms above and behind the head, thus releasing their personal odour by giving more exposure to the smell-producing underarm glands. This happens specially when someone is defending a point of view he feels strongly about: 'This largely unconscious gesture seems to express the feeling: "I have something important to say! Look at me! Listen to me! Smell me!"' (Schleidt 1992: 42).

As with some other animals, the human mutual recognition of personal scents serves to link members of closely interacting pairs and groups, distinguishing them from others. People recognise the odour of close friends and kin as pleasant and familiar, whereas others communicate themselves as (olfactory) outsiders. Again this is largely below the level of verbalised awareness but becomes explicit in some circumstances, especially crowded public settings. Here the olfactory modality is only too clearly recognised as people try to withdraw from the odours of those they classify – and smell – as strangers.

One setting where we almost unavoidably use olfaction is in close interpersonal communication. It is true that among humans (unlike some other animals) this is manifested more among those receiving a smell than in deliberate or controlled emissions. But as with the visible messages we pick up from face or body movements, so too with smells – the processes may not be conscious but may nevertheless be understood and acted on within specific contexts. Coming close enough to experience someone else's odour in contemporary western cultures suggests mutual intimacy or a close personal link (see Box 4.2 in Chapter 4). In some traditions this is an explicit dimension of close greetings. Roth comments of salutations in south-east India that 'they apply the mouth and nose to the cheek, and give a strong inhalation. In their language, they do not say "Give me a kiss" but they say, "Smell me"' (Roth 1889: 167). In *The Hidden Dimension* E. T. Hall remarks on the prominent place of olfaction in Arab communicating, used both as sign of close personal involvement and as distance-setting mechanism. In contrast to American conventions that people should avoid breathing in each other's faces, in Arab culture, he writes, 'to smell one's friend is not only nice but desirable, for to deny him your breath is to act ashamed'. The olfactory boundary 'enfolds those who want to relate and separates those who don't' (Hall 1966: 149).

People's smells and smelling are socially managed and interpreted, marked in differing ways across different groups and historical periods. In some places a person's smell has a prominent and explicit role. The Ethiopian Dassanetch, for example, attach particular importance to the personal odours of close family members. After death their remembered scent becomes the basis for their living memory.

> The objects which evoke memories among the Dassanetch . . . are usually personal objects inherited from a deceased person. In these memories odors fulfil an important role, for these heirlooms exude odors associated with the deceased who had used them for many years, sometimes decades, and thus bear the personal odor of the deceased. . . . The brothers and sisters referred to the odor of their father whom they smelled whenever they came to visit one of the siblings and entered his hut. . . . Each of them told me that a similar odor recollection happened to him or her whenever they went to visit their brothers and sisters. With the latter it was mainly the odor of their mother which was present inside the hut and was exuded from the various milk vessels which the sisters inherited.
> (Almagor 1990b: 264–5)

Another instance comes from eighteenth-century France, very different in its details but equally building on the communicative resource of smell. Alain Corbin's *The Foul and the Fragrant* (1986) recounts the vitalist views in which emanations of the various organs were held to be part of the body's constitution. The odour of sperm was notable above all, the paradigm on which all other humours were modelled. The more pungent this *aura seminalis* the greater a man's sexual attractiveness, contrasting with the odours of 'the continent priest or the assistant schoolmaster, the unsavory celibate, [which] became a commonplace of Romantic literature' (Corbin 1986: 36–7). 'Odoriferous' individuals conveyed their animal vigour through smell – something to be treasured, not spoiled by over-cleansing (when Napoleon told Josephine he was on his way he famously added 'Don't wash'). How far human bodily odour can be controlled to give off aphrodisiac signals similar to the olfactory sexual attractants among some animals is debateable, but it is clear at least that in some cultural perspectives this is felt to be possible. Here the olfactory channel becomes a purposive dimension of the presentation of self.

Social differentiation is sometimes explicitly related to odour. The Brazilian Suyá classify life-stages by smell. Young men move from being 'strong-smelling' children to having no odour after initiation, then 'pungent-smelling' when they reach grandfatherhood (Seeger 1988: 45). Eighteenth-century French writers noted that people from different occupations or areas communicated their nature by their different odours. Rural as against urban people, peasants from different regions of France, cesspool cleaners, tanners, butchers, candlestick makers and even nuns – all could be identified by their smell (Corbin 1986: 39–40).

In rain forests where vision is restricted, smell can outdistance sight. The Umeda people of New Guinea were always on the lookout for olfactory clues 'to enable them to discover things otherwise kept hidden . . . [like] the faintest hint of the smoke from a campfire in the depths of the forest' (Gell 1977: 32). The Desana living in the forests of Columbian north-west Amazonia lay particular emphasis on olfactory communication, holding that everyone sends out odour signals in periodic cycles, gradually changing as they age. They classify men and women – as well as different animal species – by their different smells (Reichel-Dolmatoff 1985: 124–6, 138). When they travel to other areas, Desana men 'continuously sniff the air and comment upon the differences'; in their experience each tribe, including themselves, has a distinctive smell and, like a deer, lays down 'odour threads' to mark out its territory (Reichel-Dolmatoff 1985: 125, 126).

Odour is a peculiarly emotive basis for social inclusion and exclusion, often invoked by powerful groups to both distinguish and stigmatise those they classify as inferior or alien. Members of lower classes, immigrants, and despised outsider groups or races are commonly said 'to smell'. It is not difficult to think of examples nearer home; but the Ethiopian Dassanetch can again be mentioned for their elaborate rationale, using olfactory labels to distinguish themselves from other peoples in the area who all 'smell differently from themselves' (Almagor 1987: 110). They make a definitive olfactory distinction between themselves, as cattle keepers, and the foul-smelling, despised fisherfolk. Fish are antithetical to cattle, the 'perfect' animals not just for subsistence but also for proper social relationships and the right cosmic order. It is therefore natural to loathe and reject those dependent on fishing for their disgusting fishy odour. 'The Dassanetch concept is that the fishermen permanently stink', threatening the cosmological cycle by their stench (Almagor 1987: 114). The nineteenth-century French 'olfactory revolution' depicted by Alain Corbin similarly involved differentiating between fragrant bourgeoisie and foul masses, defined in olfactory terms. 'The absence of intrusive odor enabled the individual to distinguish himself from the putrid masses, stinking like death, like sin, and at the same time implicitly to justify the treatment meted out to them' (Corbin 1986: 143). Such olfactory hierarchies may of course be based as much in socially generated symbolisms as in actual odour. But either way, smell is here, as elsewhere, invoked as an explicit vehicle for conveying and reinforcing conclusions about the essential nature and status of other individuals and groups encountered in social life.

Olfactory arts and artefacts

This brings us on to the more consciously contrived and externally produced uses of olfaction. Humans may not be able to emit bodily odours in the controlled way practised by insects, nor do they generally utilise faecal deposits or other odoriferous marks to define their territory. Nevertheless they can and do make deliberate use of smells produced otherwise than directly from the human body. Though less dependent on olfactory communication than some other animals, humans can discriminate many different odours, and over the millennia have taken pains to produce and utilise them. These human-made aromas are another surprisingly rich resource in human interaction.

Fragrances have long been deliberately produced from both plant and animal sources. Just as vision and audition have formed the basis for complex art forms and associated social organisation, so too has olfaction. In multiple and variegated ways human beings have developed perfumes for the beautification and display of persons, clothes, buildings and special occasions. In classical Greece and Rome and in the great Arabian cultures, the use of fragrances was highly elaborated, backed by a complex system of international trade routes, manufacture and distribution. In classical Roman theatres the stages were sprinkled with saffron and other scents, lavish banquets were scented by the fragrances of flowers, incense and perfume, and even the amphitheatre fountains sprayed out perfumed waters (Classen *et al.* 1994: 24, 26). Aromatic herbs and scented gardens exploit the atmosphere-setting properties of smell, as in the distinctive fragrances valued in some Chinese gardens (Tuan 1993: 67). In Europe, too, scents have at times been highly elaborated. Personal perfumes were mixed from different fragrances to suit individual personalities, and beautiful aromas carefully deployed to embellish feasts and public occasions.

This is not just something of the past, for fragrances are produced and manipulated worldwide today both as bottled scents and as perfumed soaps, cosmetics, oils or incense. They can be the basis for great aesthetic sophistication. The aromas used in the twentieth-century United Arab Emirates, for example, regularly included aloewood, ambergris, saffron, musk, rose, jasmine, narcissus, sandalwood, henna and civet.

> [This] basic palette of scents . . . is employed by Arab women to compose their own blends of perfume which will be applied to different parts of the body. Musk, rose and saffron are rubbed on the whole body. The hair is perfumed and oiled with a blend of walnut or sesame seed oil with ambergris or jasmine. The ears are anointed and coloured with a red mixture . . . composed of aloewood, saffron, rose, musk and civet. For the neck, aloewood, ambergris, rose, narcissus or musk are used, for the armpits ambergris or sandalwood, and on the nostrils aloewood.
>
> (Classen *et al.* 1994: 126)

Kanafani describes how each woman composes her own personal blend; her personality encompasses 'her artistic ability to create a blend of harmonious smells, and her social ability to communicate with other women . . . as an efficient creator of beautiful smells' (1983: 89). In many parts of the Near and Far East, scented oils are particularly prized; elsewhere, bottled scents and perfumed cosmetics. In one form or another fragrances are processed and distributed throughout the world, an international industry.

These externally produced sources of smell are turned to many purposes. They are sometimes elaborated with complex and cultivated artistry, as in the examples above, but even in a less heightened way can be drawn on to convey particular aspects of personal identity. Self-presentation has often included the intentional deployment of fragrance: carrying sweet-smelling flowers and other scented objects, perfuming clothes, using scented soaps and oils, steaming the body in fragrance, or applying special perfumes. Scents call attention to the wearer's presence and, if only subliminally, affect others' reactions. This form of impression management is one aspect of personal communication, a dimension well publicised by the modern perfume industry. Personal perfuming draws on current cultural expectations to convey messages, implicitly at least, about the wearer's alignment with a particular category of people and/or their intentions in a specific situation. The Arabian women's scents mentioned above were for private not public use, and a woman wearing them in public would be regarded as communicating an image of, at best, impropriety. The effectiveness of scents to convey invisible messages was explicitly recognised in an English act of 1770:

> All women, of whatever age, rank, profession or degree, whether virgins, maids or widows, that shall from and after this act impose upon, seduce and betray into matrimony any of His Majesty's subjects by the use of scents, paints, cosmetic washes . . . shall incur the penalty of the law now in force against witchcraft.
>
> (quoted in Classen *et al.* 1994: 163)

Both the use and the avoidance of particular fragrances can present a very public display of social identity and differences. Gender can be marked out by (among other things) the application of particular scent(s); the same for particular professions or sectional groups. Olfaction can also be a vehicle for communicating solidarity with others of the same beliefs. The Puritans rejected what they regarded as the unnecessary and wrongful use of fragrances in both personal and religious contexts, making this a mark of their differentiation from the odoriferous usages of other worshippers.

The deliberate use of fragrances often plays a powerful part in creating an atmosphere or defining an occasion. As Yi-Fu Tuan points out 'aromatic architecture' is a feature of some palaces and religious buildings; Solomon's temple used fragrant cedarwood and certain Indian temples are known as 'houses of fragrance', the aroma helping to frame the experience and the place (Tuan 1993: 65). A location or event can be distinguished by its wafted fragrances independent of embodied personal scents. Humans have developed the arts of exploiting the pervasive yet subtle properties of smell to good effect in such contexts, sometimes relatively unawares, sometimes quite deliberately. The scene may be set by the fragrance of particular flowers, the odours of freshly washed linen, evocative cooking smells from ceremonial foods, the odours associated with hospitals or churches, or aromatic substances like myrrh, lavender, ginger or balsam. On other occasions it is the odour of particular kinds of alcohol or the lingering smell of cigarette smoke. It is perhaps relatively seldom that smell acts as the sole marker in such cases. Its effectiveness, however, lies in its uniquely evocative power to awaken deeply held but often non-verbalised associations. These can define a situation or, alternatively, subtly convey to participants that something is 'wrong' when the hidden olfactory ambience does not match the expectation. It may not be verbally articulated but through their noses people may be in no doubt about what kind of occasion they are engaged in and the nature of their interaction.

Olfaction can be a powerful communicative tool for influencing others. In magicians' spells in the Trobriand Islands smell was pre-eminent: 'magic, in order to achieve its greatest potency, must enter through the nose. Love charms are borne into the victim on the scent of some spellbound aromatic substance' (Malinowski 1929: 378). Its use in marketing is another example, exploiting the special power of smell to create the right atmosphere. We are acquainted with the smells of certain specialist shops – shoe shops, hardware, bakers, stalls in an open-air market – with their clear but unstated encouragement to recognise this as an occasion for buying their goods. Some modern superstores are said to go further, experimenting with odoriferous messages to create an appropriate mood for shopping, and underground stations have tried special scents to convey an atmosphere of calm and security. And we have probably all heard the folk wisdom urging sellers of houses to have aromatic coffee brewing in the kitchen or, better still, the smell of freshly made bread to convey to potential buyers the unspoken but intense message of a warm-hearted place where they can feel relaxed and at home.

Smells are deliberately deployed in religious, ceremonial and therapeutic contexts. Perfumed flowers, aromatic materials and scented oils are common features of rituals and sacred sites. The wafting of fragrance is commonly the channel for communicating with gods or ancestors, bringing humans into touch with the world of the spirit. In the complex olfactory cosmology of the Batek Negrito of Peninsular Malaysia, incense and the aroma of sweet-smelling leaves and flowers bring contact between earth and firmament as the deities delight in the fragrant smoke (Endicott 1979: Chapter 2 and *passim*). The Homeric epics depict the smell of smoke from burnt offerings as delectable to the gods' nostrils and many other cultures have their own favoured aromas for spiritual communication: mint for the Trobriand Islanders, ginger among the Umeda of New Guinea, balsam in some Christian services. Incense made by burning odoriferous substances like camphor, cloves, myrrh, frankincense, sandalwood, balsam or juniper is common in religious ceremony, designed to attract the gods' attention, propitiate them, ask for blessings, or display their worshippers' devotion. Incense was the medium for appealing to the gods in Chinese Taoist healing rituals:

> Using the rising flame and smoke from the incense burner in the center of the oratory to transmit a message borne by spirits exteriorized from within his own body, the Taoist libationer submitted petitions to the appropriate bureau of the Three Heavens, where officials pronounced judgement on the appeal and mar-shaled celestial forces against the offending demons responsible for the illness.
>
> (Rahim 1987: 161)

On such occasions, furthermore, the pervasive perfume from the incense binds the worshippers into a jointly communicating nexus as well as helping to shape the specific ritual and mark its successive stages. Olfaction can be an emotive and powerful communicative dimension in these situations, the more effective because of the immediate and invasive properties of smell, harder to 'tune out' than vision or even audition.

Rites of passage are common settings both for fragrances and for their contrived denial. Many inauguration ceremonies for kings or priests include ritual bathing – casting off the odours of their prior identity – and anointing with aromatic oils. Special perfumes are chosen for wedding or initiation ceremonies. The aromas define the ritual situation, act as signals to synchronise people's activities, and publicly confirm the ceremony and its participants through the olfactory conventions.

Overlapping with its religious and ceremonial roles are the specialist usages of olfaction in therapeutic settings. Spices and aromatic oils have long played a part in medical practice, varyingly used in curing, purifying, or driving out evil spirits. In some medical perspectives smells are associated with particular diseases, a better guide than vision to what is internal; in eighteenth- and nineteenth-century France prior to microbial models of disease, smell was not only the symptom of medical conditions but also in part their definition. Curing diseases or expelling the spirits that cause them has sometimes meant utilising antagonistic odours or employing particular fragrances to protect against illness. Recent years have seen the expansion of aromatherapy and the associations with particular odours that this brings. Some therapists have similarly tried out evocative fragrances – of the seaside for example or of particular flowers – to reduce anxiety and positively communicate a sense of relaxation and well-being, others deploy the mood-altering or aphrodisiac fragrances of particular drugs.

The consciousness-altering potential of smell comes into some of these healing rituals as into ceremonies of personal transition; people move from the status of

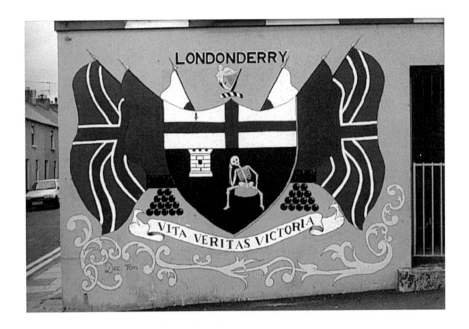

Figure 6.1 Murals from the north of Ireland

Above: Loyalist mural in Derry showing Union Jacks (spectacular in emotive red, white and blue) and Derry city's coat of arms; the skeleton recalls the famous siege of 1688, annually commemorated in the 'Apprentice Boys March' (see comment in text). Below: Nationalist mural, Belfast, with shields of the four provinces of Ireland, a stylised phoenix (predominantly green) for the republican movement, and a statement supporting the republican

diseased or devil-ridden to healthy and pure, for example, from child to adult, layman to expert, or secular being to someone imbued with the sacred. It is used explicitly in this way by the Dakota in the North American Western Plains where the shared smell of the sweet grass brewed during their rituals 'entrains so complete a transformation of awareness that all categories, all discontinuities, dissolve into the continuum of the fragrant smoke of sweet grass' (Howes 1987: 401). Through this they experience 'the ultimate unity of all . . . to "make the four-legged, the wingeds, the star peoples of the heavens and all things as relatives"' (Lee 1959: 63).

Olfaction has been claimed to be *the* liminal sense above all others (Howes 1987: 411). The experience of trance, dream or religious transcendence is certainly sometimes associated with smell. In hallucinogen-taking cultures in South America, shamans make particular use of fragrances; likewise in the ancient oracular shrine at Delphi smoke from burning bay-leaves led to trance-like communication with the gods. Through these aromas people can somehow go beyond themselves and move into contact with ultimate cosmic realities. In Alfred Gell's words, olfaction 'comes into play most when the other senses are in suspense, at moments, one could say, of *materialisation* and *dematerialisation*, the coming into being and the passing away of things' (Gell 1977: 28 [italics in original]).

It would be easy to give the impression that olfaction always involves sweet smells or redolent messages of harmony, nostalgia or ritual transcendence. But as cultural historians in particular have reminded us, smells can be unpleasant and threatening too, or at any rate interpreted as such. Corbin (1986) conveys a horrifying picture of the putridity, stench and foulness that characterised the life of the French masses and so offended the noses and the principles of the nineteenth-century reformers. As among other animals, humans too sometimes deploy smell to convey hostile or competitive intent. Gases have been deliberately loosed to warn, intimidate or control – the equivalent of the skunk's obnoxious stink. Smoke is sometimes used in a similar way, smell being one of its immediately detectable features.

A good example is an event that used to take place regularly in Derry in Northern Ireland – or so folk mythology had it, formulated in a way intelligible to all local residents in the light of the background of murals (among other things) such as those of Figure 6.1. This was during the colourful 'Apprentice Boys March'

---

prisoners then carrying on an internationally publicised hunger strike: 'The people arose in 69, they will do it again at any time. Maggie Thatcher think again, don't let our brave men die in vain.' Both draw on a vibrant Ulster tradition of using murals to present potent images, interacting with other musical, auditory, visual and material symbols, together with processions and commemorative celebrations, to convey opposing political positions and views of history (from Bill Rolston *Drawing Support. Murals in the North of Ireland,* Belfast: Beyond the Pale Publications (7 Winetavern St., Belfast BT1 1JQ), 1992); photographs: Bill Rolston 1991, 1981).

each August commemorating their 'loyalist' ancestors' refusal, three centuries and more ago, to yield the city to the Catholic besiegers. Some of the Catholic residents regard this march as a triumphalist assertion of sectarian Protestant ascendancy. Well cognisant of the prevailing winds, they set their chimneys alight. The smoke conveyed their protest, obscuring the procession and spoiling the festive atmosphere by its smell.

Olfaction is in some ways not so different from other communicative modalities. Like them it sometimes takes a central role, sometimes combines with others to present a multisensory message about an individual or occasion. But in other ways it is one of the most obscure and elusive of the human communicative channels. It is continuous, rather than bounded. It can be powerful, direct and immediate, but also hard to capture, seeming not to reside *in* things but to escape and float above them. Of all the senses it is perhaps the most intense and long-lasting in the memory, but not to be pinned down in verbal formulation or deliberately retrievable recollection. As Yi-Fu Tuan says, 'scents capture the aesthetic-emotional quality of place' (1993: 69), and we have doubtless all experienced the redolent effects of smell in stirring deeply emotive but unsought evocations of places, people and experiences – perhaps more profoundly moving and long-lasting than those given through any other sense, and yet impalpable, not to be imprisoned in words. Alfred Gell in his striking 'Magic, perfume, dream' may overstate the matter but we can sympathise with the point he is making: 'A mere aroma, in its very lack of substance is more *like* a concept than it is like a "thing" in the usual sense. . . . To manifest itself as a smell is the nearest an objective reality can go towards becoming a concept without leaving the realm of the sensible altogether' (Gell 1977: 28–9 [italics in original]).

Smell furthermore seems to take us into the inner nature of things, beyond the superficial surfaces that can be captured by vision. Some cultural traditions are especially alive to this potentiality of olfaction, not just in the context of scientific exploration or medical diagnosis but deliberately intensifying it through the mood-altering qualities of specific fragrances and, especially, the smoke from burning odoriferous substances. Here smell seems to be at the edge of reality, taking the participants into communication with something beyond the here and now of the presently tangible or visible world.

Despite these far-reaching characteristics of smell, it seems, however, that human beings have not developed their uses of olfaction into any more standardised systems of communication. There are some minor examples perhaps. Smoke signals from camp fires are sometimes exploited in situations where vision is obscured and if we are prepared to include communication with the gods, the smell of burnt offerings carries agreed meanings within particular religious contexts. But, unlike hearing, seeing and to a degree touching, there seems to be no widely recognised codification. The modern perfume industry attempts from time to time to popularise accepted meanings for their marketed scents but apparently with but little success.[6] One suggested explanation for the absence of developed olfactory coding is that smell, like touch and taste, is a 'proximity' sense and so does not need the same degree of verbalisation or codification as the 'distance senses' of sight and hearing (Howes and Lalonde 1991). Though this might possibly be true of the olfaction of embodied interactions, it could scarcely account for the more distant communication for which the wafting of smells is in fact eminently suited and, indeed, to some extent exploited by human beings. Whatever the reason, olfaction is a rich and complex human sense which nevertheless seems to have been little exploited (so far) as a *standardised* communication system in ways that could parallel those using auditory, visual and even (to some degree) tactile channels.

At a less standardised level, however, smells and their associations certainly play a role in human communication. They can shape the nature of particular forms of human interaction in both embodied and externalised forms, doing so in pervasive and often highly effective ways whether in close interpersonal communication or more public ceremonies. If communicating is to be understood as including not just message-transfer and cognition but also experiential and emotive processes it would clearly be wrong to omit smell. Even where olfactory dimensions are, as often, not verbalised there are still recognised conventions for interpreting their import, structured by the social processes and learned experiences shared within particular traditions. And it is possible that as the current research into this channel of animal communication progresses, so further insights into as yet unimagined dimensions of human olfactory interaction may perhaps also be revealed.

7 Communicating touch

Touching, by contrast, is thoroughly palpable and present, a direct mode through which living creatures interact with the environment and each other. The tactile channel is complex and multifaceted, not always easy to distinguish sharply from others (it merges into audition and vibration), and in most treatments of communication makes only a limited appearance. But the patterned and purposive uses of touch are in fact crucial in many human encounters. This is the channel through which physical co-presence is most directly embodied, the first sense experienced in the womb, a regulated mode of social interaction, and symbol as well as vehicle of human interconnectedness. Its role among animals has long been taken for granted, and its significance for human interaction now increasingly recognised. It has justly been termed 'one of the most basic and commanding forms of human communicative behavior' (McDaniel and Andersen 1998: 59).

The tactile channel and animal communication

Like other channels, touch has its own characteristics. It provides a rapid, immediate and powerful means of contact though mutual bodily interconnection. Easier to locate than sound and smell, it is specific and direct, works equally well in noisy conditions and, unlike vision, in the dark. Multiple dimensions can be detected through touch, from the identification of objects to shape, size, spatial properties, temperature, flexibility, movement and texture. There are corresponding limitations. The corollary to the immediacy of touch is that, like audition, it is not lasting and in the main disappears without trace. It is slower and more cumbersome than vision for scanning a linear series and less effective than sound for getting round physical barriers or covering distance. With some exceptions, participants must be physically close to communicate through touch.

Animals make much use of tactile communication, the strongest and most immediate of all forms of direct interconnection. They can both move parts of their bodies to touch each other and move into and out of reach of tactile contact. They make deliberate use of many bodily areas for physical contact, notably noses, teeth, lips, tongue, limbs, hands/paws, feet, tails, flanks and genitals; elongated antennae,

Figure 7.1 Monkey tails: communicating through touch
When two to four titi monkeys from the same group sit side by side they often intertwine
their tails, either just one loose turn or, as here, in a tighter corkscrew-like fashion. Through
this tactile communication they convey, enact and strengthen their social relationships (M.
Moynihan, 'Communication in the titi monkey, *Callicebus*', *Journal of Zoology,* 150, 1966,
Fig. 1 p. 83, courtesy Cambridge University Press).

tentacles and fin rays can facilitate longer stretches. They employ these tools for touching and feeling in an astounding variety of ways. They lean, press, lightly touch, push, strike, suck and embrace. Comforting, calming, protecting, suckling, copulating, fighting, threatening, competing, submitting, playing, greeting, warning, courting, and asserting or accepting a relationship – for all these forms of interaction touch is a recognised medium. It contributes to the maintenance of social bonds through cuddling, nuzzling, rubbing noses in greeting, or – common among mammals – mutual grooming. Among social insects such as ants or bees touch is used as well as olfaction, while fish grasp with their mouths and use noses or mouths to nudge. A parrot nibbles another's toes to make it move along the branch and South American titi monkeys communicate by mutual touch when they twine their long tails together (Figure 7.1).

Seismic contact can also be regarded as a form of tactile communication.[1] Many animals systematically send and receive organised vibrations through the ground to mark their territory or locate a mate, among them insects, amphibians, reptiles, rodents and some large mammals, and to a greater extent than was once realised. Prairie mole crickets use vibration to space themselves out and avoid over-crowding underground, aggressive elephant-seal bulls compete for females through seismic signals, while mole-rats in underground burrows attract mates by drumming to a specific pattern with their hind legs. Spiders communicate through the vibrations of their webs. When elephants trumpet or stomp their feet the vibrations can travel twenty or thirty miles through the ground (much further than the sounds through the air), detectable by specially sensitive cells in the trunk (Anon 2001: 76–7). Vibrations are sent across water too. Male water strider insects tap out messages on the water's surface creating a patterned ripple sequence for the female to feel; other water insects use comparable patterns to repel intruders. These seismic devices extend the otherwise limited range of the tactile channel, providing yet a further means of animal communication over distance.

Human touching as communication

Humans make little use of vibration but otherwise utilise touch for communicating in similar ways to other animals. Interaction through touching and feeling is one of the fundamentals of human social existence. The experience of physically touching something – other people, external objects – assures us of being in touch both with the world outside ourselves and with our own embodied actuality. One major way in which human beings interconnect is through the corporeal inter-presence attested above all by touch.[2]

We are well equipped to do so. Many parts of the human body can be moved and manipulated to make physical contact or to control and assess through touch. Limbs, feet, hands, elbows, genitals, head and face (and especially nose, lips, cheeks, teeth) – all are effective resources for touching. There is also contact spread through many areas of the body at once as in hugging, holding, sitting on someone's lap, and manifold sexual encounters.

The human hand has a pre-eminent place – 'by far the most informative of all our organs' (Montagu 1986: 127). The hand's position at the end of long upper limbs gives us a lengthy stretch well out from the rest of the body, comparable to the long antennae and tentacles of other species. Equally important, our upright posture and bipedal locomotion free our hands to act as highly adaptable tactile tools either singly or together. The spread and sensitivity of five fingers, together with the combined potential of two separate hands enables the detection of, for example, spatial relations, texture and irregularities as well as the manipulation of multiple objects or positions simultaneously. They make up 'an expert system' as Millar rightly calls it (1997: 16) that can be trained to a remarkable degree of sensitivity, demonstrated among other things in the skills of blind braille readers. In common with other communicative forms we use our hands in culturally mediated ways; as the so-called 'thalidomide children' remind us there are many different ways of exploiting our basic biological resources. But it seems fair to say that a characteristic of human beings across the world is to lay a heavy emphasis on the communicative powers of the hands.[3]

The outgoing and active process in which we use touch to explore and affect the world outside ourselves is matched by our capacity to *be* touched. In being so, we inescapably enter into some kind of contact with another. Our skin is crucial, 'the envelope which contains the human organism' (Frank 1957: 211). Here is the juncture between our bodies and those of others, and between ourselves and the environment outside us. Sometimes described as 'the largest human organ' (Frank 1957: 217), our skin is the extensive surface through which we engage in the deeply human experience of bodily interconnection with others. It is relatively accessible to touch from those outside it, its sensitive nerve endings enabling precise discriminations for intersomatic communication between separate human beings. Through this dermal channel we feel both moving and relatively static contacts from others – a kiss, a handshake, a slap or an embrace.

It is through the interacting combination of tactual sensation and active touching, deployed in purposive and coordinated movements, that humans take advantage of the many different dimensions brought together under the somewhat simplified terms of 'touching' and 'feeling'.[4] The potential of touch is immense, for it can come in manifold combinations of types of touching and of places touched. Through the tactile channel, sometimes on its own, sometimes interacting closely with visual or auditory processes, we experience, and to a degree share, weight, size, texture, hardness/softness, flexibility, viscosity, composition, depth, shape, spatial relations, movement and, in a slightly different sense, temperature and pain.

This complex and effective channel seldom receives any serious attention in accounts of communicating. In studies of perception it has often been regarded as just an impoverished form of vision, and the hand(s) merely 'a second-class citizen'

(Millar 1997: 15, Lederman and Klatzky 1987: 342). One reason is presumably because tactile interaction so often takes place below the level of conscious awareness, too familiar to be consciously noticed. Only when deliberate studies are undertaken does it emerge both how often we touch and are touched *and* how our attitudes and actions are in practice affected, unawares, by the touches of others. As Ashley Montagu points out (1986), we have only a small vocabulary for speaking about touch, and in contrast to the ample literary celebration of sight and hearing, touch has seldom been the subject for poetry. It is also almost impossible to envisage what it would be like to be without touch so as to give a vantage point on how we actually do use it.

> For vision and audition, one can imagine being deprived of sight or hearing, and there are, of course, blind and profoundly deaf individuals who can help us understand the nature of their experiences. A head cold lets us know the information derived from olfaction, but what would it be like to be without somesthesis?
>
> (Craig and Rollman 1999: 306)

Some perspective is provided by the experiences of Ian Waterman after he lost his sense of touch and position and had to monitor all his movements visually. *Pride and a Daily Marathon* (Cole 1991) recounts the extraordinary measures he had to take to cope with his situation, an unexpected insight into complex tactile processes we normally take for granted.

Touch, like smell, has often been ranked low in the hierarchy of the senses, body-centred experiences which modern humanity should leave behind for higher intellectual or spiritual concerns. In the late eighteenth century Schiller was echoing an accepted view when he spoke of the 'more animal senses' in his study of aesthetics: 'as long as man is still a savage he enjoys by means of these tactile senses alone'; his 'entry upon humanity' depends on greater use of eye and ear (1982 [1794–1801]: 191–5). This view still has influence, but is after all only one view of the matter. As Millar points out, in some philosophies 'touch teaches vision' and mediates between the other senses (1997: 15ff). For Bertrand Russell it is touch that 'gives us our sense of "reality". . . . Not only our geometry and physics, but our whole conception of what exists outside us, is based upon the sense of touch' (Russell 1969: 10).

Whatever our philosophies, in practice we act on the assumption that, verbalisable or not, touch is indeed a channel of communicating. Perhaps lovers appreciate this above all, but whether welcomed as joint commitment or resented as invasion – or a host of reactions in between – mutual touching is surely one of the most immediately engaged and participatory forms of corporeal interconnection between human beings. Touch is all the more effective in mutual interconnectedness because someone touched almost inevitably makes some direct tactile response. Even the seeming lack of a reaction can communicate a direct and clear sign of withdrawal or hostility. There is a sense in which, as Jones and Yarbrough claim (1985: 20), communication through touch, more so than through visual glances or gestures, conveys 'an undeniable message'.

We also recognise the communicating role of touch when we observe it in others. This fact is well exploited in pictorial representation where we regularly interpret what is shown, and especially the relations between people represented, by noting how they are shown as touching (or not touching). The many close mother-and-child portrayals in western art, for example, or the rough handling of sinners in 'doom' pictures attest to much more awareness of the significance of mutual touch than might be deduced from verbalised accounts alone.

One attempt to convey the far-reaching potential of touch is, paradoxically enough, an account of monkey grooming. The passage no doubt draws a little on imagination as well as undoubted expertise, but is worth quoting for its evocative formulation of dimensions of touching which are seldom put into words.

Figure 7.2 Seeing touch

Pictorial representations build on our awareness of the communicative importance of both touching – and particular kinds of touching – and of avoiding touch. Left: 'Noli me tangere' shows the well-known scene between Christ and Mary Magdalene in the garden after his resurrection: Mary wishes to touch him, but the newly risen Christ marks his transitional state by his gesture and the evocative words 'Do not touch me.' The picture is set into the decorated initial letter G of an illuminated fifteenth-century missal, which also includes written words and musical notation (Museo di San Marco dell'Angelico, Florence, Italy (Missal 558 f.64v)/Bridgeman Art Library). Right: 'The Virgin of Louvain' by Peter Mabuse, 1533, one of the abundant Madonna and child pictures of western art. The intimate touch between mother and child communicates potent images of love, care and close interaction for Christians and non-Christians alike (Prado, Madrid, Spain/Bridgeman Art Library).

> To be groomed by a monkey is to experience primordial emotions: the initial frisson of uncertainty in an untested relationship, the gradual surrender to another's avid fingers flickering expertly across bare skin. . . . You begin to relax into the sheer intensity of the business, ceding deliciously to the ebb and flow of the neural signals that spin their fleeting way from periphery to brain, pitter-pattering their light drumming on the mind's consciousness somewhere in the deep cores of being.
>
> (Dunbar 1996: 1)

The experience is not just physical sensation but also, Dunbar insists, a process of communication:

> A light touch, a gentle caress, can convey all the meanings in the world: one moment it can be a word of consolation, an apology, a request to be groomed, an invitation to play; on another, an assertion of privilege, a demand that you move elsewhere; on yet another, a calming influence, a declaration that intentions are friendly. Knowing which meaning to infer is the very basis of social being. . . . Here, in the minutiae of everyday life, is a point of convergence between ourselves and our nearest relatives, the monkeys and apes. Here is behaviour with which we instantly empathize, the innuendoes and subtleties of everyday social experiences.
>
> (Dunbar 1996: 1–2)

Human beings draw extensively on our capacity for tactile communication. Babies move around within the womb, touching their own bodies. Touch is an essential dimension of a newly born baby's social life, with close tactile communication between infant and nurturing adult in feeding, skin contact, holding and reassuring. Kabongo, a Kenyan Kikuyu, looks back at the age of eighty at his experience of child–mother bodily interaction:

> I can remember the comforting feel of her body as she carried me on her back and the smell of her skin in the hot sun. Everything came from her. When I was hungry or thirsty she would swing me round to where I could reach her full breasts; now when I shut my eyes I feel again with gratitude the sense of well-being that I had as I buried my head in their softness and drank the sweet milk that they gave.
>
> (Baker 1955: 18)

This is just one set of experiences; the patterns of infant feeding – that intimate area of tactile interaction – vary across time and space. Various too are the conventions about how babies and young children are carried, handled or touched, and by whom and where. There is probably always a high degree of tactile communication with and between young children, not least because of their only gradually developing skills in other communicative modalities and their initially limited mobility. Even then, however, it is likely to be limited to prescribed situations and to particular categories of people.

We may be especially aware of tactile communicating between adults and small children. This is important enough, for such processes are real, not just incipient, cases of tactile communicating; and part of the young child's development lies in its increasing control of active tactile interaction within its social and physical world and of the locally approved patterns for both touching and non-touching. But touch is a channel for communication throughout life. We already surely know from our own experience that it can communicate love, sympathy, comfort, pleasure, gratitude, reassurance or, equally, dislike, reproof, aloofness, anger, violence or rejection. We are acquainted too with the tactile language of pressure (literally) when someone is pushed or pulled to do something or go in some direction. People actively communicate by shaking hands (and shaking them in particular ways) or by kissing, embracing, leaning against each other, nudging, pinching, stroking, touching noses, squeezing, pushing, biting or wrestling. Hugging, slapping, thumping, guiding, shaking, holding or caressing – all these tactile communications convey through the skin subtle, effective but unverbalised messages of (for example) affection, support, aggression, disapproval, control, recognition, sympathy and a host of other things appropriate and intelligible within particular groups and particular situations.

Even small tactile actions can carry large meanings. Think of the light touch on the shoulder at a funeral to convey a discreet and intimate mark of sympathy or affection, or the handshake of (perhaps qualified) reconciliation and recognition between two estranged friends or competitors. A slap on the back or buffet on the shoulder can express congratulation, celebration or a friendly tease. And when we hear of the meeting of long-lost relatives, perhaps kept apart by years of ignorance or forced separation, the climax is so often 'and we fell into each other's arms' – the somatic contact conveying and affirming their mutual recognition.

Establishing tactile contact is an act of communication. It can convey intimacy, affiliation, protection, dominance, intrusion, dependence, or the giving and accepting of care. Friends touch to communicate empathy or agreement, comrades share their solidarity by an arm round the shoulders. Links of kinship or affection are expressed and reinforced in tactile processes like combing someone's hair, applying cream, tending minor hurts: 'social grooming' as Segerstråle and Molnár term it (1997: 70ff). Avoiding bodily contact where it might otherwise be expected communicates too; so does the manner of touching or being touched. And while the communicative potential of touch is not confined to erotic encounters, it is obviously of special significance in the subtle touches of courtship and love.

Touching can also acknowledge mutual participation in some experience. Even among those who would normally avoid extensive tactile contact, there are recognised situations of grief or disaster where embracing or other bodily contact is interpreted as a mark of comfort, fellow feeling or respect. A group of people joined by touch, perhaps through direct or serial hand clasps or by crowding into a small space, can experience and intend this as a symbolic mark of social, not just physical, solidarity. In public demonstrations people mutually communicate their shared commitment and corporate unity through joining hands or linking arms. Particular types of touch convey people's mutual involvement in celebration or congratulation, like the interlinked arms and hands during the singing of 'Auld lang syne' or football players' tactile rejoicing after scoring a goal.

The tactile experience of others' temperatures or movements can also enter in. Proxemic researchers have pointed to the mutual awareness of body warmth in close personal encounters within the 'intimate' proxemic zone (see p. 105). An element of tactile awareness also seems to be one dimension of coordinated group movement: religious congregations jointly rising, kneeling or prostrating, for example, a partisan crowd watching their team playing, a panic-stricken group turning together to flee, a couple walking in step, or a column of marchers. In this extended sense of touch, affected perhaps by the vibrations of movement through the air rather than direct skin-to-skin contact, the feeling of others moving in concert forms one part of their mutual interconnecting.

Touch often complements other communicative modes. It has a place in proxemic conventions. Strangers often take care to avoid physical contact by not approaching closely, thus conveying that they are not claiming familiarity; the touching or near-touching stance of close friends, by contrast, mutually declares and reinforces their shared relationship. During verbal exchanges tactile communication is often used in comparable ways to gestures or posture – emphasising, clarifying, qualifying, personalising, or on occasion contradicting the spoken words. But touch can also override other channels. It is effective where sight or hearing is difficult, or if someone wants to interrupt what is going on or communicate directly without informing others. A touch on the shoulder from behind in a crowd will probably make someone turn round at once if it follows accepted conventions (two quick taps with the finger tips for example). A grasp or push can be used as urgent warning, while a rapid nudge, kick or pull on the arm can tell a friend it is time to go. Because it can work independently of sight or hearing, touch is a good way to communicate unbeknownst to others. Lovers touch hand or foot invisibly under the table, prisoners converse secretly by touch. The famous Masonic handshake conveys secret messages to other members, unseen to those around them.

The effectiveness of tactile communicating can be illustrated from a study of communicative touching among students at a western American university (Jones and Yarbrough 1985). This identified a variety of distinct touches for communicating recognised and relatively unambiguous meanings (see Box 7.1). Particular tactile forms were used for expressing support, appreciation, inclusion, sexual interest or intent, affection, playfulness, compliance, attention getting, announcing a response, greetings and departures. 'Support touches' for instance were well understood by participants in a situation where someone was experiencing distress, used by the initiator of the touch to communicate concern for the sufferer: consoling and reassuring them and saying in tactile form something like 'It's OK' or 'Let me take care of you.' Or someone announced their current state of feeling not just verbally but by calling tactile attention to it and emphasising it by touch. Through these touches they were conveying messages like 'I'm really happy', 'I'm really glad we came', 'That's funny', 'I'm surprised', or 'I'm so excited about today', and at the same time inviting the other to reciprocate and share in the feeling (Jones and Yarbrough 1985: 42–3).

Box 7.1 Meanings of touch among American students at a western university

(based on Jones and Yarbrough 1985: esp. 29–35)

Nature of communication	Situation	Comment
Support: reassures, nurtures or promises protection	Situation calls for comfort or reassurance	Initiated by person giving support, through hand or arm, usually by holding but also spot-touches, pats, squeezes or caresses
Appreciation: expresses gratitude	Receiver has performed service for toucher	Mainly hand-to-body, holding, also brief touches. Initiator also verbalises appreciation
Inclusion: draws attention to being together, suggests closeness	Mainly between close friends or sexual intimates	Sustained touching, often at least several minutes
Sexual: expresses physical attraction, sexual interest	Mostly between sexual intimates	Holding and/or caressing

Affection: expresses generalised positive regard (beyond mere acknowledgement)	Close relationships	Holding, caressing, some spot-touches or pats
Playful affection: lightens interaction, qualifies seriousness of affection	Mainly close relationships	Mainly spot-touches and holding, but also wrestle, tickle, punch, pinch, bump, pat; often teasing and quasi-sexual
Playful aggression: lightens interaction, qualifies seriousness of aggression	Aggressive message with play signal, e.g. mock strangling, wrestling, punching, pinching, slapping, grabbing, standing on toes	Play signals conveyed by spot-touches and pats
Compliance: attempts to direct behaviour, attitudes or feelings of another	Initiated by person attempting influence	Usually spot-touch with hand accompanied by verbal request
Attention getting: directs the recipient's focus	In any kind of relationship, including strangers	Initiated by person requesting attention, mostly spot-touch by hand
Announcing a response: calls attention to and emphasises feeling by initiator, implicitly requests affect-response from another	Initiated by announcer, usually also with verbalisation	Mostly hand to body, a few hugs

Greeting: part of the act of acknowledging another at opening of an encounter	All kinds of relationship	Handshake (mainly between males) or hand to body (cross-sex or female–female), usually with verbalisation of standard greeting phrase
Greeting with affection: expresses affection and acknowledgement at opening of an encounter	Close relationship	Typically with hug plus greeting phrase
Departure: part of the act of closing an encounter	Mainly close or not-close friends, seldom between family members or intimates	Mainly pats and spot-touches, some holding and caresses, usually with verbalisation of standard departure phrase
Departure with affection: expresses affection and closes encounter	Close relationship	Typically with hug or kiss plus departure phrase

This was a study of just one social world, related to the conventions of that particular group and their circumstances. But it can alert us to something of the complex range of patterned touching through which people can communicate, even if they seldom describe it in words or notice it consciously. Tactile communication is not something unusual, nor the passive, biologically determined reaction that Schiller and similar writers implied, but a rich resource of which human beings make active use in their purposive social intercourse.

Regulating and organising tactile communication

It is perhaps not difficult to agree that touching is indeed one mode of human communication. But given the earlier views of touch as something more 'animalistic' than human, 'purely physical' rather than purposefully ordered, it is worth stressing again that it resembles other communicative modalities in being socially organised and that human tactile conventions are culturally variable. For example, interpersonal touching in public is probably more strictly controlled in many Asian societies than in contemporary western cultures (McDaniel and Andersen 1998), while tactile contact is often said to be greater in southern Europe and Latin America than in Northern Europe or America (thus sometimes labelled 'non-contact' cultures); Americans are in turn sometimes described as more 'touchy/feely' than the British. Different yet again are the West African Wolof for whom bodily contact is apparently central to interpersonal communication and the most comfortable register of interaction throughout life (Rabain 1979: 116, 79). These broad-brush comparisons provide a starting point but need to be treated with caution; tactile conventions are probably even more variegated in practice, and there are likely to be multiple usages even within a specific group according to people's differing backgrounds, beliefs, gender, age, status, contexts or mutual relationships. The main point remains however that, like vision, audition and olfaction, tactile communicating is socially shaped and mediated through culturally specific patterns.

Touch is a powerful vehicle in the interactions between human beings, with conspicuous potential for aggression, sex and physical coercion. In the 'bubble' of privacy that people maintain around themselves, touch perhaps represents the most direct invasion. It is scarcely surprising that its practice is regulated. In every group there are rules, if mostly unspoken ones, about who can touch whom, where and in what manner, and about the settings in which tactile contact may be legitimately employed. Thayer's analysis of social touching reinforces the point:

> Touch represents a confirmation of our boundaries and separateness while permitting a union or connection with others that transcends physical limits. For this reason, of all the communication channels, touch is the most carefully guarded and monitored, the most infrequently used, yet the most powerful and immediate.
>
> (Thayer 1982: 298)

Thus we follow agreed (or relatively agreed) conventions when we accord certain people the right to touch us in specific ways and interpret their and our actions accordingly. An embrace from a stranger or non-intimate conveys something very different from one by a close friend or relative, and – depending also on *how* it is done – could communicate claims you might prefer to reject. Some people are allowed to pick up and tickle your young baby, others definitely not. There are culture-specific expectations for the tactile relations between categories of people such as men and women, employer and employee, patient and doctor, or those of different statuses, ages or affiliations. As well illustrated in Routasalo and Isola's 'The right to touch and be touched' (1996), nurses have to take seriously the communicative meanings of their touches – the positive aspects of mutual touching between themselves and their patients but also their patients' personal space and the appropriateness or otherwise of touching in particular situations. When people accidentally or unavoidably touch strangers or non-intimates, especially in public places, they often apologise verbally to make clear that the intrusive claim seemingly implied through this tactile pressure was not in fact intended.

Because people more or less understand the main rules of the group(s) in which they are interacting, touch is effective for marking particular relationships. Just as only certain people are accepted into the familiarity of, say, using first names or standing within close proxemic range, so too in the tactile sphere. The extent and form of touching can indicate the nature and stage of a relationship, and people suggest, impose, accept or reject relationships through touch. A rigid armour-like tactile response to someone's unacceptable touch communicates unambiguously that the advances or assumptions conveyed in the other's touch are being refused or qualified. And I still recall the moment when as a young teenager I moved to kiss a cousin's cheek, in accordance with our elders' dragooning to kiss as children, and he avoided my touch. I realised even in my embarrassment that he was telling me he was now a young man, no longer another child.

Sometimes tactile conventions are stated quite explicitly. Seventeenth-century Dutch etiquette manuals laid down what distance different categories of people should keep from each other, who could touch whom, and how. When talking with a superior it was wrong to grab his sleeves and against the rules of etiquette to kiss a woman of higher rank without her permission; even if she offered her cheek, the kiss should be in the air without actually touching her face (Bremmer and Roodenburg 1991: 162). Ignatius Loyola's rules for the Jesuit order included the injunction that 'No one may touch another, even in jest' (quoted in Howes 1991: 69), while schoolteachers must nowadays learn strict rules governing any physical contact with their pupils to avoid any possible risk of being accused of 'improper' touching.

With its close bodily contact and erotic associations, kissing is a prominent focus for both enactment and regulation. In many western traditions its public expression has been an important symbolic stage in political or religious communication. There is the 'kiss of peace' in religious services, its use in ritual healing, and the acknowledgements conveyed by kissing the king's feet or a bishop's ring – 'respect signals' rather than greetings between equals (Firth 1973: 318). Early Christians were exhorted to salute each other with 'a holy kiss', but later the rule became that men should only kiss men and women women 'to prevent suggestion of scandal' (Parrinder 1987: 582). Frijhoff's intriguing account of 'The kiss sacred and profane' (1991) illustrates how kissing has varied from place to place and changed over time. He recounts the profusion of kisses in greetings in late fifteenth-century England – unlike in Holland – and the less inhibited use of bodily contact in Holland before the seventeenth-century takeover by courtly etiquette. The locations in which kissing takes place count too. In many Asian countries a mouth-to-mouth kiss in public, with its inevitable physical touching, is considered immoral or disgusting.

In *Behavior in Public Places,* Goffman notes that while it is 'permissible for persons at an ocean pier to kiss each other deeply, thereby withdrawing to an appreciable degree from other aspects of the situation, the same action by a suburban housewife meeting her husband at the 6:45 would be inappropriate' (1963: 167). He quotes a lively newspaper report on how a '"kiss of delight" in broad daylight in a busy Roman piazza can land you in jail':

> A court case to determine what public kissing is permissible, ended this week after nearly a year in a sentence of two months in separate reformatories for an engaged couple. The unfortunate lovers, Vittorio Grazini, 20, and his fiancee, Angelina Rossi, 22, had their fatal kiss last August at 6:30 in the afternoon. The cop who arrested them claimed they had a 'long kiss of delight' that was a menace to public morals. The judge agreed. Public kissing is against the law in Rome.
>
> (*San Francisco Chronicle* 31 July, 1961, quoted in Goffman 1963: 167)

The specific form and setting of kissing communicates much about the participants' relationship and their respective acceptance or rejection of each others' claims. Ignoring the usual rules can convey unintended messages. Raymond Firth cites a young woman's request to a newspaper for guidance because, when she greeted her American father-in-law expecting a cheek-kiss, she had been shocked by him insisting on kissing her lips (Firth 1973: 316), while an Englishman amusingly charts what happened when he married into a Greek family:

> Kissing both cheeks on greeting and parting is an ubiquitous part of Greek culture, but this is not the case in England. I have had to learn who to kiss, when to kiss, and, just as important, who and when *not* to kiss, a learning curve which has been accompanied by much dance-like gyration on my part as I look for clues in the demeanour of those for whom it is natural.
>
> (Cottrell 1999: 18)

Both these examples and the American students' uses of touch mentioned earlier (Box 7.1) illustrate how the ordered uses of touching can perform actions and confirm or develop relationships. Just as we 'do things with words' so, too, we act through our touches. Greetings and farewells are conspicuous examples. Touching can convey and acknowledge the non-aggressive nature of an encounter or the nature of the participants' relationship through a variety of forms such as touching or shaking hands, kissing, nose or cheek contact, touching someone's shoulder or foot, slapping the palms or back, arm clasps, embracing, or a playful punch or pull of the hair (at one period a common – and painful – adult greeting to children). The detailed practices vary and some groups prefer to avoid physical contact in many of their salutations, using instead the visual form of bowing or hand gestures. But in general touch is a widespread mode for marking the start and end of an encounter, one that can be subtly manipulated to suit particular settings, relationships or even individual intentions at specific moments.

The tactile greetings observed between people meeting at an American airport (Box 7.2) illustrate both the familiar ordinariness of such touches and their taken-for-granted status as the appropriate communicative action within particular contexts. Over four-fifths of the greetings involved bodily contact (Greenbaum and Rosenfeld 1980).

Box 7.2 Touch in airport greetings

Touch used in greetings observed at Kansas City International Airport (Greenbaum and Rosenfeld 1980; figures based on calculations in Argyle 1988: 221–2)

Nature of touching	Number
No touch	41
Kiss on mouth	41
Touch on head, arm or back	38
Kiss on cheek	30
Light hug	23
Solid hug	19
Arm round waist or back	15
Holding hands	12
Handshake	10
Extended embrace	10
Extended kiss	3

The presence, amount or form of physical contact during salutations publicly declares and reinforces the participants' relationship. Subordinates may greet superiors by touching their feet or knees or kissing a ring, a pontiff lightly touch the head of the faithful, an elder male pat a child on the head; in some cultures men can mutually touch in greeting but must avoid physical contact in greeting women. These tactile communications are not just trivial dimensions of social interaction but important enough to provoke serious disputes. Handshakes were an issue for serious political and religious discussion in the seventeenth century. Quakers objected to what they considered the secular deference expressed through bowing or hat-doffing and insisted on the democratic ethos conveyed by 'giving the hand' as a mark of friendship and affiliation (Bremmer and Roodenburg 1991: 176, Bauman 1983:

47). To use or not use the handshake openly communicated both political and religious commitments.

Touch is also used for ratifying contracts or relationships, both a direct performative sign in itself and with the potential for transcending linguistic and other barriers. The act of sealing a bargain is frequently communicated by a handshake. Among the Ethiopian Amhara it was conveyed by touching palms (Thayer 1989: 248), while in nineteenth-century rural Ireland the conclusion of prolonged verbal haggling was finally marked by the two parties slapping their hands together. Touching some symbolic object (like a Bible or the relics depicted in the Bayeux tapestry in Figure 4.5) can seal a promise or make an act of devotion. A touch can consecrate or confer grace, as in commissioning ordained Christian ministers to service through the laying on of hands. The Church of England bishop's touch during the ordination of priests 'gives power as well as office' (as Parrinder expresses it, 1987: 580), verbalised in the words 'Receive the Holy Ghost for the office and work of a priest in the Church of God, now committed unto thee by the imposition of our hands'. Touch often forms a significant part of rites of passage: performing the achievement of new status. Obeisance is marked by tactile acts like kissing a hand or touching a sword to convey the acceptance of a particular status and allegiance. The kiss and joining of hands at weddings, physical placing of a crown or ceremonial robe at inaugurations, kiss at a bishop's consecration, anointing of the sick or dying in Christian rituals, final kiss of farewell to the dead, shaking hands or other physical contact at graduation ceremonies, or the handling of sacred objects in religious inductions – all draw on tactile communicating at a crucial ritual juncture.

There are also the communicative uses of touch in situations of competition and conflict, playful as well as aggressive. Boys communicate through wrestling, horseplay and other physical touching: mutual testing and friendly display as much as hostile interaction. Likewise 'contact' sports with their agreed rules are a popular occasion for collaborative bodily expressiveness. In less structured situations people nudge others aside or 'elbow' their way through a crowd, recognised ways of controlling others or telling them to get out of the way, or can utilise either sustained physical pressure or a series of active pushes or strikes to communicate a threat, an act of hostility or the unapologetic exercise of power. Warfare, rape or outright physical coercion communicate through forcibly applied touch, exerting tangible bodily pressures to control others' bodies in ways usually only too well understood by the participants on both sides. Punishment can be conveyed not just through verbal admonishment but also in tactile form, just as holding someone's arms can be both a symbolic and a physical sign of restraint, and a forceful command or aggressive overture unmistakably conveyed by a shove or a blow. All are forms of tactile communication, again with their own rules.

Conventions about tactile interaction can go to the roots of social differentiation. The concept of the polluted and polluting 'untouchables' in the Hindu caste system is one notable example, but ideas and practices of touching are defining features of personhood or status in other settings too. Those of higher rank or power commonly initiate touching more freely than their subordinates (employer with employee, for example, king with subject, teacher with pupil), communicating among other things their dominance and superiority – a tactually conveyed message that may in turn be resented or rejected. That the *mode* of touching can also mark status is exemplified in the rule among West African Bambara men that the superior turned palm downwards in hand-greetings, the inferior palm upwards (Firth 1973: 321).

Political and symbolic messages are expressed and reinforced both by the actual forms of touch, and by its avoidance. Directly touching people with special status is often disapproved – flouting that expectation thus conveys insolence or defiance. There was a great outcry a few years ago when the prime minister lightly touched Queen Elizabeth II on her visit to Australia; some thought this merely a tactually expressed token of hospitable welcome, others a flagrant insult to royalty. The touching of hands between public figure and attendant crowd in royal or presidential 'walkabouts' carries special meaning, crossing the distance that separates them at other times. Kissing babies and 'pressing the flesh' to convey an image of direct contact and accessibility are communicative techniques well-known to contemporary politicians – and earlier ones too: Charles II was reputed to have employed his royal touch on almost a hundred thousand people in England to gain popular support in the seventeenth century (Parrinder 1987: 580–1). There are also the dangers or contagions sometimes believed to be conveyed through touching between human bodies – or, rather, between bodies of certain kinds and in certain circumstances; this in turn affects people's interpretations of both the practice and the avoidance of tactile contact. Washing the feet of those who in other situations might be regarded as inferior conveys a sense of service and fellowship, while Princess Diana's insistence on tactile contact with AIDS patients (then physically shunned by many) was famously interpreted as communicating a symbolic message to both sufferers and the wider public about their shared humanity.

Touch is often regarded as carrying particular power in the context of physical, spiritual and medical well-being. As well as the beliefs about the danger or pollution of certain tactile engagements, touching is also sometimes envisaged as a means of communicating comfort, healing or respite. Even in the self-consciously scientific west, TLC ('tender loving care') by nurses and other carers is often regarded as conveying comfort and improving a sufferer's condition. The famous mediaeval phrase 'the king's touch' referred to the French and English kings' powers to heal scrofula (the 'king's evil') by their divine touch on the patient's neck. In Islamic tradition the touch of kissing a holy man's foot, shoulder or, especially, hand communicates spiritual benefit (Parrinder 1987: 582), while the Christian gospels describe Jesus' power to heal by laying on his hands. One much-quoted passage depicts a woman being healed by touching the fringe of his garment in a crowd, and Jesus, realising that power had gone out from him, asking 'Who touched me?' (Luke 8: 45–6). Shamans, priests, mediums, gurus, divine kings and faith-healers are widely credited with the ability to transfer healing or spiritual power through their hands or other physical touch, and touch has been interpreted as effecting notable and otherwise unforseeable cures both in the contemporary world and in the miracle cures of biblical and saintly tradition. However controversial, it is hard to regard such instances or the beliefs about them as totally irrelevant to the subject of human tactile communication.

We can also return to the earlier point about the interconnectedness achieved through coordinated processes of bodies moving closely together. This means extending the spread of touch (and feeling) beyond the narrow meaning it is often assigned within the traditional fivefold categorisation of the senses. The experience of working, marching, playing, loving or competing together, 'in sync', is a real one in human interconnectedness, even without actual 'touch' in the literal sense. The most striking and easily comprehended examples are of the jointly felt movements of bodies working symmetrically and in parallel, as in a drilled line of marchers where the shared somatic experience surely rests on more than just sight or sound. But it can also be a matter of complementary but integrated actions between competitors, dancers, even talkers. Communication among farmers in the north of England, for example, has been interpreted as resting in part on carrying out their tasks 'through unspoken, physical coordination. Their bodies become paired in shared activities' (Christensen *et al.* 2001: 75). In the sphere of dance, analysts have sketched out for us a kind of somatic interconnectedness, rooted in the movements, subjective experience and control of the moving or still body (for example Farnell 1995a, b, Hanna 1979, Ness 1992). Perhaps we can expand Schutz's auditory-musical image of the 'mutual tuning-in relationship' at the heart of communication (1951: 92) by a 'dancing-together' image which brings out the tactual dimensions of coordinated interconnection experienced in the embodied processes of felt coordinated movement, 'a physical symbolism and practice' (Ness 1992: 232). Such an experience is to be found not just in heightened choreographic performance but also in other less stereotyped experiences of coordinated bodily rhythm, dynamic movement and (in some sense) jointly shared somatic actions. Many modalities are commonly in play here no doubt, but in some sense touch is often one of them – not touch in the strict physical sense, but a species of tactile and humanly enacted communicating nonetheless.

Systems of tactile communication and their extension over time and space

The most typical uses of tactile communication are in and through the immediate bodily presence of interacting participants; the examples so far are mainly of this kind. But humans have also made some limited attempts to exploit touch for more distant communicating and to construct formalised tactile systems.

Some of these use external devices to extend physical contact. While spiders spin their long silk strands and use their vibrations in communicating, so humans sometimes make use of other material skeins of interconnection. We tug cords to signal between underwater and surface, pull ropes to communicate between mountaineers out of mutual sight or earshot. We enlarge our tactile reach through sticks, swords or thrown weapons; over greater spans teleoperation utilises mechanical manipulation or electronic links for tactile contact at a distance. Though humans generally make little direct use of vibration for long-distance communication (unlike some other animals), we do use it over shorter spaces. Irritation can be communicated by one person shaking a table, sending the vibrations across to the other side, and, as Poyatos puts it, 'convulsive or spasmodic laughter [or] . . . someone's tense hand wringing [can be] sensed through a shared couch' (1983: 59, 60). The vibrations of morse telegraphy have covered longer distances, and in an extended but perhaps still recognisable sense, touch is perhaps also utilised in the impulses of electronic communication.

There are also the durable artefacts discussed in Chapter 5 which people can use to interconnect over both space or time. Their tactile features are commonly secondary to their visual effect, but sometimes one significant aspect nevertheless. The 'sand pictures' of the Native American Navajo may strike outsiders by their visual properties, but for the Navajo themselves their tactile dimension matters more (Howes 1991: 264–5). We are accustomed to take account not just of the *look* of clothes but also of their texture, weight, volume or richness to the touch, all properties which may communicate something about the wearer or the occasion; likewise with the delicate curves or smoothness of ceramics, or the solidity of a building. The *feel* of a piece of sculpture, a mat, a basket, an inscribed ring, an embossed seal or a richly bound book of thick expensive paper, interpreted in culture-specific ways, can all convey and reinforce shared memories or values.

The communicative role of touch for interconnecting across time can become more explicit when used by those without sight. In *The Story of my Life* the blind and deaf Helen Keller speaks of her experience of museums and art exhibitions:

> As my fingertips trace line and curve, they discover the thought and emotion which the artist has portrayed. I can feel in the faces of gods and heroes, hate, courage and love, just as I can detect them in living faces I am permitted to touch. . . . I sometimes wonder if the hand is not more sensitive to the beauties of sculpture than the eye. I should think the wonderful rhythmical flow of lines and curves could be more subtly felt than seen. . . . I know that I can feel the heart-throbs of the ancient Greeks in the marble gods and goddesses.
>
> (Keller 1923: 126–7)

Human memory is extended and embodied through our tactile as well as our visual or auditory experience. Something of a commemorative function can be performed even through the handling of familiar objects, from the feel of a heavy silver spoon inherited through the family or tangible manipulation of long-accustomed tools, to the smoothness and grip of a treasured fountain pen with its associated memories. It is even more explicit in the ritual handling of regalia or relics transmitted through the ages, the ceremonial carrying of a church Bible and careful turning of its pages, or kissing the scroll of the Torah before reading it. Icons and images are often kissed, not least the toe of St Peter in Rome now worn away after centuries of touching by devout lips. Symbolic tactile contact between humans through external artefacts is yet another way in which human beings extend their experience beyond the here and now into the longer ranges of the past. Social memory, as both Connerton (1989) and Forty and Küchler (1999) have well reminded us, is some-thing of the body not just the mind. One dimension of this lies in the human touching of long-lasting external objects.

What about more formalised systems? It seems that humans have done relatively little to develop standardised tactile systems with anything like the kind of currency over space or time so notable in the visual and auditory modes. However, some cases are worthy of note both for their ingenuity and for the effective way touch is used to transcend linguistic divisions.

Some information-processing systems have touch as their basis. We probably all have some experience of this. When we finger-count, we often rely less on sight to keep a tally than on the *feel* of the moving fingers; similarly many people build up tactile memories of how to key in familiar telephone numbers and passwords. A number of tactile calculating and scientific systems have been developed over the centuries. The famous Inca recording system (*quipu*) probably depended in part on the tactile qualities of the texture, spin and ply of the knotted cords of which it was made up. The manipulative skills of expert abacus operators – another tactile system – are sometimes claimed to match the speed of many electronic calculators. We are also nowadays familiar with the concept of 'touch' typing and the manual operating of computer keyboard, mouse and remote-control handsets – tactile as well as (or instead of) visual experiences.

One of the most striking examples is the system of 'palpable arithmetic' invented in the early eighteenth century by Nicholas Saunderson, the blind Lucasian Professor of Mathematics at Cambridge (Figure 7.3). This was 'a kind of Abacus or Calculating Table' which depended on the manipulation of moveable pegs set in a tabular board (Saunderson 1740: xx). The details need not detain us, but it is interesting to quote the assessment by his immediate successor, 'A':

> As the knowledge and use of Symbols, (or of sensible and arbitrary Signs of intellectual Ideas,) is of the greatest Importance and Extent in all Parts of the Mathematics; so he had invented a new Species of Mathematical Symbols, unknown and unheard of before, which were particularly accommodated to his own Circumstances. The sensible Symbols, commonly received and made use

of, to represent Mathematical Ideas, and to convey them to our own or to the Minds of others, are derived from two of our principal Senses, and are either audible or visible. The audible Symbols, it is true, he made good use of . . . But he was entirely deprived of the use of visible Symbols, which to us we find are so absolutely necessary. . . . What did he do under this (as it should seem) insuperable Difficulty, in order to satisfy his great Thirst after this kind of Knowledge? why, he had recourse to another of his Senses, which he had in great Perfection, and substituted Feeling in the place of Seeing; by inventing a Sort of Mathematical Symbols, which we may call palpable or tangible Symbols.

(Saunderson 1740: xxv–xxvi)

His system was not, apparently, taken up by others, but is nonetheless a striking example of human creativity in the sphere of tactile communication.

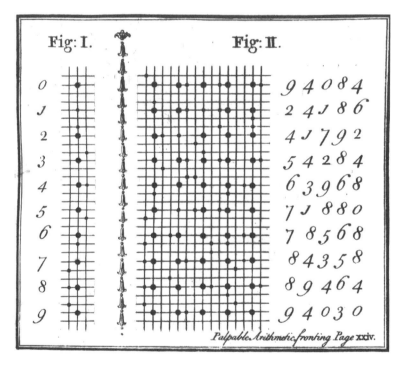

Figure 7.3 Dr Saunderson's 'Palpable Arithmetic' 1740
A 'Calculating Table' used by the blind Professor of Mathematics, University of Cambridge. He moved a series of large and small pins about the board, connecting them with threads for geometrical figures, and feeling them by 'drawing his Fingers gently over the Table'. As his successor, 'A', wrote, he employed this new system of 'palpable or tangible Symbols' to deal with 'the most abstruse and sublime Mathematical Ideas . . . and to deduce from them the most general and useful Conclusions' (Saunderson 1740: xxiii, xxvi) (Nicholas Saunderson, *The Elements of Algebra*, vol. 1, 1740 (facing p. xxiv), reproduced by permission of the Bodleian Library, University of Oxford, shelfmark GG53 Jur).

The finger-touching system once current throughout the seaports and markets of the Red Sea, Arabia and East Africa gives us another example – less far-reaching in one sense than Saunderson's 'palpable arithmetic' but at the same time of great practical use and much wider currency. The merchants conducted their commercial transactions through hand-touching in the open market-place, but kept their commercial secrets hidden from bystanders by concealing their fingers underneath a cloth or garment. They needed first to ensure they were working in the same coinage and order of magnitude, but after that the bargaining was by touch.

> If the buyer's hand touches the seller's extended index finger, this means either 1, 10, or 100. . . . Correspondingly, if the buyer touches the seller's 2 (or 3 or 4) first fingers, this means 2, 20, or 200 (3, 30, or 300; 4, 40, or 400); touching the whole hand then means 5, 50, or 500. The little finger alone means 6 (60 or 600), the ring finger alone 7, the middle finger alone 8, the bent index finger 9 and the thumb 10 (or 100 or 1000). If the buyer strokes the index finger from the middle joint knuckle toward the tip, he is saying $-\frac{1}{2}$ or 'one half off'; if he strokes the index finger toward the knuckle, this means $+\frac{1}{2}$. The fractions $(-)+\frac{1}{4}$ and $(-)+\frac{1}{8}$ are similarly indicated.
>
> (Menninger 1969: 213)

This tactile system overrides language differences and is used fluently and rapidly to reach confidential agreements on price whatever the market conditions (Menninger 1969: 214).

Further tactile systems have been developed for communicating with or between people without access to sight and hearing. Helen Keller describes how she and her family communicated through their own tactile signs after she lost sight and hearing as a young child. But, as she recounts it in a famous passage, the great breakthrough was when her teacher managed to introduce her to the more widely current manual alphabet:

> We walked down the path to the well-house, attracted by the fragrance of the honeysuckle with which it was covered. Someone was drawing water and my teacher placed my hand under the spout. As the cool stream gushed over one hand she spelled into the other the word *water*. Suddenly I felt a misty consciousness of something forgotten, a thrill of returning thought; and somehow the mystery of language was revealed to me.
>
> (Keller 1923: 23)

There are a number of such tactile communication systems. Some of the sign languages for communicating with the deaf, such as BSL, have been adapted for tactile communicating, sensed by holding the signer's arms. Makaton is another such system now developing tactile as well as visual symbols (Mountain 1987). In the distinctive deaf-blind manual alphabet, finger-spelling is conveyed through the touch of the letters being drawn out on the hand (it was a version of this that Helen Keller's teacher used). In the differently based tadoma method, speech is *felt* by putting hands on a talker's face and neck to sense the articulatory movements and vibrations. Though mostly used face-to-face, this is now also being developed in synthetic computer form.

New tactile forms are developing rapidly it seems. Tactile signs are now sometimes positioned in public places, such as raised maps and diagrams showing roads or routes, tactile symbols for landmarks, and corduroy profile surfaces warning of hazards like stairheads. Tactile maps and diagrams are being developed in educational contexts. Collages of textured materials, to be felt directly, can be reproduced in multiple copies by thermoform technology, together with 'swell paper diagrams' produced by heatcopiers and 'touch-detectable scratch' on special polymer sheets to enable rapid interaction (Hinton 1996: 7ff). New developments in computer technology are creating yet other opportunities for tactile communication and haptic scanning. One aim is to record the tactile features of something, such as its texture or spatial structure, and convey these through fingerpads (see Kaczmarek and Bach-y-Rita 1995). Some systems are apparently nearing commercial development and distribution: indeed in mid-1999 *The Times* announced a forthcoming 'motorised computer mouse that the inventors claim allows Internet surfers to feel the texture of anything from tennis rackets to corduroy trousers' (Nuttall 1999) and discussions of 'virtual reality' speak of increasing scope for tactile experience. These may well in due course lead to yet further opportunities for tactile communication.[5]

This brings us on to the more established and standardised systems specifically designed for tactile communicating over distance. These are mostly based on the systematic transfer of written forms into a tactile medium, usually presented with the same fixed and linear properties of most visible writing. Unlike several of the systems described above which (like visible gestures and sign languages) are enacted in real time, these forms are relatively permanent: like visible writing they consist of material artefacts lasting over time and portable over space.

The feel of graphic signs incised on stone or clay are partial examples, but most systems are explicitly designed for those who are visually impaired (sometimes deaf as well), structured so as to parallel and replace vision. For several centuries there have been attempts to devise systems of raised letters on paper to enable reading by touch – effective in one way but hindered by the books' bulkiness and expense. The moon system, for example (so-named after its nineteenth-century inventor), uses embossed symbols, mostly simplified forms of capital letters in the Roman alphabet. Though never fast to decipher, it is fairly easy to learn, and a 'moon-writer' device enables people to write as well as read. It still enjoys a limited currency among English speakers, but does not circulate internationally and few resources are available in it. The more recent optacon system (optical-to-tactile converter) adopts the different strategy of providing a tangible image by converting written text into vibrotactile pulses. The reader scans each line of print with a hand-held electronic-sensing camera which translates the printed letters into vibrotactile letter outlines detectable through a fingerpad. Optacon has achieved a relatively wide circulation, sometimes in combination with computing devices.

The best-known tactile system is of course that devised by Louis Braille, the nineteenth-century French teacher of the blind. This is based not on typographic forms but on a series of dots whose patterns represent alphanumeric characters. It is internationally, though not universally, used by visually impaired people and has been adapted to most languages, including Chinese. It can reproduce printed text not just from books but also from newspapers, notices, administrative papers, knitting patterns, or street and door signs (since it depends on the ability to read and to spell, it assumes literacy and linguistic competence). Musical notation too can be represented in braille, and there are now braille calculators and word processors. The expense of producing and distributing braille material has been partially overcome by computer software for transforming visual text into braille and by experiments with braille over the telephone.

Braille is not easy to learn, is not a rapid form of communication, and demands great tactile delicacy. Despite those limitations it is a far-reaching system for tactile communication, internationally recognised and used with amazing tactile skill by many thousands of people. It is impressive indeed in having become accepted as an established system of codified touch, comparable in its standardisation to the visually codified systems of visible writing.

Conclusion

The use of touch in communicating is often assumed to be primarily relevant for the blind and deaf. It is true that there is much to learn from their experience about the subtleties and complexity of touch. To quote Helen Keller again:

> Touch brings the blind many sweet certainties which our more fortunate fellows miss, because their sense of touch is uncultivated. When they look at things, they put their hands in their pockets. No doubt that is one reason why their knowledge is often so vague, inaccurate, and useless. . . . There is nothing, however, misty or uncertain about what we can touch. I know the faces of friends, the illimitable variety of straight and curved lines, all surfaces, the exuberance of the soil, the delicate shapes of flowers, the noble forms of trees and the range of mighty winds. Besides objects, surfaces, and atmospheric changes, I perceive countless vibrations.
>
> (Keller 1933: 30–1)

This is illuminating indeed. But it would be over-simplified to conclude that touch is really only a compensatory mode, making up for the deficiencies experienced by the sensorily deprived and replacing their access to the higher-ranked channels of sight and hearing. It has been turned to good use in that context, certainly. But as should have emerged in this chapter, communicative touch is emphatically not confined to any single section of humankind. It is everywhere a valuable resource for human communicating, building especially (though certainly not exclusively) on the remarkable deployment of the human hands. Touch may not be much spoken about, but it is extensively and richly used in actual practice, part of the reality of our human lives.

The most obvious characteristic of touch is its capacity for close and immediate contact – both advantage and disadvantage, for its rapidity is matched by its short life, and its close somatic immediacy by its focus on nearby interaction. Humans have pushed a little at its constraints so as to make touch usable – up to a point – both at a distance and, through relatively lasting tactile artefacts, over time. They have also gone a bit further than with olfaction, and probably (if we leave seismic systems aside) than other animals, in developing standardised tactile systems. It is striking, however, that their tactile systems have been so much less elaborated than those based on vision or audition, and that the visual rather than tactile qualities of material artefacts so often seem to the fore. The extrinsic applications of touch still take very much second place to its intrinsic uses, those located within and between interacting human bodies. But in the context of close interpersonal contact touch is a subtle and familiar resource, much used in human communicating. Here, and to a high degree, communication is indeed embodied and our tactile interactions convey a tangible message of interconnectedness, of not being alone.

Part III

The multiple creativity in human communicating

8 Communicating through the ether: a story of dreaming, death and the imaginary

I have entitled this chapter 'a story' – for that is what it is. Not hard science but stories people have drawn from ther dreams, from ther return from heaven, from shared conscousness. Counter-intuitive as it may seem we return in these stories once more to the earthly senses, the human resources so beautfully depicted in Bosch's *The Garden of Earthly Delights* (see Figure 10.5).

Death, near-death and death-and-return narratives

We can begin at an area in which, perhaps unexpectedly, there is a modicum of clear evidence. From the thousands of accounts of near-death (or, as I would rather call it, death-and-return) narratives[1] let me select just one. It is by a hard-headed scientist and neurosurgeon from Harvard Medical School, Eben Alexander, known as a sceptic of people's mistaken (he had assumed) near-death experiences. He had believed that there was good scientific evidence for the journeys described by those who narrowly escaped death – merely residual electrical impulses in the brain.

Here is what he wrote (expanded in his best-selling book, *Proof of Heaven* (2012b)):

> In the fall of 2008, after seven days in a coma during which the human part of my brain, the neocortex, was inactivated, I experienced something so profound that it gave me a scientific reason to believe in consciousness after death.
>
> On the morning of my seventh day in the hospital, as my doctors weighed whether to discontinue treatment, my eyes popped open.
>
> I'm not the first person to have discovered evidence that consciousness exists beyond the body. But as far as I know, no one before me has ever traveled to this dimension (a) while their cortex was completely shut down, and (b) while their body was under minute medical observation, as mine was for the full seven days of my coma.
>
> Toward the beginning of my adventure, I was in a place of clouds. Big, puffy, pink-white ones that showed up sharply against the deep blue-black sky. Higher than the clouds – immeasurably higher – flocks of transparent,

shimmering beings arced across the sky, leaving long, streamerlike lines behind them. A sound, huge and booming like a glorious chant, came down from above. Thinking about it later, it occurred to me that the joy of these creatures, as they soared along, was such that they had to make this noise – that if the joy didn't come out of them this way then they would simply not otherwise be able to contain it. The sound was palpable and almost material, like a rain that you can feel on your skin but doesn't get you wet.

Seeing and hearing were not separate in this place where I now was. I could hear the visual beauty of the silvery bodies of those scintillating beings above, and I could see the surging, joyful perfection of what they sang. It seemed that you could not look at or listen to anything in this world without becoming a part of it – without joining with it in some mysterious way.

It gets stranger still. For most of my journey, someone else was with me. A woman. Without using any words, she spoke to me. The message had three parts, and if I had to translate them into earthly language, I'd say they ran something like this:

'You are loved and cherished, dearly, forever.'

'You have nothing to fear.'

'There is nothing you can do wrong.'

The message flooded me with a vast and crazy sensation of relief. It was like being handed the rules to a game I'd been playing all my life without ever fully understanding it: 'We will show you many things here', the woman said 'But eventually, you will go back.'

The universe as I experienced it in my coma is . . . the same one that both Einstein and Jesus were speaking of in their (very) different ways.

(abridged from Alexander 2012b)

As he recalled later:

Every time I silently put questions, the answer came instantly in an explosion of light, color, love, and beauty that blew through me like a crashing wave. What was important about these blasts was that they didn't simply silence my questions by overwhelming them. They answered them, but in a way that bypassed language. Thoughts entered me directly. But it wasn't thought like we experience on earth. It wasn't vague, immaterial, or abstract. These thoughts were solid and immediate – hotter than fire and wetter than water – and as I received them I was able to instantly and effortlessly understand concepts that would have taken me years to fully grasp in my earthly life.

It was like the description, he said, by the seventeenth-century poet Henry Vaughan: 'There is, some say, in God a deep but dazzling darkness.'

As he concludes, in words that could sum up much of this chapter:

The plain fact is that the materialist picture of the body and brain as the producers, rather than the vehicles, of human consciousness is doomed. In its place a new view of mind and body will emerge, and in fact is emerging already. This view is scientific and spiritual in equal measure and will value what the greatest scientists of history themselves always valued above all: truth.

(Alexander 2012a)

Other cases, although each is unique, are not so different. Of the many thousands of individual cases on which data has been carefully collected the patterns of unconditional love, of being cherished, and of be unable to do any wrong have been recurrent.[2] They are found, too, in the return narratives that have been so common in our literature and myths – well illustrated in Joseph Campbell's *The Hero with a Thousand Faces* (1968), deep, it seems, in the psyche of our culture and, apparently, albeit with different details, in those of others.

'Near-death experience' is much discussed in the medico-scientific literature in which psychobiological explanations claim they are a by-product of brain functions gone awry. Apparent activity in the brain is attributed to leftover electrical traces in the temporal lobes for instance or other parts of the body – a proof of neurological explanation, sufficient evidence for the scientist. Or, alternatively, in these 'neutral' analyses are assumptions that the experiences are based in such phenomena as retinal ischaemia as a cause of tunnel vision, temporal epileptic discharges, neurotransmitter imbalances, analogies with hallucinogen effects, REM sleep intrusions and/or multisensory breakdown or – the most plausible of the materialist accounts – psychological assumptions of afterlife survival (Facco and Agrillo 2012). More promisingly, it is put down to a partial dissociation between body and mind (Van Lommel 2010, 2011), which would involve a Kuhnian revolution indeed. But, in general, interpretations incompatible with the ruling physicalist and reductionist stance are ruled out of the arena. Indeed, even mentioning it is impossible in certain circles. One researcher's assessment: 'I couldn't talk about it, or I would have been committed to an institution' (Schwartz 2012).

But narratives – not fictional – of death-and-return are manifold. Evidence is now extensive and compelling in both factual and epistemological terms through, for instance, the recent surge of interest by philosophers, physicists, information technologists, social scientists and neuroscientists in consciousness studies, robotics and cognitive issues. The experience, it seems, is much more widespread than would appear from the conventional wisdom for it is 'not done to talk about it', well exemplified in Schwartz's neat episode (2012):

At an academic conference on NDEs a few years ago, a respected cardiologist stood up and said, 'I've worked as a cardiologist for 25 years now, and I've never come across such absurd stories in my practice. I think this is complete nonsense; I don't believe a word of it.'

Whereupon, another man stood up and said, 'I'm one of your patients. A couple of years ago I survived a cardiac arrest and had an NDE, and you would be the last person I'd ever tell.'

It seems that there are thousands, indeed millions, of people worldwide with individual stories to tell on their return, communicating what they had seen, heard and felt while in that place.

It goes further, as we will see when we turn to the apparently – but only apparently – very different subject of dreaming in the next section.

Dreams, dreaming and others' voices

Let us move on, then, to the related subject of dreams. Few will fail to recall Kubla Khan and 'the man from Porlock' (may he be forever cursed!) who interrupted it: 'in Xanadu did Kubla Kahn . . .'; and some will remember Joan of Arc's power dreams and those of the Homeric heroes. And Milton too, blind, dreamed his Paradise Lost, Alexander the Great, Lincoln's and Churchill's dreams fuelled their war and peace policies, Montezuma was led by dreams and divination and writers from mediaeval saints and scholars to Mark Twain have famously been inspired by dreams. Einstein, too, for all we know and Newton were led by dreams as much as hard everyday science.

Few, however, seem to know the story of Tartini and the devil's trills.

Tartini was a baroque composer and virtuoso violinist. He wanted to compose the most beautiful and difficult violin piece in the world So, as one does, he made a pact wth the devil. Here is that very devil, so very brilliant and wicked, playing all night to Tartini (Figure 8.1).

Figure 8.1 The very wicked, very brilliant devil plays violin trills to Tartini's dream

When he awoke Tartini had forgotten much, not this time because of an interruption, but because of the nature of human memory. He did indeed compose two fine baroque-style movements, nice enough but nothing extraordinary, but then poured everything he could recall into the final movement, full of (impossible) double stopping and trills – a combination near-unplayable even for the most virtuosic performers of today. But Tartini could play it – for the devil had given him six fingers on his left hand.

What has this to do with communicating? Readers will have their own opinions. But for me, it is hard not to see these results as anything but communications from – well, use what metaphor you please – God, heaven, the divine, the unconscious either deep within ourselves or coming from somewhere outside us. Certainly not from our everyday routines or our daily earthly preoccupations. And the medium for these communications? Dreams.

Anthropologists, psychologists, writers of literature and historians (among, no doubt, many others) have much to say about dreaming and its communicative power.[3] Here is no evidence of the kind the scientific soul desires. The secure base of fieldwork informs many comparative and historical accounts, but often enough the foundations lie in literary sources and personal anecdotes (and the 'anecdotal' and 'mere' literary we have been taught to distrust for all that it forms the basis of medical 'cases'). So as some corrective let us remember the recent interests in the allied topics of quoting, allusion and meta-communication (the voices of others from outside oneself whether in dream or, perhaps, telepathy?)[4] and, allied to this, in originality, the imaginary, the dialogic qualities of language and speech[5] and, finally, in memory.[6]

As in several earlier chapters, let me start off with a case study, that long-tested strategy of the single insightful case and by now an established strategy for increasing understanding.[7] It concerns the communicative experience of dreaming by a woman not from far-off exotic 'other' realms but in the here and now of modern industrial life.

Her recovery from a seemingly unusual neurological illness – so dubbed by others at any rate, although in herself she scarcely felt ill – was complicated but beautified by the delight and imagination of night-time dreaming. It was not dreams as ordinarily understood but Dreams, powerful awakening visions that arrived with irresistible communicative force in that liminal borderland between sleeping and waking – arriving without her deliberate wish or action from somewhere seemingly beyond herself. Then as she lay half awake and later, more deliberately, during the day, they turned themselves – for they were not 'hers' – into stories.

These dream-stories came so fully formed that she became doubtful if they were really hers or plagiarised from another's hand or tradition. Anthropologists after all commonly insist that even dreams and undeliberate imaginings are shaped by the culture of present and past literary creation and its words – and, as I know well, its familiar sights and sounds. But we conclude that ultimately they do not come directly from any of those – unless perhaps from some unknown hand, some alter ego, of some other century or galaxy past or yet to come.

Then there was music (I come back to this later) and poems. The latter arrived instantaneously, fully formed and complete like the stories but, unlike the story tableaux, dynamic and linguistic, complete with rhyme, sonority and, often, a twist in the tail. Often the starting point was just a word in the by-now-familiar half-state between waking and sleeping and communicated as an order that *this* was what the poem was to be about. The ones on love or death or the earth were in their way easy. But what was she to make of an underground blind mole?, a fish?, an old grey wolf carrying a submissive cub in his mouth to his hidden cave in the west?, or, hardest of all, a *beetle!*:

> 'A beetle?'
> 'A *beetle* lord?
> a beetle POEM? you must be joking
> I don't LIKE beetles
> Not hate, but worse
> *dislike!*'

And so on . . . But – not so stupid after all. After the six legs of life's course, the unexpected wings unfurl – 'to fly me to heaven'.

Although, as always, each case is unique, the by-now-extensive investigations have uncovered, among other instances, experiences reported by a minister in a hospice for the dying. Some patients were sent terrifying guilt-drenched dream messages. But after they had in some way resolved the issues they received instead fortifying messages foretelling the tunnel (often though not always) through which they would pass on the way to heaven. Often as they neared death they dreamed of preparing to set out on a journey – putting on or taking off shoes or hat, the approach of a train, a ship – sure signs that the journey through death was approaching (Bulkeley *et al.* 2009).

Or again, as in the responses of the 200 or so Mass Observation writers (2012): for the majority of people dreams come each night, reportable with their detailed locations and relationships, sometimes but not always recurring and working out some persistent relationship issue (always with an older person, it seemed, now with children, although occasionally a close younger sibling) and (unexpected perhaps) in full colour – and, more importantly, *remembered*. Often, as we might expect from our own experience, they revolved round journeys, examinations, being lost and other testing situations. Often enough too, it seemed, the dreamers tried to interpret the dreams and, when assured of anonymity, to recall and speak of them in some detail, although rarely in Freudian terms. It was only very seldom indeed – and the Mass Observation writers, as ever, seemed to be speaking candidly – that they reported erotic dreams.

Who dreams these dreams? It seems that more often it is women than men – or perhaps it is just that women remember or speak of them more readily – among children too young to have given in to the culture-demanded vehicle of speech and in literary, philosophical or prayerful situations. Men may indeed dream less often – but they *do* have dreams. In some cultures, dream communicating is more recognised than in others: less in the contemporary west (less overtly, that is) and more in classical and mediaeval times, or in eastern religious settings. In 'traditional religions', notably in Native American cultures, drug-induced trance, dream and ritual take a prominent place, as they did, too, together with oracular interpretation and mantic divination, among the Chinese, Greeks and Romans (Devereux 1969; Harris 2000; Moss 1998, 2010; Rahim 1987). Dreams are welcome, sometimes deliberately induced in rituals around trance, shamanism, or communicating through a voice other than one's own (Bulkeley *et al.* 2009; Burke 1997a; Moss 1998, 2010; Vitebsky 1995) – and also at times strikingly powerful in relatively recent situations as in Winston Churchill's political and military guidance in dreams or Lincoln's policy-related dreams.

It emerges that it is especially in situations of danger, war or uncertainty or of some deep emotion and sense of stress or impending death, that the dream channel comes into its own and communication from outside the immediate situation so welcome.

It is not just for Kubla Kahn or similar instances that dreaming makes up a crucial stage in literary composition. In Fiji, for example, as in other Pacific islands and, indeed, in many cultures of the world, the highly revered expert poets (*daunivucu*) received their inspired dance-poems through induced trance. Sitting under a fragrant tree, they slept and the voice, sometimes also the choreography, was delivered to them, in the past through the spirit world, in the present from heaven or their own inspired genius. Sometimes it was as they lay in the magic liminal edge between reef and ocean. They spoke the words aloud for their followers to hear and remember or, more recently, to tape record word for word. For when they awoke they no longer recalled what they had heard (further elaborated in Finnegan 2011b). Are we nowadays in danger of forgetting the truths of this oneiric (dream), the elusive wisdom of the past and present?

Telepathy and communicating through the ether: is it possible?

And then we arrive at – *telepathy*.[8] Most people do not believe this is possible. Neither did I, neither, I am sure, do you. I am, after all, a scientist and all the hard evidence and the overt (but only the overt) conventional wisdom all seems to point the other way.

And yet . . . read on a little with an open mind.

Telepathy is more about *receiving* than *sending* messages (despite the earlier example – that is why it seemed so extraordinary by comparison with the usual experience of communicating).

Twins, we accept, communicate in ways we do not understand: not deliberately – or it seems not – but emotionally, spiritually, intensely.[9] They do it, somehow, 'through the ether'. Is it that twins are together in the womb (what could be closer, more intertwined, more single?), in death and even perhaps in life, chained, as it were, as one being? All Kates and Catherines, remarkably, including the dream narrator described above, seem somehow twins in this way: late-born children after false starts, the traces left from earlier unknown miscarriages in the womb, as a good (non-anthropologist but experienced) friend once suggested. I recall the African twins who appear in stories as beings with 'double eyes': insight into and power over the spirit world, those ever chained beings represented in the tiny but powerful Yoruba *ibeji* twin figurines. And do we not nowadays – even psychotherapists and counsellors seem to admit the possibility, no, the *reality* of this – accept some continuing deep connection between living and dead: different, but continuing? Have we not all known of at least one such enduring, mutually loving, relationship; between mother and dead child, born or unborn; husband and wife; passionate lovers? Or a close colleague, friend or grandparent visiting another to say a last farewell before death? Why do we exclude it between the living?

Small babies too, it seems, can communicate pre-speech with those they know and love. I have myself observed a small 4-year-old sister interpreting her 18-month younger sister's wishes to her mother. Not later, however: 'She can speak for herself now.' Is this somehow the explanation for the well-recorded telepathic communication between humans and 'dumb' animals? (Sheldrake 2002).

Let me again cite a case study, drawn, anonymously, from a male in a British town (Anon 2012–13), someone who thought little about telepathy and, if asked, would have denied its possibility.

His experience started off as general feelings of reassurance while on holiday abroad – far away in other words – mostly felt, somehow, in his lungs ('the love organs' according to one Victorian writer whose name, unfortunately, I cannot recall), then soon as references to pieces of music or particular recordings, often (perhaps) jointly (?) heard on the radio programme Classic FM.

One of the things that convinced him it was not just wishful thinking was that at night when, his wife asleep beside him, he was lonely and tried to encourage communication – nothing came. Why? The living message sender was asleep, too: as simple as that. So too with the interchanges that might have been a conversation. When, though rather seldom at first, she seemed somehow to be speaking to him – without words, perhaps in prayer? – he could not 'get a word in edgewise' until she had finished and, as it were, gone 'offline'. (It would seem that I am including the trivial here, but it is for the same reason as earlier: it illustrates that this telepathic stuff is not some profound emotive longed-for contact – or not *just* that at any rate – neither is it from some deep sexual id but it is sometimes quite funny; and, to tell the truth, sometimes just a downright nuisance.)

The next, and hugely startling, episode was when he was wakened (yes, positively shaken out of a deep sleep) by a sensation too strong to sleep through: utmost distress, guilt, bitterest desolation. He knew they were not his own emotions. At first he could do nothing but utter silent endearments and trite phrases such as 'I am here', 'I am still here.' He knew who it was, calling from her house in the north of England. He could do nothing but send out as strongly as he could messages of comfort, that he was there, would never leave her, would always be there to protect her. At first she was apparently too distressed to hear. But after a few moments, a century, a lifetime (so it seemed) but perhaps 15 minutes, she at last seemed to calm down a little, starting to listen as he went on with his silent babble. At last they both tranquilly drifted off to sleep again and in the morning, although they remembered it (he did anyway), they were, remarkably, little disturbed by the recollection. He remembered that many years before she had lost her husband to a long illness – telepathy could cross time as well as space then?

The second episode was equally precise. He remembered the exact date, partly because it was his (dead) mother's birthday, but mostly because it grew into a poem – a poem that, as with the earlier stories, was just somehow 'found'. It helps to explain what follows:

> He lifted the shell
> that opening shell
> th'pink-beautiful shell
> pearl ring'd in his tears
> So lovely, so fragile, so strong
> So washed in the sea's wild waves
> Braving the tide and the sand.[10]

Suddenly, in the deep night, a word (not, at first, an image), the word 'shell' came into his mind. It built into a picture of a beautiful shell by the sea, gathering itself somehow from the edges of his mind's orb, building the shell ring by ring. It was there, built, in his mind. Unlike his other experiences he knew it was not sent *to* him from another; it came both from outside and from his own inner self. And then came all that followed in the poem.

And here was what was new – but repeated several times since. He deliberately but without forethought reached out and somehow 'threw' the shell through the ether (not the earth or even, precisely, the sky), through the *air* – threw it to his soul-twin. He felt it seep into her mind. 'Seep' has to be the word. It took shape slowly, he could feel it. He felt it build gradually in her, taken from the edges of his mind into the beautiful shell they could both see, a shared receptacle for love.

Built gradually from his mind's edges: at first he thought this must be the typical fashion for telepathy – shared communication – to grow. But a few days later it was 'bubbling water', a spring bubbling up from the rock: In his (linguistic) mind, he associated this (verbally that is, rather than, at first, as image) with deep wells, springs, the source of great rivers, water bubbling up from the farthermost rocky depths of the sea, the waters of life. Again, this time with more confidence, he *threw*. Again, he felt it seep into her mind. But this time not, as he expected, from the edges of his mind but bubbling up from below. Why? Then he understood. The creatures that build shells make them from the sands and grit of the sea, so, of course, the shell rings build gradually, out from their edges. But water bubbles up from below.

Once it was a tricky personal question for him to consider before returning the answer she wanted, but mostly the images were of natural objects. Once it was a wolf (that was in a triumphant dream). Once when he had been frightened in the night, the morning brought the most tender, softest, curled feather you can imagine and once, just at a point when he needed reassurance about fidelity, the word 'raven' alighted in his mind. A raven? – symbol of intelligence and faithfulness, is it not, and again source for a poem:

> Ravens mate for ever
> They say, for life
> El'phants, deer, and camels,
> Man, and wife . . .

(Although it did end with a more sceptical question: all was not love and tranquillity!)

One afternoon it was a nightingale (with all those connotations of love, both divine and erotic), followed quickly by 'lark' – clearly an all-day affair. Often it was a fish: strange, as fishes were not things he much liked but even so these, too, resulted in poetry. At the same time he found that he could not transmit images, however meaningful or beautiful, that he did not in his inner self wish her to share. They remained – thankfully – separate personalities as well.

And then – photos, ones he really did not remember taking but there they were on the web. Four carried emotional vibes, never before felt in that way: one of him in his early days, close to when she would have last recalled him; three other innocuous-seeming images but when looked at in a different way carrying strong Freudian overtones, like dancing in the dark ('dancing'), one of these images hitting him with a stunning impact that was hard to resist – and it was the same every time he looked at the photograph.

Time too. He knew that she was working irregular but frequent hours as a part-time teacher, but not her days and hours. Or not at first. But why was it that he was struck with almost physical force when he was deeply concentrating on his own work on certain weekdays (never the weekend or school holidays) between 5 and 6 pm (the end of the school day?). Always unanticipated, they were *not* welcome, interrupting his chain of thought for two to three minutes or more at a time, an infinity in terms of personal power. And then there was the day when somewhat to his chagrin (did she not care any more?) there was a short burst at 5.32, cut off almost immediately, only to surge back again with immense force at 6.02. (He concluded, no doubt correctly, that her work that day came in half-hour periods and the first messages were interrupted by the arrival of the class.) They also came when she was apparently on her way home or relaxing over a drink in the evening – but never at weekends when she was with her lover in another town.

One day he was aware of a huge surge of panic. He did not know when it had arrived, it was just there. Not his own he knew. It was on the day he had had a wart removed from above his lip. It was not something he was in the least worried about for two doctors he trusted had declared it benign, just worth getting rid of when it happened to be convenient and the local GP had not kept him waiting more than a few minutes after he'd inspected it. Neither was it in the least painful even afterwards. But he then remembered that his telepathic partner had had dire experience of cancer in both herself and, fatally, in one dear to her. The utter panic continued despite his protests, but at last died down on his repeated messages of calm and reassurance. He was much touched by the messages of sympathy even while knowing he did not need them.

These hard thrusts of communication, forceful, irresistible however hard he tried to brush them aside, and always unexpected, were hard to deny. It would have been impossible for him to have just made them up – they were not even particularly pleasurable experiences to undergo. And what about his recognition, from a swiftly passing train, of the house she lived in, to be confirmed later from the map of the area? Or the park in which she walked often with her lover (not him)? The name of the dog he had found waiting on his doorstep when he most needed consolation? Or the conviction, in exactly the same words as for the death returnees, that henceforth he could 'do no wrong', not because of any predetermination or curtailment of free will but because it had already happened, was *there*, only waiting for them to experience it at the same instance for it to be fully realised?

And then there was another dream that linked telepathic and oneiric communicating. He was angry with her (it is irrelevant to pursue the reason), *very* angry, and refused for over 24 hours to open up to her hoping that would force her to contact him in this world by text or email. Predictably, she refused. But 36 or so hours later there she came, as the ancient Greeks would say, in a dream to tell him indirectly but unmistakeably in words and actions that she would *not* be bullied. Suffused with love she might be, as much his soul as her own ('as easy might I from myself depart' – Shakespeare as ever captured it). But that did *not* mean he could tell her what to think or feel. Neither, more faintly, did she wish to overcome *his* will.

This deep inner communicating did not mostly come in specific delimited messages although occasionally there were short verbal phrases such as 'She has forgiven you' and 'She is waiting for you.' But this type of comment was unusual – mostly, apart from the eventually verbal poems, the communicating was not 'linguistic', even though somehow intelligible in some other mode.

Such shared experience and communication may, it seems, only be possible with great (inclusive rather than exclusive, limited) love and understanding between two people, transcending time and place, life and death: suffusing the minds of each. And with *pain* too – this, for some reason, seems a necessary condition, perhaps part of the human condition of love? Telepathy indeed – except that that seems a trivialising word for this kind of liminal entrancement: *koinonia,* the ancient Greek and Christian word for sharing, communion may be a better term. Not tele-*mission* – sending – but *experiencing and suffering,* the true and full meanings of the ancient Greek *pathein*.

To return to the information technology metaphor: it was not so much a shared standalone computer, open to both parties, more a dropbox on the cloud – or the Garden of Eden (see Figure 8.2) – into which we can choose to put certain files and folders to be shared but keep others to ourselves – 'choose' I *think,* or anyway prefer to think – is the right term but at what level that choice is made I do not know and perhaps prefer not to enquire.

Figure 8.2 Eve sleeping in the garden to be awakened to the (?) real-er world by Adam Gustave Doré, 'The second tale of creation: the garden of Eden' (Second récit de la création: le jardin d'Eden).

What was involved, it would seem (if, that is, we can temporarily suspend disbelief), was that two intimately linked souls did not so much 'send and receive' 'messages' at a distance (*tele-*) as find themselves merged, the thoughts and feelings of the one interpenetrating the other: sharing and fellowship, rather than discrete communication. Most profoundly, it seemed, it was through music. Bach – above all the keyboard version of 'Sleepers awake' (significant words indeed) – and – *her* gift to *him* (mostly it was the other way round) – Mozart piano concertos, especially the slow movements. His to her was the songs of John Rutter, especially 'The Lord bless you and keep you . . . and give you peace'. We know from many years of experience that the deepest human communion is through sharing music.

All this is not really as novel as it appears when read in the setting of hard print. It is worth recalling the experience of twins; also, to an extent of split personalities and multiple selves; religious experience, meditation and curing strategies; studies such as those of the great anthropologists John Blacking and Vic Turner, of music, performance, experience and the multi-talented human body; of multisensory communicating (as in Howes 2011);[11] the nature of perception and of reality, well explored in long-historied philosophical thinking; the exploration (as seen earlier) of near-death experiences, miraculous cures and falling in love; the new world(s) revealed by MRI[12] (it does not *have* to be reductionist). The terms 'paranormal' and 'supernatural' seem too dismissive, begging all the questions, but studies called under that heading might carry rich rewards. And, above all, may we turn once again to the works of poetry and narrative – where better to gain insights into other worlds, other realities?

The telepathising communicating – a kind of morphing resonance to employ Rupert Sheldrake's vivid (and as so often musical) image – comes, it seems, through a similar but not the same source and medium. Despite the lengthy case described in this chapter, it is perhaps more common for women to be the more powerful partners sending messages to male partners. And dreams seem to be female carried, transmitted through the female line.

This illustrates another facet of communication: that even though I would characterise love as its main feature, it is emphatically not all loving and caring. Just as in 'real' life, telepathic communication does not stop us getting angry at times, impatient, desolate from separation, thinking the other is uncaring, unfaithful, selfish, *too* unselfish, you name it. Just like any old relationship!

From whence does this come? Can the source, the channel, somehow lie both beyond and outside human life and humans' earthly experiences? Or perhaps equally mysteriously, perhaps, hidden, unknown within ourselves? (The unconscious is a concept, long rejected, that we may find we come back to after all.) Is it that the 'psychic' and the 'physical' somehow both separate and merge? In what terms can we posit such experiences of communication to ourselves? All the words seem somehow unsatisfactory: telepathy, ESP, psychic insights, the sixth (or the seventh) sense. Shared consciousness or extended minds seem a slightly better way of phrasing it, but even those fail to hit the mark bang centre. Perhaps Vernadsky came closest, elusive though he knew his words to be, perhaps even unappealing to others, as to me, in his time-limited geological terminology. As he speculated:

> We are entering the noosphere. This new elemental geological process is taking place at a stormy time. . . . The important fact is that our democratic ideals are in tune with the elemental geological processes, with the laws of nature, and with the noosphere.
>
> (Vernadsky 2007: 414)

Are all human beings then born with the capacity for non-bodily ethereal communication irrespective of time and place but lose it as they learn to speak or become captured by the linguistic cultures of their time? And are some cultures and organisations, like the silent orders of nuns perhaps or those practised in meditation, whether east or west, more receptive to developing these latent communicative powers, either in small, submerged, ways or, at times, to a high pitch of expertise?

The answers may be misty. But if we value communication the questions are surely worth asking.

A new communications revolution – or an old one?

As so often happens, one place to look in to try to resolve our quandary is to the past experience of humankind. Can this help us understand or – at the least, and as in other chapters of this book – put our puzzles into greater, more fitting context?

We are accustomed to think of human history in terms of communication revolutions. And no, not technological solely, but cultural, political, economic, setting objects and processes in the context of technological affordances and limitations: print, modern information technology, audio books, iPads – and much more.

The channels of communication that we humans have developed – spoken, written, sonic, tactile, olfactory, pictorial, electronic and more – may look transparent. But they shape our configuration of our own and others' words and voices. The long-standing oral medium offered and offers multifaceted opportunities for human communication, ordered by the conventions of any given cultural setting as to appropriate settings, personnel, genre features and verbal register. Writing provides a different range of resources with the potential (magical as that no doubt once appeared) to be repeated and recorded in a form more or less removed from the immediate context and without the pressure of a directly present audience.

The development and spread of print technology in Europe from the fifteenth century offered additional challenges and opportunities. Books circulated more widely and in multiple copies, offering resources for individuals to copy by hand into personal commonplace books and to conflate extracts from printed sources for further publication. They also presented a threat to the existing controls over quoting exercised by church and state. These print technologies have since gone through a variety of forms, predictably matched by measures regulating printed quotation.

Together with the institutional arrangements of publishing, the book trade, educational curricula and academic hierarchies, these measures have over the centuries come to underpin the system we broadly observe today. This has meant, on the one hand, greater openings than in manuscript copying for unattributed quotations lifted from the multiply available printed publications and, on the other, scope for additional constraints over what is copied – over what is, or can and may be, communicated.

The technologies of the late twentieth and early twenty-first century add further twists. There are now substantial challenges to some of the earlier controls over the established medium and institutions of print. Photocopying, faxing, word processing, emailing, self-publication in increasingly manageable forms and the recent spread of open-access publishing have removed many of the practical constraints on copying, facilitating a spurt in the reproduction of others' words as home industry rather than specialist publication. The web and its search engines have brought new facilities for locating, reading and painlessly reproducing both short and extremely long passages and extracted quotations can be pasted seamlessly into a copyist's own documents.

These historical phases are without doubt of great importance in the history of communication. They have another dimension too. Often, it seems, it is in a period when new technologies have made possible the dissemination of words of wisdom, of messages from seers, prophets and, perhaps we may also include here, dreamers, that new religious sensibilities arise in the setting of wider ranges from human voices made possible by the spread of empires, trade routes and *linguae francae*, not without the exercise of the human power to constrain – call it 'educate' – other peoples and nations. Or take the worlds of the Roman or the British empires with their respective *linguae francae:* were these not periods of radical revolution in the channels of communication? Was it surprising that these were periods during which new truths and media were revealed to the then civilised world?

So are we now in another such period when communications are being vastly extended? And extended, as with all such technologies, within the settings of given cultures and controls/instruments of power?[13]

Are we now due for the next unveiling, crowning the half millennium that has so often in the past marked a turning point, a new revelation? It is hard not to believe that this is, indeed, the case. Is it in the end arrogant to suggest that this new uncurtaining through dreams, experiences of heaven and telepathic communication – our innovative technologies – can be counted in this same fashion?

We would do well not to ignore this heritage and the confluence of channels on which for good or ill we all draw: spoken words, written, spoken and electronic language, visual image, dance, the many modes of communication technology and (closest to my heart) song. And then – telepathy and dreams? Can we doubt that here we have resources that, using what terminology and attribution of cause we wish, are given for our celebration and understanding. What new concepts will we yet attain of brain and mind, our communicative powers or of the nature and potential of human beings through the lengthening millennia of human history?

We already accept electronic and radio waves, sound waves too. What new waves are we yet to become aware of? And are the channels we have been discussing in this chapter now still so impossible to envisage?

9   A mix of arts

Human beings, then, use a vast range of communicative modes. There is tactile communicating with its subtle immediacy of contact; the memory-holding evocations of the olfactory mode; the sonic experiences and resonances of the often underestimated auditory channel; and the multiplicity of visible actions, arts and artefacts. We share many of these basic resources with other animals and sometimes apply them in comparable ways. But humans have also fashioned them according to their own manners, drawing on them in an amazing variety of ways both nearby and at a distance: in the embodied actions of living human beings, and also, overlappingly, in human-made technologies and artefacts. These are, truly, the arts through which we maintain our human interconnectedness.

Examining the channels separately, as we have just done, gives some idea of the rich potentials, complexities and usages of each, necessary for revealing dimensions that are too often ignored or underrated. But of course they must ultimately be treated together. In practice these modes are seldom used alone and when humans interact they regularly call on a plurality of arts.

The interwoven modes of human communicating

We need only reflect a little on our own experience to recognise that in our communicating we regularly draw simultaneously on several modalities. In practical terms we know this already. But many analyses of human communication and of language take little account of it: speech has commonly been treated as a different domain from gesture, writing from pictorial representation, movement and space from the handling of tangible artefacts. This separation is now happily starting to be eroded. In particular, some sociolinguists and others now vehemently challenge the idea that language and non-verbal communication are independent domains, and increasingly include gestures and spacing in their analyses of speech and of language. All can act together, coordinated parts of the whole. Hand works with tongue, with eye, with ear. . . .[1]

Even in the would-be separate discussions in the earlier chapters it was unavoidably coming through that in practice the various channels regularly intermingle. The same point was foreshadowed in the short examples introducing Chapter 1. Now is the time to take this further, starting with some additional illustrative cases to lead into more general comment.

We could start by retracing our steps back to the indignant farmer shown in Figure 4.3 (p. 110). Earlier our focus was on the visual elements of the interaction – the gestures, stances and facial expressions of the various parties – but if we look again other dimensions, too, become obvious. There are of course the spoken words with, we can imagine, all the subtle and varying intonations, dynamics and timing which made them expressive, but also the accused girl's sobs – whether or not hypocritical they are clearly part, unspoken, of the communicating process. The positioning and spacing between the parties tell part of the story too. So far the farmer has not actually laid hands on the girl nor have she or her mother touched him in their supplication and rebuttal as they might have done (tactile communicating by its absence, so to speak); but it clearly remains an imminent question whether the farmer is on the verge of a violent touch: the threat of this extreme form of tactile communication is part of the situation. Multiple communicative channels are being used.

Or consider the many modes involved in the process of greeting in Samoa. This sounds simple enough in basic outline. A newcomer enters a house where others are already sitting, sits in the front region, is ceremonially greeted, and responds. But these are complex sequences, enacted through 'the language of bodies in social space' (as Duranti describes it in his rich analysis, 1992). They involve regulated body movements, the spatial settings of Samoan houses, conventions laying down the appropriate uttered sounds at particular junctures, and, not least, Samoans' intimate concern with status difference and its markers. To communicate their salutations effectively people must organise their positioning and movement in due fashion – for the different parts of the Samoan house are separately categorised – and integrate these with the proper spoken sounds. Where the new arrival is allowed or expected to sit during and after the greeting has crucial status connotations, communicating clearly to all participants the acceptance or – it may be – denial of the visitor's claims. The visual dimension is highly relevant too.

> Participants can be seen making their sighting of others either apparent or not apparent. . . . From the point of view of people already in the house, to see someone arriving may imply taking a stand as to where that person is expected or allowed to sit. If eye contact is made during the sighting of the new arrival, the party in the house may have to offer a particular spot [with consequential status implications], sometimes even his own. . . . Seeing one another has social significance and must thus be monitored.
>
> (Duranti 1992: 678)

What seems at first the mere utterance of a greeting turns out to have multiple facets. It operates through 'a variety of channels and media (voice, body, sight, physical space, and physical arrangement of living bodies in that space) . . . [and with] temporal as well as spatial dimensions' (Duranti 1992: 683).

Or again, think of the kind of interaction we are familiar with nearly every day. Two acquaintances meet by chance in a street or corridor. They are almost certain to draw on a plurality of visual displays: recognition signals and acknowledgements, subtly deployed and designed to be visibly noticed as the distance between the two gradually decreases; visible facial expressions as their interaction continues; proxemic placings in their mutual distance and positioning; visible postures and orientations in relation to each other; movements and gesturing of (at least) hands, limbs, heads and shoulders; purposive manipulation of clothing or other objects, like removing gloves before shaking hands, displaying some article of shared interest, glancing at a watch as prelude to farewell. Such actions go on both during the central phases and in greeting and farewell movements at start and finish, mutually understood in accordance with conventions accepted both in a general way in the social world inhabited by the participants, and, perhaps, in specific forms more, or less, recognised between this particular pair. The auditory channel is important too. One or both make sounds drawing and acknowledging attention at the outset and acoustic communicating probably extends throughout the main phase of their encounter. They interact not only through the modulations, rhythms and auditory subtleties of verbalised speech, acoustically formulated in ways that mark their specific mutual relationship and are appropriate for the sonic environment, but also through other sounds such as sighs, laughs or silences. Touching – or its studied avoidance – quite likely plays some part, most explicitly during greeting and parting. It indicates the nature and development of the participants' relationship through their respective acceptance or otherwise of particular tactile contacts and at some points may be directly used to convey, for example, shared sympathy, congratulation or rejection. Finally, smell may enter in too, if only implicitly. The (non-conscious) personal odours emanating from each can amplify or qualify the sense of familiar friendship and the olfactory ambience help to define the situation.

A full account of the sequences of even an apparently simple encounter like this could extend to many pages. The intermingling of modalities is uneven and varied, and develops in a series of detailed interactions throughout the phases of the communicating process. At any given time one (or two) of the channels, or of the specific means through which they are deployed, may be specially to the fore. But even then others may be partly in play too. They intertwine in complex and versatile ways, supporting, qualifying, illustrating, extending, deepening, perhaps contradicting the other(s). As Adam Kendon rightly says: 'Communication in interaction is a continuous multichannel process' (1990: 15). This multiplicity is something we draw on every day but, taking it for granted, we seldom notice it consciously.

These and other examples in this book are merely a few tokens of an infinitude of possible encounters. The specificities and combinations of modes vary not only in different cultural conditions but up to a point within and during each personal enactment: the detailed balance between different channels, say, or the use or avoidance of touch or smell; the patterning of visible gesture, facial expression, posture, orientation, spacing, personal adornment; or the processes of audible interaction through manipulation of volume, tone, speed, vocabulary or mood . . . and so on, and so on. The possible combinations are near-endless and in each communicative sequence the participants create their own unique mix.

It perhaps seems exaggerated to suggest that human communicating is characteristically multimodal. Even if the examples above are multifaceted, surely *some* forms of communication are typically unidimensional? Speech and music for example seem to be predominantly acoustic, reading and writing to be essentially a matter of vision, and distance communicating perhaps less rich again. It is instructive to press these cases further for, at first sight unpromising within this line of argument, they are more multiple than they seem.

Spoken expression is an illuminating example. The (relatively) informal genres of interpersonal conversation have been mentioned already – cases where, it is clear, many modes are likely to be interacting: it is emphatically *not* just an auditory process. We can extend the same point to the more explicitly performance-oriented genres such as stories, speeches, poems or spoken prayers. These seem on the face of it single-mode genres, utilising the auditory-verbal channel, and this indeed is how they have often been analysed. But once they are considered as active processes, their multidimensional nature becomes obvious. Recent studies of oral art from a performance perspective reveal the complex mix commonly deployed – auditory, kinesic, visual, participatory, perhaps also tactile and olfactory.

The processes of story-telling among the Sierra Leonean Limba people can illustrate this further. When I worked in Limba villages in the 1960s (Finnegan 1967) I began, as many did then, by assuming that the essential reality of the stories lay in their verbal make-up; transcribing them into linear written text was thus ultimately the way to capture and study them. I only gradually became aware how much else was going on besides the delivery of words.

Sound was, certainly, one channel. Audition was in one sense fundamental, for story-telling usually happened in the dark of the evening. The sound floated through the village and attracted people to join the throng crowding the outside veranda of a hut, often the chief's since that was the largest and best-lit. The focus was the spoken and sounded words uttered by the main narrator. But this was not a 'one-line' style of delivery dependent on one speaker alone. The sounds made by the leading narrator were partly shared, overlappingly, with his or her main supporter (the 'replier') who provided auditory echoes of a small selection of the utterances, para-linguistic sounds indicating attention and respect, and extra comments at moments of high drama ('. . . and all the time he didn't know she was planning to kill him . . .'). Other participants joined in the sonic occasion from time to time through murmured agreement or appreciation, laughter, exclamations of excitement or horror, or the occasional acoustic echo of the main speaker's words. From one viewpoint they were the 'audience' but from another full actors in the auditory communicative process, which they in turn were helping to co-construct.

The audible words were not just indicators of denotative propositional meaning, transmitting a one-way informational message. Story-telling depended on *how* they were sounded. Limba narrators were experts in the timing of their delivery, the grouping or separation of their spoken sounds, the deployment of speed, silence, volume, incisiveness, tone and auditory characterisation. Drastic lengthening or repetition of certain syllables added to the effect. Thus while listeners were already well acquainted with the spoken sound *piripiri* as conveying the idea of 'all night', the consciously exaggerated high, long-drawn and repeated *piripiripiripiripiri,* responded to acoustically by the audience too, created the shared auditory experience that conveyed struggling through the whole long night, hour after hour after hour after hour . . .

In western categorisations rhythm and melody are often associated with music rather than plain 'prose' (if indeed prose is ever 'plain' or absolutely distinct from verse). But Limba story-tellers, like those of many cultures, certainly used rhythmic artistry in their tellings. The sonic patterns of the rising and falling tonal contours of larger units than 'words' or phrases were part of the atmosphere and formulating of the narration, one dimension of the generic conventions of Limba story-telling. They also marked out the sequential phases of the narration through the tonal contours for opening and closing a tale, for moments of rapid action, or pauses for reflection. From time to time the sonic effects were intensified in the singing of both principal narrator and other participants, co-enacting the narrated events through joining in sung (sometimes danced) choruses. To add to the auditory experience there was the whole sonic ambience of the village, one familiar dimension of the communicative process as a whole.

But sound was not all, for vision was another crucial resource for story-tellers and one much appreciated by the participating audience. People preferred places with some light from fires or oil lanterns (in the 1960s few villages had electricity), but in any case eyes partly adjusted to the gloom and at times there was bright moonlight. The story's developing stages were communicated through the narrators' facial expressions, head position, gestures, posture, and sometimes movements of their whole bodies. Individual characterisation has sometimes been said to be weak in orally told stories – and so perhaps it might seem if verbal transcriptions are considered. But in performance Limba story-tellers conveyed it vividly, partly through sound, but also, and often brilliantly, through the visual channel. The facial expression, tilt of the head, and pretendedly modest posture depicted the outwardly sweet and innocent young girl with hidden depths, out to entrap the susceptible old chief who had killed her father. We grasped the personality of the cunning and magically endowed hunter through the teller's visual representation of his deep-set and piercing eyes, his head movements, his restrained but memorable gestures. And the sight of the other co-participants in the event – their more muted but still partly visible movements or stillnesses – added to the visually apprehended experience of the story's development.

The role of smell was harder to capture and possibly of little importance (I did not think to explore it at the time). Certainly story-telling usually took place in a particular olfactory situation. Its typical timing was after people had come home from the farm, washed and eaten, so the lingering and fading smell of cooking and of smoke from the fires, as well as the familiar odours of mingling human bodies all contributed to defining the nature of the event. At times, too, there was the sharp but sweet fragrance of palm wine, that powerful and unforgettable aromatic symbol not just of shared relaxation but also of the aesthetic and practical arts in which the Limba knew themselves to excel.

Touch did not seem to take a large part. Story-tellers sometimes slapped hands with their selected 'repliers' at particular narrative moments but otherwise did not make much play with tactile resources. Nevertheless the tactile overtones of thronging closely together during the narration, whilst observing due conventions about social touching, and of joint engagement in the sung and (sometimes) danced enactment of the story were all part of a shared and embodied experience.

Not all genres of spoken performance follow those precise processes and many other combinations are of course found. Sometimes there is more emphasis on visible accoutrements and staging or, as in some Pacific contexts, on concurrent dance, music, costume, fans and poetry. Sometimes the olfactory ambience of smoke, alcohol and old furniture are part of the occasion – think of telling tall tales in English pubs. But whatever the details, any 'oral' communicative process is highly likely to involve other channels than the purely auditory and verbal. As is now being increasingly emphasised in narrative and oral theory as well as in analysis of speech more generally, the arts of oral performance are more than just 'words'.

Music is another example: on the face of it purely auditory but in its actual practice multidimensional. Musical performances are 'multi-media events', as John Blacking put it, 'and their sound patterns are but one of several channels of communication' (1987: 123). Music speaks simultaneously 'to the head and the legs' is Gilbert Rouget's conclusion to his *Music and Trance* (Rouget 1985: 325), something of the body, not just the ear. Barthes makes a parallel point when he remarks that playing music is not so much auditive as manual and muscular, 'as if the body was listening, not the "soul"' (Barthes 1986: 261). He picks particularly on his experience of playing Schumann, whose music 'goes much further than the ear; it goes into the body, into the muscles by the beats of the rhythm, and somehow into the viscera by the voluptuous pleasure of its *melos*' (Barthes 1986: 295).

Most musical performances have a visual dimension. This is so even in genres of western classical music commonly conceptualised as purely auditory. The shine of violins, layout and decoration of hall and platform, spatial relations between participants ('performers' separated from 'audience'), posture and orientation of a singer, dress and seating of orchestral players, a flautist's stance and gestures, the kinesic formulae for starting and ending, the conductor's movements of hands, body and baton (a dance . . .) – all are part of the whole communicative experience. Leppert's *The Sight of Sound* displays 'the visual-performative aspect' of music as 'no less central to its meanings than are the visual components of . . . performing arts . . . like dance or theatre' (1993: xxi), a point further illustrated through the ample representation of music in European visual art. In some musical traditions the participants' dress, colourful display, accoutrements, visual setting, kinaesthetic movements or facial expressions are all explicitly recognised as contributing to the shared experience. This is also true of most, perhaps all, danced music. It is conspicuous in opera and musical theatre, but also appears in settings ranging from English brass-band processions to the performances (live or videoed) of contemporary rock and pop music, Limba danced ceremonies or the luxuriant displays of Pacific or Indian dance.

Tactile and olfactory expectations sometimes enter in too, if in hidden ways. In musical performance, especially dance, people touch or avoid touch, and sense their own and others' somatic dynamics. They sometimes approach close enough for personal odours to play a part, or perform in settings where olfactory expectations help to shape the scene – smoke perhaps, the smell of beer, the intertwined experiences of music, wafted fragrances and trance, or the aromatic atmosphere of a church, ritual or concert hall. Even in recorded music overtly intended just for the ear, both performers and their later listeners may observe spatial and temporal conventions which, in turn, may have their associated proxemic, kinesic and even olfactory overtones.

Writing is another multimodal resource. This may seem surprising. On the face of it writing is visual, two-dimensional and transparent. Its visibility often enters into its definitions; indeed it has mostly been presented here in the context of vision. Reading, too, is often conceived as a kind of silent mental communion between writer and reader, disembodied except for the eye.

The actual practice is more complex. Even the visual dimensions themselves are multiple, going beyond the simplified model according to which the visible marks of writing consist essentially and solely of 'words' and directly convey transparent meanings. As we saw earlier (Chapter 5), graphic, spatial and pictorial elements in practice intertwine. Asian calligraphies perhaps lay special stress on the art of visual form, but even in the apparently word-based alphabetic systems of European tradition other visual signs are salient too (again see Chapter 5). Typographical format conveys whether something is to be treated 'as verse' or 'as prose', for example, and the style of line layout is part of a poem. Written poetry is always partly conveyed through explicit or assumed visible appearance but this is sometimes deliberately marked. In George Herbert's beautiful 'Easter-wings' the shape of the poem, in wing form, matches the meaning; so too, in varying ways, do the products of various movements of 'visual' and 'concrete' poetry, illustrated in Figure 9.1.

PREMIER canonnier conducteur
Je suis au front et te salue
Non non tu n'as pas la berlue
Cinquante-neuf est mon secteur

J'entends siffler l'oiseau
Le
bel oiseau rapace

Je vois de loin
la cathédrale

```
O   C
M   H
O   E
N   A R
NDRE
BILLY
```

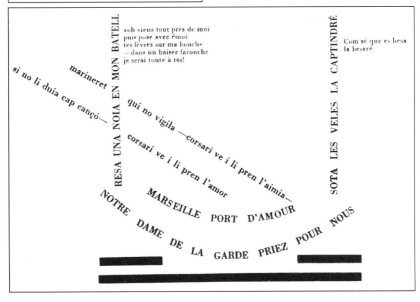

Figure 9.1 Poems as pictures
Above: Guillaume Apollinaire's letter-poem of April 1915 to André Billy: a pictorial impression of his life at the front, with the whistling shell attack from the air in the centre, then below his vision of a distant cathedral in the shape of an eye (perhaps also recalling Notre Dame in Paris where the recipient was living), and, right, an image of a cathedral's facade and twin towers – as Billy comments (1923: 81), Apollinaire had been stationed near Reims ('First gunner driver/ I am at the front and greet you/ No no you are not bedazzled/ Fifty-nine is my section./ I hear the bird whistling the beautiful bird of prey/ I see the cathedral far off/ OH MY DEAR ANDRÉ BILLY') (from André Billy, *Apollinaire vivant*, 1923, p. 81 and Guillaume Apollinaire, *Oeuvres poétiques*, Bibliothèque de la Pléiade, Gallimard, 1965, p. 771, image courtesy Éditions Gallimard). Below: The Catalan poet Joan Salvat-Papasseit's

The elaborate verbo-visual confections created on some computer screens sometimes take this even further. We are all familiar, too, with the way visual images complement the verbal, even transcend it, in comics, advertisements, newspapers or children's books, one essential dimension of their complex visual impact. And even in genres ostensibly centred on words, the inclusion of illustrations, maps, or diagrams is often not mere secondary 'decoration' to written text but – as indeed in this volume – itself part of the communication.

Writing is also an object in space. Sometimes this is more implicit than explicit, but in any written hard copy there is always *some* material dimension which in itself declares something of its purpose, genre or tone. This is evident right from the most informal of handwritten notes to the great traditions of mediaeval decorated manuscripts, Chinese painting, Islamic scripts, or the colourful pictorial realisations of Mesoamerican writing. Even in less elaborated examples the layout, material, fastenings or script of a piece of writing provide essential information about its nature: its provenance, its aims, likely participants and how it is to be read and used. Without needing to think about it we take account of the physical differences between a magazine article, Bible, poster, or religious inscription – crucial features for how we interpret them. Writing has taken many material forms besides the recent western paradigm of linear text on flat surface. As Graziella Tonfoni illustrates in her provocative *Writing as a Visual Art* (1994), it has also been presented on three-dimensional objects like cubes, pyramids, politticos (openable panels), obelisks and columns. It comes as part of the ornamentation of buildings, on carpets, on silk, on the Bayeux tapestry, all with their communicative qualities of texture, feel and structure. A multiplicity of visible shapes, colours, spatial relations, materials and artistries can be interwoven together in the apparently simple process of communicating through writing.

---

visual poem as two-masted boat with furled sails: masts in capitals, small print for the pennants at their heads, lower-case lines slanting diagonally along the sails. On one pennant the girl sings in French inviting her would-be lover who has taken her on the ship, matched by his anticipation in the other pennant; below is the poet's wry commentary on women's fickleness and the need for vigilance. The lover's amorous intentions are confirmed by the ironic reference to prayers for their sin in the heavy lower edge of the boat. 'MARSEILLE PORT D'AMOUR/ NOTRE DAME DE LA GARDE PRIEZ POUR NOUS/ RESA UNA NOIA EN MON BATELL: "oh viens tout près de moi/ puis pose avec émoi/ tes lèvres sur ma bouche/ – dans un baiser farouche/ je serai toute à toi!"/ SOTA LES VELES LA CAPTINDRÉ/ Com sé que es besa/ la besaré/ marineret qui no vigila – corsari ve i li pren l'aimia/ so no li duia cap cançó – corsari ve i li pren l'amor' ('MARSEILLES PORT OF LOVE/ OUR LADY OF THE GARDE PRAY FOR US/ A GIRL ON MY BOAT RECITES:/ "oh come close to me/ then with great emotion press/ your lips against mine/ – with a feverish kiss/ I will be entirely yours!"/ I WILL LEAD HER UNDER THE SAILS/ Since I know she likes to kiss/ I will kiss her/ The sailor-boy who is not vigilant – pirates come and take his sweetheart; if he never brought her a song – pirates come and take her love' – for translation and fuller commentary see Bohn 1986: 138–41) (from Joan Salvat-Papasseit, *La rosa als llavis*, 1923, XIII).

There are other dimensions too, some already implied in the examples above. Written texts commonly carry phonological overtones and both affect, and are affected by, the acoustic associations of speaking. Some are taken to reach their full realisation through being read aloud, performed, or used for auditory memorising and vocal repetition. Soundless reading is not everywhere the norm, indeed has not always been part even of western tradition. Parents still commonly read to small and not-so-small children, school pupils prove themselves by reading aloud, and for many worshippers the sacred text of the Bible is acoustically experienced through church 'readings'. 'Audio books' increasingly circulate, directly conveying the auditory aspects of written texts. Even 'silent' reading can have sonic dimensions and we have all doubtless had the experience of hearing with the 'inner ear', above all with poetry.

Tactile dimensions can be relevant too. Whether or not consciously, we are aware of the *feel* of newspapers, of thick or thin paper, of leather bindings, of the turn of a page. A draft computer print-out feels different – and has a different status – from a shiny bound book with the same words. The touch of writing inscribed on a memorial stone, painted on silk or indented on clay tablets; of embossed print on expensive vellum; of three-dimensional globes presenting cartographic and printed information about the world; of lavish 'coffee table' books; and of touch-based systems like braille – these tactile dimensions are all on occasion significant for written communication. Children are taught how to handle books and other written material, not just how to read them – they must 'treat' them 'properly' and the mode of touching is a crucial part of the lesson. This is not just for utilitarian preservation, for the tactile channel too carries messages about the nature and purpose of the object in question, part of its communicative power.

Smell is sometimes another clue to the nature of what we are reading. Newspapers or magazines smell different from books, paperbacks from heavy hardcover tomes. New books have a special odour, little-read ones are musty, and old books and manuscripts have distinctive smells of their own, helping to identify their period or provenance. We react to them accordingly. And the particular olfactory ambience of an archive, a private bedroom or a great public library shapes our interpretation of the books and papers we handle in those surroundings.

The 'materiality' of writing and of books is now increasingly appreciated (see for example Donatelli and Winthrop-Young 1995). Electronic forms of text have challenged the easy assumption that 'hard copy' unilinear writing is *the* transparent and universally valid medium for conveying verbal meaning over space and time, stimulating a more critical awareness of the variety of material forms in which writing has in fact been organised. Recent approaches to the study of material culture have enhanced this realisation, chiming in with current transdisciplinary interests in 'the material aspects of human existence' (Miller and Tilley 1996: 8; see also pp. 40–1 above). Far from writing being a simple monological medium of communication, it comes in a variety of material forms, each with its own multiplex dimensions in actual usage.

Electronic text may seem to escape this multi-sided materiality. It has specific characteristics of its own, certainly. Its relative lack of 'fixity' challenges definitions of writing in terms of permanent signs while the multiple paths opened up by 'hypertext' contrast with the one-way linear constraints of much writing over recent centuries (or so it has been argued). 'Cyberspace' is presented as something of the dematerialised ether which provides for the transfer and processing of data in non-material form, 'envisioned as a world of pure information' (Levinson and Ember 1996, vol. 1: 306).

But for its participants this may have its own materiality. There is the feel of the machine, the smell and atmosphere associated with its site, the skilful touch of the fingers, the tactile manipulation of mouse and screen. The auditory channel is now often used too, and tactile communication via computer is on the way. Visual conventions are also emerging here. The ingenious 'smileys' of email communication depend on juggling typographical formats to convey emotion, humour or irony, while the developing 'netiquettes' for computer-mediated interaction link to expectations among particular groups about vocabulary and procedures. Similarly the potentials of fluid computer text and hypertextual non-linear ordering are exploited to generate new forms of creative writing where 'reader' as well as 'writer' joins in the creation (Moulthrop 1995). Typography and visual format are part of the expression. 'The text is much more like an image', was how one cyber poet expressed it, going on to describe how

> she created the visual background to the poem by squashing vanilla yogurt and old hairs between two sheets of acetate and scanning them in to the computer. 'I was trying to reproduce the texture of vellum, the subject of my work at the time. . . . You can try things you would not do in print. The web is much more dynamic and closer to the process of writing'.
>
> (Catherine Byron, quoted in Utley 2000: 13)

'Cyborg poetry' creates new senses of aesthetic experience, as in the many examples currently on the web or, from slightly earlier, John Cayley's 'cybertextual transformations' which give indeterminate and changing 'performance readings' rather than frozen texts, and his 'speaking clock' which produces ever-changing verbal and spatial displays by quasi-aleatory procedures as well as telling the 'real time' (Cayley 1996, see also Danet 2001).

Increasingly people are using computer-based media for art and play, not just for 'information' transfer and retrieval, and here written text can take spectacularly multimodal forms. Ethnographic research on computer communication now adopts a different perspective from the earlier morally loaded generalisations and 'impact' studies, and is consequently revealing how people actually use it in practice. Brenda Danet's *Cyberpl@y. Communicating Online*, for example, describes playful digital communication as people construct complex and emotive art forms through creating colours, poems, sounds, banners, emblems and greetings electronically (Danet 2001). As she wrote earlier, bringing out yet again the multimodal nature of 'writing' in a computer-based setting:

> Computerization is fostering a new aesthetic based on simulation. One can customize one's reading and writing environment, by experimenting with fonts, changing color schemes, using commercial screen savers and background 'wallpaper', or even designing one's own. . . . Publication on the World Wide Web or on a CD-ROM usually involves as much attention to color, graphics and background, including many that simulate three-dimensional textures, sound and video, etc., as to the text itself.
>
> (Danet 1997: 27)

These are only a scatttering of the innumerable instances of the multimodal dimensions of communicating, emphasised here to offset the earlier focus on separate channels. Many further examples have been referred to tangentially in previous chapters or appear in the illustrative figures. The essence of legal decisions for example may seem to lie in spoken or written words; but visible gesture and bodily enactment at times play an equally important role, as shown in the Bayeux tapestry frame of Figure 4.5 (p. 116). Stories may often be spoken verbally; but for the Australian Walbiri, the sand graphics form a major part of the telling (see pp. 154–6 above), while in some Pacific islands the tactile and visual experience of making string figures intertwine with the oral narrations. Experiences of 'landscape' may seem to depend on vision but can have tactile, olfactory or auditory resonances too. Or again, we may think of a sermon or religious testimony as a verbal formulation, delivered through the auditory channel. But that other dimensions can also enter in emerges in Sidener's account (1987) of the visual, auditory, olfactory, tactile and spatial characteristics which distinguish a high Episcopal Church from a Quaker meeting house (see p. 142 above), and in the multiply contrasting elements, accoutrements and associations of evangelical and Catholic preaching encapsulated in the Reformation woodcut of Figure 5.11 (p. 168).

It is not just a matter of 'sensory channels' if we interpret that term in the narrow sense of the body's perceptual and transmissive capacities. There is also the remarkable human facility to draw human-created material objects into their modes of interconnecting. This runs through human communicating at every level, from the artefactual constructing of the human body to the visual arts of writing, the sounds of live and recorded music, tactile diagrams, wafted incense and the devices through which, as we will see further in the final chapter, humankind extends its interconnection through the expanses of time and space. Their significance, even their existence, is often obscured by the influential mentalist models of communication or, paralleling this, by the assumption that using 'material' objects is somehow artificial and secondary in human communicating. But in practice a multiplicity of material artefacts regularly form part of the complex mix of arts through which human beings interconnect.

There are also variations within the multimodal tendencies of our communicating. The various strands may not be equally salient, shaped as they are by culturally specific conventions, expected situations or even individual sensibilities as to what counts for most, or what is 'direct', what 'indirect'.[2] The accepted characteristics of some genres may lie in their stress on just *one* dimension, all the more distinctive for the way they subvert the more usual – and perhaps still underlying – tendency to multimodality. Sometimes multiple mixed strands are richly developed, spread in complex ways across many modalities; sometimes they are fewer or thinner. Some people and some circumstances bring out specific facets; others face particular constraints, not least sensorily deprived individuals or some situations of distance-communicating. Sometimes (not infrequently in fact) the different dimensions seem to work 'against' as much as 'with' each other or carry different weights for different enactors – though, rather than diminishing the multiplicities, this makes them all the more important.

The multimodal character of human communicating may by now seem too obvious to need reiterating. Birdwhistell made the point long ago that 'a mono-channel analysis of communication must ignore or deny too much evidence to gain support unless the definition of communication is limited to the wholly aware, completely purposive transmission of commonly held, explicit, and denotative verbal information between interactants' (Birdwhistell 1968: 28). It is seldom fully appreciated, however. No doubt we are partly influenced, in both our practices and our reflections, by the fact that capturing just one dimension makes for simpler analysis. More pervasively, the classificatory ideologies developed in specific cultures – or by specific parties within them – often pick out certain features rather than others for conscious attention. The importance attached to the visual (written) representation of words in recent western intellectual culture is the most familiar example: this screens out other aspects of what is going on. As a result it is easy to conclude that only one dimension 'really' matters or, notably with vision and audition, that only one facet of a complex channel is in play. But, to repeat, in people's actual practice communication is typically multiplex, often much more so than they consciously realise themselves – an inextricable combination of modes utilised not as additional extras but at the heart of the communicating process.

The scope for human creativity in each and every process of communication is thus enormous, far more than shows up in the definitions of communication which focus on single-line verbalised messages or emphasise one channel only. Each channel is itself complex and, as we saw in earlier chapters, can be exploited in a huge range of subtle, varying and emotive ways and through a multiplicity of media. This creative interweaving of many arts would indeed seem to be one of the most significant features of our human modes of interconnecting.

Multiplicity and human interconnectedness

What are the implications of this profuse multiplicity of arts for our understanding of human communication?

One response is to invoke the idea of 'redundancy'. Employing more elements than the bare minimum insures against failure. This is so even within a single channel – we cope with spoken interchanges even when we only catch *part* of what is said. Drawing on more than one modality provides an additional safeguard. In noisy airports announcements are often made through both visual and auditory channels, and using sound or touch as well as vision means a message can get through even in the dark or round obstructions. It makes for flexibility too, for individuals can interact differently according to their own particular situation or capacities. Those less competent in one modality can at least partially compensate by greater reliance on others; elders going a little deaf become adept in observing lip movements, while those whose vision is obstructed can rely more on auditory or tactile dimensions – and so with all the different permutations made possible by the 'extra' elements in communicating over and above the basic minimum.

There is something to be said for this redundancy model. But it is not the end of the matter. If communication was just a matter of transferring once-and-for-all messages, then one element might indeed provide a surrogate for another so long as the basic information got across. But if we take a processual and active view of human communicating, then the many concurrent dimensions are not alternatives but all part of the process, with as many experiences and creations, furthermore, as there are participants.

This perspective takes us beyond the substitution of one channel for another to an enlarged appreciation of the typical richness and complexity of human communicating. It is seldom that communicating consists solely in the transfer of simplex one-line messages. Much more characteristic is a process that is composite, multifarious, complicatedly interwoven, variable over time. Remember the complex mix of arts in an everyday conversation – spoken words; visible expressions of the face, gestures, body movements and spacing; manipulation of various material objects; selective use of touch; and perhaps subtle olfactory emanations. They may be reinforcing, contradicting, qualifying and/or personalising the communicating, together with a host of other possibilities – certainly complexifying and deepening it. Different participants pick up different elements and warm to them even at the same time, let alone at different moments, not least because multiple dimensions are often simultaneously in play, which in one sense may be working against or modifying each other. Amidst the thick skein of intertwined elements we cannot conclude that just *one* of these strands is self-evidently the 'right' one or carries the 'true' message. Their unwrapping will be moulded not just by differing cultural assumptions about what 'counts' but perhaps by single enactors in unique situations and in ways different from their fellows on that very occasion. Emotive as well as informational dimensions (insofar as these are different) enter in and, again, are taken up differently by the various participants, whether near or distant. And the emergent unfolding of the processes over time, and sometimes over space, adds to the plurality as different actors make their own mutually interacting contributions, perhaps unawares, to its developing multimodal formulation.

Because such interactions are multiple in time, in enactors, and in their mixture of modes, their nature is not simple. They can seldom, if ever, be confined to a single objective and predetermined meaning. It would be foolish to deny that some cases of communicating are closer to the traditional sender–message–receiver model than are others. But even there human creativity is inevitably in play through the personal weight given to one or another of the interwoven modes and the unfolding process of joint interaction. As we saw above, even apparently transparent and impersonal 'codes' like writing or ethereal computer communication are in practice often multimodal. If we look just to the transfer of a one-dimensional message, we will miss the multiplicity, depth and creativity of what is actually going on.

This mix of arts has implications for our understanding of communicating. It reminds us, for example, to consider the multiplex combinations drawn on in differing social worlds. The sermons, songs and pictorial images of the mediaeval European 'mass media', to use Morris's term (1972), differ from the electronic and print media of today, just as the performed music, dance and oratory of some African cultures contrasted with the print-focus of their European colonisers. We cannot assume that the particular array of media taken for granted in one culture – or indeed in one small social world, even a regularly interacting twosome – is universally applicable.

But despite contrasts and changes, human communicators always have *some* mix of multiple communicative resources. Certainly there have been historical shifts in the balance between different modalities or, at any rate, in the ideologies surrounding them, in the specific media to which people have commonly turned and in the constraints and opportunities within which they work. But the grandiose terms in which these are sometimes described are often simplistic – the 'great divide' between non-literate and literate societies, the 'revolution' brought by computer technologies, the heightened evaluation of sight in post-enlightenment Europe. Accounts of vast historic changes in human development linked (variously) to the 'leap' from orality to writing, from manuscript to print, or from written to electronic 'age' often miss the point that, however significant the changes and however much powerful groups promote one particular medium, other media are almost certainly in play as well – and likely in some respects to remain so. The technological determinism that focuses on just a limited selection of media to identify 'consequences' ignores the mix typical of human interaction. Every set of changes is multifaceted and manipulated by a multiplicity of human agents.

Different genres and occasions may demand their own specific mix. In certain conditions or between certain participants, one channel may indeed tend to dominate, and powerful voices in some traditions make a point of elevating one modality or one particular set of media over others. This differential deployment is yet another aspect of the multiplicity of human communicating, for the mix is not uniform and is formulated through the specifics both of accepted convention and individual performance. Adam Kendon has well described the 'gradient of explicitness' in people's actions with no sharp distinction between 'main-track' and background or unofficial dimensions, but also points to how we can perform actions in a way that makes them 'more salient than usual, that draws attention to them' (Kendon 1990: 260). The same applies to the interwoven strands within our communicative processes more generally. Some may indeed be specially 'salient' and valued, a very real factor therefore in the communicative process. But this can also be relative: they may be more so for some participants, some cultures or some occasions than for others, or emerge more, or less, explicitly at differing points over time, and in versatile ways that could not always be thoroughly predicted in advance – yet another dimension of the multiplex and elusive process of communicating.

If some mix of arts is a feature of our communicating generally, this is often intensified on occasions of high ritual or performance. Memorial celebrations, great public ceremonies, and personal rites of passage can involve heightened multisensory experiences. Ceremonial processions may display the visual properties of colour, festive dress, bodily ornamentation, visual artefacts like flags and banners, choreographed spacing and movements; draw on elaborated musical and other sounds and (at some point) the vocalisation of carefully modulated words; on systematically controlled touch, both direct and through the indirect but tangibly felt somatic movements of many participants; and perhaps on the evocativeness of wafting smells associated with the occasion. Dramatic performances often rely heavily on multiple dimensions of sound, colour, movement and display, from Shakespearean or Noh drama to the Yoruba popular plays of modern Nigeria which bring together the fragmented modes of oral genres into more linear narrative theatrical presentations using (among other things) songs, speeches, dialogue, chorus, drumming, costume, stage sets, props, mime and, not least, the vibrant interaction of the audience (Barber 2000: esp. 341–2).

In some traditions healing performances similarly draw on a range of sensuous qualities – sound, fragrance, touch and dance as well as spoken words (see for example Laderman and Roseman 1996). Or consider the familiar rituals of church weddings. They are commonly enacted through triumphal sounds from musical instrument(s); formally spoken words, both familiar and new, together with the empathetic sounds from the congregation; visual display of very special clothing and accoutrements by the principals (and often others, too); orchestrated processing, movements and spatial positionings not just of bride, bridal attendants and groom but, up to a point, of the whole congregation; ordered exercise of touch, especially between bride, groom and celebrant but also congratulatory and confirming handshakes and kisses between other participants too; and the olfactory ambience of the building and scent of flowers. It is the heightened multidimensional character of many ritual occasions that makes them so powerful – one reason no doubt why they are not only valued but also regulated and on occasion feared. And if all communicating typically involves a range of modalities, it is perhaps in these intensified nodes of mutual communication with their multisensory and perhaps cosmic dimensions that human interconnectedness is manifested at its most explicit and staged, linking people in profound ways through all their senses.

That a complex mix of arts is typically drawn on in all communicating – not just the heightened rituals – has a further important implication. Each of the elements of the mix is to some degree likely to have its own overtones for the enactors, adding yet further to the multifaceted complexity of the process. The fertile concept of intertextuality reminds us that a given text is not to be understood on its own, but that allusions, metaphors, or connotations which echo other texts carry associations which form part of their meaning; readers thus create their own meanings, at least in part, through the associations they themselves bring to their interpretations. 'Intertextuality' mostly suggests the associations of verbalised texts. But the same principle can be applied to *all* the multimodal dimensions of communicating. Taking account of all the overtones arising in multifarious ways from the participants' personal and cultural experience – visual, auditory, tactile, olfactory and, amidst all this, the engagement with material artefacts – can bring home yet further the multilayered complexities and richness of human communicating.

Such overtones are sometimes taken to be just the contingent experience of individuals or 'merely' a matter of 'context'. But as we saw earlier (Chapter 1), what is 'context' and what 'central' is hardly self-evident. It is also scarcely justified to assume that what counts must only be dimensions of which actors are fully conscious in a verbal, or perhaps visual, sense and that other elements are secondary or 'merely contextual' – elements like the spatial arrangements, the dress, the sonic ambience, the bodily touching of and between the participants, the material objects they are displaying or handling, or the architectural and (perhaps subliminal) olfactory associations. For some or all of the enactors these associational echoes may be integral to the process. So if we try to take account of the whole mix of arts in our communicating, we must also include the 'intertextual' associations that participants bring with them and that emerge during their interaction: the olfactory and tactile as well as the more obvious auditory and (in its many guises) visual overtones, expressed as they are through manifold realisations in particular cultures and on particular occasions. The multidimensional nature of communicating implies equally multidimensional 'overtonalities' (a term I prefer as bypassing the verbocentric imagery of 'intertextuality').

Thus the associations of a particular scent, visual image, sonic ambience, or personal touch can each on occasion play a part, generated both through accepted cultural conventions and – the other side of the same coin – through individuals' personal experiences and interactions. In any given cultural world there will be many potential overtones to evoke; established associations interweaving different media and

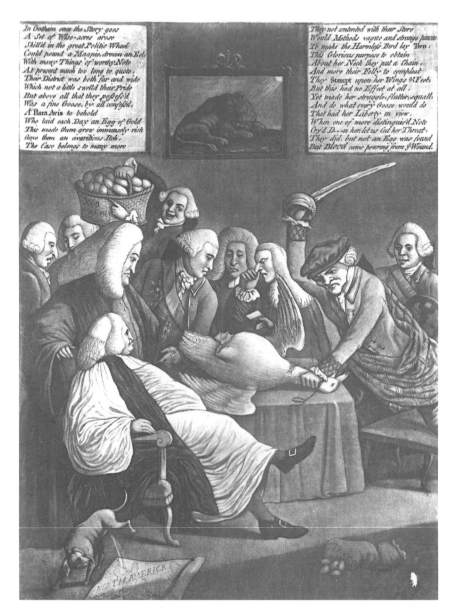

Figure 9.2 'The wise men of Gotham and their goose': the American Revolution pictured
The mix of humorous picture, artfully displayed writing and the auditory resonances of
catchy witty rhyme and popular tale made for effective propaganda for a particular political
position on current events. The 'wise' British officials, some satirically portrayed in person,
are disdainfully killing the goose (the American colonies) that lays the golden eggs – but
would do better to keep the eggs and treat the goose properly (political satire published on
16th February 1776 by W. Humphrey of Gerrard Street, Soho. By permission of the Library
of Congress, LC-US262-1514).

modalities are a regular feature of human communicating. Certain stories may have musical as well as purely verbal dimensions, cleverly evoked in Figure 9.2 for example. Here both sets of (overlapping) overtones may affect people's actual communicative experience, not least the varied sonic associations built up through other heard performances. Particular sounds are sometimes linked to specific (seen) gestures or to touch, making up a patterned set with its own associations. In the north of Ireland particular colours, images, murals, smells, flags, and commemorative rituals permeate each other so that communicating using any of these involves a thick skein of multiplex and emotive associations. Clusters of relationships are recognised in specific social worlds. Among the Native American Apache speech, thought and vision are closely linked and their historical stories sit within the physical landscape which perpetuates the stories and their moral applications (Basso 1996). For some people familiar hymns or the 'Hallelujah' chorus may carry multiple resonances that extend across many modes; for others the sounds, sights and movements of Yoruba drumming may do the same thing, expressed pictorially and poetically as well as acoustically; so too with the performance imageries and displays of Noh drama. The associations of one mode carry over into, and are intensified by, the others.

One communicative medium has often been deemed to translate into – or be representable in terms of – another one, carrying overtones from each other as they do so. One familiar example is the ever-debated association between vocalised sounds and fixed visual marks – speech and writing. Likewise some visual sign languages are equated with vocalised words, drum beats in West African and other 'drum languages' are 'heard' as speech, dance movements in some Indian classical dance forms taught and memorised through verbal terms. In the Japanese *kuchishooga* system words and ideophones are used to designate musical sounds and playing styles (especially timbre), and rhythms in western music sometimes conveyed through visual gesture or spoken counting. Recordings on gramophone, tape, or audio- and video-cassette are taken to reproduce live performances, maps to mirror spatial relations, landscape pictures to convey features of the seen environment, and visual notation (the 'score') to capture complex musical sounds and sequences – all problematic assumptions in one sense, but in another yet another dimension of our intermingled mix of associations.

Many artistic genres quite explicitly link together multiple media, as in dancing, theatre, musical drama, and many more do so implicitly – though not all in the same way, for some strands are sometimes absent or suppressed. Akan proverbs in West Africa are expressed both verbally and in the visual material form of the tiny but beautifully crafted goldweights (Figure 2.3), and among the Quiché Maya there is conscious overlap between textile and verbal text (Tedlock and Tedlock 1986). Iconographic patterns commonly interpenetrate manifold visual media and carry their own associations in each. In Oceania certain visual and material artefacts connote stories: Tongan mats, Maori treasures, and house decorations in the Caroline Islands (Figure 9.3) remind people of stories and sometimes pictorially tell them (Thomas 1995: 165ff). Likewise the Indian *Ramayana* epic, once analysed as a primarily textual form, has rich and variegated multimodal associations and processes in its actual realisations (see Figure 9.4). Without taking account of these intricately interwoven multimodal overtones it would be impossible to fully grasp the complex processes of any communication which involved them.

We saw earlier that there is no wall between the many visual practices of human beings – graphic, pictorial, scriptal, even gestural, interact and blend. So too with other human arts. Gestured movements merge into graphic signs (consider the Walbiri sand stories or the frozen pictorial representations of hand signals), into played sounds, into tactile systems. Pictorial images mingle in with danced, musical and material symbols, and with the movements and touches of human bodies. The Bayeux tapestry uses not only pictures, writing and the vivid and recognisable representation of people's actions but could itself be experienced as if it was a series of publicly enacted dramatic episodes (Maclagan 1945: 7). Through the performance dimensions of Asian literatures voice, dance and image are brought together – the artistry of 'Word, Sound, Image', as Kersenboom entitles her study of the Tamil text (1995). Deeply entrenched symbolisms and iconographies run through many cultures, finding expressions in both formal arts and everyday practices, from the linked multisensory practices of basketry, weaving, singing and narrative of the South American rainforest Yekuana (Guss 1989) to the reiteration of calligraphic symbols in Islamic culture. This unending chain of multiple connections is an essential feature of human communication, not to be dismissed as a mere secondary or contextual matter but adding yet a further set of overtones to the complexity and depth of any act of communicating. As Roy Harris has it, 'the interesting fact is not that *Homo sapiens* has available such a multiplicity of forms of communication, but that these diverse forms are not independent of one another' (1996: 16).

Figure 9.3 Story of the magical breadfruit tree
One of a series of painted wood storyboards from a house in Belau in the Caroline Islands which illustrates a locally well-known myth: the breadfruit tree that gave wonderful catches of fish to a poor old woman after her semi-divine adopted son Terkel dived down and cut a hole in the trunk and branches so the waves washed fish through in front of her house. Jealous neighbours cut down the tree. The whole island is flooded but the old woman is saved on a raft by Terkel (for further details see Thomas 1995: 173–4) (By permission of Bishop Museum, Honolulu. Photo Christine Takata).

Figure 9.4 Ramayana illustration
One of the prolific illustrations associated with the ancient and still vibrant Indian epic
Ramayana, with its multiple and variegated representations in dramatised, danced, puppet,
painted, sculptural, textual, spoken, musical and televised/filmed enactments. In the well-
known episode portrayed here the divine hero Rama miraculously shoots an arrow through
seven trees in the land of the monkeys, and supports his own ally by killing one of the two
brothers fighting for the monkey kingship (© The V & A Picture Library).

Communicating, then, is indeed a multiplex and versatile process, realised in the
many interlinked modes and arts that its enactors deploy and in the differentiated
weight and associations attached to its many interwoven strands by different people
and in different social worlds, occasions and interactions. The basis lies in the precious communicative resources of human beings – their powers of eye and ear and
movement, their embodied interactions in and with the external environment,
their capacities to interconnect along auditory, visual, tactile and perhaps olfactory
modalities, and their ability to create and manipulate objects in the world. This is
not some mechanical procedure for we take our own creative and selective part in
these multiply-'overtoned' processes of communicating, both personally flexible
and made possible by the (more or less) shared and organised human-formulated
resources on which we are jointly drawing.

This indeed may be among the distinctions of the human fashion of communicating: not our 'mental' or 'intellectual' achievements but our practice of
interconnecting at once through many modes, simultaneously, overlappingly, subtly,
differentially. This thickly woven intricate skein with its multiplex and versatile
strands is something very different from the thinner model implied in many
accounts of communicating. The processes are rich ones, dependent on our creative
and purposeful usages of a multiple range of resources. It is through this mix of
arts – patterned yet flexible, multifaceted, fluid, human-recognised, made possible
through the resources of the human body and its works in the world – that we
organise our active human interconnectedness; that – for good or ill – we continue
to create the human world in and through which we interconnect.

10 Through space and time

> We must enlarge our appreciation to encompass the formation taking place before our eyes . . . of a particular biological entity that has never existed on earth – the growth, outside and above the biosphere, of an added planetary layer, an envelope of thinking substance, to which for the sake of convenience and symmetry, I have given the name of the Noosphere.
>
> (Teilhard de Chardin, *The Future of Man*, 1964, p. 131)

This human world of communicating is not just an abstract matter. Human creatures live in space and in time, dimensions which set both the openings and the limits for their interconnectedness. They move to many places, live scattered across the globe, are born, change, mature, die. How is it then that in their individual bodies humans can span these temporal and spatial separations? And are our capacities to do so changing with the technologies of recent centuries? These issues have inevitably crept into the discussion at many points already, but we should now look at them more directly.

Covering distance, spatial and temporal

Much of the writing on communication assumes a model of immediate co-presence by the key participants. Rightly so perhaps, for humans are gregarious animals, and even at the most distant, where individuals are indeed separated by space or time, *some* bodily engagement by some enactor(s) is necessary, in this world at least, for active human interconnection. But, remarkably enough, human interconnectedness is also realised over distance, both through conventions recognised across wide spans of space and time and, overlappingly, through our human-made artefacts and technologies.

The concept of 'distance' needs some unpacking. Its opposite is commonly taken to be where people are in direct somatic contact, physically touching or able to do so. Alternatively it is where they can see each other ('face-to-face' or 'in sight' are common phrases, prioritising vision over touch) or, less often, being within mutual hearing. All these situations are a matter of degree. Once one gets beyond actual physical contact distance becomes relative; so too does 'in sight' or 'in earshot'. Clearly there *is* a difference between close and distant communicating, unmistakable at the extremes, but the boundary is fuzzy and the possible criteria complex. Like our bundle-definition of communication, it is not an all or nothing thing – we are dealing with a spectrum, not clear-cut contrasts.

For this reason it is hard to draw a sharp distinction not only between near and distant communication in general but also between the practices of humans and of other animals. Other species besides humans communicate across temporal or spatial separations. There are nests and other structures that endure over time, deposits of visual or olfactory marks on trees, ground or air, and the complex acoustic repertoire of birds – all means for communicating presence or control even in the physical absence of the originators. Some animals use chemical communication to cover wide distances or linger over time. Others communicate across many miles through vibration while the space-conquering properties of audition, especially through water, are utilised in the sonic communication of whales and other aquatic animals over even longer spans – sometimes hundreds even thousands of miles. Distance communicating is nothing extraordinary in the world of living creatures. Indeed in some respects the human potential for long-distance communicating falls far short of other animals by our terrestrial (not aquatic) habitat and our apparently poorly endowed olfactory and seismic capacities.

Still, humans *do* communicate through space and time, exploiting their resources in organised ways to do so. Like many other living creatures, they move from place to place and, as social animals, both maintain contact with their well-known fellows when separated only temporarily and by short distances, and interact with previously unknown individuals when they move over longer spans. Humans are often travellers and it is not only in recent centuries that some have moved to distant lands, explored previously unfamiliar parts of the globe, or produced maps to share and propagate their visions of the world (those in Figure 5.4 for example). For this, the local practices of small and intimate groups do not wholly suffice; interaction between less familiar people raises the need for more widely recognised patterns of interconnection.

There is also the even more elusive issue of communication across time. This is partly linked to mobility, for communicating can be after one of the participants has left the scene. Many animals employ devices like long-lasting smells, physical marks or deposits, and material structures. Humans utilise comparable strategies, especially in the form of material artefacts, enabling links between people separated by wide stretches of time, even by generations or millennia. Like other animals, humans also live and develop in time. Our habits and our capacities for interaction, as well as the cultural worlds we inhabit, vary throughout our lives. In this context too some joint expectations are needed to enable effective interconnections not just at separate points in time but also through time and even, at a quite mundane level, between co-members of our species at different stages of their life cycles.

Humans draw on a multiplicity of (relatively) shared practices to cope with these spatial and temporal barriers. Particular gestures and facial expressions have been used and recognised among huge numbers of human communicators, for

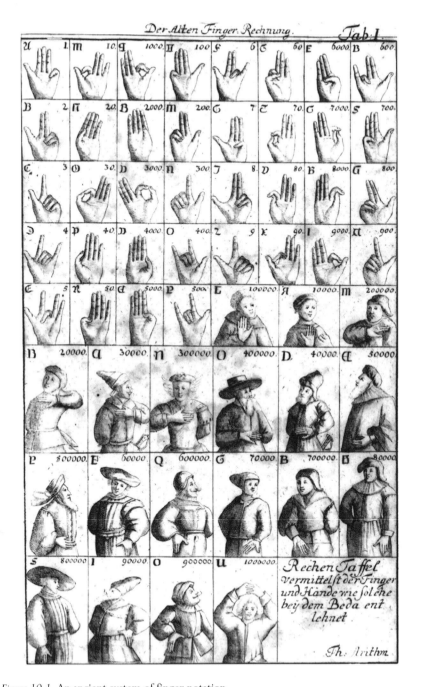

Figure 10.1 An ancient system of finger notation

The Romans had a complex system for representing numbers from 1 to 10,000 on the fingers of both hands which they also used to calculate, apparently using both place-value

example, sometimes organised into highly articulate 'sign languages'. Individuals across extensive geographical regions have shared – more, or less – similar forms of speaking or writing which have in turn persisted to a degree over time; musical and verbal genres, dance traditions and iconographies have been accepted and practised across continents and generations; artefacts like pictures, coins, jewels or books, often with multiple evocative overtones, have circulated over far areas or endured through generations; styles of architectural display are established over many areas of the globe and monuments last as tactile and visible objects through many centuries.

The span of such patterned conventions is relative, sometimes widely current, sometimes confined to small numbers of people and with little continuity over time. Nor are they in absolute terms wholly distinct from the ways in which individual animals (human or other) who are hitherto unknown to each other nevertheless seem to have some degree (more, or less) of mutual recognition as members of the same species.[1] Even long-enduring and widespread systems have fluidities and variabilities as well as continuities. Local ways of speaking, or specific processes of gesturing or greeting among small groups, even individuals, merge into more general patterns. And where the skills and practices of these (relatively) established conventions are indeed passed on over time, then this is no automatic transmission but possible only through the activated and emergent engagements of their human participants at particular times and places. People are notably separated as well as connected, furthermore, by the disparate conventions of different places or times, even by the smaller diversities of practice over small-scale temporal or spatial divisions.

So our shared communicative practices can be fluid, diverse and in a sense fragile. But given the spread of the human species over area and time, the surprise must be not the differences but that there are indeed certain shared patterns which, if only up to a point, yet facilitate interconnection among human beings over both small and (sometimes) immense spans of space and time. The long-lasting finger-counting system of Figure 10.1 is only one example of many – though an impressive one – for there are extensive shared human conventions, drawing on the many modalities discussed in earlier chapters, the material artefacts in which they are often realised, and the multiple associations with which human beings exploit them in their interconnecting. To an extent they allow us to transcend the limitations of our separate ephemeral bodies, enabling in some real sense the active bridging of spatial or temporal separation.

---

position and the concept of zero (a relaxed finger position). The system continued as part of the classical inheritance of western Europe and was used extensively in mediaeval times, a practical commercial tool between peoples speaking many different languages. The English monk Bede gave a verbal description in the eighth century, reproduced in illustrated format in Jacob Leupold's mathematical compendium nearly one thousand years later (see Menninger 1969: 201ff for a fuller account) (from Jacob Leupold, *Theatrum Arithmetico-Geometricum*, 1727, Tab. 1. By permission of the British Library, shelfmark HS 74/67).

Humans also actively extend their basic resources for distance communication through the creation of external artefacts and technologies, assisting us to inter-connect even when divided by physical location or the gap of time ('external', of course, again only a relative term). In one sense, *all* communicating, near or distant, involves the corporeal presence of at least some enactors, but in another, all artefacts contain something of ourselves, emergent as we interconnect with both them and each other. We have distinctive human-made tools which help us tussle with the divides of time and of space.

For the smaller temporal or spatial separations humans have developed ingenious ways of extending their bodily capacities (distance, remember, is relative). We raise our voices to carry effectively, make our gestures large and slow to be detectable further away, and capitalise on the distance-covering properties of audi-tion in specific environments by whistled or yodelled signals across valleys or ocean expanses. Auditory memories are trained and cultivated in a variety of ways – in some traditions more strikingly than others – so as to retain and transmit human interconnections over time. Physical objects are created or adapted to cover greater distances: projecting the human voice through loudhailers or amplifiers, setting speakers on vantage points to be better seen and heard; or utilising glasses and tele-scopes to enhance eyesight; ropes, canes or weapons to extend tactile contact; or vibrating and percussive instruments to carry sound further. All these contrivances extend the scope of human interaction, even if the distances are still relatively small and the problem of time less surmountable than that of space.

And then there are the artefacts and technologies decisively outside our bodies. The production and use of 'extrinsic' objects are by no means unknown among other animals; but among humans seem to be developed to an extraordinarily high degree. Many examples have featured in previous chapters, evident especially in the discussions of audition and of vision. Humans have long harnessed fire and reflected light to be visible across many miles, drawn on the assistance of birds, and created artefacts portable across space or enduring over time – woven, written, pictorial, shaped, forged, built. Manifold media have been utilised to link people across the far-flung cultural domains and empires of the past and present. Some highly sys-tematic forms have been developed too, such as semaphore, Native American smoke signals and flag-based systems at sea. Over even greater distances humans have exploited the visual properties of fire and heliographs. In England relays of fire beacons reported the movements of the Spanish Armada in Queen Elizabeth I's reign. Longer still was the chain of towers along the North African coast at the end of the first millennium, from Ceuta in the west to Alexandria in the east, with mes-sages taking three to four hours between Tripoli to Alexandria or a night to run the whole course (Solymar 1999: 18). The 'mechanical telegraph' for military signals in late eighteenth-century France used the same relay principle. Coded messages were signalled by mechanical arms, read through telescopes, then transmitted on to the next tower; the system covered 5000 km of line and 534 stations by the early

Figure 10.2 Indian carpet
Amritsar carpet, India, about 1870. Just one of the many Middle-Eastern and Asian carpets which have helped to spread particular decorative and, for some people, religious visions and evocations so widely through the world (Courtesy of the Atlantic Bay Gallery, London).

nineteenth century (Solymar 1999: 20ff, 302–3). Similar systems were installed elsewhere in Europe and America before succumbing to competition from the faster electrical telegraph and the developing technologies of what Mattelart (2000) calls the 'networking of the world' over the last two centuries.

In this, the visual channel has taken a leading role, from 'humble', beautiful artefacts (Figure 10.2) to the great figures of the Greek Parthenon. For if vision in itself cannot take human interconnectedness through far distances, it is a different matter when external and transportable visible objects are used. As we saw in Chapters 4 and 5 humans make effective use of this channel and have done so for millennia. Pictures, weapons, writing, clothes, flags, carpets – all have on occasion served to connect human beings both in day-to-day close interactions and, at times, over even the furthest stretches of space. These visible devices also have that other important property of durability (more, or less) through time. This vastly extends our powers of distance communicating, taking it not just across space but also time, sometimes immensely long tracts of time. We are well acquainted with this use of, for example, carvings, buildings, graphics, the images of film and television, and the material forms of writing. We can interact both nearby and at a distance through material tokens which link us to others and share in their actions and experiences. Interconnection becomes possible even between enactors far removed in time, the more so because of the subtle overtones – the clusters of associated evocations – with which such artefacts are often in practice connected.

Externalised acoustic communication across time and space seems to be less established than for vision. But among the most striking developments of the last couple of centuries are the expanding technologies for far-reaching auditory communication through telephones, radio and television. By now there are also materialised ways both to transport sounds and, equally important, to lengthen their life through mechanical and electronic audio-recording. Other modalities have been drawn on as well, if in a limited way. Scents have long been produced, stored and used in areas far from their original provenance. The tactile channel, too, is sometimes exploited well beyond the direct contact of bodies at a single place or moment, notably in tactile systems like the braille alphabet, usable in communicating over both space and time.

Some of these material resources and our ways of using them are organised into standardised and explicit systems, sometimes widely current over space and time. There are graphic or pictorial designs, film conventions, computer displays, braille and other tactile systems, and the many versions of visible writing. Some utilise complex permutations and combinations of units, as in forms of visible and tangible writing or the relatively substitutable gestures of some 'sign languages', articulated and applied quite explicitly as a common currency among people who are otherwise widely separated. None, of course, makes up an automatic and one-to-one mechanism for 'recording the world', so to speak (as perhaps implied by the term 'code' which is often used to describe them). Various notations and recording devices have been mentioned or illustrated earlier that have endeavoured to capture, for example, sounds, places or movements (for instance Figures 3.4, 5.4, 5.8); all represent just one 'fix' on the world – useful indeed on occasion for certain purposes and dimensions but inevitably partial. It is the same for pictures and photographs, or the Noh play performance script in Figure 10.3. This applies to writing too. At one point this was assumed (especially in its alphabetic form) to be the perfect transparent form for directly capturing reality. And it is true that the various writing systems have made up a vast and fertile range of communicative forms with great potential to interconnect over space and time. But they are nothing inevitable and even the most long-lasting are rooted in human artifice rather than predestined outcome. The same must apply to the many acoustic, tactile or visual systems that have no doubt been developed in the past, just as others will be in the future. None provide 'complete' coverage nor, probably, can any achieve universal or permanent currency; as communicative devices they are realised only in the specificities of their actual human usages. Despite the qualifications, however, these (relatively) standardised and codified systems do indeed provide hugely impressive and readily manipulable tools for human communicating. The explicit systems, together with all the other less articulated conventions of human interaction and the notable human-made external artefacts outside their own bodies, provide remarkable vehicles by which human beings interconnect with others both nearby and at a distance.

Like other forms of communicating, interconnection at a distance draws on a mix of arts. It is true that this is sometimes less prominent than with more immediate interaction – communicating after all is a relative matter. Some situations limit or preclude multimodal expression. Telephoning is one example: though visible gesture and facial expressions do play some part in quite complex ways, the emphasis is certainly centred on audition. But distance does not always mean single-channel contact. Sound recordings are often implicitly linked to visual and perhaps olfactory experiences too, and are now commonly supported by visual packaging and print. As we saw in the last chapter, writing systems which on the surface may seem purely visual are often multidimensional when considered within the actual process of communicating. And even when vision is, as so often, the dominant channel over distance, in actual practice it is not always the only one in play nor – an important point – without its associated multiple overtonalities.

The same applies to the multiple modes of communicating through which human contacts are realised and shared over time. Memory – 'the time dimension of culture' as Hannerz has it (1992: 147) – is often now analysed not as some entity in the mind or as necessarily confined to the cognitive or verbalisable. Rather (like the view of communication here), it is envisaged as a creative and culturally shaped human process, potentially multisensory and open to many human modalities including the use of material objects.[2] Unsurprisingly, the modes vary among different groups and historical periods as well as in different situations. Frances Yates (1966) describes the trained 'art of memory', developed by the Greeks and continuing in earlier centuries of European history, which relied centrally on visual images and places. The fixed visible marks of writing have played a large part in recent times – though again, some would see memory as still essentially 'a language of images' (Annette Kuhn in Radstone 2000: 188). Elsewhere (but in Europe, too) auditory memory has been strongly developed, as in the amazing memories of early Irish bards and of South

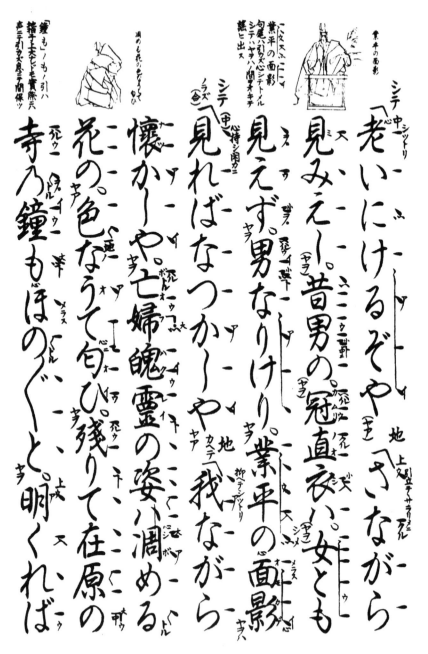

Figure 10.3 Performance script for the Japanese Noh play *Izutsu*

Elements of performance – both auditory and kinesic – are presented and encapsulated in fixed visual format. The page is from an 'utaibon', a libretto text printed in 1977 by the Kanze School of Noh with musical notation for voice (running down alongside the text) and illustrations for movement, designed for amateurs or budding professionals. Learning to

Pacific dwellers like the Maori experts with their trained capacity to memorise huge corpora of oral poetry. In less systematic ways we are also probably all familiar with the acoustic resonances of our everyday recall and of 'learning by rote'. And perhaps we would even be wrong to dismiss the experiential dimensions in multimodal rituals where through sound and scent, and perhaps other modalities too, people are carried beyond the here and now into other space and time.

As eloquently illustrated in recent collections (such as Forty and Küchler 1999, Kwint *et al.* 1999) 'material memories' are important, too: memorial representation through objects. Over many millennia a multitude of material forms have been used to carry visible and tangible records and evocations across the ages. We have contact with the pictures, carpets, carvings or writings not just from far-off places but also from people long dead. Places, scenes and the visible and tactile material objects around us play a part in materialising our memories and carrying continuities and evocations of the past and of our own place within this larger temporal order. There are some long-lasting and spectacular forms through which such continuities are mediated, like the laughing Buddha statues, great architectural monuments or – another example of the 'picture book' of the Christian church – the wonderful narrative window of St William's deeds in York Minster (Figure 10.4). But it is not just a case of specialised artistic genres. Rapoport describes the 'mnemonics' of the built environment (1990), while for agricultural families in northern England the material layout of farms, cottages and village streets are a continual reminder of their ancestry (Christensen *et al.* 2001: 76), and spoken stories and ritual actions are associated with abiding features of the landscape. Bodily enactments enter in too, for the connections with the past are not seldom formulated and symbolised through embodied ritual performances. As Connerton points out, performative memory is one dimension of 'how societies remember' (1989).

People interconnect across time through the sharing, to a degree, of ideas, aesthetic experiences and communicative genres across the ages. There are many inherited continuities. This is an elusive process, true, but nevertheless a real part of human experience. Here the enactors include both those who in some senses created the

---

perform Noh plays was from the sixteenth century a popular hobby and came to be an important element of samurai education; 'reading' a Noh play has until very recently meant learning to chant it as a performance. *Izutsu*, composed by Zeami in the fifteenth century, is from an episode in the ninth-century 'Tales of Ise' (like most Noh plays, the story comes from a well-known tale). It portrays an elegant woman's passion for the famous poet/lover Narihira. As children they played around a well curb (*izutsu*) and later became husband and wife. She continues her love for him even long after their deaths and at the play's climax dons his formal robes while dancing and looks into the water's reflection and sees his face. Her spirit is unable to give up her love and gain rebirth in nirvana. The illustration at top right shows her looking into the well (Courtesy Hinoki Publishing Company, Tokyo, and (also for caption) C. Andrew Gerstle).

forms in the first place (if it is ever totally accurate to speak of 'the' form or the 'first place' . . .), and those others who have participated over time, developing partially shared and/or disputed understandings and continuities of experience. Bahktin speaks of literary and spoken genres (though I would not confine it just to those), which

> throughout the centuries of their life accumulate forms of seeing and interpreting particular aspects of the world. . . . A work of literature . . . is revealed primarily in the differentiated unity of the culture of the epoch in which it was created, but it cannot be closed off in this epoch: its fullness is revealed only in *great time*.
> (Bakhtin 1986: 5)

Figure 10.4 From the St William window, York Minster
In 1415 John Thornton designed a stained glass window in York Minster with one hundred panels recounting the life, times and miracles of St William, the patron saint of York; his first miracle was to save hundreds of people from the river Ouse after a wooden bridge collapsed in 1154. Now being restored, it has for centuries visually displayed the story of a Christian saint's deeds. Interpreted somewhat variously no doubt over the ages and by different individuals, it still carries evocative pictorial representations, imbued with both Christian and everyday imagery, even to many modern viewers (Photograph © Andrew Crowley).

Likewise an art form, like that summed up as the *Ramayana*, can be used to inter-link people through many centuries, not by the mechanical reception of unchanging text but through multifarious different creative enactments and experiences by living people in a multiplicity of media. So too with the reading even of more fixed and entextualised forms – not passive reception but, again, active experiencing, co-constructing, and, no doubt, interacting with yet other agents during the process (and if not something like this, then it would fall beyond the edge of even that wide and rel-ative spectrum that I include as 'communicating'). People do make active uses of multiple media for interconnecting over distant time as well as nearby. They work through visual artefacts (not least the visible written, graphic and pictorial systems), through recorded sounds, material memories and somatic performances. All these can again evoke multiple overtones as they connect human creatures across time as well as space, bringing them into that 'great time', in Bakhtin's poignant image, and link-ing human beings over centuries and millennia from the far past to the further reaches of the future. Interconnecting across distance may, like all communicating, be a com-plex and elusive affair; but it is a regular feature of human living.

What now?

The history of human communicating, far and near, is still often presented as a one-way path leading humankind up and away from animals and progressively separating the modern from the uncivilised, the literate from the oral, the higher cognitive abilities from lowlier sensual experiences. Parallel narratives recount tales of salva-tion (or, alternatively, damnation) through the imminent electronic 'revolution', those 'information and communication technologies' destined to bring new global interconnections and sweep away the older cultures of the book. And then there is the long-told darker side, telling of the costs as humankind loses its 'older' modes of face-to-face and oral interaction.

These great stories still stir us. But we are rightly more cautious nowadays about their implicit paradigms of progress and their ethnocentric and often ill-informed evaluations. The human strategies for communicating are too variegated to be ranked on hierarchical and chronological ladders. Over the ages human beings have tried manifold strategies to initiate and maintain their interconnect-edness, overlapping as well as relatively distinct, and (depending on your viewpoint) with deplorable as well as laudable consequences. Even when appar-ently large changes have affected particular groups and usages or been trumpeted by particular parties with their own interests – the spread of western moveable print for example or of telegraphy – in actual practice many other communicative modes continued to be drawn on concurrently by multiple actors in the multifar-ious diversities that make up the world of human communicating. Unidimensional swathes through the multiplex processes of human interconnecting are inevitably over-simplified.

Nevertheless there *are* changes which our justified suspicion of unilinear narratives of human history should not make us ignore. It is illuminating to reflect on recent developments and on the mix of resources now available to humans. The vast amount of commentary on current technologies, much (not all) couched in generalised and often speculative terms, is too large to treat here.[3] Instead let me pick out a few points related to these same issues of interconnecting across spatial and temporal barriers.

First, audition has been significantly extended by recent technologies for capturing sound in recorded form and transmitting it over distance. Since the nineteenth century, the space-conquering potential of audition has been progressively enlarged by telephonic, radio and most recently computer technologies. Even more strikingly, the property usually missing in acoustic communicating – endurance over time – has been to an extent achieved through gramophone records, tapes and other audio-recording devices. Like other visible and tangible artefacts, these can be physically carried in material and relatively permanent form from place to place (as well as transmitted over the air), and retained over time. Furthermore the combination of both spatial spread and recordability means that humans can now engage in long-distance *auditory* communicating, both more or less instantaneously and across a period of time. There are opportunities, that is, for both synchronous (same-time) communication, through live broadcast transmissions and fixed or mobile telephones, and for the storing of sound for later retrieval (asynchronously), as in 'voice mail' and other audio-recorded forms. All this opens new resources for long-distance interconnection unavailable in the past.

Second, rapid communication over space has been extended over the last centuries. There have been telegraph systems (both semaphore and electric), telegrams, fax, emails, and a variety of computer-mediated interactions both synchronous and asynchronous. The increasing means of *rapid* travel across wide distances has meant that individuals, families and other groups directly known to each, have endeavoured to keep in frequent and direct touch despite their separation – small wonder perhaps that it is during much the same period that humans have developed fast, even instantaneous, modes of distant contact. The speed with which even the furthest distances can now in principle be overcome is striking indeed.

Third, electronic technologies offer new ways for interweaving different forms of communication. Though much computerised material is still primarily visual and in printed (largely alphabetic) format, pictorial, non-linear and audio forms are increasingly intermingling with this. The visual displays of networked computers offer openings to expand communication through iconic (or semasiographic) formats with the potential to transcend language divisions. They can also capitalise on the pictorial and diagrammatic representation of, for example, juxtaposition and contrast, conveying this with an immediacy and economy often lacking in print or speech. Computer technologies may perhaps also lead to greater opportunities for multisensory communication at a distance. Up to a point this is already happening through the 'multimedia' (i.e. audio-visual) displays in both networked and CD-ROM formulations, but it may be that the technological potential of computers will be exploited for distance communicating in channels not as yet much systematised by humans – tactile and olfactory.

Computer technologies have implications for writing, that long-established if diverse visual medium for communication over time and space. The relatively fixed or 'permanent' quality often taken as its unquestioned characteristic, even part of writing's definition, is being broken up by the fluidity of electronic text. One much-acclaimed result is the new flexibility this offers readers, no longer constrained by one-way linear arrangements of fixed text but able to proceed through multiply branching paths selected by each reader individually. This is obviously a significant development. Its novelty has been somewhat exaggerated, however. In the past, too, readers have at times exploited the opportunity for scanning and skipping, and non-linear, multiple ways of reading have long been the norm for written works like encyclopaedias and dictionaries. There have been many formats for presenting, reading and illustrating texts besides the straight one-line presentation of written words. In any case, texts closely linked to performance traditions have probably always had more versatility. Kersenboom notes the 'dynamic nature' of the Tamil text, the basis for performance, where (for example) three lines noted down in a manuscript

> serve as seeds for the organic growth of the stem, branches and foliage of a tree. The text develops branches, sub-branches and rich foliage that fans out like a peacock's tale, displaying the splendour of its imagery.
>
> (Kersenboom 1995: 31)

Following on from this, it could be argued than an even more important quality is that computer text, not being fixed, can similarly be changed, manipulated and realised in multiple transformations. It takes on something of the transient and performative quality that has in the past more often been associated with oral formulations, with far-reaching implications, perhaps, for current relationships between spoken and written forms.[4]

All these trends have probably been intensified through the development of the internet and world wide web. This has attracted great attention from commentators. Some regard the internet as the central communication symbol of our time, even as encapsulating more or less all human knowledge. Thus if it can be suggested, following Marie-Laure Ryan, that

> every period has its monument to a totalizing vision: in the Middle Ages it was the Cathedral, complex architecture whose windows and sculptures encompassed all of space and all of history; in the Enlightenment it was the Encyclopedia, immense compendium of knowledge
>
> (Ryan 1999: 14)

then in the early twenty-first century might it be the apparently unending prolifer-ation of databases of the world wide web? At any rate this computerised resource enables (in principle) the rapid access by participants from just about all over the human world to a colossal amount of material from many sources. It gives people the potential to interact with others, whether near or afar. They can arrange for commercial, political and other transactions which interconnect with other people's actions, organise direct contact between named individuals today and/or have experience of their productions both in the present and, through web versions of books, manuscripts or works of art, from the past.

Computer technologies, then, have markedly widened human resources for rapid, sometimes near-instantaneous, contact over far distances. They may not always be fully exploited to this end, true, but in principle offer truly brilliant strategies for interconnecting human beings separated by even the furthest of spa-tial distances, on land, in air, in space, and on or under the sea.

On the temporal front they are less impressive. Certainly they can be useful over relatively small timescales, enabling the storage of both audio and video records and their usage at different points of time. Visual records from long ago can be put on the web for wider distribution. But for interaction through longer temporal spans or the persistence of enduring records over many years, let alone generations or centuries, electronic communication has serious limitations. Admittedly all human arts and artefacts are liable to go out of usage, and most are subject to the ravages of decay, accident, even deliberate destruction. Textiles have perished, pictures been painted over, libraries – even the greatest – been burned. Even long-lasting forms like architectural monuments, cuneiform tablets or, it must be said, printed books do not last for ever. But computerised records have additional vulnerabilities. These partly lie in the fluidity of electronic text: once deleted or changed the 'original' version may be gone for ever. Equally important is the ephemerality of hardware and software systems. Records from even a few decades back sometimes cannot be deciphered easily, if at all, because expertise and equipment in 'obsolete' technologies have gone. And then there is the well-known susceptibility of com-puter records to being attacked. The wiping of the whole web system by virus or hacker is an engaging topic for science fiction and for horrified (or gloating) spec-ulation. But the loss or corruption of computer data is regularly reported, sometimes on a large scale, occurrences that can only reinforce the impression of the likely fragility of electronic systems for communication over lengthy periods of time. Computer technologies, in short, provide a wonderful resource for commu-nication over space, but over time may prove much more limited.

The overall significance of these developments is controversial. They have great potential for human modes of communicating both today and in the future. Human technologies for rapid contact across great spatial spans, and (if to a lesser extent) over time, have without doubt widened human resources, giving us yet more ways to push at the limits of our human-endowed capacities. More important still, it seems, are the overlapping technologies for rendering sound more lasting, enabling us to partly bypass one long-standing limitation of audition as a communicative mode. This development, even more than other changes, might be the real break-through.

But it would be equally true to say that in a wider perspective such technologies add only marginally to the mix of communicative arts already developed by human beings and in principle available to them. Rhetoric about the 'electronic revolution', 'the information age', or some great move to 'virtual reality' (often in high-flown, even mystical terms) overlooks the immensely rich, variegated and changing human take-up of communicative resources already developed and flourishing through the ages. Now as in the past technological changes can be presented as more uniform and all-embracing than they ever were or are in practice. Moveable type did not supplant speech, pictures, music and gestures; telephones may have affected the specific uses of written communication but did not destroy it; television or computers will not do away with books. It is also worth highlighting the 'in principle' phrase much used above. Certain resources may indeed be 'available', whether in the form of human capacities, specific artefacts, technologies or social practices – but that is far from saying they are equally accessible to all, used (or indeed desired) by everyone, widespread among all groupings or individuals in particular social contexts, or suitable for all human purposes. As with all resources, they are only relevant in the real-world processes of human interconnection insofar as they are actively deployed by human practitioners.

The basic characteristics of human communication are likely to persist despite passing enthusiasms for whatever 'new revolution' is fashionable among particular groups or specific interests. Humans will continue their many-sided mix of arts in both nearby communication and interconnections across space and time. The age-old human practice of travelling, and thus of direct embodied interaction with people who are at other times far away, will not disappear (whatever our 'virtual' resources); nor will those other long-used vehicles for distance communication in the form of material objects, with all their varying associations. People will go on finding means of mediating their interconnections with others over long spans of time, including across the generations of those long passed away, through human-made material resources extrinsic to the individual human body. There is no reason to believe they will cease to engage in multiplex, differential and multiply-used interactions both within and alongside new developments.

The senses – again: earthly and heavenly

Human experience, we would surely now agree across a range of humanistic and social disciplines, is a matter not just of beautiful literature, although that has been a feature of human culture since – I almost said since the world began – certainly since the human world began. It is eminently mind *and* body and all the senses that we humans have been blessed with. Too often overlooked even by anthropologists, our human communication and expression are fundamentally multisensory. It is well expressed in Hieronymus Bosch's *The Garden of Earthly Delights* (see Figure 10.5) which in its way sums up the resources that humans so wonderfully draw on in their communicating – before that inspired picture this book is scarcely necessary.

But in our human settings words must strive to convey this, so let me use language to explain, a little, of how, even in non-bodily communication the senses can still – however counter-intuitively – be as fully in play as in 'normal' communicating.

First, it takes place through verbalised language. This brings up some interesting points. Out-of-the-body – 'psychic' – communicating proved to be in very different style, vocabulary and grammar from my 'normal' (academic) writing. In the end, unintentionally and at first unnoticed, much turned out, like so many African and Native American narratives, to be mangled in their transcription (Hymes 1996), but really a species of poetry. Given the traditions in which I grew up and the Bible- and Bunyan-rich Quaker school I attended, the language, cadences and images of my own communicating, both earthly and heavenly, could not avoid being biblical, although often in ways I was not aware of when I was writing them down – sometimes, as it felt, from dictation. Like the dream-narrator of Chapter 8, I too have worked – hard – at trying to put dreams into the narrative language in which I grew up, influenced, I now see, by my experience of African narrative forms, especially the Sierra Leonean Limba and their wonderful story-teller Karanke Dema (Finnegan 1967, 1970, 2007, 2012): their verbal stylistics lack for the most part what we might term prepositions, conjunctions and adverbs but there are other, perhaps richer, resources in their place, together with musical cadences and interpolated songs, personalities (twins, including three twins, figured often) and characterisation, dramatic moves, everyday style and setting, above all perhaps the ubiquity of repetitions – repetitions both within and between words.

This has made me more aware of the creativity of language, both spoken and written. I used to picture language use as drawing out from a tangle of wired words in the brain, already there, perhaps even in a Chomskian way (as in Chomsky 2012). My present image is more of an empty sphere and around the dark edges the words – and chunks of words – and sounds of words and phrases lurking for me to draw them out into the light. And share with others. Beyond that the great sphere of words and stars and creations lies waiting; waiting for the curtain to be drawn back, the darkness to be lifted to human communicating.

One remarkable point worth noting is that during ethereal 'conversations' the resemblance to earthly turn-taking is striking. While the other is speaking I cannot utter – even in my mind (although at a deeper level I know, and perhaps subliminally convey – what I want to say). I do, however, find myself silently nodding and smiling automatically to show I am attending. Then it is my turn, speaking to a silent but receptive auditor (audition, I realise, is the main sense here (silent as it is), although, as in any conversation, vision and kinesics come in too).

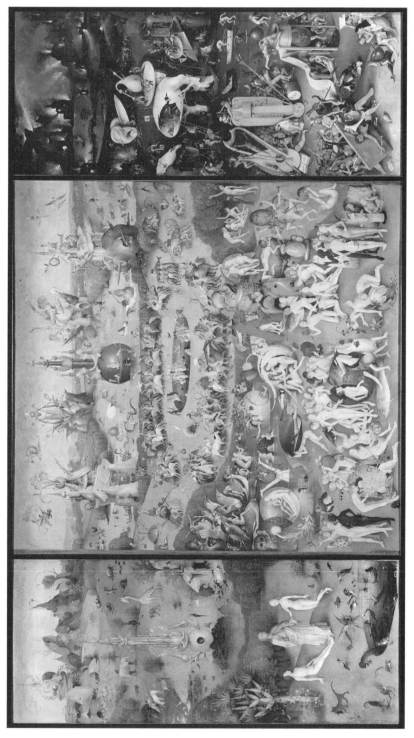

Figure 10.5 A wonderful vision encompassing our human resources for communication, our lovely multisensory world Hieronymus Bosch, *The Garden of Earthly Delights (El jardín de las Delicias)*. © Madrid, Museo Nacional del Prado.

And then music. Clearly of central importance in the ether – and in heaven – it also plays a crucial part in dreaming and creation: In my own case – parallel to that of many others – I find myself drawing on the culture in which I have been fortunate to grow up, Irish, English and European alike, with a touch of African music too.

To illustrate with just one example: one day in autumn, away from home, I drifted up from deep sleep with the tune and sung words of *Deo gratias* ringing in my head. Unwinding it sceptically to its start I found it was the last line of a fifteenth-century carol, one I knew well but had not thought about since the previous Christmas. It was 'Adam lay ybounden' with its stunning – heretical? – conclusion: 'Blessed by the day / that apple taken bin'. At first it seemed irrelevant, a distraction. But sleeping and waking through that night I saw that it was a crucial part of a story that before had seemed, although completed, so thin and uninteresting.

I was puzzled, for surely music comes before words in human experience? I had always believed so. But I should not have been surprised by the music fighting to come up to my consciousness. For if music is somehow more fundamental than verbal language is it surprising we have to dig deeper and come to it later?

The stories and dreams – and poems too – were, like the performed art forms I had studied before and indeed all human experience, notably multidimensional, only fully realised in their sounds and sights and movements – landscape, sea and sky; birds both strong and weak, trees and their tracery of branches; wild flowers, streams and still waters. And the glowing light of pearl catching pearl, whirling timeless skies and great oceans, the pain of birth, separation and sacrifice. Water was rippling sound, too – somehow auditory as well as formed in dazzling rainbow colours, symbol of the delights, less often of the pains, of love, frozen ice of the shock of lover's tears withdrawn: a painful theme.

In dreaming and in many death experiences, vision seems to be the main channel, just as we have seen it is dominant in much human experience: light, colour, striking heavenly figures, dazzlement mixed with calmness. But there is also travel – motion (human indeed) – and, resonant moreover, audition, with the singing of angels and the spoken messages of reassurance. Scent and touch? Less often mentioned (as indeed less, however unconsciously powerful in both presence and remembrance, in our human experience) but perhaps implicit in heaven's felt and fragrant atmosphere, reminiscent of incense, loving touch and the perfume of trance and fragrant leaves in many parts of the world, the background to dream and inspiration. But the abiding themes, as I say, seem, as in human communicating, to be visual, verbal and – most potent of all – musical, working always together.

Humans as communicators

At the most mundane as well as the most high-flown levels, then, human creatures have developed ways to exploit and extend their bodily capacities, among them the amazing practices by which they can interconnect through vast tracts of space and over many generations. Some practices have small temporal or geographic currency or relatively narrow scope. Others, more widely recognised, standardised or codified, have the potential to relate to a broad range of human experience and to help formulate people's interaction over great areas. And all are intertwined in complex and multifaceted ways both with each other and with the multisensory experiences, materialities and overtonalities of the enactors who actually use them at given times and places.

Are humans distinctive in developing and exploiting this multiple range of resources? Given our relative lack of knowledge, it behoves us to be cautious about sweeping comparisons with other animals; different species have different resources and challenges and it is scarcely acceptable to rank them in any simple, inevitably humano-centric, hierarchy. Nonetheless it is fair to say that certain characteristics of human communicating do indeed seem unparalleled – not only their multiply overlapping communicative modes but their ability to span far space and time through their material creations.

It is worth recalling the particular resources of the human species sketched out in Chapter 2 (pp. 52ff): among them, the human audio-visual capacities, extensively developed in an astonishing variety of communicative forms; the respiratory-vocal tract with all its implications for vocal communication; relatively large size; and bipedal locomotion freeing our hands not just for a series of subtle gesturing systems but also for the creation and manipulation of objects – our hands are crucial communicative tools indeed, too often underestimated in our respect for mentalist models. We lack the distance-communicating abilities of some other animals, true, in particular olfactory and vibrational resources and avian flight. But we have other skills to compensate, especially our arts and artefacts for crossing space and time. It is a striking array of resources, both in their combination and in the effective ways that humans exploit them.

Two further features are also almost certainly in play: our human propensity to live in social groups and our relative longevity.[5] As social animals, humans like to remain in contact (not that this is always harmonious or equitable . . .) and the shared social processes that we engage in depend on – consist in – a high degree of mutual communication; our interconnectedness is an inescapable fact of our humanity. We live, often, in dense settlements, needing effective communication for spacing ourselves at close quarters. But we also constantly exploit our capacities for mobility, using our bodies for signalling in a multitude of ways, actively constructing external media and technologies usable for keeping contact, and moving from place to place. The human species is widely distributed over the globe and has for long created networks of communication to suit this, possibly, as suggested above, with a particular surge in this direction over recent centuries. Humans, in short, are a gregarious, dense but also scattered species who like and need to keep in regulated contact and to work and express themselves jointly with others. They have actively developed numerous ways through which they can do so, interconnecting with others both now and in the past and future.

The generally long lives of human beings facilitate lengthy processes of learning and of manipulating and shaping the world around them. At the same time they make possible the joint involvements in the creation and usages of cultural and material artefacts for handing on – mostly – to those who follow. So perhaps our longevity, combined with our other attributes of sociality, energy and the active production of extrinsic material resources, is also related to the striking continuities as well as the changes and diversities in human life. Human beings interactively hand on their conventions, their practices and their evocative material artefacts over the generations: linguistic patterns, kinesic conventions, written and pictorial marks, literary and performance genres, architectural monuments, built edifices, conventions for shared experiences, and our multiply decorated *oikoumene* (to use the beautiful Greek word for the inhabited world). There are changes, certainly, and the essential condition for human interaction also lies in the individual creativities and unique experiences through which their communicating is in practice enacted – there is something to be said for the view that we do not step twice in the same river. But the continuities are striking too, and the diverse yet overlapping cultural products created by human beings are, to one degree or another, spread between different localities and handed on between different generations.

It is a characteristic and striking human capacity both to create new resources and flexible ways of using them *and* to share them with others. Think of the multifarious communicative modes developed by human action – the subtle and diverse gestural systems, the manifold sign languages, the verbalised forms of vocal speech, tactile systems like braille, visible writing of many kinds, pictorial and graphic systems, cartographic techniques, mood-altering processes through olfaction . . . the existence of all these systems and practices is actually something extraordinary. So long as we could just think of them as the result of predestined evolution blindly working its way up, or of traits laid down in our prehistoric brains, there was really no challenge to consider the human means by which they were created. But when one recalls our manifold communicative practices and, amidst them, standardised arts like the diverse forms of writing, sign languages, or iconographic, musical and choreographic systems, we might well wonder how these and other systems really got created and, more or less, kept going. It is a staggering question, worth raising even if we cannot tell the answer.

Speculation can too easily turn into hopeful myth. But if we can surmise a little from the recent evidence, deliberate human input certainly had much to do with it. Some systems, we know, got going by organised human inventiveness. There are the tactile systems for the blind, the deaf signing languages, the new scripts invented over recent centuries in Africa, Asia or Native America, or the many writing systems – reputedly and perhaps truly – developed by earlier saints, rulers or reformers (see above p. 165; Gaur 1992: 130ff). In such cases we sometimes know names and can appreciate the human innovating and establishing that created them. There is no reason why other systems should not have been due, at least in part, to similar elements of deliberate invention by individuals or small groups in the past: our own ignorance and our 'dimwit model' of earlier humanity should not tempt us to underestimate the potential for human inventiveness in eras less familiar to ourselves.

Human systems are also developed with the flow, so to speak, created over time by innumerable small actions in the emergent processes of human interconnecting. There are constant adaptations of existing practices, mergings, new twists on what is already practised – a trend made the more viable by the many continuities between different communicative forms noted earlier. One flows into another: pictorial, graphic, musical, danced, voiced, gestured, felt. Some element of this no doubt played a part even in the more purposively designed innovations. To say this is not to minimise the human input involved – in fact the opposite. Some practices may have been shaped slowly (more, or less), but their organised patternings are no less the result of human creativity in both their incremental development and, in some cases, their successful establishment in widely current systems.

Many other systems will, presumably, be created in similar ways in the future – we have certainly not reached the end of human innovation. But neither new systems nor those already developed come automatically: only as a result of human action. Our present communicative modes are in fact stunning, their constraints as well as their creativities. They are all the more amazing when we ask, as we have just done, about the human actions through many eras in the past which must underlie so many of them, and the consolidation of communicative conventions brought about through these actions – not forgetting those other systems and practices which have doubtless fallen into disuse or failed to take off.

This capacity for both innovation and its continuing establishment over space and time must be counted as among the great achievements of the human species – sometimes unevenly tapped and certainly not always achieving wide circulation, but exploited, in however diverse or contested ways, by the many many generations of human communicators. Our variegated modes of communicating necessarily take us beyond the narrower vision of humans as essentially sites for mental representations or unidimensional information-transfers, to appreciate them as full multisensory beings actively living in the world. It is in these embodied and mediational practices, not in our brains, that (to follow Tim Ingold's phrasing, 2000: 69) we experience 'the ongoing, temporal interweaving of our lives with one another and with the manifold constituents of our environment'.

To what purposes we use our interconnectedness is another question. So is how each of us might wish in the last analysis to judge the directions of these countless acts of human interconnecting now and in the past and the future. But that, as humans, we have developed manifold and marvellous modes of communicating is incontrovertible. We have pushed at our basic communicative resources and continue to do so. We have extended them through creative uses of our bodily capacities intertwined with human-made artefacts; communicated nearby and at a distance; enlarged the possibilities of sound; mingled the different modalities in both fluid and more standardised ways; and exploited a wonderful multimodal and evocative mix of arts. We have developed not a thin fashion of communicating but a richly stranded mix of multimodal interactions, marked by multiple overtones and creative enactments. Through all these modes, muddled and vulnerable as they sometimes are, we human communicators continue to forge our active inter-connectedness and in doing so have fashioned routes towards transcending our bodily separations and interconnecting with other human creatures, those nearby as well as those at other places and times.

We have gone through many developments in our understanding of the universe. Just to consider the shortened millennia in western history we may recall the three-fold Greek concept of the soul, moving to Newtonian physics, the Cartesian duality of mind and matter, the twentieth century collapsing into single-dimensional mate-riality and now – notably – to the break-up of our certainties in quantum theory, relativity, indeterminism, MRI imaging of the brain (the soul?) and the concept of myriad 'bits', separating and joining, in the ether. Einstein (1977) could scarcely have foreseen our most recent developments, but surely he grasped their import when he wrote:

> A human being is a part of the whole, called by us 'Universe,' a part limited in time and space. He experiences himself, his thoughts and feelings as something separated from the rest a kind of optical delusion of his consciousness. This delusion is a kind of prison for us, restricting us to our personal desires and to affection for a few persons nearest to us. Our task must be to free ourselves from this prison by widening our circle of compassion to embrace all living creatures and the whole of nature in its beauty (2005: 206).

We now accept – magic to past generations – the reality of sound and light waves in the ether, telegraphic, electrical and electronic impulses interpenetrating the world's web of communication – the 'cloud(s)' – and the million and more ways in which we experience one another's extended minds. We might envisage this shared consciousness as a kind of layer between heaven and earth – nothing less than miraculous – filled with the sounds and sights and fragrances of human messages and memories, reaching as far as the universe and all its wonders, but as close and familiar as the quiet space between eyelid and eye, sleeping and waking – Teilhard de Chardin's planetary layer, an envelope of thinking substance (1964: 131).

Is this really any less 'scientific' or any more of a miracle than those other amaz-ing forms of communicating that form the subject of this book?

Notes

1 Communicating humans . . . but what does that mean?

1 Based on fieldwork in Sierra Leone in early 1960s (see Finnegan 1967). Field studies of this kind have traditionally been presented in the present tense but this is now rightly queried as giving a misleadingly timeless and homogenising impression. In citing examples here I have sometimes adopted this 'ethnographic present', especially of course in direct quotations, but sometimes used past tenses; it is hard to be completely consistent so I hope that in this book, as in many comparable ones, the reader will treat examples as indeed true of certain situations or traditions at some point in time but not necessarily as uniformly or literally true of the present.

2 For illuminating overviews of these developments see for example Budwig *et al.* 2000: Introduction, Clark 1992, Duranti 1997, Duranti and Goodwin 1992: Introduction, Hanks 1996: Chapter 1, Knoblauch and Kotthoff 2001: Introduction, Ochs *et al.* 1996: Introduction, Potter 1996; see also Malinowski's 1923 essay on 'meaning in primitive languages', sometimes regarded as anticipating these recent emphases with his insistence on the 'context of situation' and his view of language (albeit focused on 'primitive uses') as 'a mode of action and not an instrument of reflection' (Malinowski 1923: 306, 312).

3 For examples see Burke 1993, 1997b, Camporesi 1994, Corbin 1986, 1999 (history); Schiffer 1999 (archaeology and anthropology); Hibbitts 1992, 1995 (law); Tuan 1993, Rodaway 1994 ('sensuous geography'). For sociolinguistics and linguistic anthropology see specially Besnier 1990, Gumperz and Levinson 1996, Kendon 1990, 1994, Sheldon 1999, Streeck and Knapp 1992, Tracey 1999 and the journal *Research on Language and Social Interaction*, and for recent work in the anthropology of the senses Classen 1997.

4 For current introductions or overviews see for example Cobley 1996, Corner and Hawthorn 1993, Fiske 1990, Mantovani 1996, Mattelart and Mattelart 1998, O'Sullivan *et al.* 1994, Price 1996, Rosengren 1999, Schirato and Yell 2000, Watson and Hill 1997 (all interesting but taking a different view of communication from my own, or focusing just on certain types of communication, specially verbal/linguistic or 'mass' and/or computer-based media). Sociology textbooks mostly examine only limited aspects (the chapters in Giddens 1997 and Fulcher and Scott 1999, for example, concentrate mainly on the 'mass media'). Some texts include sections on non-verbal dimensions (e.g. Adler and Rodman 2000, Burgoon *et al.* 1994, DeVito 2000, Gudykunst 1998, Ketrow 1999, Tubbs and Moss 1994) but these are often ghettoised, as if secondary to the 'verbal' norm, and (with a few partial exceptions, notably Salzmann 1998) seldom include communication at a distance. Other recent treatments of 'communication' are basically 'how to do it' manuals or focus primarily on new technologies.

5 Reference works in anthropology (as distinct from more detailed monographs) often assume the sender–message–receiver model, focus almost exclusively on language, or else (as in Barnard and Spencer 1996, Ingold 1994, Levinson and Ember 1996) have no explicit discussion of 'communication' as such (Barfield 1997 is a partial exception). Textbooks follow a similar pattern (see Note 8 below) or use 'communication' mainly as a term for analysing practices such as marriage or ritual (e.g. Hendry 1999). More substantive works include Sperber and Wilson's cognitivist analysis (1995) (discussed further, pp. 20–1), Rothenbuhler 1998 (concerned with ritual rather than with communication), Hendry and Watson 2001 (on 'indirect communication'), and Duranti's *Linguistic Anthropology* 1997, which overlaps with the perspective here but understandably focuses on language.

6 Recent exceptions or partial exceptions include the short but stimulating overview in Bauman 1992 (Introduction), Beeman 1997 (despite its information-transfer start), Budwig *et al.* 2000, Carrithers 1992 (in some respects, esp. 66ff), Lindlof 1995 (introductory chapters), Roy Harris's 'integrationist' analyses (1996 and elsewhere, also Harris and Wolf 1998), Hendry and Watson 2001 (on 'indirect communication'), Knoblauch and Kotthoff 2001, and Schiffer 1999 (with special reference to material life), together with other more specific studies mentioned in the text in due course. There are some excellent studies of interpersonal and small-group communication, mainly by psychologists (e.g. Argyle 1988, Hargie 1997, Hartley 1999, Trenholm and Jensen 2000) but again these mostly omit the distance dimensions. An increasing number of books or collections now treat the 'non-verbal' as a specialist topic on its own (e.g. Burgoon *et al.* 1996, Knapp and Hall 1997, Poyatos 1983, 1992, Richmond *et al.* 1987), as well as separate chapters on this within more general books (see Note 4 above).

7 Windahl and Signitzer (1992: 17–18) cite Merten's analysis (1977) of 160 definitions of communication; no doubt these could be multiplied.

8 For example Cheater 1989, Ember and Ember 1998, Keesing and Strathern 1998, Kehoe 1998, Scupin 1998, Whitten and Hunter 1993, Womack 1998.

9 On this topic see especially Bauman and Briggs 2000.

10 For more active and multiple approaches to the concept of audience see, variously, Abercrombie and Longhurst 1998: Chap. 1, Finnegan 1992: 94ff, Schechner 1988: esp. 193ff, Streeck 1994; work on the ethnography and history of reading similarly queries the presupposition that this necessarily entails passive or mechanical reception (e.g. Boyarin 1993, Cavallo and Chartier 1999).

11 This is also why I cannot follow some scholars' generic use of the term 'discourse': though sometimes used illuminatingly to indicate the emergent and/or multisensory qualities of communicating (for example Burke 1997b, Hudson 1999: 12, Sherzer 1987, Urban 1991), I prefer not to rely on it much here because of its textual/ linguistic/propositional connotations as well as its close associations (in Britain at least) with specific theories about language and power.

12 For examples and discussion of current approaches in evolutionary psychology see (among many others) Buss 1999, Mithen 1996, Pinker 1997, Plotkin 1997, Wright 1996, and some of the papers in Runciman *et al.* 1996; also the vigorous critique in Rose and Rose 2000.

13 For further discussion of controversies surrounding the so-called 'orality/literacy debate' see Finnegan 1988, 2001, Keller-Cohen 1994, Olson and Torrance 1991, Street 1993 and further references there, also Chapter 5 below.

14 For recent work on the related topic of 'the emotions' see for example Barbalet 1998,

Bendelow and Williams 1997, Harré and Parrott 1996, Hetherington 1998 (on identity and space), James 1997, Karim 1991, Kotthoff 2001, Lupton 1998, Lutz and White 1986, Lutz and Abu-Lughod 1990, Schwartz *et al*. 1992, *Terrain* 1994, Wentworth and Ryan 1994, Williams 2000; also influential earlier work by Robert Plant Armstrong on 'affect' in human experience (1975 and elsewhere).

2 How can we communicate? The basic resources of humans and other animals

1 For work on these lines see especially Classen 1993, 1997, Classen *et al*. 1994, Howes 1991, Järviluoma 1994, Seeger 1981, Stoller 1984, 1989, also additional references mentioned in the text and (in more celebratory tone) Ackerman 1990, Tuan 1993.

2 For recent reviews of debates on perception see Akins 1996, Bruce *et al*. 1996: Chapter 17; see also the active approach emphasised in, for example, Classen 1997, Rodaway 1994, Stewart 1999, Stockfelt 1994, and, earlier, in Goodman's pertinently titled *Ways of Worldmaking* (1978); also examples at specific points in later chapters.

3 Alternative and partly overlapping taxonomies are given in Burgoon *et al*. 1996: esp. 18–19, Hartley 1999: 143ff, Ketrow 1999: 252–3; see also the more elaborate approach in Poyatos 1983: 58 and elsewhere.

4 See also Larry Gross's similar paradigm of 'modes of communication' (lexical; social-gestural; iconic; logico-mathematical; musical – Gross 1974, also 1989), to which Gardner notes his indebtedness.

5 In common with several other authors I will, however, mostly be using 'medium/a' in a more concrete sense than 'modality' (the latter implying broader concepts such as vision, audition or olfaction).

6 For material culture see especially the stimulating analysis in Schiffer 1999, also Arnoldi *et al*. 1996, Graves-Brown 2000, Hodder 1989, *Journal of Material Culture* (1996–) and other references at appropriate places in the text. The term 'artefacts' (American spelling 'artifacts') was once mainly the preserve of archaeologists but is now increasingly used with the general sense of human-made or -modified objects.

7 Here and elsewhere 'animal' is to be understood in the broad sense in which it contrasts with 'plants' rather than in the narrower meaning that would distinguish animals from (for example) fishes or insects. I also mostly use the unqualified 'animal' to *include* humans, but occasionally, especially in later chapters, use 'animals' to mean non-humans when the context makes this unambiguous.

8 Examples of the proliferating literature on or relevant to animal communication include Balda *et al*. 1998, Bekoff and Jamieson 1996, Cheney and Seyfarth 1990, Dawkins 1995, Griffin 1984, Hauser 1996, Hepper 1991, Marler and Evans 1997, Owings *et al*. 1997, Pepperberg 1999, Ristau 1991, Smith 1997, Smith *et al*. 1989, Whiten *et al*. 1999 (others are mentioned at appropriate places in the text here and/or in later chapters). Some readers will doubtless be able to add their own (anecdotal) experience of, for example, the purposive signalling used by domestic dogs or the many distinctive calls, squawks, clucks, twitters and 'lullabies' among hens.

9 See especially Goodenough *et al*. 1993: 568ff, also Agosta 1992, Griffin 1986, Hauser 1996: 5, Maryanski 1997, Ridley 1995: Chapter 7, Siiter 1999: Chap. 9, and references in previous note.

3 The sounding world and its creation

1　This remains true in general despite the existence of individuals fully or partially deprived of access to this resource. As in the complementary case of vision, illuminating analyses have come both from those lacking the capacity and those extensively relying on it because of other disabilities.

2　For recent treatments see, for example, Bailey 1996, Bull 2000, Corbin 1999, Smith 1999, as well as the excellent overview in Van Leeuwen 1999 and the publications of Steven Feld (1986, 1989, 1990, 1995, 1996, among others) and of Anthony Seeger (1981, 1987, 1994). On the other hand Schirato and Yell's otherwise stimulating treatment of 'communication and culture' (2000) includes no treatment either of music or of sound as such. See also further references and examples in the text, together with insightful earlier publications such as Ostwald 1973, Schafer 1977, Truax 1984, Zukerkandl 1958.

3　The terms 'sonic, 'auditory' and 'acoustic' can have slightly different connotations but in this chapter I am mostly using them as broadly interchangeable.

4　For animal acoustic communication see Goodenough *et al.* 1993, Griffin 1986, Hopp *et al.* 1998, Morton and Page 1992, Papousek *et al.* 1992, Ridley 1995, Siiter 1999: Chapter 9, and Smith *et al.* 1989: 74–5; also, for particular species or mechanisms, Cheney and Seyfarth 1990, Griffin 1986, Kroodsma and Miller 1996, Pepperberg 1999, Popper and Fay 1995, Whitlow 1993.

5　Elements of acoustically experienced echolocation have sometimes been reported by blind individuals, however (for example Hull 1997: 22–4) .

6　Ostwald elsewhere (1973: 18) states that it is principally men that whistle, but in general uses 'he' to include 'she'.

7　For further discussion and references to follow up this brief summary of a vast subject see Bauman and Briggs 2000, Besnier 1990, Bloomaert 1999, Clark 1992, Couper-Kuhlen and Selting 1996, Duranti 1997, Fox 2000, Ochs *et al.* 1996; also Van Leeuwen 1999 and the general trends discussed in Chapter 1 above. Since this chapter focuses on sonic dimensions, visual and tactile aspects are left until later chapters; the important topic of the mingling of these modes is taken up in Part III.

8　On ideophones see Finnegan 1970: 64–6, 71–2, Okpewho 1992: 92ff, and for a more comparative perspective – for they are by no means confined to Africa – Kawada 1996, Besnier 1990: 423ff.

9　For further examples and discussion see, among many other works, Feld 1995, Finnegan 1992, 2001, Knoblauch and Kotthoff 2001, Okpewho 1992, Sherzer and Woodbury 1987, Tedlock 1983.

10　Further studies include those on Quechua speakers in Ecuador (Nuckolls 1996), Southeast Asia (Roseman 1988, 1991, Laderman and Roseman 1996), and the role of sound in Native American cultures more generally, especially in verbal art (Tedlock 1983, Sherzer and Woodbury 1987).

4 Shaping the sights: vision and the communicating body

1　With some striking exceptions among earlier writers (notably Simmel, Goffman, E. T. Hall, and ethnographers of communication such as Birdwhistell) most studies of the visual have focused on only certain categories within this range. Treatments of visual art mostly emphasise stationary and pictorial forms (often two-dimensional), but ignore performance arts and 'everyday' objects such as domestic utensils, house styles or streetscapes. Till recently 'visual anthropology' meant film and photography (see Hockings 1995 and earlier issues of *Visual Anthropology*), while in sociology and cultural studies photography, film and theories of 'the image' take pride of place (see Evans and Hall 1999). Studies of writing systems have operated mainly as a separate domain (e.g. Brown 1998, Coulmas 1996, Daniels and Bright 1996, Robinson 1995). Recently however, there have been more attempts to bring these scattered elements together (Banks and Morphy 1997, Emmison and Smith 2000, Kress and Van Leeuwen 1996, the *Journal of Material Culture* (1996–) and perhaps the new *Journal of Visual Culture* (2002–); also, up to a point Forty and Küchler 1999, Gombrich 1996, Lester 2000, Tufte 1983, 1990, 1997); see also other references in the text, and insightful studies by blind and by deaf writers such as Hull 1997, Sacks 1991.

2 Or at least that is the joined-up experience of the viewers even if the physiological process is more gappy.

3 For references on animal visual communication see relevant portions of works cited in Chapter 2, Note 8; other sources used in this section include Bateson 1990, Bruce *et al.* 1996, Hailman 1989, Hewes 1996.

4 For some overview of the flood of writing on aspects of 'the body' see Turner 1996, Introduction to the 2nd edition (written from a largely postmodernist perspective); also, among many other publications spanning a variety of viewpoints, Argyle 1988, Benthall and Polhemus 1975, Blacking 1977, Comaroff 1985, Csordas 1994, Douglas 1966, 1973, Entwistle 2000, Farnell 1995a, Featherstone 2000, Featherstone *et al.* 1991, Mauss 1979 [1935], Strathern and Stewart 1998, the journal *Body and Society* 1995 – and the Berg series 'Dress, Body, Culture'; also references throughout this chapter. In most of this writing the main (though not always sole) focus is on visual aspects.

5 The degree to which certain facial expressions are invariant across the human species is still debated (see for example Ekman and Keltner 1997).

6 Hall 1959. Proxemics as the spatial dimension of communication was pioneered by E. T. Hall (1959, 1966, 1974), see also parallel studies by Goffman (1963, 1971) and, more recently, Duranti 1992, Kendon 1990, Lebaron and Streeck 1997 (among others). Initially used of the mutual sensory involvement of people in face-to-face encounters, proxemics is now often widened to cover all types of human spatial behaviour in social interaction.

7 There is a growing literature on kinesics and related topics: see especially Adam Kendon's publications (e.g. 1988, 1989, 1990, 1994, 1997, 2000); also, among many others, Bremmer and Roodenburg 1991, Burke 1997b, Ekman 1976, Farnell 1995b, McNeill 1992, 2000 (a stimulating interdisciplinary work that only became available to me as I finished the first edition of this book), Morris *et al.* 1979, and the classic work by Andrea de Jorio (2000 [1832]), plus other references in the text.

8 For further comment and references on sign languages etc. see especially Kendon 1988: Chapter 13, also Brun 1969, Critchley 1975, Farnell 1995b, Gregory 1996: 40ff (on makaton), Lock and Peters 1996: 555ff, Morris *et al.* 1979, Rée 1999: 271ff.

9 Dance is typically a multiplex activity, operating in several channels, but in that sight usually plays a crucial role it is included here. The widespread logocentric approach to communication has meant that the role of dance is often seriously underplayed; for recent analyses see (among others) Farnell 1995a, 1995b, Hanna 1979, Hughes-Freeland 1997, Ness 1992, Seeger 1994, Spencer 1985, 1996, plus other references in the text.

10 There is a large and polemical literature on deaf signing; for some recent reflections see Rée 1999, Sacks 1991.

5 Creating and sharing sights: human arts and artefacts

1 On landscape and place see for example Basso 1996, Cosgrove and Daniels 1985, Feld and Basso 1996, Frake 1996, Glowczewski 1999, Hanks 1990: Chapter 7, Hirsch and O'Hanlon 1995 (unfortunately there is not space to pursue this important body of work here).

2 From the large literature on the social and cosmological significance of dwellings and their layout see also Bahloul 1999, Bourdieu 1973, 1977: 89ff, Bowden 1992, Carsten and Hugh-Jones 1995, Comaroff 1985: 54ff, Littlejohn 1967, Thomas 1996, Waterson 1990.

3 For further examples and comment on cloth see Perani and Wolff 1999, Tedlock and Tedlock 1986, Weiner and Schneider 1989, and, on clothing, Chapter 4 above.

4 For a down-to earth comparative discussion of issues concerning 'representation', 'reality' and 'iconicity', see Morphy 1994: 664ff.

5 The term is based on the Greek *sema* (sign) combined with a 'graphic' presentation (see Boone and Mignolo 1994: 15ff, Sampson 1985). Definitions, terminologies and classifications for writing systems remain controversial, however, including those used here. For influential recent accounts presenting the current state of play, variously discussing the issues, and/or taking particular stands on the debates see Basso 1989, Boone and Mignolo 1994, Brown 1998, Coulmas 1996, Crystal 1997: esp. 199ff, Daniels and Bright 1996: esp. 8ff, DeFrancis 1989, Gaur 1992, Harris 1995, 2000, Robinson 1995, Wagner *et al.* 1999, also the journal *Written Language and Literacy* (1998–).

6 Studies in the history and ethnography of reading, and of the performance traditions of some literatures, have demonstrated that the actual *practices* of reading and of interacting with written texts are more varied than often assumed and not necessarily in a linear form (see for example Boyarin 1993, Cavallo and Chartier 1999, Coleman 1996, Kersenboom 1995). Consider too, dear reader, how you have been approaching this (or any) book – in linear and one-way manner only?

7 These blurred boundaries make it difficult if not impossible to lay down any satisfactory verbal definition of 'writing' (though there is something to be said for Boone and Mignolo's inclusive wording of 'the communication of relatively specific ideas in a conventional manner by means of permanent, visible marks' (1994: 15) [nowadays we might question 'permanent', however]). For terminologies and classifications more generally see references in Note 5 above.

8 In a number of cases, perhaps significantly, there were links between the creation of these scripts and cloth-workers (tailors, weavers) with their interest in cloth stamps and other graphic symbols (Dalby 1968: 181). For further discussion and examples of recently invented writing systems see Coulmas 1996: 4, 73ff, 94ff, 213ff, Dalby 1967–9, Daniels and Bright 1996: Part IX.

9 There is a large literature on various aspects of western visualism; for commentary and examples (and in some cases critical assessment) see Clifford and Marcus 1986: 11ff, Emmison and Smith 2000, Fabian 1983: 105ff, Howes and Lalonde 1991, Jay 1986, 1992, Lester 2000, Levin 1993, Poteat 1974, Reed 1999, Stoller 1989; also other references in the text and Chapter 3, pp. 82–4 above.

6 Sensing the odour

1 For example Almagor 1987, 1990a, b, Classen 1993, 1997, Classen *et al.* 1994, Corbin 1986, Howes 1987, Howes and Lalonde 1991, Rindisbacher 1992, Schleidt 1992, Seeger 1988.

2 For further examples, references and discussion see the very useful overview in Classen *et al.* 1994 which has been much relied on in this section.

3 Among the many recent publications on food and related topics (now a rapidly growing area) see, for example, Bell and Valentine 1997, Counihan 1999, Counihan and Kaplan 1998, Scholliers 2001, Warde 1997.

4 For fuller accounts of the expanding research on chemical communication in animals see especially Agosta 1992, Johnston *et al.* 1999, Sussman 1992, Vander Meer *et al.* 1998, also Goodenough *et al.* 1993: 571ff and the accessible account in Watson 1999.

5 The literature on human uses of smell is somewhat scattered but see references in Note 1 above, also Doty 1981, Engen 1991, Gell 1977, Rahim 1987, Russell 1976, Stoddart 1990, Tuan 1993: 55ff, Van Toller and Dodd 1988, 1992, Watson 1999, plus other citations in the text.

6 The so-called 'language of flowers' might seem one candidate. But insofar as this ever really circulated (and Goody argues convincingly (1993: 232ff) that it was probably restricted to a small elite in nineteenth-century France), the symbolism seems to be centred on sight and literary verbal associations rather than a scent-based code.

7 Communicating touch

1 Research on seismic (vibrational) communication has apparently been blossoming recently (see the report in Anon 2001); some analysts separate it off as a communication channel in its own right, others treat it with touch or sound.

2 Touch is still relatively underplayed in studies both of communication and the related topic of perception. Recentish publications I have found especially useful include Craig and Rollman 1999, Lederman and Klatzky 1987, McDaniel and Andersen 1998, Millar 1997, Montagu 1986, Parrinder 1987, Stewart 1999, Thayer 1982, 1989, and, on tactile perception in infancy, Kellman and Arterberry 1998: 216ff; also relevant sections in Argyle 1988, Burgoon *et al.* 1996, Ketrow 1999, Poyatos 1983.

3 The hand is of course also important in other areas of communication besides touch: recall its uses in gesticulation, sign languages (see the various figures illustrating this) and, from another viewpoint, in the manipulation and creation of artefacts.

4 A contrast is sometimes made between the terms 'tactual' (relatively passive) and 'haptic' (more active) as psychologists now increasingly explore the active processes undertaken by the hand(s) (see Craig and Rollman 1999: 314ff, Kellman and Arterberry 1998: 216ff, Millar 1997: 21ff, also Lederman and Klatzky 1987). Despite this useful distinction I mostly use 'tactile' to cover both dimensions ('haptic' tends to be particularly associated with manipulative activity by the *hands*, whereas I envisage tactile communicating as sometimes involving other parts of the body as well; also the term 'tactual sensation/perception' carries more passive overtones than applicable in many (perhaps all) cases of mutual touching/being touched).

5 For this section I am especially indebted to accounts of tactile systems in Hinton 1996, Kaczmarek and Bach-y-Rita 1995, Millar 1997, Summers 1992, and the magazine *Talking Sense* published by Sense, The National Deafblind and Rubella Association [UK]. Computer technologies change rapidly so examples here will need to be supplemented by more recent accounts.

8 Communicating through the ether: a story of dreaming, death and the imaginary

1 See, for example, Alexander 2012a, b, and the useful overview and references in Facco and Agrillo 2012.
2 See, for example, the evidence of such works as Alexander 2012b, Appleby 1989, Bardy 2002, Belanti *et al.* 2008, Blackmore 1996, French 2001, Gabbard and Twemlow 1991, Greyson 2010, Greyson *et al.* 2009, Holden *et al.* 2009, Mobbs and Watt 2011, Morse *et al.* 1986, Schroeter-Kunhardt 1993, Van Lommel 2010. Schwartz (2012) also remarks on the further telling episode at a recent conference where a leading researcher was challenged to pick an experiment and say what was wrong about it. 'I had said to him: "Pick an experiment we both know, and you tell me what is wrong with it, and I will respond." Without a moment's hesitation he shot back in the most deliberately condescending act I have ever had directed at me and said: "You don't think I actually read this stuff, do you?"' I have seldom myself spoken of the subject in public or private without at least one person adding to the discussion with an example from their own knowledge, in keeping with the patterns noted by Eben Alexander.
3 See, among much else, Abraham 1979, Basso 1992, Bulkeley *et al.* 2009, Burke 1997a, Devereux 1969, Edgar 1995, 1999, 2009, Finnegan 2012, Harris 2009, Jedrej and Shaw 1992, Lohmann 2003, Moss 1998, 2010, Tedlock *et al.* 1987 (together with Basso 1992, the classic anthropological account). The relaying of deep-seated human myths, stories that, for all their fictional form, may be directly pertinent for historical and social scientific analyses.

   This is reinforced by my interest not only in linguistic and literary expression/performance, oral and written (as in Bauman 2004, Bauman and Briggs 1990, Duranti 2001, Duranti and Goodwin 1992, Hanks 1996, Hill and Irvine 1993, Hymes 1996, Lucy 1993, Mannheim and Tedlock 1995, Schieffelin 2007, Silverstein and Urban 1996) but also, more especially in quoting (see for example Bakhtin 1981, Barthes 1977, Bazerman 1989, Becker 1995, Bublitz and Hübler 2007, Compagnon 1979, Conte 1986, De Grazia 1991, Duranti 1997, 2001, Eisner and Vicinus 2008, Eliot 1975, Feld 1989, 2010, Finnegan 1967, 1992, 1998, 2007, 2011a, 2012, Foucault 1977, Garber 2003, Goffman 1981, Graham 1987, Hanks 1990, Harris 1998, Heath 1983, Hymes 1964, Irvine 1996, Irwin 2001, Kotthoff 1998, Lucy 2001, Lunsford and Ede 1990, Mannheim and Tedlock 1995, Merton 1965, Olson and Kamawar 2002, Pennycock 1996, Perdue 2008, Perri 1978, Putnam 1894, Regier 2011, Ricks 2002, Scollon 1994, Shuman 1999, Silk 2003, Silverstein and Urban 1996, Swales 1990, Urban 1989, Wilson 2000, Woodmansee and Jaszi 1994.
4 Having been engaged for several years in the study of quoting, meta-communication and the dialogic and pragmatic qualities of language, I have garnered a mass of reading on the subject, including, among many others, Bakhtin 1986, Compagnon 1979, Conte 1986, Conte and Most 2003, De Grazia 1991, Duranti 1997, 2001, Emerson 1876, Finnegan 2011b, Gans 1981, Garber, 2003, Grafton 1999, Graham 1987, Hymes 1964, Irvine 1996, Kellett 1933, Kotthoff 1998, Lucy 1993, 2001, Olson and Kamawar 2002, Perri 1978, Regier 2011, Reynolds 2003, Ricks 2002, Savran 1988, Wilson 2000, Yankah 1995.
5 Barthes 1977, Conte 1986, Conte and Most 2003, De Graza 1991, Duranti 1997, 2001, Emerson 1876, Foucault 1977, Goffman 1981, Hanks 1990, Harris 1998, Heath 1983, Hill and Irvine 1993, Homer 2009, Howard 1999, Howard and Robillard 2008, Hymes 1964, Putnam 1894, Scollon 1994, Silverstein and Urban 1996, Urban 1989, 1991, Voloshinov 1986.

6 Among others Carruthers 1990, Goody 1977, Lord 1960, Olson and Torrance 1996, Perdue 2008.

7 See, for example, Atkinson *et al.* 2003, Bryman 2008, Chamberlayne *et al.* 2000, Denzin and Lincoln 2005, Madden 2010, Murray 1975, Stake 2005.

8 In conventional anthropology, this has received far less attention than dreaming. But, surprising as it may seem, there is a serious interdisciplinary literature on the subject – elusive as it is, much but not all of it by psychologists: see, for example, Anon 2012c, Butler 1998, 2012, Goswami 2001, Howes 2011, Playfair 2002, Sheldrake 2002, Ullman *et al.* 1989, Zangrilli 2012. Furthermore, there is growing interest in the subject among general readers; see, for example, Anon 2012c, Baumann 2012, Butler 1998, 2012, Hewitt 1996, Howes 2011, Society for Psychical Research 2012; on the related topic of MRI scans (the imaginative, not the purely technical) see Anon 2012a, National High Magnetic Field Laboratory 2012. And even the US Defence Department has become interested and, I believe, is currently pouring millions of dollars into research into the subject (Anon 2012b).

9 This remains controversial, but there is much anecdotal evidence; see, for instance, Fierro 2012, Playfair 2002, Wagner 2012 – and, of course, twins personally known to me (and perhaps to you?).

10 Here and earlier I have hesitated about including extracts from poems as too personal and perhaps too 'arty' for this book. But I have remembered that as fieldworkers cite 'texts' from their field experience, historians too use quotations from their primary, valued, sources, and that these too form part of the data (the reader can always ignore any that seem intrusive: they are included, after all, not for their intrinsic value or artistic merit but in illustration of the overall argument).

11 See, among much else (coming from various perspectives but largely from the pragmatist tradition), Basso 1992, Bulkeley *et al.* 2009, Burke 1997a, Edgar 1995, 1999, 2009, Finnegan 2012, Jedrej and Shaw 1992, Lohmann 2003, Moss 1998, Tedlock 1987.

12 See, for example, Anon 2012a, National High Magnetic Field Laboratory 2012.

13 It may be no accident that the largest current expenditure on telepathy research seems to be by the American military (with perhaps Russia a very close second).

9 A mix of arts

1 See the critique of separate domains summarised in Burgoon *et al.* 1996: 152 and references there, also important analyses such as Farnell 1995a, b, Kendon 1994, McNeill 1992, 2000, Sheldon 1999, Streeck and Knapp 1992.

2 This is why, much though I warm to the approach and examples in Hendry and Watson's *Anthropology of Indirect Communication* (2001), I part company with the implication, apparent at least at times, that verbalised statements make up 'direct' communicating, the non-verbal the 'indirect'; for some people and on some occasions it might be the other way round (or in any case more complicated), something to be investigated rather than assumed.

10 Through space and time

1 Some psychologists suggest there is a widely recognised, possibly universal, codified system of facial expression (see for example the overview and references in Ekman and Keltner 1997) though its extent and interpretation remain controversial.

2 For recent discussions of memory see Antze and Lambek 1996, Bloch 1998, Carruthers 1990, Coleman 1992, Connerton 1989, Fentress and Wickham 1992, Forty and Küchler 1999, Kwint *et al.* 1999, Radstone 2000, Tonkin 1992, Virilio 1994.

3 See the recent accounts now reacting against the earlier hype and/or taking a welcome ethnographic approach, such as Danet 2001, Miller and Slater 2000, Pemberton and Shurville 2000, Van Dijk 1997; also the incisive analysis in Harris 2000.

4 Arguments stated persuasively in the (otherwise different) analyses by Baron 2000, Harris 2000.

5 Both these points are stressed in Irene Pepperberg's stimulating comparative conclusion to her account of the outstanding communication skills of African grey parrots (Pepperberg 1999: 322).

Bibliography

Abercrombie, N. and Longhurst, B. (1998) *Audiences. A Sociological Theory of Performance and Imagination*, London: Sage.

Abraham, K. (1979) 'Dreams and myths: a study in folk psychology', in *Clinical Papers and Essays on Psychoanalysis*, London: Hogarth Press.

Ackerman, D. (1990) *A Natural History of the Senses*, New York: Random House.

Adler, R. B. and Rodman, G. (2000) *Understanding Human Communication*, Fort Worth: Harcourt College Publishers.

Agosta, W. C. (1992) *Chemical Communication, the Language of Pheromones*, New York: Scientific American Library.

Agrillo, C. (2011) 'Near-death experience: out-of-body and out-of-brain?', *Review of General Psychology* 15: 1–10.

Akins, K. (ed.) (1996) *Perception*, Oxford: Oxford University Press.

Alexander, E. (2012a) *Newsweek*, October 2012.

Alexander, E. (2012b) *Proof of Heaven. A Neurosurgeon's Journey into the Afterlife*, London: Piatkus.

Allenby, B. (2013) 'What will "truth" mean in the future?', *Slate*, February 2013.

Almagor, U. (1987) 'The cycle and stagnation of smells: pastoralists–fishermen relationships in an East African society', *RES* 13: 106–21.

Almagor, U. (1990a) 'Some thoughts on common scents', *Journal for the Theory of Social Behaviour* 20: 181–95.

Almagor, U. (1990b) 'Odors and private language: observations on the phenomenology of scent', *Human Studies* 13: 253–74.

Anderson, M. D. (1971) *History and Imagery in British Churches*, London: Murray.

Anon (2001) 'Extra sensory perception', *The Economist*, 6 Jan: 76–7.

Anon (2012–13) Personal communications.

Anon (2012a) Magnetic resonance imaging, online, http://en.wikipedia.org/wiki/Magnetic_resonance_imaging

Anon (2012b) Online, http://www.synthetictelepathy.net/brain-computer-interface/defence-research-nanotechnology-a-cloud-of-dust-listens-to-you/

Anon (2012c) Online, http://en.wikipedia.org/wiki/Telepathy

Anon (2012d) 'Telepathic love therapy', online, http://www.vibrational-alchemy.com/telepathic/intro.htm

Anon (2012e) Personal communications.

Antze, P. and Lambek, M. (eds) (1996) *Tense Past. Cultural Essays in Trauma and Memory*, New York: Routledge.

Apollinaire, G. (1965) *Oeuvres poétiques*, Bibliothèque de la Pléiade, Paris: Editions Gallimard.

Applbaum, R. L., Anatol, K. W. E., Hays, E. R., Jenson, O. O., Porter, R. E. and Mandel, J. E. (1973) *Fundamental Concepts in Human Communication*, New York: Canfield Press.

Appleby, L. (1989) 'Near death experience', *British Medical Journal* 298: 976–7.

Arguillees, J. (2011) *Manifesto for the Noosphere*, Berkeley: Evolver.

Argyle, M. (1988) *Bodily Communication*, 2nd edn, London: Methuen.

Argyle, M. and Cook, M. (1976) *Gaze and Mutual Gaze*, Cambridge: Cambridge University Press.

Armstrong, R. P. (1975) *Wellspring. On the Myth and Source of Culture*, Berkeley: University of California Press.

Arnoldi, M. J. (1995) 'Introduction', in Arnoldi, M. J. and Kreamer, C. M. (eds) *Crowning Achievements: African Arts of Dressing the Head*, Los Angeles: Fowler Museum of Cultural History, UCLA.

Arnoldi, M. J., Geary, C. M. and Hardin, K. L. (eds) (1996) *African Material Culture*, Bloomington: Indiana University Press.

Arthur, L. B. (ed.) (1999) *Religion, Dress and the Body*, Oxford: Berg.

Atkinson, P., Coffey, A. and Delamont, S. (2003) *Key Themes in Qualitative Research. Continuities and Changes*, Walnut Creek: Altamira Press.

Aveni, A. F. (1986) 'Non-Western notational frameworks and the role of anthropology in our understanding of literacy', in Wrolstad and Fisher.

Bahloul, J. (1999) 'The memory house: time and place in Jewish immigrant culture in France', in Birdwell-Pheasant and Lawrence-Zúñiga.

Bailey, P. (1996) 'Breaking the sound barrier: a historian listens to noise', *Body and Society* 2, 2: 49–66.

Baker, R. St B. (1955) *Kabongo. The Story of a Kikuyu Chief*, Oxford: George Ronald.

Bakhtin, M. M. (1981) *The Dialogic Imagination*, Austin: University of Texas Press.

Bakhtin, M. M. (1986) *Speech Genres and Other Late Essays,* Eng. transl., ed. C. Emerson and M. Holquist, Austin: University of Texas Press.

Balda, R. P., Pepperberg, I. M. and Kamil A. C. (eds) (1998) *Animal Cognition in Nature. The Convergence of Psychology and Biology in Laboratory and Field*, San Diego and London: Academic Press.

Banks, M. and Morphy, H. (eds) (1997) *Rethinking Visual Anthropology*, New Haven: Yale University Press.

Barbalet, J. M. (1998) *Emotion, Social Theory and Social Structure*, Cambridge: Cambridge University Press.

Barber, K. (2000) *The Generation of Plays. Yoruba Popular Life in Theater*, Bloomington: Indiana University Press.

Bardy, A. H. (2002) 'Near-death experiences', *Lancet* 359: 2116.

Barfield, T. (ed.) (1997) *The Dictionary of Anthropology*, Oxford: Blackwell.

Barnard, A. and Spencer, J. (eds) (1996) *Encyclopedia of Social and Cultural Anthropology*, London: Routledge.

Barnard, M. (1998) *Art, Design and Visual Culture*, Basingstoke and London: Macmillan.

Barnes, R. and Eicher, J. B. (eds) (1992) *Dress and Gender: Making and Meaning in Cultural Contexts*, Oxford: Berg.

Barnouw, E. with Gerbner, G., Schramm, W., Worth, T. L. and Gross, L. (eds) (1989) *International Encyclopedia of Communications,* 4 vols, New York and Oxford: Oxford University Press.

Baron, N. S. (2000) *Alphabet to Email. How Written English Evolved and Where It's Heading*, London: Routledge.

Barthes, R. (1964) 'Eléménts de sémiologie', *Communications* 4: 1–3, 91–134.

Barthes, R. (1972) *Mythologies*, London: Cape.

Barthes, R. (1977) 'The death of the author', in Barthes, R. *Image – Music – Text*, London: Fontana.

Barthes, R. (1983) *The Fashion System*, Eng. transl., New York: Hill and Wang.

Barthes, R. (1986) *The Responsibility of Forms: Critical Essays on Music, Art, and Representation*, Eng. transl., Oxford: Blackwell.

Basso, B. (1985) *A Musical View of the Universe: Kalapalo Myth and Ritual Performance*, Philadelphia: University of Pennsylvania Press.

Basso, E. *et al.* (1992) *Dreaming: Anthropological and Psychological Interpretations*, School of American Research Press.

Basso, K. H. (1989) 'The ethnography of writing', in Bauman and Sherzer.

Basso, K. H. (1996) *Wisdom Sits in Places: Landscapes and Language among the Western Apache*, Albuquerque: University of New Mexico Press.

Bateson, P. (1990) 'Animal communication', in Mellor.

Baudrillard, J. (1988) *Jean Baudrillard. Selected Works*, Cambridge: Polity.

Bauman, R. (1977) *Verbal Art as Performance*, Rowley MA: Newbury House.

Bauman, R. (1983) *Let your Words be Few. Symbolism of Speaking and Silence among Seventeenth-Century Quakers*, Cambridge: Cambridge University Press.

Bauman, R. (2001) 'Mediational performance, traditionalization, and the authorization of discourse', in Knoblauch and Kotthoff.

Bauman, R. (2004) *A World of Others' Words. Cross-Cultural Perspectives on Intertextuality*, Oxford: Blackwell.

Bauman, R. (ed.) (1992) *Folklore, Cultural Performances, and Popular Entertainments: a Communications-Centered Handbook*, New York and Oxford: Oxford University Press.

Bauman, R. and Briggs, C. L. (1990) 'Poetics and performance as critical perspectives on language and social life', *Annual Review of Anthropology* 19: 59–88.

Bauman, R. and Briggs, C. L. (2000) 'Language philosophy as language ideology: John Locke and Johann Gottfried Herder', in Kroskrity, P. (ed.) *Regimes of Language. Ideologies, Polities, Identities*, Oxford: James Currey.

Bauman, R. and Sherzer, J. (eds) (1989) *Explorations in the Ethnography of Speaking*, 2nd edn, London: Cambridge University Press.

Baumann, G. (2012) Personal communications.

Bazerman, C. (1989) *Shaping Written Knowledge*, Madison: University of Wisconsin Press.

Bean, S. S. (1989) 'Gandhi and *khadi*, the fabric of Indian Independence', in Weiner and Schneider.

Becker, A. L. (1995) *Beyond Translation. Essays toward a Modern Philology*, Ann Arbor: University of Michigan Press.

Becker, H. (1986) *Writing for Social Scientists*, Chicago: University of Chicago Press.

Becker, H. S. (1982) *Art Worlds*, Berkeley and Los Angeles: University of California Press.

Beeman, W. (1997) 'Communication', in Barfield.

Bekoff, M. and Jamieson, D. (eds) (1996) *Readings in Animal Cognition*, Cambridge MA: MIT Press.

Belanti, J., Perera, M. and Jagadheesan, K. (2008) 'Phenomenology of near-death experiences: a cross-cultural perspective', *Transcultural Psychiatry* 45: 121–33.

Bell, D. and Valentine, G. (1997) *Consuming Geographies: We are What We Eat*, London: Routledge.

Bendelow, G. and Williams, S. J. (eds) (1997) *Emotions in Social Life: Critical Themes and Contemporary Issues*, London: Routledge.

Benson, S. (2000) 'Inscriptions of the self: reflections on tattooing and piercing in contemporary Euro-America', in Caplan.

Benthall, J. and Polhemus, T. (eds) (1975) *The Body as a Medium of Expression*, London: Allen Lane.

Berger, A. A. (2000) *Media and Communication Research Methods*, Thousand Oaks: Sage.

Besnier, N. (1990) 'Language and affect', *Annual Review of Anthropology* 19: 419–51.

Bickerton, D. (1996) *Language and Human Behaviour*, London: UCL Press.

Billy, A. (1923) *Apollinaire vivant*, Paris: La Sirène.

Birdwell-Pheasant, D. and Lawrence-Zúñiga, D. (eds) (1999) *House Life. Space, Place and Family in Europe*, Oxford: Berg.

Birdwhistell, R. L. (1968) 'Communication', in Sills vol. 3: 24–9.

Birdwhistell, R. L. (1970) *Kinesics and Context: Essays on Body Motion Communication*, Philadelphia: University of Pennsylvania Press.

Blacking, J. (1967) *Venda Children's Songs: a Study in Ethnomusicological Analysis,* Johannesburg: Witwatersrand University Press.

Blacking, J. (1976) *How Musical is Man?* London: Faber and Faber.

Blacking, J. (1985) 'Movement, dance, music, and the Venda girls' initiation cycle', in Spencer.

Blacking, J. (1987) *'A Commonsense View of All Music'. Reflections on Percy Grainger's Contribution to Ethnomusicology and Music Education*, Cambridge: Cambridge University Press.

Blacking, J. (1991) 'Towards a reintegration of musicology', in Buckley, A., Edström, K. O. and Nixon P. (eds) *Proceedings of the British–Swedish Conference on Musicology: Ethnomusicology*, Institute of Musicology: Göteborgs Universitet.

Blacking, J. (ed.) (1977) *The Anthropology of the Body,* New York and London: Academic Press.

Blackmore, S. J. (1996) 'Near-death experiences', *Journal of the Royal Society of Medicine* 89: 73–6.

Blanke, O. and Mohr, C. (2005) 'Out-of-body experience, heautoscopy, and autoscopic hallucination of neurological origin. Implications for neurocognitive mechanisms of corporeal awareness and self-consciousness', *Brain Research Reviews* 50: 184–99.

Blavatsky, H. (1888) *The Secret Doctrine*, New Delhi: Theosophical Publishing Company.

Blavatsky, H. (1933) [1889] *The Voice of the Silence*, New Delhi: Theosophy Publishing Company.

Bloch, M. (1991) 'Language, anthropology and cognitive science', *Man* 26: 183–98.

Bloch, M. (1998) *How We Think They Think. Anthropological Approaches to Cognition, Memory, and Literacy*, Boulder: Westview.

Bloomaert, J. (1999) 'Reconstructing the sociolinguistic image of Africa: grassroots writing in Shaba (Congo)', *Text* 19, 2: 175–200.

Bohn, W. (1986) *The Aesthetics of Visual Poetry 1914–1928*, Cambridge: Cambridge University Press.

Boone, E. H. and Mignolo, W. D. (eds) (1994) *Writing without Words. Alternative Literacies in Mesoamerica and the Andes*, Durham and London: Duke University Press.

Boow, J. (1988) *Symbol and Status in Javanese Batik*, Nedlands: Asian Studies Centre, University of Western Australia.

Bourdieu, P. (1973) 'The Berber house', in Douglas, M. (ed.) *Rules and Meanings. The Anthropology of Everyday Knowledge*, Harmondsworth: Penguin.

Bourdieu, P. (1977) *Outline of a Theory of Practice*, Eng. transl., Cambridge: Cambridge University Press.

Bowden, R. (1992) 'Art, architecture, and collective representation in a New Guinea society', in Coote and Shelton.

Boyarin, J. (ed.) (1993) *The Ethnography of Reading*, Berkeley: University of California Press.

Brain, R. (1979) *The Decorated Body*, New York: Harper and Row.

Bremmer, J. and Roodenburg, H. (eds) (1991) *A Cultural History of Gesture from Antiquity to the Present Day,* Cambridge: Polity.

Brown, M. P. (1998) *The British Library Guide to Writing and Scripts: History and Techniques*, London: British Library.

Brown, S. D. and Stenner, P. (2009) *Psychology without Foundations*, London: Sage.

Bruce, V., Green, P. R. and Georgeson, M. A. (eds) (1996) *Visual Perception. Physiology, Psychology, and Ecology*, 3rd edn, Hove: Psychology Press.

Brugger, P. and Mohr, C. (2009) 'Out of the body, but not out of mind, *Cortex* 45: 137–40.

Brun, T. (1969) *The International Dictionary of Sign Language: a Study of Human Behaviour*, London: Wolfe.

Bryman, A. (2008) *Social Research Methods*, 3rd edn, Oxford: Oxford University Press.

Bublitz, W. and Hübler, A. (eds) (2007) *Metapragmatics in Use*, Amsterdam: John Benjamins.

Budwig, N., Uzgiris, I. C. and Wertsch, J. V. (eds) (2000) *Communication. An Arena of Development*, Stamford: Ablex.

Bulkeley, K., Adams, K. and Davis, P. M. (2009) *Dreaming in Christianity and Islam*, New Brunswick: Rutgers University Press.

Bull, M. (2000) *Sounding Out the City. Personal Stereos and the Management of Everyday Life*, Oxford: Berg.

Bull, P. E. (1987) *Posture and Gesture*, Oxford: Pergamon.

Bunge, M. (2010) 'Matter and mind', *Boston Studies in the Philosophy of Science* 287: 143–57.

Burgoon, J. K. and Guerrero, L. K. (1994) 'Nonverbal communication', in Burgoon *et al.*

Burgoon, J. K., Buller, D. B. and Woodall, D. (1996) *Nonverbal Communication. The Unspoken Dialogue*, 2nd edn, New York: McGraw-Hill.

Burgoon, M., Hunsaker, F. G. and Dawson, E. J. (1994) *Human Communication*, 3rd edn Thousand Oaks: Sage.

Burke, P. (1993) *The Art of Conversation*, Cambridge: Polity.

Burke, P. (1997a) 'The cultural history of dreams', in *Varieties of Cultural History*, New York: Cornell University Press.

Burke, P. (1997b) *Varieties of Cultural History,* Cambridge: Polity.

Buss, D. (1999) *Evolutionary Psychology: The New Science of Mind*, Boston: Allyn and Bacon.

Butler, W. E. (1998) *How to Read the Aura and Practice Psychometry, Telepathy and Clairvoyance*, Destiny.

Butler, W. E. (2012) *Telepathy Will Change Your Life*, online.

Cameron, D. (2000) *Good to Talk? Living and Working in a Communication Culture*, London: Sage.

Campbell, J. (1968) *The Hero with a Thousand Faces*, Princeton: Princeton University Press.

Camporesi, P. (1989) *Bread of Dreams. Food and Fantasy in Early Modern Europe*, Eng. transl., Cambridge: Polity.

Camporesi, P. (1994) *The Anatomy of the Senses. Natural Symbols in Medieval and Early Modern Italy*, Eng. transl., Cambridge: Polity.

Cannadine, D. (2001) *Ornamentalism. How the British Saw their Empire*, London: Allen Lane.

Caplan, J. (ed.) (2000) *Written on the Body. The Tattoo in European and American History*, London: Reaktion.

Carey, E. S. (1996) 'How to get from space to place in a fairly short stretch of time: phenomenological prolegomena', in Feld and Basso.

Carey, J. W. (1989) *Communication as Culture. Essays on Media and Society*, Unwin-Hyman: Boston.

Carpenter, E. and McLuhan, M. (eds) (1960) *Explorations in Communication*, Boston: Beacon Press.

Carrier, J. and A. (1995) 'Every picture tells a story: visual alternatives to oral tradition in Ponam society', in Finnegan and Orbell.

Carrington, J. F. (1949) *Talking Drums of Africa*, London: Carey Kingsgate Press.

Carrithers, M. (1992) *Why Humans Have Cultures. Explaining Anthropology and Social Diversity*, Oxford: Oxford University Press.

Carruthers, M. J. (1990) *The Book of Memory. A Study of Memory in Medieval Culture*, Cambridge: Cambridge University Press.

Carsten, J. and Hugh-Jones, S. (eds) (1995) *About the House. Lévi-Strauss and Beyond*, Cambridge: Cambridge University Press.

Cavallo, G. and Chartier, R. (eds) (1999) *A History of Reading in the West,* Eng. transl., Cambridge: Polity.

Cayley, J. (c. 1996) *Indra's Net or Holography. A Cybertextual Project by John Cayley,* online, http://www.shadoof.net/in/incat.html

Chalmers, D. J. (1995) 'The puzzle of conscious experience', *Scientific American* 273: 80–86.

Chalmers, D. J. (1999) *The Conscious Mind*, Oxford: Oxford University Press.

Chamberlayne, P., Bornat, J. and Wengraf, T. (eds) (2000) *The Turn to Biographical Methods in Social Science: Comparative Issues and Examples*, London: Routledge.

Cheater, A. P. (1989) *Social Anthropology, an Alternative Introduction*, 2nd edn, London: Routledge.

Cheney, D. L. and Seyfarth, R. M. (1990) *How Monkeys See the World. Inside the Mind of Another Species*, Chicago: University of Chicago Press.

Chomsky, N. (2000) *New Horizons in the Study of Language and Mind*, Cambridge: Cambridge University Press.

Chomsky, N. (2012) *The Science of Language*, Cambridge: Cambridge University Press.

Chorost, M. (2011) *Worldwide Mind*, New York: Free Press.

Christensen, P., Hockey, J. and James, A. (2001) 'Talk, silence and the material world: patterns of indirect communication among agricultural families in northern England', in Hendry and Watson.

Clark, H. H. (1992) *Arenas of Language Use*, Chicago: University of Chicago Press.

Classen, C. (1993) *Worlds of Sense. Exploring the Senses in History and across Cultures*, London: Routledge.

Classen, C. (1997) 'Foundations for an anthropology of the senses', *International Social Science Journal* 153: 401–12.

Classen, C., Howes, D. and Synnott, A. (1994) *Aroma. The Cultural History of Smell,* London: Routledge.

Clifford, J. and Marcus, G. E. (eds) (1986) *Writing Culture: the Poetics and Politics of Ethnography*, Berkeley: University of California Press.

Cobley, P. (ed.) (1996) *The Communication Theory Reader*, London: Routledge.

Cohn, N. (1957) *The Pursuit of the Millennium*, London: Secker & Warburg.

Cole, J. (1991) *Pride and a Daily Marathon*, London: Duckworth.

Coleman, Janet (1992) *Ancient and Medieval Memories. Studies in the Reconstruction of the Past*, Cambridge: Cambridge University Press.

Coleman, Joyce (1996) *Public Reading and the Reading Public in Late Medieval England and France*, Cambridge: Cambridge University Press.

Collias, N. E. and E. C. (1984) *Nest Building and Bird Behavior*, Princeton: Princeton University Press.

Comaroff, J. (1985) *Body of Power, Spirit of Resistance. The Culture and History of a South African People*, Chicago: University of Chicago Press.

Compagnon, A. (1979) *La seconde main, ou le travail de la citation*, Paris: Edition du Seuil.

Comrie, B. (1997), 'Language', in Barfield.

Connerton, P. (1989) *How Societies Remember*, Cambridge: Cambridge University Press.

Conte, G. B. (1986) *The Rhetoric of Imitation. Genre and Poetic Memory in Virgil and Other Latin Poets*, transl. and ed. Charles Segal, Ithaca and London: Cornell University Press.

Conte, G. B. and Most, G. W. (2003) 'Imitatio', in Hornblower and Spawforth.

Coote, J. (1992) '"Marvels of everyday vision": the anthropology of aesthetics and the cattle-keeping Nuer', in Coote and Shelton.

Coote, J. and Shelton, A. (eds) (1992) *Anthropology, Art and Aesthetics*, Oxford: Clarendon Press.

Corbin, A. (1986) *The Foul and the Fragrant. Odor and the French Social Imagination*, English trans., Cambridge MA: Harvard University Press.

Corbin, A. (1999) *Village Bells*, Eng. transl., London: Macmillan.

Corner, J. and Hawthorn, J. (eds) (1993) *Communication Studies. An Introductory Reader*, 4th edn, London: Arnold.

Cosgrove, D. and Daniels, S. (eds) (1985) *The Iconography of Landscape*, Cambridge: Cambridge University Press.

Cottrell, S. J. (1999) 'The ethnography of experience: professional music-making in London', unpublished PhD thesis, University of London.

Coulmas, F. (1996) *Blackwell Encyclopedia of Writing Systems*, Oxford: Blackwell.

Counihan, C. M. (1999) *The Anthropology of Food and the Body. Gender, Meaning, and Power*, London: Routledge.

Counihan, C. M. and Kaplan, S. L. (1998) *Food and Gender. Identity and Power*, Newark: Gordon and Breach.

Couper-Kuhlen, E. and Selting, M. (eds) (1996) *Prosody in Conversation. Interactional Studies*, Cambridge: Cambridge University Press.

Craig, J. C. and Rollman, G. B. (1999) 'Somesthesis', *Annual Review of Psychology* 50: 305–31.

Crapanzano, V. (1994) 'Réflexions sur une anthropologie des émotions', *Terrain: carnets du patrimoine ethnologique 22.*

Critchley, M. (1975) *Silent Language*, London: Butterworths.

Crystal, D. (ed.) (1997) *The Cambridge Encyclopedia of Language*, 2nd edn, Cambridge: Cambridge University Press.

Csordas, T. J. (ed.) (1994) *Embodiment and Experience: the Existential Ground of Culture and Self*, Cambridge: Cambridge University Press.

Dalby, D. (1967–9) 'A survey of the indigenous scripts of Liberia and Sierra Leone: Vai, Mende, Loma, Kpelle and Bassa', 'The indigenous scripts of West Africa and Surinam: their inspiration and design', 'Further indigenous scripts of West Africa: Manding,

Wolof and Fula alphabets and Yoruba "holy" writing', *African Language Studies* 8: 1–52, 9: 156–97, 10: 161–81.

Danet, B. (1997) 'Books, letters, documents: the changing aesthetics of texts in late print culture', *Journal of Material Culture* 2: 5–38.

Danet, B. (2001) *Cyberpl@y. Communicating Online*, Oxford: Berg.

Daniels, P. T. and Bright, W. (eds) (1996) *The World's Writing Systems*, New York: Oxford University Press.

Darwin, C. R. (1872) *The Expression of the Emotions in Man and Animals*, London: John Murray.

Davies, A. (1988) 'Talking in silence: ministry in Quaker Meetings', in Coupland, N. (ed.) *Styles of Discourse*, Beckenham: Croom Helm.

Davies, J. (1996) 'A reluctant guru on matters between the ears', *The Times Higher*, 19 Jan.

Dawkins, M. S. (1995) *Unravelling Animal Behaviour,* 2nd edn, Harlow: Longman Scientific and Technical.

De Grazia, M. (1991) 'Sanctioning voice: quotation marks, the abolition of torture, and the fifth amendment', in Woodmansee and Jaszi.

De Jorio, A. (2000) *Andrea de Jorio, Gesture in Naples and Gesture in Classical Antiquity*, transl. and ed. Kendon, A., Bloomington: Indiana University Press (1st pub. 1832).

DeFrancis, J. (1989) *Visible Speech. The Diverse Oneness of Writing Systems*, Honolulu: University of Hawaii Press.

Delano-Smith, C. and Kain, R. J. P. (1999) *English Maps. A History*, London: British Library.

Denny, F. M. (1987), 'Gestures and postures', in Eliade vol. 11: 461–5.

Denzin, N. K. and Lincoln, Y. S. (eds) (2005) *The Sage Handbook of Qualitative Research*, 3rd edn, London: Sage.

Derrida, J. (1976) *Of Grammatology*, Eng. transl., Baltimore: Johns Hopkins University Press.

Devereux, G. (1969) *Reality and Dream. Psychotherapy of a Plains Indian*, New York: International Universities Press.

Devereux, L. and Hillman, R. (eds) (1995) *Fields of Vision. Essays in Film Studies, Visual Anthropology, and Photography,* Berkeley, London: University of California Press.

DeVito, J. A. (2000) *Human Communication, the Basic Course*, 8th edn, London: Longman.

Dewey, J. (1958) *Art as Experience*, New York: Putnam (1st pub. 1934).

Diringer, D. (1968) *The Alphabet. A Key to the History of Mankind*, 2 vols, 3rd edn, London: Hutchinson.

Donatelli, J. and Winthrop-Young, G. (eds) (1995) *Media Matters. Technologies of Literary Production*, special issue, *Mosaic* 28: 4.

Doniger, W., Eliade, M. and Trask, W. (2004) *Shamanism. Archaic Techniques of Ecstasy*, Princeton: Princeton University Press.

Doty, R. L. (1981) 'Olfactory communication in humans', *Chemical Senses* 6: 351–76.

Douglas, M. (1966) *Purity and Danger*, London: Routledge.

Douglas, M. (1973) *Natural Symbols*, Harmondsworth: Penguin.

Douglas, M. (1975) *Implicit Meanings. Essays in Anthropology*, London: Routledge and Kegan Paul.

Douglas, M. (1982) 'Food as a system of communication', in *In the Active Voice*, London: Routledge.

Douglas, M. and Isherwood, B. (1980) *The World of Goods. Towards an Anthropology of Consumption*, Harmondsworth: Penguin.

Drake, S. (1986) 'Literacy and scientific notations', in Wrolstad and Fisher.

Dunbar, R. (1996) *Grooming, Gossip and the Evolution of Language*, London: Faber and Faber.

Dunbar, R., Knight, C. and Power, C. (eds) (1999) *The Evolution of Culture*, Edinburgh: Edinburgh University Press.

Duranti, A. (1992) 'Language and bodies in social space: Samoan ceremonial greetings', *American Anthropologist* 94: 657–91.

Duranti, A. (1997) *Linguistic Anthropology*, Cambridge: Cambridge University Press.

Duranti, A. (ed.) (2001) *Key Terms in Language and Culture*, Oxford: Blackwell.

Duranti, A. and Goodwin, C. (eds) (1992) *Rethinking Context. Language as an Interactive Phenomenon*, Cambridge: Cambridge University Press.

Dutton, W. H. (ed.) (1996) *Information and Communication Technologies: Visions and Realities*, Oxford: Oxford University Press.

Ebin, V. (1979) *The Body Decorated*, London: Thames and Hudson.

Edgar, I. (1995) *Dreamwork, Anthropology and the Caring Professions: A Cultural Approach to Dreamwork*. Aldershot: Avebury.

Edgar, I. (1999) 'Dream fact and real fiction: the realisation of the imagined self', *Anthropology of Consciousness* 10, 1: 28–42.

Edgar, I. (2000) 'Cultural dreaming or dreaming cultures? The anthropologist and the dream', *Zeitschrift für Kulturwissenschaften* 13: 1–20.

Edgar, I. (2004) *Guide to Imagework: Imagination-based Research Methods*. London: Routledge.

Edgar, I. (2006) 'Encountering the "true dream" in Islam: a journey to Turkey and Pakistan', *British Academy Review* 9: 7–9.

Edgar, I. (2008) 'The inspirational night dream in the motivation and justification of jihad', *Left Curve* 32: 27–34.

Edgar, I. (2009) 'A comparison of Islamic and Western psychological dream theories', in K. Bulkeley, K. Adams and P. Davis, *Dreaming in Christianity and Islam: Culture, Conflict, and Creativity*. New Brunswick: Rutgers.

Edgar, I. (2011) *The Dream in Islam: From Qur'anic Tradition to Jihadist Inspiration*, Oxford: Berghahn Books.

Efron, D. (1972) *Gesture, Race and Culture*, The Hague: Mouton (1st pub. 1941).

Ehn, B. and Löfgren, O. (2010) 'Daydreaming', in *The Secret World of Doing Nothing*, Berkeley: University of California Press.

Eicher, J. B. and Roach-Higgins, M. E. (1992) 'Definition and classification of dress', in Barnes and Eicher.

Einstein, A. (1977) *Mathematical Circles Adieu*, ed. H. Eves, Boston: Prindle Weber Schmidt.

Eisner, C. and Vicinus, M. (eds) (2008) *Originality, Imitation, and Plagiarism. Teaching Writing in the Digital Age*, Ann Arbor: University of Michigan Press.

Ekman, P. (1976) 'Movements with precise meanings', *Journal of Communication* 26, 3: 14–26.

Ekman, P. and Keltner, D. (1997) 'Universal facial expressions of emotion: an old controversy and new findings', in Segerstråle and Molnár.

Eliade, M. (ed.) (1987) *Encyclopedia of Religion*, New York: Macmillan.

Elias, N. (1991) 'On human beings and their emotions: a process-sociological essay', in Featherstone *et al.*

Eliot, T. S. (1975) 'Tradition and the individual talent', in Kermode, F. (ed.) *Selected Prose of T. S. Eliot*, New York: Harcourt Brace.

Ellen, R. and Fukui, K. (eds) (1996) *Redefining Nature*, Oxford: Berg.

Ellingson, T. (1986) 'Buddhist musical notations', in Tokumaru and Yamaguti.

Ellis, A. and Beattie, G. (1986) *The Psychology of Language and Communication*, London: Weidenfeld and Nicolson.

Ember, C. and M. (1998) *Cultural Anthropology*, 9th edn, Upper Saddle River: Prentice-Hall.

Emerson, R. W. (1876) 'Quotation and originality', in *Letters and Social Aims*, London: Chatto and Windus.

Emmison, M. and Smith, P. (2000) *Researching the Visual. Images, Objects, Contexts and Interactions in Social and Cultural Inquiry*, London: Sage.

Endicott, K. (1979) *Batek Negrito Religion. The World-view and Rituals of a Hunting and Gathering People of Peninsular Malaysia*, Oxford: Clarendon Press.

Engen, T. (1991) *Odor Sensation and Memory*, New York: Praeger.

Entwistle, J. (2000) *The Fashioned Body*, Cambridge: Polity.

Evans, J. and Hall, S. (eds) (1999) *Visual Culture: the Reader*, London: Sage.

Evans-Pritchard, E. E. (1940) *The Nuer*, Oxford: Clarendon Press.

Fabian, J. (1983) *Time and the Other. How Anthropology Makes its Object*, New York: Columbia University Press.

Fabian, J. (1996) *Remembering the Present. Painting and Popular History in Zaire*, Berkeley: University of California Press.

Facco, E. and Agrillo, C. (2012) 'Near-death experiences between science and prejudice', *Frontiers in Human Neuroscience*, 18 July.

Farnell, B. (1995a) *Do You See What I Mean? Plains Indian Sign Talk and the Embodiment of Action*, Austin: University of Texas Press.

Farnell, B. (ed.) (1995b) *Human Action Signs in Cultural Context. The Visible and the Invisible in Movement and Dance*, Metuchen NJ and London: Scarecrow Press.

Featherstone, M. (ed.) (2000) *Body Modification*, London: Sage.

Featherstone, M., Hepworth, M. and Turner, B. (eds) (1991) *The Body. Social Process and Cultural Theory,* London: Sage.

Feld, S. (1986) 'Orality and consciousness', in Tokumaru and Yamaguti.

Feld, S. (1989, 2010) Personal communications.

Feld, S. (1989) 'Sound', in Barnouw *et al.* vol. 4: 101–7.

Feld, S. (1990) *Sound and Sentiment. Birds, Weeping, Poetics and Song in Kaluli Experience*, 2nd edn, Philadelphia: University of Pennsylvania Press.

Feld, S. (1995) 'Wept thoughts: the voicing of Kaluli memories', in Finnegan and Orbell.

Feld, S. (1996) 'A poetics of place: ecological and aesthetic co-evolution in a Papua New Guinea rainforest community', in Ellen and Fukui.

Feld, S. and Basso, K. H. (eds) (1996) *Senses of Place*, Santa Fe: School of American Research Press.

Feld, S. *et al.* (1991) *Voices of the Rainforest*, audio-cassette and insert leaflet [no pagination], Rykodisc RACS 0173.

Fentress, J. and Wickham, C. (1992) *Social Memory*, Oxford: Blackwell.

Fernald, A. (1992) 'Meaningful melodies in mothers' speech to infants', in Papousek *et al.*

Fierro, P. (2012) 'Do twins have ESP?', online, http://multiples.about.com/od/funfacts/a/twintelepathy.htm

Finnegan, R. (1967) *Limba Stories and Story-Telling*, Oxford: Clarendon Press.

Finnegan, R. (1970) *Oral Literature in Africa,* Oxford: Clarendon Press.

Finnegan, R. (1988) *Literacy and Orality. Studies in the Technology of Communication,* Oxford: Blackwell.

Finnegan, R. (1992) *Oral Poetry. Its Nature, Significance and Social Context*, 2nd edn, Bloomington: Indiana University Press.

Finnegan, R. (1998) *Tales of the City: A Study of Narrative and Urban Life*, Cambridge: Cambridge University Press.

Finnegan, R. (2001) 'Oral and literate expression', *International Encyclopedia of the Social and Behavioral Sciences*, Oxford: Pergamon.

Finnegan, R. (2003) *Communicating. The Multiple Modes of Human Interaction*, London: Routledge.

Finnegan, R. (2007) *The Oral and Beyond: Doing Things with Words in Africa*, Oxford: James Currey.

Finnegan, R. (2011a) *Why Do We Quote? The Culture and History of Quotation*, Cambridge: Open Book.

Finnegan, R. (2011b) 'What migrates and who does it? A mini case study from Fiji', in Toynbee, J. and Dueck, B. (eds) *Migrating Music*, London: Routledge.

Finnegan, R. (2012) *Oral Literature in Africa*, 2nd (illustrated) edn, Cambridge: Open Book.

Finnegan, R. (ed.) (forthcoming) *Entrancement: Dreaming, Waking and Human Imagination*.

Finnegan, R. and Orbell, M. (eds) (1995) *South Pacific Oral Traditions*, Bloomington: Indiana University Press.

Firth, R. (1973) *Symbols, Public and Private*, London: Allen and Unwin.

Firth, R. (1992) 'Art and anthropology', in Coote and Shelton.

Fiske, J. (1990) *Introduction to Communication Studies*, 2nd edn, London: Routledge.

Fodor, G. (1983) *The Modularity of Mind. An Essay on Faculty Psychology*, Cambridge MA: MIT Press.

Forrest, J. (1988) *Lord I'm Coming Home. Everyday Aesthetics in Tidewater North Carolina*, Ithaca and London: Cornell University Press.

Forty, A. and Küchler, S. (eds) (1999) *The Art of Forgetting*, Oxford: Berg.

Foucault, M. (1970) *The Order of Things. An Archaeology of the Human Sciences*, Eng. transl., New York: Random House.

Foucault, M. (1977) *Discipline and Punish: The Birth of the Prison*, Eng. transl., London: Allen Lane.

Fox, A. (2000) *Prosodic Features and Prosodic Structure*, Oxford: Oxford University Press.

Frake, C. O. (1996) 'A church too far near a bridge oddly placed: the cultural construction of the Norfolk countryside', in Ellen and Fukui.

Frank, L. K. (1957) 'Tactile communication', *Genetic Psychology Monographs* 56: 201–55.

French, C. C. (2001) 'Dying to know the truth: visions of a dying brain, or false memories?', *Lancet* 358: 2010–11.

Frey, L. R. (ed.) (1999) *The Handbook of Group Communication Theory and Research*, Thousand Oaks: Sage.

Frijhoff, W. (1991) 'The kiss sacred and profane: reflections on a cross-cultural confrontation', in Bremmer and Roodenburg.

Fulcher, J. and Scott, J. (1999) *Sociology*, Oxford: Oxford University Press.

Gabbard, G. O. and Twemlow, S. W. (1991) 'Do "near-death experiences" occur only near-death?' *Journal of Near-Death Studies* 10: 41–7.

Gans, E. (1981) *The Origin of Language*, University of California Press.

Garber, M. (2003) *Quotation Marks*, London: Routledge.

Gardner, H. (1980) *Artful Scribble. The Significance of Children's Drawings*, London: Norman.

Gardner, H. (1983) *Frames of Mind. The Theory of Multiple Intelligences*, New York: Basic Books.

Gaur, A. (1992) *A History of Writing*, 2nd edn, London: British Library.

Gell, A. (1977) 'Magic, perfume, dream . . .', in Lewis, I. M. (ed.) *Symbols and Sentiments. Cross-Cultural Studies in Symbolism*, London: Academic Press.

Gell, A. (1992) 'The technology of enchantment . . .', in Coote and Shelton.

Gell, A. (1993) *Wrapping in Images: Tattooing in Polynesia*, Oxford: Clarendon Press.

Gell, A. (1995) 'The language of the forest: landscape and phonological iconism in Umeda', in Hirsch and O'Hanlon.

Gerbner, G. (1956) 'Toward a general model of communication', *Audio Visual Communication Review* 4, 3: 173–99.

Giddens, A. (1997) *Sociology*, 3rd edn, Cambridge: Polity.

Gladwin, T. (1970) *East is a Big Bird. Navigation and Logic on Puluwat Atoll*, Cambridge MA: Harvard University Press.

Glassie, H. (1997) *Art and Life in Bangladesh*, Bloomington: Indiana University Press.

Gleick, J. (2011) *The Information. A History, a Theory, a Flood*, London: HarperCollins.

Glowczewski, B. (1999) 'Dynamic cosmologies and Aboriginal heritage', *Anthropology Today* 15, 1: 3–9.

Goffman, E. (1963) *Behavior in Public Places*, New York: Free Press of Glencoe.

Goffman, E. (1971) *Relations in Public*, New York: Basic Books.

Goffman, E. (1981) *Forms of Talk*, Philadelphia: University of Pennsylvania Press.

Gombrich, E. (1996) 'The visual image: its place in communication', reprinted in Woodfield, R. (ed.) *The Essential Gombrich: Selected Writings on Art and Culture*, London: Phaidon (1st pub. 1972).

Goodenough, J., McGuire, B. and Wallace, R. A. (1993) *Perspectives on Animal Behavior*, New York: Wiley.

Goodman, N. (1978) *Ways of Worldmaking*, Hassocks: Harvester Press.

Goody, E. N. (ed.) (1995) *Social Intelligence and Interaction. Expressions and Implications of the Social Bias in Human Intelligence,* Cambridge: Cambridge University Press.

Goody, J. (1977) *The Domestication of the Savage Mind*, Cambridge: Cambridge University Press.

Goody, J. (1982) *Cooking, Cuisine and Class. A Study in Comparative Sociology*, Cambridge: Cambridge University Press.

Goody, J. (1993) *The Culture of Flowers*, Cambridge: Cambridge University Press.

Goody, J. (1997) *Representations and Contradictions: Ambivalence Towards Images, Theatre, Fiction, Relics and Sexuality*, Oxford: Blackwell.

Goswami, A. (2001) *Physics of the Soul*, Charlottesville: Hampton Roads.

Gow, P. (1995) 'Land, people, and paper in Western Amazonia', in Hirsch and O'Hanlon.

Graf, F. (1991) 'Gestures and conventions: the gestures of Roman actors and orators', in Bremmer and Roodenburg.

Grafton, A. (1999) *The Footnote. A Curious History*, Cambridge MA: Harvard University Press.

Graham, W. (1987) *Beyond the Written Word. Oral Aspects of Scripture in the History of Religion*, Cambridge: Cambridge University Press.

Graves-Brown, P. M. (ed.) (2000) *Matter, Materiality and Modern Culture*, London: Routledge.

Gray, P. M., Krause, B., Atema, J., Payne, R., Krumhansl, C. and Baptista, L. (2001) 'The music of nature and the nature of music', *Science* 291: 52–4.

Greenbaum, P. E. and Rosenfeld, H. W. (1980) 'Varieties of touching in greeting: sequential structure and sex-related differences', *Journal of Nonverbal Behavior* 5: 13–25.

Gregory, W. (1996) *The Informability Manual,* London: HMSO.

Greyson, B. (2010) 'Implications of near-death experiences for a postmaterialist psychology', *Psychology of Religion and Spirituality* 2: 37–45.

Greyson, B., Kelly, E. W. and Kelly, E. F. (2009) 'Explanatory models for near-death experiences', in Holden, J. M., Greyson, B. and James, D. (eds) *The Handbook of Near-Death Experiences*, Santa Barbara: Praeger/ABC-CLIO.

Griffin, D. A. (1984) *Animal Thinking*, Cambridge MA: Harvard University Press.

Griffin, D. A. (1986) *Listening in the Dark. The Acoustic Orientation of Bats and Men*, 2nd edn, Ithaca and London: Cornell University Press.

Gröning, K. (1997) *Decorated Skin. A World Survey of Body Art*, London: Thames and Hudson.

Gross, L. (1974) 'Modes of communication and the acquisition of symbolic capacities', in Olson.

Gross, L. (1989) 'Modes', in Barnouw *et al.* vol. 3: 32–6.

Gudykunst, W. G. (1998) *Bridging Differences. Effective Intergroup Communication*, 3rd edn, Thousand Oaks: Sage.

Gulliver, P. H. (1958) 'Counting with the fingers by two East African tribes', *Tanganyika Notes and Records* 51: 259–62.

Gumperz, J. J. and Levinson, S. C. (eds) (1996) *Rethinking Linguistic Relativity*, Cambridge: Cambridge University Press.

Guss, D. M. (1989) *To Weave and Sing. Art, Symbol, and Narrative in the South American Rain Forest*, Berkeley: University of California Press.

Habermas, J. (1998) *On the Pragmatics of Communication*, Eng. transl., Cambridge: Polity (selected articles first published 1976–96).

Hailman, J. P. (1989) 'Visible signals', in Barnouw *et al.* vol. 1: 83–88.

Hailman, J. P. and Ficken, M. S. (1996) 'Comparative analysis of vocal repertoires, with reference to chickadees', in Kroodsma and Miller.

Hall, E. T. (1959) *The Silent Language,* New York: Doubleday.

Hall, E. T. (1960) 'The language of space', *Landscape* 10: 41–5.

Hall, E. T. (1966) *The Hidden Dimension,* New York: Doubleday.

Hall, E. T. (1974) *Handbook for Proxemic Research,* Washington: Society for the Anthropology of Visual Communication.

Hall, S. (ed.) (1997) *Representation. Cultural Representations and Signifying Practices*, London: Sage/The Open University.

Hanks, W. F. (1990) *Referential Practice. Language and Lived Space among the Maya*, Chicago: University of Chicago Press.

Hanks, W. F. (1996) *Language and Communicative Practices*, Boulder: Westview Press.

Hanna, J. L. (1979) *To Dance is Human. A Theory of Nonverbal Communication*, Austin and London: University of Texas Press.

Hannerz, U. (1992) *Cultural Complexity. Studies in the Social Organization of Meaning*, New York: Columbia University Press.

Hargie, O. D. W. (ed.) (1997) *The Handbook of Communication Skills*, 2nd edn, London: Routledge.

Harley, J. B. (1985) 'Maps, knowledge and power', in Cosgrove and Daniels.

Harré, R. and Parrott, W. G. (eds) (1996) *The Emotions*, London: Sage.

Harris, Robert L. (1999) *Information Graphics. Visual Tools for Analyzing, Managing, and Communicating*, New York: Oxford.

Harris, Roy (1986) *The Origin of Writing*, London: Duckworth.

Harris, Roy (1995) *Signs of Writing*, London: Routledge.

Harris, Roy (1996) *Signs, Language and Communication. Integrational and Segregational Approaches*, London: Routledge.

Harris, Roy (1998) *Introduction to Integrational Linguistics*, Oxford: Pergamon.

Harris, Roy (2000) *Rethinking Writing*, London: Athlone Press.

Harris, Roy and Wolf, G. (eds) (1998) *Integrational Linguistics. A First Reader*, Oxford: Pergamon.

Harris, W. (2009) *Dreaming and Experience in Classical Antiquity*, Harvard: Harvard University Press.

Hartley, P. (1999) *Interpersonal Communication*, 2nd edn, London: Routledge.

Hauser, M. D. (1996) *The Evolution of Communication*, Cambridge MA: MIT Press.

Hayward, G. (2013) 'Chanting as one: the synchrony of sonorous community', PhD thesis, University of Cambridge.

Heath, S. B. (1983) *Ways with Words. Language, Life and Work in Communities and Classrooms*, Cambridge: Cambridge University Press.

Henderson, K. (1999) *On Line and on Paper. Visual Representations, Visual Culture, and Computer Graphics in Design Engineering*, Cambridge MA: MIT Press.

Hendry, J. (1999) *An Introduction to Social Anthropology. Other People's Worlds*, Basingstoke: Macmillan.

Hendry, J. and Watson, C. W. (eds) (2001) *An Anthropology of Indirect Communication*, London: Routledge.

Henecy, D. (2008) *The ESP Enigma: The Scientific Case for Psychic Phenomena*, New York: Walker & Company.

Hepper, P. G. (ed.) (1991) *Kin Recognition*, Cambridge: Cambridge University Press.

Hetherington, K. (1998) *Expressions of Identity: Space, Performance, Politics*, London: Sage.

Hewes, G. (1978) 'Visual learning, thinking, and communication in human biosocial evolution', in Randhawa and Coffman.

Hewes, G. W. (1996) 'A history of the study of language origins and the gestural primacy hypothesis', in Lock and Peters.

Hewitt, W. (1996) *Psychic Development for Beginners: An Easy Guide to Releasing and Developing Your Psychic Abilities*, Llewellyn.

Heywood, I. and Sandywell, B. (eds) (1999) *Interpreting Visual Culture. Explorations in the Hermeneutics of the Visual*, London: Routledge.

Hibbitts, B. J. (1992) '"Coming to our senses": communication and legal expression in performance cultures', *Emory Law Journal* 41, 4: 873–960.

Hibbitts, B. J. (1995) 'Making motions: the embodiment of law in gesture', *Journal of Contemporary Legal Issues* 6: 51–81.

Hill, J. H. and Irvine, J. T. (eds) (1993) *Responsibility and Evidence in Oral Discourse*, Cambridge: Cambridge University Press.

Hinde, R. A. (1975) 'The comparative study of non-verbal communication', in Benthall and Polhemus.

Hinton, R. (1996) *Tactile Graphics in Education*, Edinburgh: Moray House.

Hirsch, E. and O'Hanlon, M. (eds) (1995) *The Anthropology of Landscape*, Clarendon Press: Oxford.

Hirschfeld, L. A. and Gelman, S. A. (eds) (1994) *Mapping the Mind. Domain Specificity in Cognition and Culture*, Cambridge: Cambridge University Press.

Hockings, P. (ed.) (1995) *Principles of Visual Anthropology,* 2nd edn, Berlin: Mouton de Gruyter (1st edn 1975).

Hodder, I. (ed.) (1989) *The Meanings of Things. Material Culture and Symbolic Expression*, London: Unwin Hyman.

Hofmeyr, I. (1993) *'We Spend our Years as a Tale that is Told'. Oral Historical Narrative in a South African Chiefdom*, Johannesburg: Witwatersrand University Press.

Holden, J. M., Greyson, B. and James, D. (2009) *The Handbook of Near-Death Experiences*, Santa Barbara: Praeger/ABC-CLIO.

Homer, B. D. (2009) 'Literacy and metalinguistic development', in Olson and Torrance.

Hopp, S. L., Owren, M. J. and Evans, C. S. (eds) (1998) *Animal Acoustic Communication. Sound Analysis and Research Methods*, Berlin: Springer.

Hornblower, S. and Spawforth, A. (eds) (2003) *The Oxford Classical Dictionary*, Oxford: Oxford University Press.

Horton, R. (1967) 'Ikaki – the Tortoise masquerade', *Nigeria Magazine* 94, Sept.: 226–39.

Horton, R. and Finnegan, R. (eds) (1973) *Modes of Thought. Essays on Thinking in Western and Non-Western Societies*, London: Faber.

Howard, R. M. (1999) *Standing in the Shadow of Giants: Plagiarists, Authors, Collaborators*, Stamford: Ablex.

Howard, R. M. and Robillard, A. E. (eds) (2008) *Pluralizing Plagiarism. Identities, Contexts, Pedagogies*, Portsmouth NH: Heinemann.

Howes, D. (1987) 'Olfaction and transition: an essay on the ritual uses of smell', *Canadian Review of Sociology and Anthropology* 24: 398–416.

Howes, D. (ed.) (1991) *The Varieties of Sensory Experience. A Sourcebook in the Anthropology of the Senses,* Toronto: University of Toronto Press.

Howes, D. (ed.) (2011) *The Sixth Sense Reader*, Oxford: Berg.

Howes, D. and Lalonde, M. (1991) 'The history of sensibilities: of the standard of taste in mid-eighteenth century England and the circulation of smells in post-revolutionary France', *Dialectical Anthropology* 16: 125–35.

Hudson, P. (1999) 'Industrialization in Britain: the challenge of micro-history', *Family and Community History* 2: 5–16.

Hughes-Freeland, F. (1997) 'Art and politics: from Javanese court dance to Indonesian art', *Journal of the Royal Anthropological Institute* 3, 3: 473–95.

Hughes-Freeland, F. (ed.) (1998) *Ritual, Performance, Media*, London: Routledge.

Hull, J. (1997) *On Sight and Insight, a Journey into the World of Blindness*, Oxford: Oneworld.

Humphrey, C. (1974) 'Inside a Mongolian tent', *New Society* 31 October: 273–5.

Hymes, D. (1964) 'Introduction: toward ethnographies of communication', *American Anthropologist* 66, 6: 1–34.

Hymes, D. (1996) *Ethnography, Linguistics, Narrative Inequality*, London: Taylor & Francis.

Ingold, T. (1996) 'Social relations, human ecology, and the evolution of culture', in Lock and Peters.

Ingold, T. (2000) 'Making culture and weaving the world', in Graves-Brown.

Ingold, T. (2012) Personal communication.

Ingold, T. (ed.) (1994) *Companion Encyclopedia of Anthropology: Humanity, Culture and Social Life,* London: Routledge.

Irvine, J. T. (1996) 'Shadow conversations: the indeterminacy of participant roles', in Silverstein and Urban.

Irwin, W. (2001) 'What is an allusion?', *Journal of Aesthetics and Art Criticism* 59, 3: 287–97.

Ivins, W. M. (1953) *Prints and Visual Communication*, Cambridge MA: Harvard University Press.

James, W. (1997) 'The names of fear: memory, history, and the ethnography of feeling among Uduk refugees', *Journal of the Royal Anthropological Institute* 3: 115–31.

Järviluoma, H. (ed.) (1994) *Soundscapes: Essays on Vroom and Moo*, Tampere: Department of Folk Tradition University of Tampere and Institute of Rhythm Music.

Jaworski, A. (1993) *The Power of Silence. Social and Pragmatic Perspectives*, Newbury Park: Sage.

Jay, M. (1986) 'In the empire of the gaze: Foucault and the denigration of vision in twentieth-century French thought', in Couzen-Hoy, D. (ed.) *Foucault: A Critical Reader*, Oxford: Blackwell.

Jay, M. (1992) 'Scopic regimes of modernity', in Lash and Friedman.

Jedrej, M. and Shaw, R. (eds) (1992), *Dreaming, Religion and Society in Africa*, Leiden: Brill.

John, E. R. (2002) 'The neurophysics of consciousness', *Brain Research Reviews* 39: 1–28.

Johnson-Laird, P. N. (1990) 'Introduction: what is communication?', in Mellor.

Johnston, R. E., Müller-Schwarze, D. and Sorensen, P. W. (eds) (1999) *Advances in Chemical Signals in Vertebrates*, New York: Kluwer Academic.

Jones, S. E. and Yarbrough, A. E. (1985) 'A naturalistic study of the meanings of touch', *Communications Monographs* 52: 19–56.

Jones, S., Martin, R. and Pilbeam, D. (eds) (1992) *The Cambridge Encyclopedia of Human Evolution*, Cambridge: Cambridge University Press.

Jung, C. G. (2001) *Dreams*, Abingdon: Routledge.

Jussim, E. (1983) *Visual Communication and the Graphic Arts. Photographic Technologies in the Nineteenth Century*, New York: Bowker.

Kacapyr, S. (2013) 'Brain creates and uses personality models to predict behavior', *Cerebral Cortex*, March.

Kaczmarek, K. A. and Bach-y-Rita, P. (1995) 'Tactile displays', in Barfield, W. and Furness, T. A. (eds) *Virtual Environments and Advanced Interface Design*, New York: Oxford University Press.

Kaeppler, A. L. (1993) *Poetry in Motion: Studies of Tongan Dance*, Nuku'alofa, Tonga: Vava'u Press.

Kaeppler, A. L. (1996) 'Dance', in Levinson and Ember.

Kanafani, A. S. (1983) *Aesthetics and Ritual in the United Arab Emirates. The Anthropology of Food and Personal Adornment among Arabian Women*, Beirut: American University of Beirut.

Kant, I. (1978 [1798]) *Anthropology from a Pragmatic Point of View*, Eng. transl., Carbondale: Southern Illinois University Press.

Karim, Wazir Jahan (ed.) (1991) *Emotions of Culture: a Malay Perspective*, Singapore: Oxford University Press.

Kassam, A. and Megerssa, G. (1996) 'Sticks, self, and society in Booran Oromo: a symbolic interpretation', in Arnoldi *et al.*

Kawada, Junzo (1996) 'Human dimensions in the sound universe', in Ellen and Fukui.

Keane, W. (2013) 'On spirit writing: materialities of language and the religious work of transduction', *Journal of the Royal Anthropological Institute* 19: 1–17.

Keenan, W. J. F. (ed.) (2001) *Dressed to Impress. Looking the Part*, Oxford: Berg.

Keesing, R. M. and Strathern, A. J. (1998) *Cultural Anthropology. A Contemporary Perspective*, 3rd edn (updated), Fort Worth: Brace College.

Kehoe, A. B. (1998) *Humans. An Introduction to Four-Field Anthropology*, London: Routledge.

Keil, C. and Feld, S. (1994) *Music Grooves*, Chicago and London: Chicago University Press.

Keller-Cohen, D. (ed.) (1994) *Literacy. Interdisciplinary Conversations*, New York: Hampton Press.

Keller, H. (1923) *The Story of My Life*, London: Harrap.

Keller, H. (1933) *The World I Live in*, London: Methuen.

Kellett, E. E. (1933) *Literary Quotation and Allusion*, Cambridge: W. Heffer and Sons.

Kellman, P. J. and Arterberry, M. E. (1998) *The Cradle of Knowledge. Development of Perception in Infancy*, Cambridge MA: MIT Press.

Kelly, E. W., Crabtree, A., Gauld, A., Grosso, M. and Greyson, B. (2007) *Irreducible Mind: Toward a Psychology for the 21st Century*, Lanham: Rowman & Littlefield.

Kendon, A. (1988) *Sign Languages of Aboriginal Australia, Cultural, Semiotic and Communicative Perspectives*, Cambridge: Cambridge University Press.

Kendon, A. (1989) 'Nonverbal communication', in Barnouw *et al.* vol. 3: 209–10.

Kendon, A. (1990) *Conducting Interaction. Patterns of Behavior in Focused Encounters*, Cambridge: Cambridge University Press.

Kendon, A. (1991) 'Some considerations for a theory of language origins', *Man* 26: 199–221.

Kendon, A. (1997) 'Gesture', *Annual Review of Anthropology* 26: 109–28.

Kendon, A. (2000) 'Editor's introduction', in De Jorio.

Kendon, A. (ed.) (1994) *Gesture and Understanding in Social Interaction,* Special issue, *Research on Language and Social Interaction* 27, 3: 171–267.

Kersenboom, S. (1995) *Word, Sound, Image: the Life of the Tamil Text*, Oxford: Berg.

Ketrow, S. M. (1999) 'Nonverbal aspects of group communication', in Frey.

Khatibi, A. and Sijelmassi, M. (1995) *The Splendour of Islamic Calligraphy*, Eng. transl., London: Thames and Hudson.

Kigotho, W. (2001) 'If you hear a rumble in the jungle it's probably just the elephants talking', *The Times Higher*, 20 April: 19.

Knapp, M. L. and Hall, J. A. (1997) *Nonverbal Communication in Human Interaction*, 4th edn, Fort Worth: Harcourt Brace College Publishers.

Knoblauch, H. and Kotthoff, H. (eds) (2001) *Verbal Art across Cultures. The Aesthetics and Proto-Aesthetics of Communication*, Tübingen: Narr.

Kotthoff, H. (1998) *Irony, Quotation, and Other forms of Staged Intertextuality. Double or Contrastive Perspectivation in Discourse*, Konstanz: Universität Konstanz, InLiST-Arbeitspapier, 5.

Kotthoff, H. (2000) 'Gender, emotion and poeticity in Georgian mourning rituals', in Baron, B. and Kotthoff, H. (eds) *Gender in Interaction*, Amsterdam: Benjamins.

Kotthoff, H. (2001) 'Aesthetic dimensions of Georgian grief rituals: on the artful display of emotions in lamentation', in Knoblauch and Kotthoff.

Kracke, W. (1987a) 'Myths in dreams, thought in images: an Amazonian contribution to the psychoanalytic theory of primary process', in Tedlock *et al.* 1987.

Kracke, W. (1987b) 'Selfhood and discourse in Sambia dream sharing', in Tedlock *et al.* 1987.

Kress, G. (2000) *Early Spelling. Between Convention and Creativity*, London: Routledge.

Kress, G. and Van Leeuwen, T. (1996) *Reading Images. The Grammar of Visual Design*, London: Routledge.

Kripal, G. (2011) *Authors of the Impossible*, Chicago: University of Chicago Press.

Krippendorff, K. (1993) 'Major metaphors of communication and some constructivist reflections on their use', *Cybernetics and Human Knowing* 2, 1: 3–25.

Kroodsma, D. E. and Miller, E. H. (eds) (1996) *Ecology and Evolution of Acoustic Communication in Birds*, Ithaca: Cornell University Press.

Kwint, M., Breward, C. and Aynsely, J. (eds) (1999) *Material Memories. Design and Evocation*, Oxford: Berg.

Laderman, C. and Roseman, M. (eds) (1996) *The Performance of Healing*, London: Routledge.

Lambert, H. (2001) 'Not talking about sex in India', in Hendry and Watson.

Lang, A. (1898 [reprint 2012]) 'Anthropology and hallucination', in *The Making of Religion*, London: Longman.

Larwood, J. and Hotten, J. C. (1866) *The History of Signboards*, London: John Camden Hotten.

Lash, S. and Friedman, J. (eds) (1992) *Modernity and Identity*, Oxford: Blackwell.

Lasswell, H. D. (1948) 'The structure and function of communication in society', in Bryson, L. (ed.) *The Communication of Ideas*, New York: Harper and Brothers.

Layton, R. (1991) *The Anthropology of Art*, 2nd edn, Cambridge: Cambridge University Press.

Lebaron, C. D. and Streeck, J. (1997) 'Built space and the interactional framing of experience during a murder interrogation', *Human Studies* 20: 1–25.

Lederman, S. J. and Klatzky, R. L. (1987) 'Hand movements: a window into haptic object recognition', *Cognitive Psychology* 19: 342–68.

Lee, D. C. (1959) *Freedom and Culture*, Englewood Cliffs: Prentice-Hall.

Leppert, R. (1993) *The Sight of Sound: Music, Representation, and the History of the Body*, Berkeley: University of California Press.

Lester, P. M. (2000) *Visual Communication. Images with Messages*, 2nd edn, London: Wadsworth.

Leupold, J. (1727) *Theatrum Arithmetico-Geometricum*, Leipzig.

Lévi-Strauss, C. (1970) *The Raw and the Cooked*, Eng. transl., London: Cape.

Levin, D. (1988) *The Opening of Vision: Nihilism and the Postmodern Situation*, New York: Routledge.

Levin, D. M. (ed.) (1993) *Modernity and the Hegemony of Vision*, Berkeley: University of California Press.

Levinson, D. and Ember, M. (eds) (1996) *An Encyclopedia of Cultural Anthropology*, 4 vols, New York: Henry Holt.

Lindlof, T. R. (1995) *Qualitative Communication Research Methods*, Thousand Oaks: Sage.

Lithgow, W. (1906) *The Totall Discourse of The Rare Adventures and Painefull Peregrinations of long Nineteene Yeares Travayles from Scotland to the most famous Kingdomes in Europe, Asia and Affrica*, Glasgow: MacLehose (1st pub. London 1640).

Littlejohn, J. (1967) 'The Temne house', in Middleton, J. (ed.) *Myth and Cosmos*, New York: Natural History Press.

Lock, A. and Peters, C. R. (eds) (1996) *Handbook of Human Symbolic Evolution*, Oxford: Clarendon Press.

Lohmann, R. I. (ed.) (2003) *Dream Travelers: Sleep Experiences and Culture in the Western Pacific*, Basingstoke: Palgrave.

Lord, A. B. (1960) *The Singer of Tales*, Cambridge MA: Harvard University Press.

Lowe, D. M. (1982) *History of Bourgeois Perception*, Chicago: University of Chicago Press.

Luckmann, T. (1995) 'Interaction planning and intersubjective adjustment of perspective by communicative genres', in Goody, E.

Lucy, J. A. (2001) 'Reflexivity', in Duranti.

Lucy, J. A. (ed.) (1993) *Reflexive Language. Reported Speech and Metapragmatics*, New York: Cambridge University Press.

Lull, J. (ed.) (2001) *Culture in the Communication Age*, London: Routledge.

Lunsford, A. A. and Ede, L. (1990) *Singular Texts/Plural Authors. Perspectives on Collaborative Writing*, Carbondale: Southern Illinois University Press.

Lupton, D. (1998) *The Emotional Self*, London: Sage.

Lutz, C. A. and Abu-Lughod, L. (eds) (1990) *Language and the Politics of Emotion*, Cambridge: Cambridge University Press.

Lutz, C. A. and White, G. (1986) 'The anthropology of emotions', *Annual Review of Anthropology* 15, 405–36.

Maclagan, E. (1945) *The Bayeux Tapestry*, Harmondsworth: Penguin.

Madden, R. (2010) *Being Ethnographic: A Guide to the Theory and Practice of Ethnography*, London: Sage.

Malinowski, B. (1923) 'The problem of meaning in primitive languages', in Ogden, C. K. and Richards, I. A. (eds) *The Meaning of Meaning*, New York: Harcourt, Brace and World.

Malinowski, B. (1929) *The Sexual Life of Savages in North-Western Melanesia*, London: Routledge.

Mallery, G. (1881) *Sign Language among North American Indians Compared with that among Other Peoples and Deaf-Mutes*, Washington: Smithsonian Institution.

Mallery, G. (1893) *Picture-Writing of the American Indians*, Washington: Smithsonian Institution.

Mallon, T. (1989) *Stolen Words. Forays into the Origins and Ravages of Plagiarism*, New York: Ticknor and Fields.

Manguel, A. (1996) *A History of Reading*, London: HarperCollins.

Mannheim, B. and Tedlock, D. (1995) (eds) *The Dialogic Emergence of Culture*, Urbana: University of Illinois Press.

Mantovani, G. (1996) *New Communication Environments, from Everyday to Virtual*, London: Taylor and Francis.

Marler, P. and Evans, C. S. (1997) 'Communication signals of animals: contributions of emotion and reference', in Segerstråle and Molnár.

Marler, P., Evans, C. S. and Hauser, M. D. (1992) 'Animal signals: motivational, referential, or both?', in Papousek *et al.*

Martial, *Epigrams*, ed. and transl. in Bailey, D. R. S. (1993) *Martial Epigrams*, vol. 1, Loeb Classical Library, Cambridge MA: Harvard University Press.

Maryanski, A. (1997) 'Primate communication and the ecology of a language niche', in Segerstråle and Molnár.

Mass Observation (1970) *The Pub and the People. A Worktown Study,* Welwyn Garden City: Seven Dials Press.

Mass Observation (2012) *Responses to 'Directive' on Dreams*, Brighton: Mass Observation Archive, University of Sussex.

Mass Observation Writers Panel (2012–13) Commentaries.

Mattelart, A. (2000) *Networking the World 1794–2000*, Eng. transl., Minneapolis: University of Minnesota Press.

Mattelart, A. and M. (1998) *Theories of Communication. A Short Introduction*, Eng. transl., London: Sage.

Mauss, M. (1979) 'Body techniques', in *Sociology and Psychology: Essays*, Eng. transl., London: Routledge (1st pub. 1935).

McAdams, S. and Bigand, E. (eds) (1993) *Thinking in Sound. The Cognitive Psychology of Human Audition*, Oxford: Clarendon Press.

McDaniel, E. and Andersen, P. A. (1998) 'The international patterns of interpersonal tactile communication: a field study', *Journal of Nonverbal Behavior* 22: 59–75.

McKenzie, D. (1923) *Aromatics and the Soul. A Study of Smells*, London: Heinemann.

McLeod, M. D. (1981) *The Asante*, London: British Museum.

McLuhan, M. (1964) *Understanding Media. The Extensions of Man*, London: Routledge and Kegan Paul.

McNeill, D. (1992) *Hand and Mind. What Gestures Reveal about Thought*, Chicago: University of Chicago Press.

McNeill, D. (ed.) (2000) *Language and Gesture*, Cambridge: Cambridge University Press.

Mellor, D. H. (ed.) (1990) *Ways of Communicating*, Cambridge: Cambridge University Press.

Menninger, K. (1969) *Number Words and Number Symbols. A Cultural History of Numbers*, Eng. transl., Cambridge MA: MIT Press.

Merten, K. (1977) *Kommunikation. Eine Begriffs- und Prozessanalyse*, Opladen: Westdeutscher Verlag.

Merton, R. K. (1965) *On the Shoulders of Giants: A Shandean Postscript*, New York: Free Press.

Millar, S. (1997) *Reading by Touch*, London: Routledge.

Miller, D. (1994) 'Artefacts and the meaning of things', in Ingold.

Miller, D. and Slater, D. (2000) *The Internet. An Ethnographic Approach*, Oxford: Berg.

Miller, D. and Tilley, C. (1996) 'Editorial', *Journal of Material Culture* 1: 5–14.

Mirzoeff, N. (1999) *An Introduction to Visual Culture*, London: Routledge.

Mirzoeff, N. (ed.) (1998) *The Visual Culture Reader*, London: Routledge.

Mitchell, W. J. T. (1986) *Iconology: Image, Text, Ideology*, Chicago: University of Chicago Press.

Mitchell, W. J. T. (1994) *Picture Theory*, Chicago: University of Chicago Press.

Mithen, S. (1996) *The Prehistory of Mind. A Search for the Origins of Art, Religion and Science*, London: Thames and Hudson.

Mobbs, D. and Watt, C. (2011) 'There is nothing paranormal about near-death experiences: how neuroscience can explain seeing bright lights, meeting the dead, or being convinced you are one of them', *Trends in Cognitive Science* 15: 447–9.

Moffitt, A., Kramer, M. and Hoffman, R. (1993) *The Functions of Dreaming*, Albany: State University of New York Press.

Montagu, A. (1986) *Touching: The Human Significance of the Skin*, 3rd edn, New York: Harper and Row.

Moody, R. A. and Perry, P. (2010) *Glimpse of Eternity*. New York: Guideposts.

Morgan, A. (2001) 'The roar that leaves victims scared stiff', *The Sunday Telegraph*, 14 Jan: 16.

Morgan, V. (1999) 'The construction of civic memory in early modern Norwich', in Kwint *et al.*

Morphy, H. (1991) *Ancestral Connections. Art and an Aboriginal System of Knowledge*, Chicago: Chicago University Press.

Morphy, H. (1994) 'The anthropology of art', in Ingold.

Morris, C. (1972) *Medieval Media. Mass Communication in the Making of Europe*, Inaugural lecture: University of Southampton.

Morris, D. (1977) *Manwatching. A Field Guide to Human Behaviour*, London: Cape.

Morris, D., Collett, P., Marsh, P. and O'Shaughnessy, M. (1979) *Gestures, their Origins and Distribution*, London: Cape.

Morris, R. L. (2001) 'Research methods in experimental parapsychology: problems and prospects', *European Journal of Parapsychology* 16: 8–18.

Morse, M., Castillo, P., Venecia, D., Milstein, J. and Tyler, D. C. (1986) 'Childhood near-death experiences', *American Journal of Diseases of Children* 140: 1110–14.

Morson, G. S. and Emerson, C. (1990) *Mikhail Bakhtin. Creation of a Prosaics*, Stanford: Stanford University Press.

Morton, E. S. and Page, J. (1992) *Animal Talk. Science and the Voices of Nature*, New York: Random House.

Moss, R. (1998) *Dreamgates*, Novato: New World Library.

Moss, R. (2010) *The Secret History of Dreaming*, Novato: New World Library.

Moulthrop, S. (1995) 'Traveling in the breakdown lane: a principle of resistance for hyper-text', in Donatelli and Winthrop-Young: 55–77.

Mountain, M. (1987) 'Working with Makaton', *Talking Sense*, winter: 10–11.

Moynihan, M. (1966) 'Communication in the titi monkey, *Callicebus*', *Journal of Zoology* 150: 77–127.

Munn, N. D. (1973) *Walbiri Iconography. Graphic Representation and Cultural Symbolism in a Central Australian Society*, Ithaca: Cornell University Press.

Murray, D. J. (1975) 'Case studies as a form of enquiry', in J. M. Lee, *Approaches to the Study of Public Administration, Part 4: The Historical Approach*, Milton Keynes: Open University Press.

National High Magnetic Field Laboratory (2012) *A Guided Tour of MRI: An Introduction for Laypeople*, Tallahassee: National High Magnetic Field Laboratory.

Ness, S. A. (1992) *Body, Movement, and Culture*, Philadelphia: University of Pennsylvania Press.

Nketia, J. H. K. (1963) *Drumming in Akan Communities of Ghana*, Edinburgh: Nelson.

Nuckolls, J. B. (1996) *Sounds Like Life. Sound-Symbolic Grammar, Performance, and Cognition in Pastaza Quechua*, Oxford and New York: Oxford University Press.

Nuttall, N. (1999) 'Motor mouse makes web a touch more fun', *The Times* [London], 8 July.

O'Hanlon, M. (1989) *Reading the Skin. Adornment, Display and Society among the Wahgi*, London: British Museum Publications.

O'Sullivan, T., Hartley, J., Saunders, D., Montgomery, M. and Fiske, J. (eds) (1994) *Key Concepts in Communication and Cultural Studies*, 2nd edn, London: Routledge.

Ochs, E., Schegloff, E. A. and Thompson, S. A. (eds) (1996) *Interaction and Grammar*, Cambridge: Cambridge University Press.

Okpewho, I. (1992) *African Oral Literature. Backgrounds, Character and Continuity*, Bloomington: Indiana University Press.

Olson, D. R. (ed.) (1974) *Media and Symbols. The Forms of Expression, Communication, and Education*, Yearbook of the National Society for the Study of Education, vol. 3 Part 1, Chicago: Chicago University Press.

Olson, D. R. and Kamawar, D. (2002) 'Writing as a form of quotation', in Brockmeier, J., Wang, M. and Olson, D. R. (eds) *Literacy, Narrative and Culture*, Richmond: Curzon.

Olson, D. R. and Torrance, N. (eds) (1991) *Literacy and Orality*, Cambridge: Cambridge University Press.

Olson, D. R. and Torrance, N. (eds) (1996) *Modes of Thought. Explorations in Culture and Cognition*, Cambridge: Cambridge University Press.

Olson, D. R. and Torrance, N. (eds) (2009) *The Cambridge Handbook of Literacy*, Cambridge: Cambridge University Press.

Olson, L. C. (1987) 'British visions of American colonies as an animal: a study in rhetori-cal iconology', in Taureg and Ruby.

Olson, L. C. (1991) *Emblems of American Community in the Revolutionary Era. A Study in Rhetorical Iconology*, Washington: Smithsonian Institution Press.

Ong, W. J. (1967) *The Presence of the Word*, New Haven: Yale University Press.

Ong, W. J. (1977) *Interfaces of the Word*, Ithaca: Cornell University Press.

Ong, W. J. (1982) *Orality and Literacy. The Technologizing of the Word*, London and New York: Methuen.

Ostwald, P. F. (1973) *The Semiotics of Human Sound*, The Hague: Mouton.

Ottenberg, S. (1996) *Seeing with Music. The Lives of Three Blind African Musicians*, Seattle: University of Washington Press.

Owen, C. L. (1986) 'Technology, literacy, and graphic systems', in Wrolstad and Fisher.

Owen, R. (1999) 'Colosseum's animal magic was high art', *The Times* [London], 8 March.

Owings, D. H., Beecher, M. D. and Thompson, N. S. (eds) (1997) *Communication*, in *Perspectives in Ethology* 12.

Papousek, H., Jürgens, U. and Papousek, M. (eds) (1992) *Nonverbal Vocal Communication. Comparative and Developmental Approaches*, Cambridge: Cambridge University Press.

Parkin, D., Caplan, L. and Fisher, H. (eds) (1996) *The Politics of Cultural Performance*, Providence and Oxford: Berghahn Books.

Parrinder, G. (1987) 'Touching', in Eliade vol. 14: 578–83.

Peek, P. (1994) 'The sounds of silence; cross-world communication and the auditory arts in African societies', *American Ethnologist* 21, 3: 474–94.

Pemberton, L. and Shurville, S. (eds) (2000) *Words on the Web. Computer Mediated Communication*, Exeter: Intellect.

Pennycock, A. (1996) 'Borrowing others' words. Text, ownership, memory and plagiarism', *TESOL Quarterly* 30, 2: 201–30.

Pepperberg, I. M. (1993) 'Cognition and communication in an African grey parrot', in Roitblat *et al.*

Pepperberg, I. M. (1999) *The Alex Studies, Cognitive and Communicative Abilities of Grey Parrots*, Cambridge MA: Harvard University Press.

Perani, J. and Wolff, N. K. (1999) *Cloth, Dress and Art Patronage in Africa*, Oxford: Berg.

Perdue, L. G. (ed.) (2008) *Scribes, Sages and Seers: The Sage in the Eastern Mediterranean*, Göttingen: Vandenhoeck & Ruprecht.

Perri, C. (1978) 'On alluding', *Poetics* 7: 289–307.

Pinker, S. (1994) *The Language Instinct. The New Science of Language and Mind*, London: Allen Lane.

Pinker, S. (1997) *How the Mind Works*, New York and London: Norton.

Playfair, G. L. (2002) *Twin Telepathy. The Psychic Connection*, London: Vega.

Ploog, D. W. (1992) 'The evolution of vocal communication', in Papousek *et al.*

Plotkin, H. (1997) *Evolution in Mind. An Introduction to Evolutionary Psychology*, London: Allen Lane.

Poe, M. R. (2011) *A History of Communications*, Cambridge: Cambridge University Press.

Polanyi, M. (1958) *Personal Knowledge*, Chicago: Chicago University Press.

Popper, A. N. and Fay, R. R. (eds) (1995) *Hearing by Bats*, New York: Springer-Verlag.

Poteat, W. H. (1974) 'Persons and places: paradigms in communication', in Waddell, J. and Dillistone, F. W. (eds) *Art and Religion as Communication*, Atlanta: John Knox Press.

Potter, J. (1996) *Representing Reality. Discourse, Rhetoric and Social Construction*, London: Sage.

Poyatos, F. (1983) *New Perspectives in Nonverbal Communication*, Oxford: Pergamon Press.

Poyatos, F. (ed.) (1992) *Advances in Nonverbal Communication*, Amsterdam: Benjamins.

Price, S. (1996) *Communication Studies*, Harlow: Longman.

Putnam, G. H. (1894) *Authors and their Public in Ancient Times*, London: Knickerbocker Press.

Quintilian, *Institutio Oratoria,* ed. and transl. in Butler, H. E. (1922) *The Institutio Oratoria of Quintilian*, Loeb Classical Library, 4 vols, London: Heinemann.

Rabain, J. (1979) *L'enfant du lignage, du sevrage à la classe d'âge chez les Wolof du Sénégal*, Paris: Payot.

Radin, D. (2006) *Entangled Minds*, Chicago: Pocket Books.

Radin, D. (2009) *The Conscious Universe: The Scientific Truth of Psychic Phenomena*, London: HarperCollins.

Radstone, S. (ed.) (2000) *Memory and Methodology*, Oxford: Berg.

Ragin, C. and Becker, H. (eds) (1992) *What is a Case? Exploring the Foundations of Social Inquiry*, Cambridge: Cambridge University Press.

Rahim, H. (1987) 'Incense', in Eliade vol. 7: 161–3.

Randhawa, B. S. and Coffman, W. E. (eds) (1978) *Visual Learning, Thinking, and Communication*, New York: Academic Press.

Rapoport, A. (1990) *The Meaning of the Built Environment. A Nonverbal Communication Approach*, 2nd edn, Tucson: University of Arizona Press.

Rée, J. (1999) *I See a Voice. A Philosophical History of Language, Deafness and the Senses*, London: HarperCollins.

Reed, A. (1999) 'Anticipating individuals: modes of vision and their social consequences in a Papua New Guinea prison', *Journal of the Royal Anthropological Institute* 5: 43–56.

Regier, W. G. (2011) *Quotology*, Lincoln: University of Nebraska Press.

Reichel-Dolmatoff, G. (1985) 'Tapir avoidance in the Columbian Northwest Amazon', in Urton, G. (ed.) *Animal Myths and Metaphors in South America*, Salt Lake City: University of Utah Press.

Reynolds, C. A. (2003) *Motives for Allusion. Context and Content in Nineteenth-Century Music*, Cambridge MA: Harvard University Press.

Richmond, V. P., McCroskey, J. C. and Payne, S. K. (1987) *Nonverbal Behavior in Interpersonal Relations*, 2nd edn, Englewood Cliffs: Prentice Hall.

Ricks, C. (2002) *Allusion to the Poets*, Oxford: Oxford University Press.

Ridley, M. (1995) *Animal Behavior*, 2nd edn, Oxford: Blackwell Scientific Publications.

Rindisbacher, H. J. (1992) *The Smell of Books. A Cultural-Historical Study of Olfactory Perception in Literature*, Ann Arbor: University of Michigan Press.

Ristau, C. A. (ed.) (1991) *Cognitive Ethology. The Minds of Other Animals,* Hillsdale NJ: Erlbaum.

Ritchie, I. (1991) 'Fusion of the faculties: a study of the language of the senses in Hausaland', in Howes.

Robinson, A. (1995) *The Story of Writing*, London: Thames and Hudson.

Robley, H. G. (1896) *Moko or Maori Tattooing*, London: Chapman and Hall.

Rodaway, P. (1994) *Sensuous Geographies. Body, Sense and Place*, London: Routledge.

Roitblat, H. L., Herman, L. M. and Nachtigall, P. E. (eds) (1993) *Language and Communication. Comparative Perspectives*, Hillsdale: Lawrence Erlbaum.

Rolston, B. (1992) *Drawing Support. Murals in the North of Ireland,* Belfast: Beyond the Pale Publications.

Rorty, R. (1980) *Philosophy and the Mirror of Nature,* Oxford: Blackwell.

Rose, H. and S. (eds) (2000) *Alas, Poor Darwin. Arguments against Evolutionary Psychology*, London: Cape.

Roseman, M. (1988) 'The pragmatics of aesthetics: the performance of healing among the Senoi Temiar', *Social Science and Medicine* 27: 811–18.

Roseman, M. (1991) *Healing Sounds from the Malaysian Rainforest. Temiar Music and Medicine*, Berkeley: University of California Press.

Rosengren, K. E. (1999) *Communication. An Introduction*, Thousand Oaks: Sage.

Rosenwein, B. H. (1999) *Negotiating Space, Power, Restraint, and Privileges of Immunity in Early Medieval England*, Manchester: Manchester University Press.

Roth, H. L. (1889) 'On salutations', *Journal of the Anthropological Institute* 19: 164–81.

Roth, W. E. (1897) *Ethnological Studies among the North-West-Central Queensland Aborigines*, London: Queensland Agent-General's Office.

Rothenbuhler, E. W. (1998) *Ritual Communication. From Everyday Conversation to Mediated Ceremony*, Thousand Oaks: Sage.

Rouget, G. (1985) *Music and Trance. A Theory of the Relations between Music and Possession*, Chicago: University of Chicago Press.

Routasalo, P. and Isola, A. (1996) 'The right to touch and to be touched', *Nursing Ethics* 3: 165–76.

Runciman, W. G., Maynard Smith, J. and Dunbar, R. I. M. (eds) (1996) *Evolution of Social Behaviour Patterns in Primates and Man*, Oxford: Oxford University Press.

Russell, B. (1969) *The ABC of Relativity*, 3rd edn, London: Allen and Unwin.

Russell, M. J. (1976) 'Human olfactory communication', *Nature* 260: 520–2.

Ryan, M-L. (ed.) (1999) *Cyberspace Textuality. Computer Technology and Literary Theory*, Bloomington: Indiana University Press.

Sachs, O. (2012) *Hallucinations*, New York: Knopf.

Sacks, O. (1991) *Seeing Voices. A Journey into the World of the Deaf*, London: Pan.

Salahub, J. E. (1999) 'Embroidering the ties of Empire: the Lord Grey banners', in Kwint et al.

Salvat-Papasseit, J. (1923) *La rosa als llavis*, Barcelona: Llibreria Nacional Catalana.

Salzmann, Z. (1998) *Language, Culture, and Society: An Introduction to Linguistic Anthropology*, 2nd edn, Boulder: Westview Press.

Sampson, G. (1985) *Writing Systems. A Linguistic Introduction*, London: Hutchinson.

Sandars, N. K. (trans.) (1964) *The Epic of Gilgamesh*, Harmondsworth: Penguin.

Sanford, J. (1990) *Dreams: God's Forgotten Language*, London: HarperCollins.

Sassoon, R. and Gaur, A. (1997) *Signs, Symbols and Icons*, Exeter: Intellect.

Saunderson, N. (1740) *The Elements of Algebra*, Cambridge: Cambridge University Press.

Saussure, F. de (1960) *Course in General Linguistics*, London: Owen.

Saville-Troike, M. (1989) *The Ethnography of Communication*, 2nd edn, Oxford: Blackwell.

Savran, G. W. (1988) *Telling and Retelling. Quotation in Biblical Narrative*, Bloomington: Indiana University Press.

Schafer, R. M. (1977) *The Tuning of the World*, Toronto: McClelland and Steward.

Schafer, R. M. (1994) 'The soundscape designer', in Järviluoma.

Schechner, R. (1988) *Performance Theory*, New York: Routledge.

Schieffelin, B. B. (2007) 'Found in translating: reflexive language across time and texts in Bosavi, Papua New Guinea', in Makihara, M. and Schieffelin, B. B. (eds) *Consequences of Contact. Language Ideologies and Sociocultural Transformations in Pacific Societies*, New York: Oxford University Press.

Schieffelin, E. L. (1985) 'Performance and the cultural construction of reality', *American Ethnologist* 12, 4: 707–24.

Schieffelin, E. L. (1998) 'Problematizing performance', in Hughes-Freeland.

Schiff, W. and Foulkes, E. (eds) (1982) *Tactual Perception: a Sourcebook*, Cambridge: Cambridge University Press.

Schiffer, M. B. (1999) *The Material Life of Human Beings. Artifacts, Behavior, and Communication*, London: Routledge.

Schiller, F. (1982) *On the Aesthetic Education of Man*, Eng. transl., Oxford: Clarendon Press (1st pub. 1794–1801).

Schirato, T. and Yell, S. (2000) *Communication and Culture. An Introduction*, London: Sage.

Schleidt, M. (1992) 'The semiotic relevance of human olfaction: a biological approach', in Van Toller and Dodd.

Schmitt, J.-C. (1991) 'The rationale of gestures in the west: third to thirteenth centuries', in Bremmer and Roodenburg.

Scholliers, P. (ed.) (2001) *Food, Drink and Identity. Cooking, Eating and Drinking in Europe since the Middle Ages*, Oxford: Berg.

Schroeter-Kunhardt, M. (1993) 'A review of near death experiences', *Journal of Scientific Experiment* 7: 219–39.

Schutz, A. (1951) 'Making music together: a study in social relationship', *Social Research* 18: 76–97.

Schwartz, S. (2012) 'Nonlocality, near-death experiences, and the challenge of consciousness', *Explore, The Journal of Science and Healing*, 8, 6: 226–30.

Schwartz, T., White, G. M. and Lutz, C. A. (eds) (1992) *New Directions in Psychological Anthropology*, Cambridge, Cambridge University Press.

Scollon, R. (1994) 'As a matter of fact: the changing ideology of authorship and responsibility in discourse', *World Englishes* 13: 33–46.

Scollon, R. (1999) 'Mediated discourse and social interaction', in Tracey.

Scribner, R. W. (1981) *For the Sake of Simple Folk. Popular Propaganda for the German Reformation*, Cambridge: Cambridge University Press.

Scupin, R. (1998) *Cultural Anthropology, a Global Perspective*, 3rd edn, Upper Saddle River NJ: Prentice-Hall.

Searle, J. R. (1984) *Minds, Brains and Science*, London: BBC Publications.

Sebeok, T. A. and Umiker-Sebeok, D. J. (eds) (1976) *Speech Surrogates: Drum and Whistle Systems*, 2 vols, The Hague: Mouton.

Seeger, A. (1981) *Nature and Society in Central Brazil: the Suyá Indians of Mato Grosso*, Cambridge MA: Harvard University Press.

Seeger, A. (1987) *Why Suyá Sing: a Musical Anthropology of an Amazonian People*, Cambridge: Cambridge University Press.

Seeger, A. (1988) 'Anthropology and odor: from Manhattan to Mato Grosso', *Perfumer and Flavorist* 13: 41–8.

Seeger, A. (1994) 'Music and dance', in Ingold.

Segerstråle, U. and Molnár, P. (eds) (1997) *Nonverbal Communication. Where Nature Meets Culture*, Mahwah NJ: Erlbaum.

Shannon, C. E. and Weaver, W. (1964) *The Mathematical Theory of Communication*, Urbana: University of Illinois Press (1st pub. 1949).

Sheldon, A. (1999) 'Approaching the future', in Tracey.

Sheldrake, R. (2002) *Dogs That Know When Their Owners Are Coming Home: And Other Unexplained Powers of Animals*, London: Arrow.

Sheldrake, R. (2004) *The Sense of Being Stared At*, London: Arrow.

Sheldrake, R. (2009) *A New Science of Life*, London: Icon Books.

Sheldrake, R. (2012) *The Science Delusion*, London: Coronet.

Sherzer, D. and J. (1976) 'Mormaknamaloe: the Cuna *mola*', in Young, P. and Howe, J. (eds) *Ritual and Symbol in Native Central America*, University of Oregon Anthropological Papers 9: 23–42.

Sherzer, J. (1987) 'A discourse-centered approach to language and culture', *American Anthropologist* 89: 295–309.

Sherzer, J. and Woodbury, A. C. (eds) (1987) *Native American Discourse: Poetics and Rhetoric*, Cambridge: Cambridge University Press.

Shuman, A. (1999) 'Ethnography of writing', in Wagner *et al.*

Sidener, D. (1987) 'The function and meaning of visual form in religious structures', in Taureg and Ruby.

Siiter, R. J. (1999) *Introduction to Animal Behavior*, Pacific Grove CA: Brooks Cole.

Silk, M. S. (2003) 'Plagiarism', in Hornblower and Spawforth.

Sillitoe, P. (1988) *Made in Niugini. Technology in the Highlands of Papua New Guinea*, London: British Museum.

Sills, D. L. (ed.) (1968) *International Encyclopedia of the Social Sciences*, 17 vols, New York: Macmillan and Free Press.

Silverstein, M. and Urban, G. (1996) *Natural Histories of Discourse*, Chicago: Chicago University Press.

Silverstone, R. (1999) *Why Study the Media?* London: Sage.

Simmel, G. (1924) 'Sociology of the senses; visual interaction', Eng. transl, in Park, R. E. and Burgess, E. W. (eds) (1924), *Introduction to the Science of Sociology*, 2nd edn, Chicago: University of Chicago Press (1st pub. in German 1908).

Simmel, G. (1997) 'Sociology of the meal', Eng. transl., in Frisby, D. and Featherstone, M. (eds) (1997) *Simmel on Culture*, London: Sage (1st pub. in German 1910).

Simpson, J. M. Y. (1994) 'Language', in Asher, R. E. (ed.) *Encyclopedia of Language and Linguistics*, Oxford: Pergamon Press, vol. 4: 1893–7.

Singer, W. (1998) 'Consciousness and the structure of neuronal representations', *Philosophical Transactions of the Royal Society, London, B*, 353: 1829–40.

Siskind, J. (1975) *To Hunt in the Morning*, Oxford: Oxford University Press.

Slater, P. J. B. (1986) 'Communication', in *The Collins Encyclopedia of Animal Behaviour*, London: Collins.

Sless, D. (1981) *Learning and Visual Communication*, London: Croom Helm.

Smith, A. (1976) *The Theory of Moral Sentiments*, eds Raphael, D. D. and Macfie, A. L., Oxford: Clarendon Press (1st pub. 1759).

Smith, B. H. (2000) 'Sewing up the mind: the claims of evolutionary psychology', in Rose and Rose.

Smith, B. R. (1999) *The Acoustic World of Early Modern England. Attending to the O-Factor*, Chicago: Chicago University Press.

Smith, W. J. (1997) 'The behavior of communicating, after twenty years', in Owings, D. H. and Thompson, N. (eds) *Perspectives in Ethology* 12: 7–53.

Smith, W. J., Wiley, R. H., Johnston, R. E. and Hailman, J. P. (1989) 'Animal signals', in Barnouw *et al.* vol. 1: 68–88.

Society for Psychical Research (2012) Online, http://www.spr.ac.uk

Solymar, L. (1999) *Getting the Message. A History of Communications*, Oxford: Oxford University Press.

Spencer, P. (1996) 'Dance and the cosmology of confidence', in Parkin *et al.*

Spencer, P. (ed.) (1985) *Society and the Dance. The Social Anthropology of Process and Performance,* Cambridge: Cambridge University Press.

Sperber, D. (1996) *Explaining Culture. A Naturalistic Approach*, Oxford: Blackwell.

Sperber, D. and Wilson, D. (1995) *Relevance. Communication and Cognition*, 2nd edn, Oxford: Blackwell.

Stake, R. E. (2005) 'Qualitative case studies', in Denzin and Lincoln.

Stevens, J. (1996) 'Asian calligraphy', in Daniels and Bright.

Stewart, S. (1999) 'Prologue: from the museum of touch', in Kwint *et al.*

Stockfelt, O. (1994) 'Cars, buildings and soundscapes', in Järviluoma.

Stoddart, D. M. (1990) *The Scented Ape. The Biology and Culture of Human Odour*, Cambridge: Cambridge University Press.

Stoller, P. (1984) 'Sound in Songhay cultural experience', *American Ethnologist* 11: 559–70.

Stoller, P. (1989) *The Taste of Ethnographic Things: the Senses in Anthropology,* Philadelphia: University of Pennsylvania Press.

Stothard, P. (1999) 'The moment that changed a memorial', *The Times* [London] 14 May: 24.

Strathern, A. and Stewart, P. J. (1998) 'Embodiment and communication: two frames for the analysis of ritual', *Social Anthropology* 6, 2: 237–51.

Strathern, M. (1979) 'The self in self-decoration', *Oceania* 49: 241–57.

Streeck, J. (1994) 'Gesture as communication II: the audience as co-author', in Kendon.

Streeck, J. (1996) 'How to do things with things', *Human Studies* 19: 365–84.

Streeck, J. (2012) 'Interaction and the living body: embodiment and emplacement', *Journal of Pragmatics*, Special Issue on Multimodal Interaction.

Streeck, J. and Knapp, M. L. (1992) 'The interaction of visual and verbal features in human communication', in Poyatos.

Street, B. (ed.) (1993) *Cross-Cultural Approaches to Literacy*. Cambridge: Cambridge University Press.

Summers, I. R. (ed.) (1992) *Tactile Aids for the Hearing Impaired*, London: Whurr.

Sussman, R. W. (1992) 'Smell as a signal', in Jones *et al.*

Swales, J. (1990) *Genre Analysis. English in Academic and Research Settings*, Cambridge: Cambridge University Press.

Synnott, A. (1991) 'Puzzling over the senses: from Plato to Marx', in Howes.

Tannen, D. (1989) *Talking Voices. Repetition, Dialogue, and Imagery in Conversational Discourse*, Cambridge: Cambridge University Press.

Taureg, M. and Ruby, J. (eds) (1987) *Visual Explorations of the World*, Aachen: Rader.

Tedlock, B. (ed.) (1987) *Dreaming. Anthropological and Psychological Interpretations*, Santa Fé: School of American Research Press.

Tedlock, B. and Tedlock, D. (1986) 'Text and textile: language and technology in the arts of the Quiché Maya', *Journal of Anthropological Research* 41: 121–46.

Tedlock, B., Basso, E. B., Brown, M. F., Herdt, G., Homiak, J. P., Kilborne, B. *et al.* (eds) (1987) *Dreaming. Anthropological and Psychological Interpretations*, Santa Fé: School of American Research Press.

Tedlock, D. (1983) *The Spoken Word and the Work of Interpretation,* Philadelphia: University of Pennsylvania Press.

Teilhard de Chardin, P. (1964) *The Future of man*, New York: Doubleday.

Terrain: carnets du patrimoine ethnologique (1994), special issue *Les émotions*, 22.

Thayer, S. (1982) 'Social touching', in Schiff and Foulkes.

Thayer, S. (1989) 'Touch', in Barnouw *et al.* vol. 4 : 246–9.

Thomas, C. (1884) *Notes on Certain Maya and Mexican Manuscripts*, Third Annual Report of Bureau of Ethnology, Smithsonian Institution, Washington: Government Printing Office.

Thomas, K. (1991) 'Introduction', in Bremmer and Roodenburg.

Thomas, N. (1995) *Oceanic Art*, Melbourne: Thames and Hudson.

Thomas, P. (1996) 'House', in Barnard and Spencer.

Tilley, C. (1989) 'Interpreting material culture', in Hodder.

Todt, D. and Hultsch, H. (1996) 'Acquisition and performance of song repertoires: ways of coping with diversity and versatility', in Kroodsma and Miller.

Tokumaru, Yosihiko and Yamaguti, Osamu (eds) (1986) *The Oral and the Literate in Music*, Tokyo: Academia Music.

Tonfoni, G., with Richardson, J. E. (1994) *Writing as a Visual Art*, Exeter: Intellect.

Tonkin, E. (1992) *Narrating our Pasts. The Social Construction of Oral History*, Cambridge: Cambridge University Press.

Tracey, K. (ed.) (1999) *Language and Social Interaction at the Century's Turn*, special issue *Research on Language and Social Interaction*, 32, 1/2.

Trenholm, S. and Jensen, A. (2000) *Interpersonal Communication*, Belmont: Wadsworth.

Truax, B. (1984) *Acoustic Communication*, Norwood: Ablex.

Tuan, Yi-Fu (1993) *Passing Strange and Wonderful. Aesthetics, Nature, and Culture*, Washington DC: Island Press.

Tubbs, S. and Moss, S. (1994) *Human Communication*, 7th edn, New York: McGraw-Hill.

Tufte, E. R. (1983) *The Visual Display of Quantitative Information*, Cheshire, Connecticut: Graphics Press.

Tufte, E. R. (1990) *Envisioning Information*, Cheshire, Connecticut: Graphics Press.

Tufte, E. R. (1997) *Visual Explanations. Images and Quantities, Evidence and Narrative*, Cheshire, Connecticut: Graphics Press.

Turner, B. S. (1996) *The Body and Society. Explorations in Social Theory*, 2nd edn, London: Sage.

Turner, V. W. and Bruner, E. M. (eds) (1986) *The Anthropology of Experience*, Urbana and Chicago: University of Illinois Press.

Tyack, P. L. (1998) 'Acoustic communication under the sea', in Hopp *et al.*

Ullman, M., Krippner, S. and Vaughan, A. (1989) *Dream Telepathy*, Jefferson: McFarland.

Umiker-Sebeok, D. J. and Sebeok, T. A. (eds) (1978) *Aboriginal Sign Languages of the Americas and Australia*, 2 vols, New York: Plenum Press.

Umiker-Sebeok, D. J. and Sebeok, T. A. (eds) (1987) *Monastic Sign Languages*, Berlin: Mouton de Gruyter.

Urban, G. (1989) 'The "I" of discourse', in Lee, B. and Urban, G. (eds) *Semiotics, Self, and Society*, Berlin: Mouton de Gruyter.

Urban, G. (1991) *A Discourse-Centered Approach to Culture: Native South American Myths and Rituals*, Austin: University of Texas Press.

Utley, A. (2000) 'Yogurt and hairs inspire web art', *The Times Higher* 1445, 21 July: 13.

Van Dijk, T. A. (ed.) (1997) *Discourse as Social Interaction*, London: Sage.

Van Dyck, J. (1999) *The Network Society. Social Aspects of New Media*, London: Sage.

Van Leeuwen, T. (1999) *Speech, Music, Sound*, Basingstoke: Macmillan.

Van Lommel, P. (2010) *Consciousness beyond Life. The Science of the Near-Death Experience*, New York: HarperCollins.

Van Lommel, P. (2011) 'Near-death experiences: the experience of the self as real and not as an illusion', *Annals of the New York Academy of Science*, 1234: 19–28.

Van Toller, S. and Dodd, G. H. (eds) (1988) *Perfumery. The Psychology and Biology of Fragrance*, London: Chapman and Hall.

Van Toller, S. and Dodd, G. H. (eds) (1992) *Fragrance. The Psychology and Biology of Perfume*, London: Elsevier.

Vander Meer, R. K., Breed, M. D., Espelie, K. E. and Winston, M. L. (eds) (1998) *Pheromone Communication in Social Insects. Ants, Wasps, Bees, and Termites*, Boulder: Westview.

Veber, H. (1996) 'External inducement and non-Westernization in the uses of the Ashéninka cushma', *Journal of Material Culture* 1: 155–82.

Vernadsky, V. (2007) *Geochemistry and the Biosphere*, Santa Fé: Synergetics Press.

Vinge, L. (1975) *The Five Senses. Studies in a Literary Tradition*, Lund: Publications of the Royal Society of Letters at Lund, vol. 72.

Virilio, P. (1994) *Vision Machine*, Eng. transl., Bloomington: Indiana University Press.

Vitebsky, P. (1995) *The Shaman: Voyages of the Soul – Trance, Ecstasy and Healing from Siberia to the Amazon*, Basingstoke: Macmillan.

Voloshinov, V. N. [/Bakhtin, M. M.] (1986) *Marxism and the Philosophy of Language*, Cambridge MA: Harvard University Press.

Von den Steinen, K. (1925–28) *Die Marquesaner und ihre Kunst*, 3 vols. Berlin: Reimer.

Waal, F. B. M. de (1999) 'Cultural primatology comes of age', *Nature* 399, 17 June: 635–6.

Wagner, D. A., Venezky, R. L. and Street, B. V. (eds) (1999) *Literacy. An International Handbook*, Boulder: Westview Press.

Wagner, S. (2012) 'Twin telepathy: the best evidence', online, http://paranormal.about.com/od/espandtelepathy/a/Twin-Telepathy-Best-Evidence.htm/

Walach, H., Schmidt, S. and Jonas, W. B. E. (2011) *Neuroscience, Consciousness and Spirituality*, Heidelberg: Springer.

Warde, A. (1997) *Consumption, Food and Taste: Culinary Antimonies and Commodity Culture*, London: Sage.

Warren, J. (2013) 'Enlightenment: is science ready to take it seriously?', *Psychology Tomorrow*, January.

Waterson, R. (1990) *The Living House. An Anthropology of Architecture in South-East Asia*, Singapore: Oxford University Press.

Watson, J. and Hill, A. (eds) (1997) *A Dictionary of Communication and Media Studies*, London: Arnold.

Watson, L. (1999) *Jacobson's Organ and the Remarkable Nature of Smell*, London: Allen Lane.

Weiner, A. B. and Schneider, J. (eds) (1989) *Cloth and Human Experience*, Washington DC and London: Smithsonian Institution Press.

Wentworth, W. W. and Ryan, J. (eds) (1994) *Social Perspectives on Emotion*, vol. 2, Greenwich CT: JAI Press.

Whiten, A., Goodall, J., McGrew, W. C., Nishida, T., Reynolds, V., Sugiyama, Y., Tutin, C. E. G., Wrangham, R. W. and Boesch, C. (1999) 'Cultures in chimpanzees', *Nature* 399, 17 June: 682–5.

Whitlow, W. L. A. (1993) *The Sonar of Dolphins*, New York: Springer-Verlag.

Whitten, P. and Hunter, D. E. K. (1993) *Anthropology: Contemporary Perspectives*, 7th edn, New York: HarperCollins.

Wilcox, R. and Jackson, R. R. (1998) 'Cognitive abilities of araneophagic jumping spiders', in Balda *et al.*

Williams, J. G. (1996) *The Two-Headed Deer. Illustrations of the* Ramayana *in Orissa,* Berkeley: University of California Press.

Williams, S. (2000) *Emotion and Social Theory. Corporeal Reflections on the (Ir)Rational*, London: Sage.

Wilson, D. (2000) 'Metarepresentation in linguistic communication', in Sperber, D. (ed.) *Metarepresentations: A Multidisciplinary Perspective*, Oxford: Oxford University Press.

Wilson, E. O. (1975) *Sociobiology. The New Synthesis*, Cambridge MA: Harvard University Press.

Windahl, S. and Signitzer, B. (1992) *Using Communication Theory*, London: Sage.

Wintle, M. (1996) 'Europe's image: visual representations of Europe from the earliest times to the twentieth century', in Wintle, M. (ed.) *Culture and Identity in Europe*, Aldershot: Avebury Press.

Womack, M. (1998) *Being Human. An Introduction to Cultural Anthropology*, Upper Saddle River NJ: Prentice-Hall.

Woodmansee, M. and Jaszi, P. (eds) (1994) *The Construction of Authorship: Textual Appropriation in Law and Literature*, Durham: Duke University Press

Wooldridge, H. E. (1929) *The Oxford History of Music*, vol. 1, *The Polyphonic Period*, 2nd edn, London: Oxford University Press.

Woolfson, P. (1988) 'Non-verbal interaction of Anglo-Canadian, Jewish-Canadian and French-Canadian physicians with their young, middle-aged and elderly patients', *Visual Anthropology* 1: 401–14.

Wright, R. (1996) *The Moral Animal. Evolutionary Psychology and Everyday Life*, London: Little, Brown.

Wrolstad, M. E. and Fisher, D. F. (eds) (1986) *Toward a New Understanding of Literacy*, New York: Praeger.

Wulf, C. (1993) 'Das mimetische Ohr', *Paragrana* 1, 1/2: 9–15.

Wynn, T. (1994) 'Tools and tool behaviour', in Ingold.

Yankah, K. (1995) *Speaking for the Chief*, Bloomington: Indiana University Press.

Yates, F. A. (1966) *The Art of Memory,* London: Routledge and Kegan Paul.

Zangrilli, Q. (2012) 'Dream and telepathy', *Science and Psychoanalysis*, online, http://www.psicoanalisi.it/psicoanalisi/psicosomatica/articoli/psomaing1117.htm

Zaslavsky, C. (1973) *Africa Counts. Number and Pattern in African Culture*, Boston: Prindle, Weber and Schmidt.

Zeman, A. (2003) *Consciousness*, Harvard: Yale University Press.

Zukerkandl, V. (1958) *Sound and Symbol: Music and the External World*, Eng. transl., Princeton: Princeton University Press.

Index